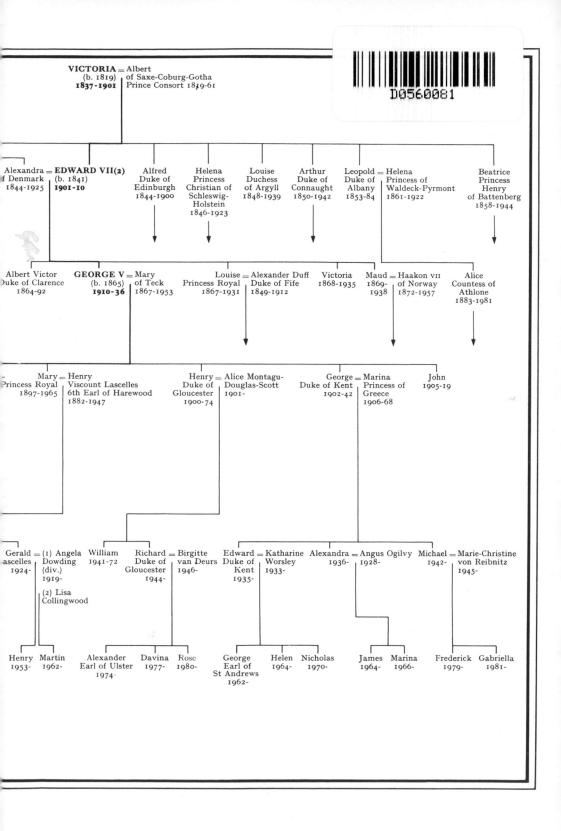

VICTORIA = Albert
(b. 1819) of Saxe-Coburg-Gotha
1837-1901 Prince Consort 1819-61

Alexandra = **EDWARD VII(2)**   Alfred   Helena   Louise   Arthur   Leopold = Helena   Beatrice
f Denmark   (b. 1841)   Duke of   Princess   Duchess   Duke of   Duke of   Princess of   Princess
1844-1925   **1901-10**   Edinburgh   Christian of   of Argyll   Connaught   Albany   Waldeck-Pyrmont   Henry
            1844-1900   Schleswig-   1848-1939   1850-1942   1853-84   1861-1922   of Battenberg
                        Holstein   1858-1944
                        1846-1923

Albert Victor   **GEORGE V** = Mary   Louise = Alexander Duff   Victoria   Maud = Haakon VII   Alice
Duke of Clarence   (b. 1865)   of Teck   Princess Royal   Duke of Fife   1868-1935   1869-   of Norway   Countess of
1864-92   **1910-36**   1867-1953   1867-1931   1849-1912   1938   1872-1957   Athlone
                                                                                            1883-1981

Mary = Henry   Henry = Alice Montagu-   George = Marina   John
Princess Royal   Viscount Lascelles   Duke of   Douglas-Scott   Duke of Kent   Princess of   1905-19
1897-1965   6th Earl of Harewood   Gloucester   1901-   1902-42   Greece
            1882-1947   1900-74   1906-68

Gerald = (1) Angela   William   Richard = Birgitte   Edward = Katharine   Alexandra = Angus Ogilvy   Michael = Marie-Christine
Lascelles   Dowding   1941-72   Duke of   van Deurs   Duke of   Worsley   1936-   1928-   1942-   von Reibnitz
1924-   (div.)   Gloucester   1946-   Kent   1933-   1945-
         1919-   1944-   1935-

         (2) Lisa
         Collingwood

Henry   Martin   Alexander   Davina   Rose   George   Helen   Nicholas   James   Marina   Frederick   Gabriella
1953-   1962-   Earl of Ulster   1977-   1980-   Earl of   1964-   1970-   1964-   1966-   1979-   1981-
                1974-   St Andrews
                                                1962-

THE ULTIMATE FAMILY

Also by John Pearson

NON-FICTION

BLUEBIRD AND THE DEAD LAKE
THE PERSUASION INDUSTRY
(with Graham Turner)
ARENA
THE PROFESSION OF VIOLENCE
THE LIFE OF IAN FLEMING
EDWARD THE RAKE
FAÇADES
STAGS AND SERPENTS

FICTION

GONE TO TIMBUCTOO
THE BELLAMY SAGA
THE AUTOBIOGRAPHY OF JAMES BOND
THE KINDNESS OF DR AVICENNA

THE ULTIMATE FAMILY

The Making of the
Royal House of Windsor

JOHN PEARSON

MICHAEL JOSEPH

LONDON

First published in Great Britain by Michael Joseph Ltd
44 Bedford Square, London WC1
1986

British Library Cataloguing in Publication Data

Pearson, John
    The ultimate family : the making of the Royal House of Windsor.
    1. Windsor, (House of) 2. Great Britain—
    Kings and rulers
    I. Title
    941.082′092′2   DA566.9.A1

    ISBN 0–7181–2612–2

Phototypeset by Input Typesetting Ltd, London
Printed and bound by Billings Ltd, Worcester

For my step-sons,
Nick, Mathew and Adam.

CONTENTS

Acknowledgements   ix

PART ONE: FOUNDATIONS
1   'Daylight upon Magic'   3
2   Queen Mary and the Sacred Kingship   9
3   Mother   23
4   Coronation and the Magic Monarchy   41

PART TWO: DECLINE
5   Philip   67
6   Margaret   96
7   'Things Fall Apart'   114
8   The Snowdon Factor   134

PART THREE: REVIVAL
9   'God Bless the Prince of Wales!'   171
10 The Price of Popularity   200
11 Divorce   218
12 Changing Faces   234
13 Prince in Waiting   245
14 A Megastar is Made   263
15 The Ultimate Family   279

Index   297

ACKNOWLEDGEMENTS

As I soon discovered when starting to research this book, royalty is something of a magic zone, in which an old dictum of Cyril Connolly's very much applies — 'Those who tell don't know: those who know don't tell'. Many of those I wished to see, like Willie Hamilton MP, refused to see me, and many more who did were anxious I should not reveal my sources. Because of this it would be misleading and invidious to list those I am free to name as having helped me. All I can do is to express my deepest gratitude to all who, on or off the record, gave me their time and their assistance.

This does not preclude my paying tribute to the few who really made this book a possibility — Edda Tasiemka of the unique and extraordinary Hans Tasiemka Archive; my friend and agent, Ed Victor, for his unfailing guidance; my indefatigable researcher, Joyce Quarrie, who corrected me from untold errors; and my editor emeritus, Max Eilenberg, to whose judgement, competence and indefatigable good humour I owe a considerable debt. I must also thank the executors of the late Admiral Baillie-Grohman for permission to publish the excerpt from his wartime diary on pages 81–2. Finally I must thank my wife, Lynette, for sympathy and help even beyond the call of marital duty as I wrote what proved to be the most exacting book of my career.

J.P.

Princes do what we dream of, hence the extremes of self-display to which they are driven . . . Of course we reward them. We stand in our streets and cheer and wave our little flags when they pass, we put their pictures on our walls and on our coins. Why shouldn't we? That is how we pay them for carrying out our wishes so zealously.

Dan Jacobson, *The Rape of Tamar*

PART ONE

FOUNDATIONS

1

'DAYLIGHT UPON MAGIC'

'The royal scene is simply a presentation of ourselves
behaving well. If anyone is being honoured, it is the human
race.'

Rebecca West

On July 29, 1981, on America's west coast, television went on the
air at 4.30 a.m. and soon an estimated 38.8 million U.S. households
were switching on their sets to watch a wedding in the heart of
London which, during the following five hours, would be simultaneously viewed by something like an eighth of the population of
the world.

In London the day had been declared a public holiday. At Knights-
bridge Barracks, reveille sounded for the Household Cavalry at 4.45,
and on the pavement of the Mall near Buckingham Palace Mrs Avril
Harrison and her daughter, Rosemary, were finishing the third night
of their vigil in the open air to guarantee their view of the procession.
For richer visitors to London, room service at the Dorchester Hotel
was serving free champagne with breakfast for those who could face
it; and the underwriters at Lloyds of London would soon congratulate themselves at not needing to pay out twelve million pounds to
those makers of commemorative pottery who had insured themselves
in case the whole event was cancelled.

In order to be present, Mrs Nancy Reagan – together with five
hatboxes and twelve personal security men – had left the President
of the United States for the longest period since their marriage
twenty-nine years before. As his representative at the actual wedding
in St Paul's Cathedral, she would be among the sovereigns of
Norway, Sweden and the Netherlands, the Presidents of Germany
and France, and Princess Grace of Monaco. There would also be
the twenty-eight stone King of Tonga, who had thought it wise to
bring his own specially reinforced chair; but the King of Spain
had not turned up because his government was currently disputing

Britain's ownership of Gibraltar. To show there was nothing personal to his absence, he had, however, sent a present.

Over a thousand other presents had also reached the Palace from around the world, including a microwave oven from Toshiba, a painting by Raoul Dufy from the President of France, and a *large* dog basket from the Marquis of Zetland.

During the night the London sewers had been searched by men from Scotland Yard for IRA terrorists, and, to be on the safe side, armed policemen dressed as footmen would be riding on the royal carriages. Extra surgeons and supplies of plasma were in readiness throughout the day at nearby hospitals.

The Pope, recovering from an assassination bid himself, had sent a special blessing from his bed in Rome. His representative, Cardinal Basil Hume, would be the first Roman Catholic prelate present at a royal wedding since the Reformation – the prospect of which had brought a rousing outburst from the Northern Ireland Protestant, the Reverend Ian Paisley:

> May God bless the Prince of Wales and his bride to be, but may God deliver the House of Windsor from the conspiracy of Rome to subvert the Protestant monarchy.

Soviet television was virtually unique in not showing any of the day's proceedings, having condescended to inform its viewers the night before that 'London hopes the wedding bells will drown out the sound of the shooting in Ireland'. But apart from Moscow and the Reverend Ian Paisley (and a *divorcé* from Shropshire who saw fit to hang himself because the bride reminded him so strongly of his former wife), the marriage of Charles Philip Arthur George Mountbatten-Windsor, Prince of Wales, to Lady Diana Frances Spencer was regarded by a troubled world as the most engrossing celebration ever shared on such a scale in history.

One effect of this 'village wedding in the presence of millions through TV', as the Dean of St Paul's somewhat curiously described it, was to endow the twenty-year-old bride with a mythical status all her own. Her televised marriage was like the greatest movie première in history, and her closest rivals were the screen stars whom she outshone for glamour and mystique; so that today, as the still shy and stringently protected mother of two small children, she has become the owner of the world's most instantly recognisable female face, with world-wide surveys showing her to be more famous, more admired and envied than any other woman in the world.

But Diana is not the only member of the British royal family to be established in the role of world-wide megastar by now. In February 1983, her parents-in-law, the Queen of England and Prince Philip, Duke of Edinburgh, arrived at Los Angeles to be greeted by the Reagans at the start of an official visit to the USA Her Majesty had casually and tactfully expressed a wish for her host to show her something of the scenes of his youthful triumphs, with the result that the high spot of the brief royal stay in California was the presidential evening spent in Hollywood itself.

The President and his First Lady personally arranged a party for the Queen to meet the stars in one of the last remaining old-time studios – stage 9 at Twentieth Century-Fox, where shooting had just finished on the latest episode of *Mash*. Banks of plastic flowers, fairy-lights and a 24-foot high fountain which had featured in *Hullo Dolly!* were hurriedly installed to make the royal couple feel at home, and five hundred of the most famous and acceptable names in Hollywood flocked to meet the Queen of England and her husband.

Roy Rogers, Fred Astaire, Gene Kelly, Lucille Ball, Bette Davis and Loretta Young, arrived together with James Mason, Julie Andrews, Dudley Moore, and Fred McMurray at the head of a glittering contingent of the brightest, best and richest Hollywood could muster. Together with Her Majesty they dutifully munched a sit-down dinner of the President's own favourite chicken-pot pie, followed by 'Snowballs' – ice-cream rolled in toasted coconut and dunked in chocolate sauce. Then just as dutifully the stars applauded the President's favourite comedian, George Burns, and an extemporary pop-song medley from his favourite vocal duo, Perry Como and Frank Sinatra.

History does not record what Elizabeth of England truly thought of the chicken-pot pie and the pop-song medley – let alone George Burns's jokes. Hers is a reserved public presence at the best of times, which reveals its full potential for enthusiasm only when one of her horses looks like winning at the races. But unlike her sister, Princess Margaret, who eighteen years before had left a more informal Hollywood party almost as dawn was breaking, the Queen and her husband did not linger, and the royal Rolls, with standard flying, made its regal exit through the famous gates of Twentieth Century-Fox long before midnight struck.

It had been a most unlikely evening, but in its own uncomfortable way it had also been a professional tribute of a sort from the reigning stars of Hollywood to a star whose reign was so much more impressive than their own. Something of this had been clearly evident the previous June, during an official visit by the Reagans as part of the important presidential tour of the leading NATO allies. By the time America's first citizen and his lady reached London, they had already met the Pope and a group of European presidents and prime ministers, and had maintained themselves as considerably more than the equals of their European hosts. No less was to be expected of a president who is one of the greatest self-projectors of our times, and the elected head of the richest nation in the world.

But when they arrived as guests of Her Majesty at Windsor Castle, the Reagans seemed to change. The presidential magic was no match for the magic of the monarchy, and suddenly the Reagans seemed not merely powerfully impressed, but rather unimpressive. When Queen and President – accomplished horseback riders both – took a morning ride in Windsor Park for the benefit of the television cameras, the world's most famous former movie star was firmly in a supporting role to his rather ordinary-looking fellow rider.

It was a strange reversal of the true power of these two heads of state and their respective nations; but it was also a clear indication of their relative standing as celebrities, and the extent to which the Queen has now become more of a star than the kingdom over which she reigns. Like Diana's wedding, it was evidence of how the royal family of Mountbatten-Windsor now enjoys a quite unique, sublimely lustrous status – yet its members apparently defy the rules of the boundless super-stardom they possess. They dance not, neither do they sing; nor do they seem to pursue the fame which, on the contrary, appears intent upon voraciously pursuing them.

Artists, statesmen, film stars, generals, religious leaders and even criminals are required to accomplish something to achieve their mede of notoriety; but the members of this one family are unique in being headline news from the moment of their birth – or even earlier, judging by the publicity which followed Diana through her pregnancies. 'I am that I am!' proclaimed Jehovah in one of his more impenetrable utterances, and the status of the British royal family seems rather similar.

The whole phenomenon remains something of a mystery. The family itself is exceptionally rich, and its members live in considerable style, yet in their private lives they offer the impression of a group of rather ordinary people, none of them abnormally intelligent or witty or accomplished, or remarkable for anything but what they are. The Queen is symbolic head of state in Britain and parts of the Commonwealth, but she possesses less true power than almost any republican president, and her role – and her dutiful advisers – keep her firmly out of virtually all controversy. The monarchical principles resoundingly proclaimed at her state occasions are relics from a long-dead age of kingship, with at best a sentimental relevance to the modern world we live in. And Britain too has long declined from its noontide glory: a small disgruntled member of the European community, it could hardly be more different from the worldwide British empire, whose power and splendour were reflected in the reverence accorded Queen Victoria in the last years of her reign.

So what is the secret of the universal fascination in the doings of the British royal family? Why are its members seen as superstars? And how to account for the survival and unparalleled prestige of this single European royal house when almost every other monarchy has foundered or abandoned all but a shadow of its ancient royal pretensions?

There is no simple answer, for the subject is bedevilled by the terrible taboos and secrecy that shroud the institution of the British monarchy. 'Its mystery is its life. We must not let in daylight upon magic,' counselled the influential theorist of the Victorian monarchy, Walter Bagehot, in the 1860s and the Court has firmly followed his advice. But due deference to the crown cannot hide the fact that the world's consuming interest in the Mountbatten-Windsors has not happened by some happy accident, nor by the operation of the mystic forces of tradition.

From the days of Queen Victoria the monarchy, which in so many way appears a living relic from the past, has shown one most surprising quality. For all its obsession with its traditional identity, it has always summoned up a sharp capacity for change and a rarely noticed genius for extracting the maximum advantage from developments within society. It has made its own determined use of the steady growth of mass communications, from the penny press in Queen Victoria's day to the television satellites which now beam the family's ceremonies of state to multimillion audiences round the world. And, most paradoxical of all, it has seen its most far-reaching changes under a Queen whose influence and private inclinations have always rested firmly on the side of keeping the institution of the Crown in the pristine state in which she inherited it from her much loved father, George VI, in 1952.

This has made the steady transformation of the modern British monarchy one of the strangest untold stories of our time. For although the main characters involved have been remorselessly admired, censured and described, their real achievements in the process have been curiously overlooked; and the story starts much earlier in the century with Queen Mary, the royal matriarch who, after Victoria herself, did most to set the stage for everything that followed.

2

QUEEN MARY AND
THE SACRED KINGSHIP

'The different fates of the British and French royal families
are not due to fundamentally different popular mentalities in
the two countries, but to the skill of one family and the
incompetence of another.'

Theodore Zeldin, *The French*

On February 7, 1952, only hours after the return from Kenya of the
new Queen Elizabeth and her husband, Philip, Duke of Edinburgh,
following the unexpected death of George VI the previous night, a
venerable, rectangular, black Rolls-Royce drew up at Clarence
House, their London residence. It had come from nearby Marlborough House and in it was the upright figure of eighty-four-year-old
Queen Mary. Despite her grief at the passing of her favourite son,
from which she would never fully recover, the indomitable old lady
was insistent that 'Her old Grannie and subject must be the first to
kiss Her hand.'

It was a touching moment as this great-granddaughter of King
George III made her obeisance to the daughter of the son and king
she was mourning; but there was more to it than that. Sentiment
apart, this curiously feudal act summed up the royal code Queen
Mary had lived by all her adult life. Her long and strict adherence
to this code had made her what she was – the mainstay and mentor
of the Royal House of Windsor.

People tended to discount Queen Mary. With her toque, her
ramrod presence, and those extraordinary Edwardian dresses which
had been part of her unchanging public image since the 1910s, she
had inevitably come to be regarded in old age as something of a
relic from a very distant royal past. Nothing could have been further
from the truth. For over fifty years, despite her age and appearance,
this remarkable woman had been virtual prime mover of the modern
monarchy, witnessing its growth and playing a crucial part behind
the scenes in the development of its public image.

Asked to sum Queen Mary up, the Duchess of Beaufort, who had
known her extremely well, offered a perceptive verdict. 'You must

remember,' said Her Grace, 'that she was very, very German', which was true, for there was not a drop of English blood within those very regal veins. Born in Kensington Palace in 1867, she was the daughter of Queen Victoria's stout first cousin, Princess Adelaide of Teck, and the dashing but dispirited Prince Franz, son of the dispossessed heir to the royal house of Württemburg. Her maternal grandparents were George III's seventh son, Adolphus, and his wife, Augusta, daughter of the Landgrave of Hesse-Cassel.

The German racial influence upon Queen Mary's character is debatable; what is beyond dispute is the profound and almost superstitious reverence for royalty she acquired from her obscure but pedigree-obsessed relations. 'To my mother,' wrote her son, the Duke of Windsor, who by then had cause to be painfully aware of it, 'the monarchy was something sacred and the Sovereign a personage apart.'

Such an exalted belief in the sacred person of the monarch was quite foreign to the English constitution and to the history of the crown in Britain over the previous two centuries, and yet it obsessed Queen Mary all her life, coloured all her contacts with her family, and became increasingly adopted by everyone around her. It was to be the greatest of the many legacies of this stately royal matriarch to the development of the modern British monarchy: her influence would be as relevant to the new reign of her granddaughter as it had been half a century earlier.

Queen Mary's faith had its origins in the seventeenth century post-Renaissance European doctrines of the Divine Right of Kings which cost Charles I his head; and the last British monarch who tried to act upon them was the Catholic James II, who was promptly disposed of by the English aristocracy in the 'Glorious Whig Revolution' of 1688. It was a blow from which the former power and status of the Crown would not recover.

In 1714, on the death of Protestant Queen Anne, parliament overrode the claims of a legitimate and sacred royal person to the throne. As the son and heir of a crowned and anointed English monarch, James II's son, Charles Stuart, 'the Old Pretender', had every right to inherit the crown – except that as a Catholic he was unacceptable to the Protestant ascendancy in parliament. The crown of England was offered to the distantly related German Electoral House of Hanover instead.

As kings of England, the Hanoverians were often casually ignored – and kept firmly in their places – by the great Whig families who ran the country, and for whom the principles of 1688 were far more sacrosanct than the disposable person of the monarch. Far from seeming 'sacred and revered', the first two Georges were disreputable and dull, and not even the determined efforts of King George III could break the power and privilege of the Whig grandees who, often richer and more arrogant than the King himself, filled the ministries of state and ruled society.

By the nineteenth century, what was left of the power and prestige of the British monarchy seemed doomed to extinction. George IV died, universally reviled, in 1830, and his brother and successor, William IV, was positively embarrassed by his royal trappings. The simplest of men, who rejoiced in the popular appellation of 'Sailor Bill', he even did his best to reduce his own coronation to its skimpiest essentials – hence its description as the 'Half-Crownation'.

This demystification of royalty seemed to have reached its peak with the accession of the eighteen-year-old Victoria in 1837. Her adored mentor and Prime Minister, Lord Melbourne, was a traditional Whig politician who instilled into his ready royal pupil the full theory of the subordination of the royal will to parliament – which the Queen accepted with occasional objections for the remainder of her life. After the death of worthy but unpopular Prince Albert in 1861, and her virtual retirement into sorrowing seclusion for the following two decades, whatever royal magic she possessed seemed to have gone for good. She was openly referred to in the press as the boring widow, 'Mrs Brown' – a sly dig at her overdependence on her Scots servant, John Brown. The scandalous existence of the Prince of Wales – which brought him into the Divorce Court as a witness, and involved him in the gambling cause célèbre of Tranby Croft – shed little lustre on the throne. By the 1870s republicanism was becoming widely mooted.

Writing in the 1860s, Walter Bagehot had described the sovereign as the crowned and largely 'ornamental' president of a developing democracy. To a monarchy divested of virtually all political power by successive Whig governments since 1688, ornament indeed seemed all that it had left. But if the Crown was disheartened and politically all but impotent, it took a politician to see the potential in its being not simply 'ornamental', but magnificently so; and the consequences of this insight have never been forgotten either by royalty or politicians since. For now occurred the great event that totally transformed the image of the monarchy and set it firmly on course for the singular developments of this century – the coaxing from sorrowing widowhood of the reluctant Queen by the ruthless flatterer and showman, Benjamin Disraeli, for her Golden Jubilee of 1887.

To put the seal upon his great imperial ambitions, Disraeli had already had parliament proclaim Victoria 'Empress of India' the year before – an extra title that she found she soon enjoyed – and during the last years of her reign, 'the Widow of Windsor' was magically transformed into the mother figure of a boundless and expanding empire. The process reached its ceremonial apotheosis ten years later in the Diamond Jubilee organised by Joseph Chamberlain, who started life a convinced republican and ended it, shrewdly responsive to popular sentiment, a passionate imperialist and royalist. As Queen Victoria drove through the streets of London to her great thanksgiving service at St Paul's, the plump little woman in the open landau was the focus for a burst of popular enthusiasm, national allegiance and imperial splendour on a scale reminiscent of the Roman Empire in its prime. At the far briefer zenith of the British Empire, it was this rediscovered monarch who suddenly enshrined the patriotic pride of a nation now exalted by the prospect of its wealth, possessions and imperial destiny.

'To be born an Englishman,' said Cecil Rhodes, 'is to draw a winning ticket in the lottery of life'; and if God himself was still not quite an Englishman, the English Queen was worshipped as 'the Great White Goddess' by her countless unseen subjects beyond the seas. Flattered, revered, beloved on a scale unknown by any previous English monarch, the former political disciple of Lord Melbourne ended her days at Osborne House on the Isle of Wight, tended by turbanned servants in a drawing-room decorated by Kipling's father like a throne-room in Kashmir. The power of 'ornamental' monarchy could hardly have been clearer.

The paradox behind this was that the monarch reigned, but did not rule. During her final years, Victoria had infinitely enhanced the splendour and the prestige of the Crown, but her long reign had also finally confirmed that the ultimate authority in government rested with the prime minister and cabinet responsible to parliament. But far from lessening the sovereign's dignity, it was this final affirmation of virtual royal impotence in politics that made the growing cult of monarchy acceptable. Simply because the Crown no longer dared − or even cared − to interfere in politics (save on rare and carefully circumscribed occasions), there seemed no danger in the rapidly inflating splendour and self-importance of the court. And, after many years of weary waiting in the wings, Victoria's successor, Edward, was perfectly suited to make the most of it. As far back as 1887, he had done his best to persuade his mother to don her crown and jewels of state for the great procession of her Golden Jubilee, but she had insisted on the simplest black widow's dress with the blue sash of the Order of the Garter. Now he could joyfully indulge in the splendour and regalia himself.

As King, there was not really a great deal Edward wished to *do*: it was sufficient simply and splendidly to *be* − crowned, fêted, richly fed, admired on horseback in one of those scarlet uniforms he wore so well, cheered in the paddock with his double Derby winner, Persimmon, and regally entertained with his mistresses and cronies at Tring, Chatsworth or Kimbolton Castle. His 'somewhat perplexing popularity,' according to Harold Nicolson, 'was largely based on the fact that again and again did he give the crowds occasion to enjoy the spectacle of splendid processions, with sleek horses and the chink and glitter of scarlet and gold.'

King Edward had a natural talent for such things. Something of an actor *manqué*, with a strong sense of the dignity of his position, he played out his role to its full theatrical extent. He had a passion for the ornamental minutiae of monarchy, and enjoyed such fine medieval touches as being called not 'sir' but 'sire' − even by his mistresses. He liked to talk of *le métier du roi*, the profession of kingship; but apart from meeting other heads of state, generally *en route* to his frequent holidays at Homburg, Spa or Biarritz, it pleased him to adopt the undemanding, politically passive role of constitutional monarch, while revelling in the flamboyant ceremony that the populace was growing to expect.

He was, in fact, the ideal monarch for his times, and something of a model for the other kings of Europe who were doing much the same in Rome, Berlin, St Petersburg and Bucharest (not to mention Vienna, Athens, Stockholm, Brussels and Madrid). Most of them were his relations, and the rapidly developing nation states of Europe were acquiring a taste for popular, impressive styles of leadership, as well as needing patriotic figureheads for their expanding empires.

Until now, the old-style European sovereigns had always kept their distance from the masses, so that kings were remote creatures, barely glimpsed by the common herd. But this was changing fast. Widespread education and the swift expansion of the popular press, replete with cheap and rapid news photography, meant that the royal features, habits and activities were becoming common knowledge on an unprecedented scale. Royalty was widely in demand: and royalty responded.

Mass popularity was positively courted, and processions, coronations, grandiose state occasions were more and more the order of the day, to satisfy the patriotic longings of rapidly increasing city populations. It was around this time that most of Europe's royal cities were rearranged especially to stage them. (Here London actually lagged behind the rest of Europe, and it was not until just before the First World War that the Mall was laid out as a grand imperial avenue, Admiralty Arch constructed, and Buckingham Palace solemnly refaced in Portland stone.)

But for all the trouble they were taking to impress their subjects, the kings of Europe were uneasy and exposed amid this unaccustomed grandeur in a swiftly changing century. For all their regal plumage and their fiercely cheering subjects, they knew that they were vulnerable, and their ranks were being thinned by violence long before the assassination of Archduke Ferdinand of Austria in 1914 marked the end of so many European dynasties. Edward, while still Prince of Wales, had been shot at in Brussels in 1900, and Italy's King Umberto assassinated that same year. The King and Queen of Serbia were butchered in their beds three years later, and the King of Greece was assassinated in 1913. Shortly before he died himself in 1910, King Edward confided to a courtier that he feared his son, poor George, would be the final King of England. He had not counted on Queen Mary.

Mary, as a young princess, had been a close witness of Victoria's grand apotheosis. Those exciting years at the turn of the century had come as simple confirmation of what she had always known to be the truth, as the lost continental creed of the Divine Right of Kings resurfaced, reinvigorated and magically transformed into an assured belief in the Divine Role of Kingship.

The young Princess of Teck was something of a favourite of Victoria, who approved of her intelligence, her sense of effortless decorum, and above all of her passion for the throne. The Queen had been enthusiastic at the engagement of so devout a monarchist to her eldest grandson, the dissolute, lethargic Duke of Clarence, trusting she would prove the Duke's salvation. No one could save the Duke of Clarence, who promptly died of a mysterious disease in 1892. But when the princess switched attention and affections to her dead fiancé's brother, George, and duly married him in 1893, few were more thoroughly relieved than Queen Victoria. She recognised the value of such dedication to the monarchy, both for the future of the family and for the happiness and prospects of her grandson, George.

King Edward was equally impressed. According to Queen Mary's official biographer, 'her reverence for the Monarchy as an institution, and thus for the person of the Monarch himself, invested her father-in-law in her eyes with an aura so bright it almost made her blink.' As a daughter-in-law, May was admittedly a touch too serious for Edward's tastes – and even more for those of his feather-brained consort, Alexandra. But the old King could appreciate dedication in others, and he insisted that the Princess of Wales be honoured by seeing the official 'boxes' which contained the documents from the main offices of state sent regularly for royal approval. Foreseeing her all-important role when she would be queen, it was King Edward's wish that she should understand the detailed work of government, and be thoroughly prepared to play her part behind the scenes.

Once she was on the throne beside her sailor king, George V, Queen Mary's hour had come – and during the twenty-six years they reigned together it was her influence that stabilised the monarchy and helped disprove King Edward's gloomy prophesy. For as well as supporting the King with absolute devotion, Queen Mary had a sort of genius for sensing how the British monarchy itself could best survive and prosper.

Under Mary, the image of the British monarchy was virtually recreated. She was German, but she saw her family become ineradicably British. To the vast and vulnerable show of finery she brought the assurance of a sacred destiny. She oversaw the development of a public cult that combined sublime regal ceremony with the humdrum family virtues of decency and duty. She set fundamental patterns for the future that her granddaughter would inherit, and it is largely due to her that the British Crown neither expired nor became one of those unassumingly 'human' modern monarchies of Scandinavia or the Netherlands, where the status of the sovereign is so little different from that of the average citizen.

Mary's first influence, predictably, was all for heightening the outward splendour of the throne and the regal dignity of Court and King. King George had little of his father's easygoing bonhomie, and none of that flamboyant vanity which had made the old king positively relish his great state appearances. Left to pursue his private inclinations, he would happily have continued as the squire of Sandringham; but his Queen was always there to remind him of his kingly duties and he bravely, if reluctantly, accepted them.

Far from the ceremony of royalty easing off with the King's accession, it became still more impressive, and was more and more extended to include that great but dwindling entity, the Empire. King Edward had not been particularly interested in the Empire, preferring Europe with its spas and courtesans: but his son, who had no need of either, was excited at the idea of those far-off lands he ruled, and whose postage stamps he compulsively collected.

More than this, the concept of the King mystically uniting the imperial brotherhood of nations became a further and important article of royal faith, continuing the work begun by the great Queen Empress. One of the most indelible of Queen Mary's memories was of what would prove a grand finale for the British Empire as it passed its peak – the Delhi Durbar of 1911. With superb self-confidence and showmanship, the sort of splendid royal event London had witnessed with Victoria's jubilees was triumphantly re-staged in the great sub-continent. Here was the show of kingship on a scale no English monarch had experienced in history.

Crowned, garbed in their coronation robes and bearing their imperial regalia, the King Emperor and his Empress on their dais solemnly displayed themselves before their subject races and accepted tribute from the Indian princes. Back in England, George might be subject to the will of parliament; here on the sweltering Delhi plain, he could have been some mogul emperor, his army passing in immaculate review and elephants with jewelled howdahs kneeling for their master's salutation. Queen Mary's sense of royal destiny was solemnly confirmed, as the acclamation of the Empire enhanced her beloved King and Emperor and the sacred institution of the Crown.

At home, too, life continued amid surroundings of unabated splendour and fabulous wealth. When the court made its annual migration to Balmoral in August by rail, seventeen locomotives would be placed along the royal route with steam up just in case His Majesty's train broke down. For the royal picnics, Daimlers with gold-plated radiators delivered baskets of food and wine served by footmen, and Buckingham Palace was maintained by a permanent staff of one hundred upper and four hundred lower servants, with the upper servants sitting down each day to a four-course meal with white wine and sherry.

Had Queen Mary been frivolous, conceited or indulgent, life on such a scale must certainly have proved disastrous – both to herself and to the future of the monarchy – but she was nothing of the kind. Queen Mary was essentially a puritan romantic. All the considerable strength of purpose she possessed now went into ensuring that the public reputation of the Crown remained unblemished.

As far as her husband was concerned, this proved no great problem. Service in the Royal Navy had done little to improve King George's brain, but it had left him with a sense of duty equal to her own. He had inherited few of his father's royal vices: abstemious and uxorious, he was wedded to routine, hated high society, and was faithful to his wife. Possessed of a deep sense of kingly dignity, he saw nothing remotely funny in her reverence for his person. Honest, sober, decent and hard-working, he had reached manhood in the approving shadow of his grandmother, Victoria. Now he continued with the firm approval of another great royal matriarch, his wife.

What was left of high Edwardian society might scoff at this royal exercise of middle-class morality, raffish aristocrats deplore the sudden boredom of the Court, but this was how Queen Mary intended it to be and this was how it was. The self-indulgent world of good King Edward and his racy friends withered beneath Queen Mary's slightly puzzled stare. Irreproachable herself, she embodied as few English queens had done before, the formidable ideals of middle-class British womanhood – thrift, service, self-control and unshakeable devotion to the royal hearth and home.

Royalty ceased to lead 'smart' fashionable society. More often than not, Queen Mary and the faithful George would dine frugally alone together at the Palace, he in white tie and tails with the Order of the Garter, she in majestic evening dress. They would be punctually in bed by eleven-fifteen. Gluttony, adultery, extravagance vanished from the royal presence, and it was something of an article of royal faith that *divorcées* be kept as firmly from the court as from the Ascot royal enclosure.

Uncomfortable as this may seem today, and distinctly hypocritical against the standards of contemporary upper-class society, there can be no question but that Queen Mary's prudery helped guarantee the British monarchy through the perilous years that lay ahead of it. It helped endear the Crown to the growing middle-classes who liked their betters to behave themselves; and at a time when arrogance, blatant extravagance and open immorality were discrediting so many European royal houses on the eve of war, the British monarchy remained above popular reproach.

In 1914 this proved to be of great importance. As anti-German feeling reached levels of hysteria, the war against the royal family's compatriots and the King's cousin, Kaiser William, might seriously have undermined the British monarchy. Instead there was a growing public emphasis on the family's national identity. Despite his Germanic ancestry, George V 'considered himself to be wholly and impregnably British', and with the war he naturally became increasingly touchy on the subject. When H. G. Wells had the exceptional temerity to criticise his 'alien and uninspiring court', he retorted angrily, 'I may be uninspiring but I'm damned if I'm an alien'.

However, the patriotism of the royal family was never seriously called in doubt, and the only casualty to anti-German feeling among the British royal relations was another cousin, Louis, Prince of Battenberg. A loyal member of the Royal Navy who had married into the British royal family and settled in England as his adopted country, he had risen, more or less by merit, to the position of First Sea Lord: but with the outbreak of war, his undisguisably Germanic surname forced him into ignominious resignation – an event which would have repercussions on the royal family even two generations later.

Nonetheless, the Battenberg affair did show how vulnerable the Crown might be over its Germanic origins and raised the question of its official name. The only problem was that no one was altogether certain what it was, as the King had never had to use a surname in his life – nor had his father, nor had Queen Victoria. The patronymic of the House of Hanover was Guelf, and that of Prince Albert, Wettin. Neither was particularly suitable during a war with Germany, and it was finally the King's secretary, a former rector's son called Arthur Bigge and now Lord Stamfordham, who hit upon the perfect brand name to proclaim the sturdy British nature of its royal family. In 1917 it was officially announced that henceforth it would call itself the Royal House of Windsor.

It was exactly what was needed, for it made the all-important point not just that the royal family had cut its ties with Germany, but that it had also changed from a distant continental dynasty into a firmly British institution as foursquare and dependable as that most ancient and evocative of royal symbols, Windsor Castle. And just as the war had brought about this change in the symbolism of the royal family, so it had also brought a transformation in its contact with the public. For the war – which might easily have wrecked the monarchy in Britain, as it did in Russia, Germany and Austria – actually strengthened the sense of national identity with the royal family, and made the Court itself more conscious of the need to create a clear impression that this family, though royal, also shared the sufferings and loyal aspirations of every ordinary family in the land.

This was something royalty had rarely bothered with before, and a radical advance in the developing myth of the modern British monarchy. It was possible, of course, only through the relatively new media of popular press and magazines, but equally it could not have happened without those homely royal virtues so steadfastly implanted by resolute Queen Mary. For the war was essentially her finest hour, and she showed considerable imagination in demonstrating that the royal family positively cared about 'their peoples' ' sufferings. The first Christmas of the war, it was her idea to send each serving soldier at the front a gift – an expensively produced and gilded cigarette box with her monogram and features on the lid and cigarettes, sweets and Queen Mary's photograph tucked inside, together with a cheering Christmas message.

It was thoughtful of Her Majesty. It was also an adroit piece of royal public relations, and the monarchy became an important force in wartime popular morale. The Queen was particularly responsive to the public mood. She and the King decided that the court would foreswear alcohol 'for the duration of hostilities'. This was a little hard on poor King George, who rather relied on his whisky and soda, but with Queen Mary always present it was rigidly enforced. The sacrifice was widely reported in the press and did much to forestall rumours that royalty lived in luxury while the common people did without.

Thanks again to widespread coverage in the popular press – which was constantly encouraged by the wartime government – people soon realised how much Queen Mary shared the anxieties of ordinary wives and mothers. Her eldest son, the dashing Prince of Wales, was at the Front – as the official press photographers made very clear; her second son, Prince Albert, commanded a gun-turret at Jutland; and the King himself made many weary visits to his troops in France, during one of which he was thrown from his horse and badly injured.

Duty and dedication had apparently become a royal religion, thanks in large part to the impressive influence of the Queen. Indefatigable in her work among the British wounded, she forced other female members of the family to follow her example until one of them finally complained, 'I'm tired and I hate hospitals.' Back snapped Queen Mary: 'You are a member of the British Royal Family. We are *never* tired, and we all *love* hospitals!'

Here was the authentic voice of the unrelenting royal matriarch herself, and it was this powerful example which was of key importance in changing the style of monarchy to meet the social and political upheavals of the time. No one did more than Queen Mary to advance the monarchy beyond those 'ornamental' qualities described by Bagehot. What in fact she did was to show how the British monarchy could flourish by combining two apparently irreconcilable elements in its public image.

On the one hand lay the concepts she herself embodied, of duty, morality and family – the everyday classless virtues which the mass of decent citizens would naturally applaud, and made the royal family appear 'just like us'. They were paragons, but human paragons, with whom the simplest of people could identify.

But while acting out this role herself, Queen Mary could never for a moment overlook the sacred nature of the royal calling – particularly where the monarch was concerned – and this she persistently impressed upon her husband, gruff King George. The most human, often irritable of men, neither he nor those around him were allowed to forget those extra-human qualities he alone embodied – king-priest, father of his people, sacred and anointed heir to what was rapidly appearing as the last, most colourful and traditional monarchy in Europe.

This dual nature of the monarch was the great invention of the House of Windsor, and it became widely accepted as quite natural,

thanks to the response of the royal couple to the developing technology of mass communications. This became particularly clear in
the early 1930s, when John Reith, the ambitious and authoritarian
chairman of the recently created national broadcasting system, the
BBC, was keenly anxious to establish his fledgling organisation as a
respectable organ of the state. As well he knew, nothing would do
this better than active royal participation; and in 1932 he got it,
when George V agreed to deliver on the radio a Christmas message
to his beloved Empire.

With his resonant diction and nautical sincerity, the King proved
an effective broadcaster; and as is the way with royalty, what was
in reality a modern innovation rapidly acquired the status of one
more monarchical tradition, so that people annually looked forward
to the royal message after lunch as part of the ritual of Christmas.

It seemed so natural and obvious at the time; yet the broadcast
marked in fact a further radical advance in the transformation of
the monarchy by the mass media. After that first technological revolution which had relayed Victoria's features and activities to the mass
readership of the penny press, King George V could now seem even
closer to his people as the nation heard its sovereign's greeting live
across the ether:

> Through one of the marvels of science, I am enabled this Christmas
> Day to speak to all my people throughout the Empire . . .

The actual words – although written for the King by Rudyard
Kipling – were not particularly important: what mattered was that
an entire population – instead of just a handful of courtiers and
servants – was hearing the royal voice addressing it in person, so
that George suddenly became something no monarch had ever been
before in history, an intimately appreciated, widely known human
being, a simple king in the age of the common man.

In one sense this was absolutely true; but it was also based on an
extraordinary illusion. George was a very simple man; with Queen
Mary firmly at his side, he was also a very sacred king, and all the
trappings and ceremony of monarchy were rigorously maintained.
None of this, however, apparently affected his popularity in the
least. On the contrary, he was widely regarded as a real king with
all the trimmings, who had brought the experience of monarchy to
ordinary people. And the full success of this illusion became clear

in May of 1935, when the National Government – thinking, as Claud Cockburn said, 'that it was in need of a tonic' – decided on a joyful celebration of the quarter-century of King George's reign.

There had never been a Silver Jubilee before, and a fiasco was predicted. Instead, the people 'ate together at long trestle tables in the streets and drank from Jubilee mugs. They had bonfires and danced and kissed in the streets. The park attendants had to call for extra trolleys to cart away the huge litter of discarded condoms. It was a genuine jamboree!'

Almost everyone seemed genuinely surprised by the old King's popularity – not least himself. 'I never realised they felt like that about me,' he said, clearly overcome, after driving through the cheering crowds of the poorest quarters of East End London.

But did they really, and why this popular enthusiasm at King George's Silver Jubilee? Cockburn, who was both a contemporary observer and some sort of Marxist at the time, offered his own intriguing explanation:

> What they were expressing was not reverence for the King because he was powerful, but fellow-feeling because he was harassed, and supposed to be powerless. He had become paradoxically, virtually one of US – endlessly harried, deceived, deprived and generally done down by Them – i.e. the bloody politicians!

As Cockburn said, the King's popularity at the Jubilee was something of a paradox, like the extraordinary illusion which enabled ordinary people to identify with him. But it was an illusion on which the standing of the monarchy was going to depend for many years to come, and which would need continual efforts to maintain once George died, as he did just one year later. At his death, a further paradox arose when it appeared that Queen Mary's work for the monarchy was not complete. For despite the outward impression of domestic happiness she had tried to cultivate, she had been nursing a potential family disaster.

3

MOTHER

'The reign of George VI,' said the Duchess of Windsor
bitterly, 'is a split-level matriarchy in pants. Queen Mary runs
the King's wife and the King's wife runs the King.'
Bryan and Murphy, *The Windsor Story*

For all Queen Mary's dedication to the myth of the British monarchy
and the sacred person of the King, there was one all-important
problem she had never managed to resolve – relations with her
children. Worse still, King George's eldest son and heir rejected
almost everything his parents stood for, so that his short and bumpy
reign – from January to December 1936 – came as the biggest crisis
the Royal House of Windsor has so far had to face. His abdication
was a royal trauma, which has haunted the family as such a dread
example ever since that it remains something of a key to understanding how the monarchy has grown to the present day.

For it was only after King Edward's abdication that Queen Mary's
highly popular successor, Queen Elizabeth, the former Duchess of
York, was able to repair the damage to her predecessor's work. In
doing so, she effectively completed what might be called 'the
Windsor Formula' – that magic dispensation which has enabled the
monarchy not merely to survive, but to attain its unparalleled heights
of super-stardom in the 1980s. To understand the full significance
of what she did, it is necessary first to appreciate why and how
Queen Mary failed – and just how large a threat her eldest son
presented to the growing reputation of the Royal House of Windsor.

As parents, George V and Queen Mary had both clearly been at
fault, and most of their troubles with their children seemed to stem
from their royal situation. The autocratic sailor-king regarded the
faintest show of childish misbehaviour as mutiny, to be dealt with
in the style of Captain Bligh: and Queen Mary, far from soothing
father-son relations, had usually made matters worse by her overriding dedication to the sacred royal person. By nature she was not

particularly maternal, having borne six children more as a royal duty
than from more commonplace female motives, and her reverence for
her husband invariably made her side with him against their
offspring. 'I have always to remember that their father is also their
King,' she told a friend when discussing the boys' behaviour; not
surprisingly, her lady-in-waiting, Lady Airlie, wrote that 'with the
exception of Princess Mary, they were strangers to her emotionally
. . . and she remained tragically inhibited with them.'

The qualities that made her so successfully a queen, made her a
disaster as a mother, and there is something positively chilling in
the way she agreed to have her epileptic youngest son, Prince John,
consigned to a small house on the Sandringham estate, where he
died, unnoticed and virtually unmourned, except by his devoted
nurse, in 1919.

All her four elder sons were to suffer in their different ways. Prince
Albert, Duke of York, was something of a nervous wreck, with
severe digestive troubles as well as an appalling stammer. Prince
George, Duke of Kent, found himself involved in several youthful
'scrapes' which were much talked about by people 'in the know',
was widely rumoured to be bisexual, and had eventually to be cured
of an addiction to cocaine. And Prince Henry, Duke of Gloucester,
soon embarked upon that life-long addiction to the bottle which
was to leave him fit for little save the less demanding sorts of military
ceremonial and the Governor Generalship of Australia, where his
weakness was not noticed. 'Just look at us!' the Prince of Wales is
said to have burst out to a friend after a family row at the Palace.
'Bertie stammers, George takes drugs, Henry drinks, and now I'm
told I'm a disgrace to the family!'

But significantly, Edward, Princes of Wales, was probably the
most intelligent of the royal brood, and he had other virtues that
his parents and siblings for the most part lacked – abundant charm,
some glamour, and a lively if selective sense of humour. During his
teens he had also acquired that most perilous of royal acquisitions
– a mind of his own. It led him almost inevitably to reject what he
saw as the oppressive influence of his parents and, along with that,
most of the principles that made the House of Windsor what it was.
It was this that made – and still makes – his melancholy story such
an instructive one for the future of the British monarchy.

In retrospect, the Duke of Windsor seems in many ways a
distinctly silly man – petulant, disloyal to his friends and erratic in

his judgements (outstandingly in his contacts with the Nazis just before and at the beginning of the war). But as a young man he enjoyed immense success as Prince of Wales, particularly in his tours of the Empire, where he swiftly developed a royal style of his own in sharp contrast with the relatively stuffy image of his parents.

His sense of fun often proved stronger than his sense of the dignity of his position, and he had a genuine aversion to all but the simplest forms of royal ceremonial. 'What rot and a waste of time, money and energy all these state visits are,' he had confided to his diary even before the First World War. His mother's arguments about the sacred nature of the royal person predictably weighed little with him, and instead of the role of god-like father of the people typified by George V, his personal inclinations tended towards a livelier, more informal sort of monarchy.

'Only two rules really count,' he wrote. 'Never miss an opportunity to relieve yourself, and never miss an opportunity to sit down and rest your feet.'

Popular, irreverent, and thoroughly enjoying his freedom from the Palace and the courtiers, he showed little inclination towards marriage, procreation and the domestic virtues of the Royal House of Windsor. To make matters worse, his private life was faintly scandalous, with a number of unsatisfactory affairs, invariably with married women. Though barely mentioned in the loyal British press, they were deeply disturbing to his parents, who received regular reports from their son's detectives of what was going on.

In fact like all his brothers and his father, he was ready to be dominated by a powerful, emphatic woman. Ironically, when he found her, she was divorced, American, still living with her second husband, and totally at odds with the ethos of that sober, country-loving family, the House of Windsor.

Ten years earlier, Edward might just have got away with his infatuation for Mrs Ernest Simpson, married her and kept the crown. During the lively 1920s, his sense of style had epitomised an exuberant decade. But the 1930s were very different. Wall Street had crashed, and two million unemployed touched the conscience of the nation. By 1936, coming so abruptly after the demise of King George V, the revelation in a *Times* leader that the dear old king's successor was involved with a *divorcée*, indignantly described by Queen Mary as an 'American adventuresss', seriously threatened the worthy moral image on which the monarchy depended for its public support.

Thanks to the Abdication crisis, King Edward was now revealed to the nation for what he was – a frivolous, distinctly selfish man, surrounded by a set of rich, fast-living sycophants. The same had applied to his grandfather and namesake, Edward VII, and he had lived to reign successfully after much early unpopularity. But 'King Tum-Tum' had reigned in a very different world from the anxious Thirties, and even he would have drawn the line at receiving at court a friend so ill-advised as to dream of marrying his twice-divorced mistress.

The prospect of a thrice-married lady from Baltimore following Queen Mary as royal consort was hard to contemplate with total seriousness. Edith Sitwell summed the situation up with caustic understatement when she wrote, 'I think she has been divorced twice too often for a Queen, and I don't think "Queen Wally" would sound well.'

More was actually at stake than this. For all his faults, Edward VIII was intent on bringing changes to the monarchy which would have brought it more in touch with popular opinion, and done much to end its sacred and ceremonial functions. He was averse to the idea of royalty as beings set apart, and was more than willing to speak his mind in public – even if this meant upsetting the politicians and involving the Crown itself in controversy – as he did with his outburst when visiting the South Wales unemployed: 'Something must be done!' Had he managed to continue reigning with 'Queen Wally' on the throne beside him, the nature of the monarchy would certainly have changed abruptly. Had it survived, it would have tended to become far closer to the democratic style of kingship the countries of Scandinavia enjoy today.

But in 1936 the Conservative prime minister, Stanley Baldwin, made it absolutely clear that this was not a possibility. Like it or not, the King of England was no ordinary mortal with the normal man's right to marry as and whom he wanted. Baldwin bluntly told the King that Mrs Simpson would be unacceptable as a royal consort to the parliaments of Britain and the Commonwealth; and on this point of principle and passion Edward VIII departed, leaving his crown to his brother, Bertie. He spent the remainder of his life in luxurious but bitter exile, with the title of the Duke of Windsor,

and the former Mrs Simpson as his Duchess, until his death at home
in Paris in 1972.

For a crisis that aroused such passions at the time, one of the
strangest things about the Abdication is how swiftly the public
adjusted to the brisk departure of the uncrowned King. But within
the Court things appeared differently, and there was a feeling of
profound betrayal and bitterness towards the Duke of Windsor – as
the exiled former King had now become – which would not diminish
with the years. Recently both Spain and Greece had lost their kings,
and for the Windsors, who had seen so many of their royal relations
murdered or deposed, the Abdication crisis had an element of private
nightmare, with their whole position and possibly their safety placed
wantonly at risk. Within the family it could not be amiably
forgotten.

For the essence of the Abdication crisis was that the King had
attempted to overthrow the solid structure, together with those
matriarchal virtues of home, family and duty, on which the reputation of the Crown was based in everyday awareness. Before he
abdicated the throne, Edward had refused the responsibilities
imposed by Queen Mary's royal code. The consequences were to
have a crucial influence upon the House of Windsor for years to
come, as that unhappy man became a sort of royal phantom,
haunting the members of his family as a ghastly warning of the
perils of almost everything he stood for.

One immediate effect of the affair was a new and lasting mood
of solidarity and seriousness within the royal family. On the actual
evening of the Abdication, Edward had a final farewell dinner with
his brothers at Windsor before driving down to Portsmouth and the
destroyer that would carry him to France. It was an emotional
occasion, and when the former king had gone, the Duke of Kent
burst out impulsively that he and the remaining members of the
family must now 'pull themselves together' to support the throne.

This, to the best of their abilities, they did, reinforced by a sense
of gratified relief for the person of the former Duke of York, the
second son who now emerged as the unlikely-seeming saviour of the
family. Like his father before him, he was prepared to do his duty;
but unlike his extrovert brother, he had not been trained for kingship. He knew he needed guidance, and he needed emotional
support.

Created Duke of York in 1920, Prince Albert Edward Michael George – 'Bertie', as the family always called him – had lived his first quarter-century as something of a casualty to his unenviable situation. Shy, sensitive, and not particularly bright (he came 68th out of 68 in his class as a cadet at Osborne Naval College), he had been frightened by his father, overshadowed by his elder brother, and bullied by his larger classmates in the Navy. He smoked compulsively (his sixteenth birthday present from his mother was a royally engraved cigarette case) and seemed a lonely, introspective figure on the royal landscape.

A plodder rather than a self-assertive rebel like his elder brother, Bertie was more in tune than his brother Edward with those public attitudes which had earned his parents their popular respect. In many ways he resembled his father as a young man, and made determined efforts of his own to 'be of use'. He became genuinely interested in British industry, and his factory visits earned him the faintly mocking family nickname of 'the Foreman'. He had also something of a social conscience, and on his own initiative started the royal family's admirable and enduring concern with Youth. Shocked, like his father, by the harrowing effect of post-war unemployment, particularly upon the urban young, he was the moving force behind the 'Duke of York Camps' for boys. These were held each summer from 1921 until the outbreak of the Second World War. Here, under canvas in healthy open country, boys of the working-classes could enjoy a free fortnight's holiday in the company of equal numbers of their social betters from the public schools. And every year, in sober knee-length shorts, the Duke of York would conscientiously attend, leading the boys on bracing walks, joining in their games, and – his stammer totally forgotten – contributing lustily to their sing-songs round a log-fire in the evenings.

From the viewpoint of the 1980s, there seems something faintly comic, even condescending in these royal attempts to alleviate unrest and bring 'better social understanding' through the gung-ho methods of an annual youth camp. But it is important to remember how extremely unsophisticated the majority of people were in this pre-war, pre-television era, and the efforts of this very worthy, shy young prince roused little of the youthful cynicism they would undoubtedly attract today. More to the point, they were very much in line with the ideals of conscientious 'service' and public duty which had earned the monarchy such popularity in the war. His work did something to endear him to his parents, and as King George's relations with his eldest son declined, those with his second son steadily improved.

For, mellowing with age, the King could appreciate Bertie's earnest attitude to life, and nothing had received more approbation than his nervous wooing of the youngest daughter of the 14th Earl of Strathmore, Lady Elizabeth Bowes-Lyon. As one of the prettiest debutantes of the year, she had not been short of suitors, and had twice rejected him. 'I said to him I was afraid, as royalty, never, never again to be free to think or speak or act as I feel I ought to think or speak or act.'

But the Prince had persevered, with the King's encouragement: 'You'll be a lucky fellow, Bertie, if she accepts you.' Lady Elizabeth's fears about retaining her individuality were overcome, and the first royal wedding of the House of Windsor was celebrated with notable panache in 1923.

The wedding marked one more significant advance in the public cult of British monarchy. The Court was beginning to exploit the popular potential of romantic ceremonial, and with the Prince of Wales already starting to attract at this time unfavourable comment by his evident unwillingness to marry, his brother's wedding to a pretty bride was something to be made the most of. Most previous royal marriages had been strictly family events, performed in the relative privacy of the Chapel Royal, Windsor; but this was a full-blown state occasion, and Lord Strathmore's daughter had the honour of becoming, besides Duchess of York, the first bride of a royal prince to be married in Westminster Abbey since Richard II wed Anne of Bohemia in 1382.

With the arrival of the two Princesses – Elizabeth in 1926 and Margaret Rose in 1930 – the Yorks became still more of an asset to the public image of the Crown, a living demonstration that the monarchy – the Prince of Wales notwithstanding – still embodied all the calm and radiant domestic virtues the times required of an ideal royal family.

The Yorks were ready to be magically transformed into the model young English family of the Thirties, and the constant impression that emerges from the press and newsreels of the period is of the faintly dreamlike domesticity also found in contemporary advertisements for Ovaltine or patent medicines: slender caring father, always neatly dressed and faintly worried, adoring mother with the loveliest of smiles, and two beautifully behaved and dressed small girls who are a credit to their doting parents. Love seems to radiate from their devotion for each other, and they appear effortlessly and always happy.

It was a dream the nation could sentimentally subscribe to, and with an eager press now avid for the slightest morsel of the home life of this happiest of families, the Duchess willingly responded to requests for decorous publicity. With her encouragement the distinguished London publisher, John Murray, produced in 1930 the first full-length 'biography' of her four-year-old eldest daughter: *The Story of Princess Elizabeth, told with the Sanction of Her Parents by Anne Ring, formerly attached to HRH the Duchess of York's Household.* Miss Ring had worked for several years as assistant secretary to the Duchess, and this short, skilfully written book, produced from within the household, shows that the future Queen Elizabeth was not averse to the creation of the legend of her perfect family.

> From the moment of her birth not only has our little Princess been wrapped about with the tender love of parents and devoted grand-parents, of cousins and uncles and friends, but she has been the admiring object of affection from thousands in this country and beyond the seas who have never seen her.

She was 'the World's best known baby', but the whole message of the book is that, far from allowing this to spoil her daughter, the gentle Duchess has wisely brought her up to mirror all the virtues of an ideal childhood. Take the description of the royal bedtime:

> When Princess Elizabeth's nurse descending to the Morning Room or the Drawing Room, says in quiet tones, 'I think it is bedtime now, Elizabeth,' there are no poutings or protests, just a few joyous skips and impromptu dance steps, a few last minute laughs at Mummy's delicious bedtime jokes, and then Princess Elizabeth's hand slips into her Nurse's hand, and the two go off gaily together across the deep chestnut pile of the Hall carpet to the accommo-dating lift, which in two seconds has whisked them off to the familiar dear domain, which is theirs to hold and to share.

The great wealth of the royal family could have been a problem for anyone intent on presenting them as the epitome of simple virtues to a faithful nation – particularly if the nation itself was racked by unemployment, economic slump and social discontent. But it was a difficulty Miss Ring could cope with. Just as King George V had been presented by the press as the embodiment of the simplest of manly virtues in positive contrast with the protocol at Court and those seventeen patient locomotives, so the young Princess's 'joyous skips' and calm obedience were actually enhanced in contrast with those royal temptations she and her devoted mother could so sensibly resist. Typical was the all-important subject of the Princess's toys. Miss Ring admitted the danger that the Princess might easily be spoiled, particularly by Queen Mary who 'whenever she sees any fascinating toy can seldom resist the pleasure of buying it for her grand-daughter.'

> But the Princess's Mother is wise; no one knows better than the Duchess of York, whose own childhood was simple and yet so happy, that it is neither the number of a child's toys nor their expensiveness which makes him happy, and she never allows the Princess to be bewildered by too many toys at once.

This contrast between the Duchess and her mother-in-law is intriguing, for it highlights an important difference the future Queen Elizabeth seemed intent on emphasising in her life. Where Queen Mary was an unsuccessful mother, her successor was determined to become the royal embodiment of maternal virtue – and evidently anxious to make everyone aware of it. Anne Ring's biography was only the beginning of a spate of articles and books which followed, with the cooperation and active sponsorship of the gracious Duchess.

Best-known of these was Lady Cynthia Asquith's *The Married Life of HRH the Duchess of York*. 'Written and Published with the PERSONAL APPROVAL of Her Royal Highness', this loyal paean to the most 'joyous', 'delightful' and 'radiant' of families must occasionally have stretched the credibility of even its most royalist reader, as with the assurance that on wet days the Duchess liked nothing better than 'to visit the still-room to revive her Scotch (*sic*) skill in the making of scones and cakes – an excellent relaxation.'

Such calm improbabilities apart, the most revealing fact about the devout confections of ladies like Miss Ring and Lady Cynthia is that they show how seriously the future royal family, and in particular the Queen herself, were already taking the creation of a starring role around the sacred person of the young Princess.

Long before Princess Elizabeth could walk she knew how to smile strangers into slavery; and while still unable to speak, she gave unmistakable signs of a laudable desire to set others at their ease.

America had Shirley Temple: Britain had Princess Lilibet – 'utterly unspoiled and in every respect a typical English child', according to an article in the *News Chronicle* in early 1935 – and Lady Cynthia soon found herself wondering whether 'even the most glittering film star has a wider circle of adorers than Princess Elizabeth . . . the most celebrated and best loved child in the world.'

Several years before they reached the throne, the Yorks had already managed to become the first royal family in history to be widely presented like characters in a modern mass-circulation family romance. Fed by the press and radio, public curiosity about the family was intense by the time the new Queen Elizabeth reached the throne, and after the Abdication she was more than prepared to go on satisfying this loyal appetite in ways Queen Mary would never have considered. Her warmth and natural ease of manner made her a favourite with journalists, and their detailed, often sugary concoctions on the daily lives of the royal parents and their young Princesses confirmed the Windsors as the best-known, best-loved household in Britain.

A few favoured, highly popular journalists like the late Godfrey Winn received facilities for reporting the resultant scene with a freedom inconceivable today. One of his first 'intimate' royal assignments was to attend the family's own Christmas pantomime at Windsor and describe how the two Princesses 'brought the house down' with their lead performances in 'Old Mother Red Riding Boots'. At the same time, 'Sources Close to the Palace' – usually ladies-in-waiting or family friends earning pin-money from daily journalism – found themselves quite free to describe the happy lives of the royal children. It was from them that the public learned about the young Princesses' keen participation in the Buckingham Palace Brownie Pack, their devotion for the royal corgis, Carol and Crackers, and their extraordinarily well-behaved enjoyment of their royal dolls' house, paid for as a special gift from 'the people of the Principality of Wales' and constructed, half life-size, in the grounds of Windsor Royal Lodge.

Queen Elizabeth had a natural flair for the public relations of royalty, and throughout the immense coverage her family received it is hard to find a disrespectful, still less a cynical or critical remark. More than ever now the family seemed 'good', the natural and effortless embodiment of all those family-based virtues which radiated from its loving mother. But there was an element of obvious illusion here. The more lovingly and loyally it was presented to the quintessentially 'ordinary' British family, the less ordinary it really was. It could not afford to be. Edward had tried to behave with 'ordinary' freedom, and the result had been disaster. Nowhere was the illusion more tested than at the Abdication; and nowhere was the influence of Elizabeth more crucial to restoring the reputation of the British monarchy. For at this point of royal crisis, another aspect of her character came into play. Being Queen of England called for sterner stuff than simply being Queen of Mothers.

While it is going too far to believe, as one of King George VI's latest biographers has written, that this simple man 'would have been perfectly content in a mock-Tudor semi-detached house with his family, his stamp collection and the radio' (in itself a revealing example of the persistence of the Yorks' image as an idealised suburban family), he had certainly been very happy with life in their mansion at the Hyde Park end of Piccadilly. But in his sudden lonely eminence, this insecure and anxious man relied upon his wife as never before; and once it was clear that life would have to change, an intriguing transformation occurred with the smiling, gentle-seeming Duchess. For Elizabeth herself, the prospect of the throne was far from daunting: she was the opposite of insecure and nobody could call her weak.

During the final stages of the Abdication, she had been ill with influenza; but on learning that she would soon be Queen, she snuffled, 'Well, we must make the best of it!' Make the best of it she did, and from the start she showed the sort of royal resolution her husband seemed to lack. A few weeks afterwards, she wrote a letter to Archbishop Cosmo Lang, the cleric who himself had played a leading part in edging godless Edward from the throne:

> The curious thing is that we are not afraid. God has enabled us to face the situation calmly.

It might have been Queen Mary speaking, and in fact the old Queen had remained an important influence upon her daughter-in-

law from before her marriage, when she had made her something
of a *protégée*, teaching her her role as a member of the royal family.
During this process a great deal of Queen Mary's perennial philosophy about the monarchy had inevitably rubbed off on the future
Queen Elizabeth, and despite their very different characters they
were united in their sense of mission to the Crown. In many ways
the young Queen had consciously modelled herself upon the old: in
particular, as an outsider to the royal family, she adopted Mary's
sense of the 'sanctity and mystery' of monarchy with all the dedication of a convert.

She also shared Queen Mary's absolute resolve to repair the
damage to the monarchy, and this, combined with her determination
to buttress the fragile person of the King, produced the steely sense
of purpose with which she treated both the Duke of Windsor and
his Duchess.

Whatever part personal antipathy may have played in this, it
would be doing Queen Elizabeth a considerable injustice to see her
attitude in terms of the family vendetta the Duke bitterly maintained
it to be. Far more than her private feelings were at stake. She was
realistic enough to understand that Edward, with his random charm
and easy manner, would be certain to attract great public sympathy
if he were once allowed back in England: with his popularity
restored, he would invite unfavourable comparisons with the King
– and might still overshadow him. Clearly it was safest for the Duke
and his lady to be kept in gilded exile in Paris and the South of
France, while the serious work of reinforcing the monarchy
continued.

The Duke of course disagreed. Naive as ever, he was not the man
to comprehend the implacable resolve of the amiable sister-in-law
who had now become Queen of England. He was no longer dealing
with his stammering younger brother, but with the two formidable
royal ladies who protected him. With all the ruthlessness the Palace
can exhibit when the need arises, its doors slammed shut against its
former king.

The break was as total as the ingenuity of royal advisers could
ensure. As King, Edward had personally inherited the two royal
residences which remain the private property of the royal family –
Balmoral Castle, built by Albert and Victoria in the 1850s, and
Sandringham, Edward VII's ugly, much-loved Norfolk country
house, purchased for £220,000 in 1863, then totally rebuilt. To

provide the Duke with the funds he desperately needed, the family agreed to buy back the two estates for around £1,000,000, on the strictest understanding that he settled permanently out of England.

Personal contact ceased as well. The Duke's letters, even to his mother, went unanswered. After 1937, his regular telephone calls to the King were no longer accepted at the Palace, and later in the year when he and Mrs Simpson married, the royal family ignored it. The Duke of Windsor interpreted as spite the failure of any member of his family to attend, and the refusal of the title 'Royal Highness' to his Duchess. But the important point was that the Palace now had no intention of doing anything that might restore the Royal Non-person and his ambitious consort in the public eye.

With the Duke and his Duchess effectively disposed of, it was time to prepare for the act which would set the seal of mystical authority upon the King: his Coronation. Set for May, 1937, it was planned with even greater splendour and solemnity than that of his parents a quarter of a century before, for it was a unique opportunity to establish the sacred image of the sovereign in the folk memory of his subjects, and unanswerable proof that the new King George was more truly a monarch than his uncrowned brother ever had been.

After the trauma of the Abdication this seemed particularly necessary. Edward's departure had been uncomfortably reminiscent of those unfashionable old Whig principles of 1688. He had abdicated when he was forced to accept that his royal power did not include the simple right to marry as he wished – a fact which was bluntly spelled out by the Prime Minister, Stanley Baldwin, who told him that Mrs Simpson would be unacceptable to the parliaments of Britain and the Commonwealth as royal consort. Like James II before him, Edward VIII finally departed thanks to the effective will of parliament.

This harsh, human truth was hard to reconcile with belief in the sacred status of the sovereign; but the Coronation would make it possible. In a profoundly British way, it would disguise this basic contradiction by enveloping the new monarch, his family and Court in such an overwhelming panoply of royal splendour that the actual limits on his right to reign would be totally obscured behind the resounding ritual of the Abbey. Military precision, monarchical tradition, the acclamation of the aristocracy and the cheering crowds along the route would abundantly proclaim the true majesty of

George VI. Even the Almighty would be there to offer irrefutable support at the climax of the beautifully staged service – the anointing of the royal breast and forehead with the sacred oil.

The only doubt among those nearest to the throne was the ability of the principal participant to see it through with appropriate panache. For anyone, the strain of the three-hour ritual would be intense: for a man of King George's temperament, it might well become a form of public torture.

Once again it was the moment for the female power beside the throne to help the image of the monarchy. Elizabeth had proved herself a natural actress, with the presence and self-confidence of one born to her position, and during the months before the king's ordeal it was she who encouraged and rehearsed him for his role. She did this with the true Svengali touch, convincing him that when the moment came he would possess the calmness and confidence to act the part demanded of a British King and Emperor.

The Coronation proved a triumph for them both – and also for Queen Mary who, breaking with a centuries-old tradition that no dowager queen was present at a crowning, decided to attend. With his Queen reassuringly beside him and his mother close at hand, this shyest of English kings was never seen to falter; and by the end of that day of heady national rejoicing, when the King, the two royal matriarchs and the two Princesses stood together on the Palace balcony, acknowledging the cheering multitude beneath, the monarchy had never seemed more firmly anchored in the hearts and imaginations of its subjects.

From this moment any doubts about King George's fitness to succeed his brother vanished, and at the end of 1937 came another demonstration of Queen Elizabeth's importance in promoting her husband's public image. The Christmas radio message to the nation was one of the rituals the King had particularly dreaded at his accession, and there had been no question of doing it that year. His stammer had long been seen as a serious impediment to a full public role in the royal family and, soon after his marriage, his wife persuaded him to have treatment from Lionel Logue, an unorthodox Australian speech therapist. Thanks to Logue's treatment and Elizabeth's powerful support, Bertie's diction had slowly, if painfully, improved; and after the Coronation she encouraged him to follow the example of his father and face the agony of delivering his Christmas message before the family enjoyed the festivities themselves at Sandringham.

Archbishop Lang, in a broadcast of his own, had unctuously warned the nation what they were in for.

When his people listen to him they will notice an occasional and momentary hesitation in his speech. But he has brought it under full control, and to those who hear him it need cause no embarrassment, for it causes none to him who speaks.

This was patent nonsense, and that Christmas – and for many to come – the nation shared the King's ordeal as he struggled, with the Queen silently beside him, to deliver his Christmas greeting exactly as his father had. His obvious discomfort added greatly to his popularity, arousing widespread sympathy for this vulnerably human sovereign trying his best to do his duty by his subjects.

But the illusion of ordinariness could not be allowed to outshine the 'sanctity' of the throne to which Queen Elizabeth, as a pupil of Queen Mary's, wholeheartedly subscribed. The British Crown was emphatically not on course to become the sort of Scandinavian-style monarchy it might have been had Edward VIII's reign continued. King George VI must be assured of the same reverence and respect his father had received from all around him, and the 'mystery of monarchy' demanded that he always keep his kingly distance from the subjects over whom he reigned.

Queen Elizabeth had been particularly insistent on this from the beginning. According to Dermot Morrah (in a book he wrote later with the *imprimatur* of the Palace), she 'always impressed upon the King the necessity for him to preserve a certain degree of aloofness' even within the family, 'and insisted that the crowned and anointed king must not be too ready to step down from his pedestal.'

Essentially the same applied to all the royal family. They met but did not mix with ordinary people. They lived their lives apart in the profoundly deferential ethos of the court. Their few close friends were courtiers and very rich aristocrats who treated them with deep respect, and they took their hieratic role for granted– as did everyone they met.

Queen Elizabeth's influence on all of this was central, as it was in the idealised public presentation of the 'ordinary', classless family itself. Her eldest daughter was now heiress presumptive to the throne, and would one day be the richest woman in the world; but much was made of the careful 'Scotch' economy the Queen supposedly instilled in both her children. 'When Elizabeth was a growing schoolgirl,' the *Express* assured its readers, 'her clothes were lengthened to "make do" longer, and when she grew out of them, Margaret wore them – just like a younger sister the world over.'

The particular genius of Queen Elizabeth lay in the way she always managed to combine the rarified world of monarchy with the manner of the democratic world outside – and taught her family to do the same. 'Your work,' she was widely reported to have told her daughters in a powerful restatement of Queen Mary's royal doctrine, 'is the rent you pay for the room you occupy on earth'; and her work was to combine to extraordinary effect elements that should have been completely incompatible.

The reward was a monarchy stronger than before, one that seemed to have adapted to the times while foreign thrones were crumbling. At once humdrum and profoundly regal, it was familiar yet still mysterious; popular yet sacrosanct; supremely privileged yet classless; all but powerless, yet automatically endowed with the sort of reverence accorded the most autocratic monarchies of years gone by.

By 1939 it was clear that the Royal House of Windsor had managed to perform some sort of minor miracle, having repaired the damage of the Abdication while keeping the best of all regal worlds without yielding an inch. The King was popular, the family virtually immune to criticism – which would have seemed akin to blasphemy – and the royal life-style followed the principles established in the reign of George V. The family remained essentially 'simple' people – dedicated, unsophisticated, still shunning 'fast' fashionable society and making no attempt to fraternise with even the most low-brow intellectuals. George V, thinking the word 'high-brow' was spelt 'eyebrow', had been baffled by its meaning all his life, and when an aide suggested to George VI that it might be diplomatic occasionally to patronise the opera, the king reportedly threw a book at him.

Thanks partly to the Queen's own Anglo-Scottish ancestry, the family's Germanic background had been more or less forgotten – and for this British dynasty there were no dangerous holidays abroad. For the King himself, 'abroad' had come to mean his tours of Commonwealth and Empire on behalf of those 'loyal subjects far beyond the seas'. For the House of Windsor was still taking the Empire as seriously as in the days of George V. With the royal stamp collection dutifully maintained at the Palace by the King himself (with the aid of the Keeper of the Royal Stamps, Sir John Wilson), George VI, like his father, could enjoy the unique experience of studying his likeness on the postage stamps of nearly one hundred colonies and nations of the British Commonwealth, starting alphabetically with Aden and finishing with Zanzibar. One of his major disappointments the year the war broke out was that it meant the cancellation of another Delhi Durbar, planned to repeat the triumph of his parents' Indian visit in 1911.

He would have been still more upset had he foreseen the way the war would spell the dissolution of his beloved Commonwealth and Empire – the most rapid and spectacular loss of power on such a scale in history. But in compensation the war gave him and his family a position as the focus for patriotic feeling similar to that his parents had experienced a quarter of a century before: and once more, like his parents, he and his family set out firmly – if a shade self-consciously – to do their wartime duty.

The Queen – who had a taste for good champagne – had no intention of repeating Queen Mary's uncomfortable example of foreswearing the demon drink for the duration. Instead there was a serious, much publicised attempt to apply food rationing rigorously to the royal menu, while the King personally painted lines inside the Windsor bath-tubs to ensure that the royal hot water was not wasted.

The Princesses were photographed together 'digging for victory' in their very own garden at Windsor: 'Every particle of the work has been done by their own hands', applauds the caption in another fulsome pictorial biography, *Our Princesses* by Lisa Sheridan, published in 1942, yet again 'by authority of Her Majesty the Queen'. Later Princess Elizabeth donned the khaki of a junior officer in the ATS, and although still spending all her nights at home, attended Windsor barracks for a period. Many photographs were taken of her peering at the engine of an army lorry.

Although overshadowed as the leader of his wartime nation by Winston Churchill – in a way his father never was by either Asquith or Lloyd George – King George VI was rarely out of the uniforms that suited him so well of one of the three services. He visited his troops as often as his government would let him, and maintained the resolute impression that he and his family were still firmly at the head of a united patriotic nation. The Palace had been bombed, the family itself suffered loss when his brother, George, Duke of Kent, died in an aircraft crash in Northern Scotland, and with the ending of the war, the monarchy appeared firmly in its place at the head of a victorious nation. It seemed right and natural that the victory celebrations should culminate with milling crowds along the Mall cheering the royal family and Winston Churchill on the Palace balcony.

By now the King had finally matured in experience and self-confidence, and seemed firmly set within the Windsor mould created so largely by his mother and his wife. He was very much a man of habit and with late middle-age had grown increasingly like his father – with the same short temper, jealous adoration for his wife, and an eye for the smallest detail of dress and royal ceremony. (He was rather pleased when he alone spotted that one of the Balmoral guards had ironed the pleats on his kilt the wrong way round.) He remained doggedly conscientious in working through official state papers, and towards the end appears to have caught that pessimism for the future of the monarchy which had afflicted both his father and grandfather in old age before him. When Vita Sackville-West told him that Knole, her great family house, had been given to the National Trust, he raised his hands in sad despair:

'Everything is going now. Before long I shall have to go as well.'

He spoke truer than he knew, and had he lived longer it is hard to see how he would have faced the social change he hated and the loss of the Empire that he loved. But the two remarkable women in his life – his mother and his wife – had no such doubts about the future of the Crown. He, like so much of the modern monarchy itself, was in a sense their joint creation; and they could still ensure that the monarchy continued, stronger than ever, with his daughter.

4

CORONATION AND
THE MAGIC MONARCHY

'The more democratic we get, the more we shall get to like
state and show which have ever pleased the vulgar.'
Walter Bagehot

Thanks largely to her mother's influence and to the homely, classless
presentation of the House of Windsor, Elizabeth II was already
highly popular at her accession. No other monarch in history had
begun a reign with such detailed public awareness of her personality,
giving people the illusion that they really knew her. She and her
sister had grown up before her subjects' fascinated gaze, and the
more people had learned to identify with that ideal English family,
the Windsors, the more this serious, shy, sensibly-dressed, corgi-
loving child of the Thirties had come to represent the most reassuring
aspects of the monarchy itself.

Like her parents, she was obviously 'good' – for nothing bad was
ever said against her. She had matured in the shared ordeal of the
war, romantically married the one man she had ever been in love
with, and automatically become the most celebrated mother of two
small children in the land. Everyone knew the way she smiled, or
rode a horse, or glanced at her husband on a state occasion; and
she effortlessly possessed qualities her father sadly lacked in the
years before his death – youth, glamour, energy and health – so that
her sudden arrival on the throne brought the greatest surge of hope
and popular excitement since the war had ended.

Her accession also fired a genuine sense of national renewal
focussed on the monarchy: as Winston Churchill put it, in his somewhat windy rhetoric, 'a fair and youthful figure, princess, wife and
mother, is the heir to all our glories and traditions.' But rhetoric
apart – outside the wonderfully discreet circle of family and few
close friends – strangely little was actually revealed about the real
wishes of this 'fair and youthful figure'. In fact, public assumptions
were considerably at odds with her private inclinations now that she

was Queen – inclinations shaped by the events that had dominated her childhood.

She had just reached the impressionable age of ten when her favourite Uncle David caused the earthquake that transformed the world she knew. 'Is Uncle David in trouble?' she had anxiously inquired. She swiftly learned that Uncle David was taboo within the family; and as each year passed and it became increasingly improbable that a younger brother would arrive to oust her from the succession, she and her father came to share the unique bond between sovereign and carefully prepared heir. In character she was rather like him and instinctively adopted most of his attitudes to life – and in particular towards the Crown. Now he was dead, his memory demanded that she carry on his work, and nothing was going to deter her.

But the aftermath of the Abdication had produced another all-important element within the family itself – a sort of royal siege mentality towards the world outside. The Windsors would perform their public duties to perfection, smile, be photographed, act graciously to all they met: but behind this there would always be the simple, very private family united in their mission to keep the monarchy intact after the near-disaster Uncle David had created. In this they were carefully protected by their courtiers, and inspired by Queen Mary's unshakeable belief in the sacred nature of the crown. But the strength that bound the family together had unquestionably been the all-absorbing love of Queen Elizabeth.

George VI made this clear in the letter he wrote his elder daughter just before her marriage to Philip, former Prince of Greece, in 1947. 'Our family, us four, the "Royal Family", must remain together with additions of course at suitable moments! I have watched you grow up all these years with pride under the skilful direction of Mummy, who as you know, is the most wonderful person in the world in my eyes.'

Like Elizabeth herself, Philip was a great-great-grandchild of Victoria: he was also the nephew and *protégé* of the King's influential kinsman, Louis, Lord Mountbatten. But the strangest thing about this marriage is how little change it really introduced at Court. Philip was a man of strong and independent character. He and his wife were patently in love. But even after they had established a household of their own at Clarence House and produced their first two children, he had done nothing to impinge upon the fixed mentality which had come to rule 'Us Four'.

'Let us hope there will now be a clean out, a clean sweep,' the Chicago-born socialite and politician, Sir Henry 'Chips' Channon, ever hopeful, wrote in his diary about the Palace at the time of King George's death. Someone who knew the chief participants as well as he did might have known better.

'The King is dead! Long live the Queen Mother!' a cynical courtier is said to have exclaimed after King George's death, and it was obvious that the royal widow could be of key importance to the new reign if she wanted to – but at first it was far from certain that she did. She was profoundly shaken by her husband's death and her immediate reaction was to retire from the world, exchanging public life for that of a private individual and leaving her daughter and son-in-law to shoulder the royal role between them.

There were strong precedents for doing this. Victoria herself had virtually retired for many years, nursing her sorrow after Albert's death. More recently, Queen Mary had withdrawn from the court when Edward VIII took over at the Palace, and even after George VI's succession had tended to remain more or less discreetly in the background as the new royal couple proceeded to rebuild the monarchy. But there was one crucial difference in the situation of the widowed Queen Mary and the new Queen Mother. Queen Mary had been absolutely certain that she could rely upon a strong-willed *protégée* in the person of the new royal consort, her daughter-in-law, Elizabeth. Philip was also a strong-willed consort, but in no sense was he the *protégé* of his royal mother-in-law. Quite the reverse. He was outspoken, radical, irreverent. He had made little secret of his impatience with the Palace protocol, which both bored and depressed him, and he had clashed already with several of the older courtiers. If anyone was going to initiate that 'clean sweep' Channon hoped for, it needed little imagination to foresee who would wield the broom.

There must have been a noticeable whiff of panic in the Palace air in the weeks following George VI's funeral, as reports from Sandringham confirmed the extent of the Queen Mother's grief. She was said to be genuinely inconsolable, and even rumoured to have turned to spiritualism in an attempt to contact the departed king. Concern began to mount, and by the time it reached the government, the Prime Minister himself, the aged Winston Churchill, saw that something clearly needed to be done.

A Conservative government required a monarchy it could rely on. So, as he saw it, did the future stability and unity of the country, whatever government might be in power, and this was not the moment to permit any changes that might shake the legacy of George VI. Certainly the most reliable and influential guarantee of royal continuity could hardly be allowed to retire now without a struggle to prevent it.

The seventy-nine-year-old Prime Minister went off to Sandringham himself and, as so often in the past, his powers of persuasion won the day: the fifty-one-year-old Queen Mother was finally convinced that however much she missed her husband, he would have wanted her to carry on the work they had begun together.

All talk of her retirement abruptly ceased: so did Prince Philip's hopes of keeping Clarence House as a separate home for the family and using Buckingham Palace as a sort of working Royal Head-quarters. For Clarence House was now scheduled as the London home for the Queen Mother, who had graciously decided to return to public life, and it would soon be lavishly refurbished in accordance with her wishes at a public cost of £55,000. (This included a total change of colour scheme and the bringing of a valuable fireplace from her bedroom at the Palace because, as she insisted, it had been the private gift of George VI.)

A generous allowance from the Civil List – £90,000 a year – was also allocated by a grateful government to the royal dowager and her household, which was to include the full royal complement of Private Secretary, Comptroller, ADC and lady-in-waiting, apart from all the lesser staff. The government still needed her, the monarchy required her, and Queen Elizabeth the Queen Mother was once again prepared to do her duty.

'All I wish now,' she said, 'is to be able to continue the work I started.' Continue it she did. Her daughter had replaced her husband on the throne, but the royal dispensation so carefully worked out for George VI was piously preserved for Elizabeth II. Existing court-iers stayed in their old positions. George VI's influential Private Secretary, Sir Alan Lascelles, was confirmed as Private Secretary to the Queen. And every morning, when she had finished reading the newspapers, Her Majesty would discuss events of the forthcoming day with mother on the telephone.

There are times when changes are produced by those most anxious to believe that they are standing still – and this was one of them. For those forces which had produced such extraordinary developments in the British monarchy during the previous three reigns were far from spent, and, barely aware that she was doing anything at all unusual, this new and most cautiously traditional of queens soon found herself at the centre of the most dramatic innovation to involve the royal house of Windsor since its creation.

For the perceptive, there had already been certain indications of what was building up: the 'Crawfie business' for example, the full significance of which was largely obscured at the time by the indignation it created in the family.

Marion Crawford was the dark-haired, former primary-school teacher from Peebleshire who in 1935, while still in her mid-twenties, was engaged as governess to the two Princesses. An earnest, unsophisticated Scottish spinster, she was a great walker and a fresh-air fiend, whose views on most things seemed to coincide with those of her employers. When one learns that for a long period she had total charge of the two Princesses' education, one understands why Queen Mary was a little worried and felt it wise to supplement Miss Crawford's teaching with visits to art galleries and museums, and special instruction in English constitutional history for Elizabeth from Sir Henry Marten, the eccentric but thoroughly reliable old vice-provost of Eton.

Queen Elizabeth herself had no wish to see her daughters turned into bluestockings, and since there was no danger of this occurring while Miss Crawford ruled the Palace schoolroom, the governess remained there in a position of considerable trust and intimacy with the family until just after Princess Margaret's eighteenth birthday in 1948. She then retired.

It would be wrong to blame the Windsors for ingratitude in the way they treated Miss Crawford, but they do seem to have been guilty of a lack of understanding of basic human nature – which has recurred to sour relations with their ex-employees on a number of occasions since. Senior courtiers almost automatically received honours and generous treatment on their retirement from the Palace (they still do), but the servant classes fared noticeably worse. Lionel

Logue, the speech therapist, who over twenty years did as much for George VI as any courtier, was lucky to receive a humble MVO. And Miss Crawford, who had also given long and faithful service to the family, received no honour for those years in the Palace classroom to accompany her meagre pension.

As English literature suggests, the British governess has always been a tricky breed, uncomfortably suspended as she is between the servants and the gentry. Miss Crawford was no exception. Once back in Aberdeen, with little but her memories and no restrictions on her fountain pen, she decided to write a book. She entitled it *The Little Princesses*, and it appeared early in 1950.

It was firmly in the tradition of those deferential books about the young Princesses written by gushing ladies like Miss Ring, Miss Sheridan and Lady Cynthia Asquith, and published with Her Majesty's encouragement in years gone by. It had much the same flavouring of intimacy and patriotic saccharine, and although much longer and more detailed than those early works, was profoundly loyal and in no way even hinted at the slightest impropriety among any of its royal subjects. But the royal family – and the Queen Mother in particular – were furious. The wall around the sacrosanct family had been breached, trust betrayed, and a hazardous precedent established. Other ex-employees who decided to finance their declining years by 'doing a Crawfie' might not be so painfully discreet in future.

But there was nothing anyone could do to stop the publication, and with the Palace in a pother over the ethics of the former governess, and the Queen Mother telling her friends that poor Crawfie had clearly lost her senses, nobody at Court appeared to spot the true significance of Crawfie's revelations. Her simple book was a phenomenal success. *Women's Own*, which shrewdly serialised it, ran it for eighteen consecutive issues and put on more than half a million readers in the process. Its editor exaggerated when he claimed that 'before then we had *no* royal stories' (in fact there had been lots), but none had had anything like the impact of *The Little Princesses*.

As the editor of *Women's Own* explained, 'The author was right, so was the timing, the background and the subject'. The passion to identify with members of the royal family was even stronger than before the war, and interest in the young Elizabeth was something of a national phenomenon. Ignoring the disapproval of the Palace,

Miss Crawford wisely made the most of it. She went on to make a fortune before her unique career as chronicler *emeritus* of royalty abruptly ceased when, against her finer Scottish scruples, she described in advance for magazine publication the Queen's appearance at Trooping the Colour on the very year the parade was finally postponed through heavy rain. But by then the national obsession with the royal family had reached levels of intensity which would require more than Miss Crawford's gentle memories to satisfy – and in the spring of 1953, on the eve of her former pupil's coronation, came a fresh reminder of the strange extent to which this public mania was building up.

The idea of putting on display the revered remains of a defunct ruler, so that members of the public can file past and offer their respects is an interesting symptom of the way the popular cult of leadership has been actively encouraged in the twentieth century. Lenin's remains were placed on public view. Queen Victoria's were not. Nor, for that matter, were those of any of Victoria's Hanoverian predecessors on the throne; and the first royal, British coffin to be placed on solemn public view, was that of King Edward VII in 1910. This was at the suggestion of the imaginative Lord Esher, who did so much to enhance the public ceremonial associated with the Crown – and the impressive vigil in the hushed medieval splendour of Westminster Hall was repeated on the deaths of George V and George VI, like some great tradition unbroken from the middle ages.

On her death in April 1953, Queen Mary became the first royal British consort in modern times to receive this honour, and could she have witnessed the fervour of the crowds who shuffled past her bier, she would have been gratified to see how widely shared her views on the sanctity of royalty had become. To an extraordinary degree, religion and royalty were now associated in loyal, patriotic minds. Even the left-wing *Reynolds News* remarked on it:

For three days and nights they bowed, saluted, wept, crossed themselves and knelt to pray for the departed Queen. 'No religious service in recent years has ever evoked such a show of mass reverence,' said a priest. 'The Church has certainly not canonised her. But the public sanctified her as no saint was publicly venerated at Westminster before.

With the old Queen's son, the Duke of Windsor, briefly permitted back to London for the funeral (his Duchess tactfully remained behind in their Paris mansion on the Boulevard Suchet), it might have seemed the ideal moment to permit the family wounds to heal; and as a gesture he might well have been invited to attend his niece's Coronation scheduled for the summer. But that unhappy man remained as much a source of bitterness – and dread example – to the family as ever.

Some of them even blamed him for his brother's death, through the strains of kingship he had thrust upon George by his abdication. Grey-faced and clad in the unaccustomed uniform of a British Admiral of the Fleet (to which the Duke was still curiously entitled), he stayed long enough to witness the remains of his unforgiving mother safely interred beside his father in St George's Chapel, Windsor. Then he departed like the ghost he was, and proceedings could continue for the one great ceremony of state his own brief reign had lacked.

According to the constitution, Edward, though uncrowned, had been as legitimate a king as his brother after his Coronation; for at the moment of the accession all the royal authority, possessions and prerogatives of the former monarch pass intact to his successor. But the actual Coronation is the public and religious demonstration of these kingly powers, and from the so-called 'mists of time' monarchs have always had some form of crowning, although its form has changed considerably during English history.

In fact, the idea of the Coronation as a great and wonderfully enacted public spectacle has been largely the invention of this present century. Tudor kings had been crowned in Westminster Abbey in the presence of a small gathering of bishops and favoured nobility, the public part of the ceremony coming later at the banquet at Westminster Hall when the Royal Champion entered, fully armed on horseback, to assert the royal authority. Muddles inevitably followed with the Hanoverians. With George III the Sword of State was lost and the chairs even failed to arrive for the Coronation banquet; and for Victoria's relatively simple but still muddled Coronation, the Westminster banquet and the champion's challenge were dispensed with – nor was the National Anthem sung within the Abbey.

It was not until the crowning of Edward VII that the Coronation started to become the moving ceremony we see today, and the

Coronation of Elizabeth II was designed to surpass its predecessors in orchestrated pageantry and public splendour. This was certainly the avowed intention of the major courtiers involved, and in particular of Bernard Marmaduke FitzAlan Howard, 16th Duke of Norfolk, who as Hereditary Marshal and Chief Butler of England had inherited the task of organising the event. This noble martinet with a lurking resemblance to the late Alfred Hitchcock was that rarity, the head of a famous English family who was also a devout Roman Catholic, and the elements within his character undoubtedly inspired the sort of Coronation he envisaged. As a great nobleman, he intended it to be a notable feudal pageant: as a skilful impressario who had already directed George V's Silver Jubilee and George VI's Coronation, a wonderfully coordinated spectacle: and as the country's leading Roman Catholic layman, an occasion which would find its echo only in the enthronement of a Pope in the ancient imperial Roman ceremonial of the Vatican.

The Queen herself regarded the Coronation as essentially a repetition of her parents' crowning. Lady Longford tells us that during the rehearsals her comments were invariably the same: 'Did my father do it? Then I will too.' For she saw the whole ceremony as a solemnly traditional event for which she had prepared herself since girlhood, when Queen Mary, practical as ever, had given her a detailed model of Victoria's Coronation with all the principal participants in miniature. She took it extremely seriously, discussing the religious implications of the ceremony at length with Archbishop Fisher, learning her responses from recordings of her father, and practising her movements in the throne room at the Palace with a sheet around her shoulders. She believed that this would be the most important moment of her life, and with typical determination set herself to make the most of it.

So did the other major characters involved, and it is worth noting the extraordinary extent to which this great popular event in a mid-twentieth century democracy was so jealously guarded for – and by – the members of the upper aristocracy. The populace of course would be permitted outside the Abbey, to cheer and line the streets. To keep them happy, Her Majesty's Government would spend £1.2 million on the festivities. There would be street decorations in the city centre, tape-recorded nightingales to sing all night to waiting crowds in Berkeley Square, and 40 large boxes of exotic flowers flown in specially from Australia to enliven the exterior of parliament. But, royalty and clergymen apart, the main participants within the Abbey would almost all be the hereditary heads of ancient families taken out of memory's mothballs for the great occasion.

St Edward's staff would be carried by the Earl of Ancaster, the spurs by Lord Hastings and Lord Churston, and the swords of Temporal Justice, Spiritual Justice, and Mercy, by the Duke of Buccleuch and Queensbury, the Earl of Home, and the Duke of Northumberland respectively. Even 'the girls the whole world envied – the six fresh-faced young women who carried the Queen's train', as the *Sunday Times* described them, were specifically required by the Palace to be the unmarried and preferably untarnished daughters of earls, at least.

As for the Abbey congregation, it consisted predominantly of the aristocracy, seated in rows in order of the strictest precedence: dukes behind royal dukes, and behind them the marquises, the earls, the viscounts and finally the barons. Not even the most obscure member of the House of Lords was refused a seat, but only fifty backbench members of the House of Commons were given places – well towards the back.

In fact the politicians, having loyally approved such lavish public expenditure on the celebrations, and sensing the growing mood of popular excitement, were more than willing to go along with whatever the Crown decided. Eight months earlier, the Conservatives under Churchill had returned to power with a majority of only seventeen. With the balance still so delicately poised, no Labour politician would willingly upset the electorate by even the faintest criticism of this cheerfully inegalitarian royal occasion. And the Conservatives, who traditionally tended to regard the Crown as their party's personal possession, undoubtedly saw the Coronation and the new Queen's popularity as a boost to their position after six grey years of postwar socialism. As Chips Channon noted in his invaluable diary:

A wave of enthusiastic relief has surged over the House and later over the City. There is a new Festival spirit about. A young Queen; an old Prime Minister and a brave, buoyant Butler budget. Has he [R. A. Butler, Chancellor of the Exchequer] put us in for a generation?

He very nearly had. The Conservatives remained in power until

1964 and certainly took advantage of the mood of optimism and national revival being spread around the Coronation.

The coincidence between the new Queen's name and title and that of the greatest of all English queens three centuries earlier was too much for any publicist to miss, and the dream of the so-called 'New Elizabethan Age' began. The sovereigns' names apart, the two periods could in reality have hardly had less in common. Elizabeth I had reigned at her country's greatest moment of expansion and intellectual daring: her namesake had inherited a nation at a point of great decline – an imperial power whose empire had almost vanished, the richest island in the world, which was suddenly becoming rather poor. But this only made the concept of a great Elizabethan revival all the more appealing.

Much was made of the idea in the run-up to the Coronation, so that the new reign suddenly appeared to offer some mystical salvation from the nation's troubles. The essence of this hope was summed up in a full-page advertisement loyally inserted by the Schweppes company in the special Coronation number of *Punch*. It took the form of a page reproduced from a hypothetical 'New History of Britain' published in the year 2003. Under the heading, *Chapter XII – The New Renaissance 1953–2003*, it boldly stated:

> Just fifty years ago – in June 1953 – Elizabeth II was crowned Queen at Westminster. From this, the year of her coronation, date the first steps towards Britain's recovery. At long last the nation's pride, the nation's will to leadership asserted themselves. The second Elizabethan age was to witness, like the first, a far-reaching renaissance of the spirit . . .

Such were the sort of widespread hopes with which the general public, swept up in a mood of very wishful thinking round the person of their youthful Queen, were encouraged to regard the coming Coronation – and none seemed more involved in this national euphoria than the Prime Minister himself, Winston Churchill. The old war-horse had acknowledged his mistake since those far-off days when he boldly championed the Duke of Windsor, and all his romantic and nostalgic fervour suddenly seemed roused at the prospect of his young Queen's Coronation. 'I,' he declaimed, 'whose youth was passed in the august, unchallenged and tranquil glare of the Victorian era, may feel a thrill in invoking once again the prayer and anthem, "God Save the Queen!" '

According to Churchill's private secretary, Sir John Colville, the statesman's feelings for his monarch were even more emotional than this suggested. 'Churchill', he wrote, 'was an old man whose passions were spent, but there is no doubt that at a respectful distance he fell in love with the Queen'. His weekly prime ministerial interviews with the monarch had become increasingly lengthy in the months since the accession, and speculation grew that he was envisaging himself as the aged Melbourne to Elizabeth's young Victoria.

If so, it was not an idea that particularly appealed to Her Majesty. Asked about it by an old Court favourite, she replied conclusively, 'Not at all. I find him rather obstinate.'

Nowhere was his obstinacy more pronounced than over the discussions of the role of television in the Coronation. As far as he was concerned, arrangements should be kept exactly as they were and the television cameras firmly excluded from the privileged and sacred happenings within the Abbey. As he rather practically put it, 'I don't see why the BBC should have a better view of my monarch being crowned than me', and general opinion at the Palace seems to have agreed with him. There had long been profound suspicions of the cheapening effect of television on solemn royal occasions, and George VI had briskly and irritably rejected the suggestion of televising his daughter's wedding inside the Abbey in 1947.

When the matter of the Coronation coverage was first discussed in Cabinet, Churchill's influence led to a similar unanimous conclusion on the grounds that TV cameras in the Abbey would be a vulgar intrusion and impose too great a burden on the Queen herself. Better far to have the ceremony discreetly filmed instead. Television could content itself with showing the subsequent procession live, the invaluable Archbishop Fisher could check the film to cut out any unforeseen unseemliness, and the populace would be perfectly happy watching this edited version of the crowning on television in the evening.

Thus the rights of the aristocracy would be preserved, BBC TV kept firmly in its place, and the public presentation of this all-important royal happening kept in the hands of the establishment.

This produced predictable indignation in the press. The people's tribune, John Gordon of the *Sunday Express*, picked as his target not the politicians but 'that tight-knit group of Palace officials whose determination to keep the people as far as possible away from the throne never diminishes . . . What a bunch of codheads to run the Queen's business!' More effective was the shrewd and influential lobbying behind the scenes that instantly began from the BBC and the television companies. Marmaduke Norfolk began to waver. Unspeakably vulgar though it undoubtedly was, he saw that television could have its uses in presenting the royal family to their people 'if only it was properly controlled', and as a showman he was professional enough to respond to the prospect of the enormous audience on offer for the greatest royal ceremony of his long career.

Archbishop Fisher, who was another showman in his way, guardedly agreed. The Duke of Edinburgh's uncle, Lord Mountbatten, was powerfully in favour and his nephew was converted to the perilous idea. But it was the Queen herself who made her own decision in the end, concluding that the 'burden' of the television cameras in the Abbey was something that she could – and on this one occasion positively should – endure for the sake of all her loyal subjects.

It was relayed to Churchill that 'Her Majesty believed all her subjects should have the opportunity of seeing the Coronation', and he informed his Cabinet accordingly. With deep misgivings, its earlier decision was reversed. 'It was, after all, the Queen who was being crowned, and not the Cabinet,' Churchill told them, and the ultimate decision had to rest with her.

This was one of the key decisions of her reign. It meant that the Coronation of Elizabeth II on June 2, 1953, would be unique in the annals of the monarchy, the first time in history a sovereign had been crowned with an estimated 300 million close and fascinated witnesses to the strange and powerful event. It would generate a tidal wave of vast emotion round the twenty-six-year-old Queen, and be the first great demonstration of the force created when the rising tide of feeling for the monarchy was carried forward by the gathering winds of television. But one of its most immediate effects would be to guarantee that the crucial figure among all those so eagerly involved would not be a statesman nor a churchman, nor a courtier, but a fat man from the middle-classes with a romantic obsession with the monarchy and a sort of genius for conveying it to millions. Malcolm Muggeridge maliciously entitled him 'Gold Microphone in Waiting', and as usual with the sage of Robertsbridge there was some truth behind the malice. As the greatest television commentator on the royal scene, Richard Frederick Dimbleby would do more to spread the gospel of the monarchy than any courtier since Lord Esher.

Dimbleby was already famous as a war correspondent for the BBC and the most successful broadcasting commentator of his day, but few can have possibly foreseen the way his commentary would come to dominate the Coronation, or how far-reaching the effect of television would suddenly become for the future of the monarchy itself.

To be fair to the BBC, its interest in the monarchy was more profound – and far less vulgar and intrusive – than the palace and the politicians thought, and there were those who had already seen that the Crown and the broadcasters had certain interests in common. From the pre-war days when its first director-general, John Reith, had persuaded George V to deliver his Christmas message to the Empire, the BBC had shown nothing but the deepest reverence and respect towards the throne – and as Jonathan Dimbleby has pointed out, there was a fascinating, self-serving element within this loyalty.

> Out of politics, usually above controversy, stable and permanent, [the monarchy] embodied every virtue to which the BBC most aspired. The BBC could give unswerving and uncritical allegiance to the Crown, yet maintain its integrity and independence. In the process, by its open devotion to the system which worship of the Crown implied, the Corporation was able to establish itself the more securely as a mature and responsible if junior pillar of the state.

As a loyal and lifelong servant of the BBC, Richard Dimbleby would certainly have seen the point, but there was more in his attitude towards the Crown than this. Over the years he had become a convinced evangelist for the British monarchy, believing in his earthly sovereign rather as Billy Graham does in his heavenly one.

His father had been owner and editor of the family paper, the *Richmond and Twickenham Herald*, and in the early Twenties was also Lloyd George's director of political publicity. The young Dimbleby left minor public school without going on to university, and joined the fledgling BBC as one of its earliest reporters in 1934. Five years later his conversion to the monarchy occurred in the improbable town of Banff, while reporting the royal tour of Canada. It was there that the King and Queen relaxed one evening by singing songs with Dimbleby around a hotel piano, and before His Majesty retired he and the young reporter had a casual conversation. It was Dimbleby's first direct encounter with the monarchy, and one he was never to forget.

It stayed with him through his years as war correspondent, when the Crown came to symbolise the freedoms and traditions he saw at risk on the battlefields of Europe. Later, when he started reading history to rectify his lack of higher education, he was even more impressed by the historic role of the English monarchy. This was the theme of the short book he wrote himself as his contribution to the Coronation, advancing the somewhat shaky proposition that throughout his country's past 'the Crown has remained steadfast, guided by the same basic principles that have applied equally to the national characteristics and way of life, whether arrow, cannon-ball, or atom-bomb have been the latest weapon.'

His attitude to Elizabeth II was unequivocal, matching the highest hopes of any New Elizabethan:

A new era for Britain opened in Feburary 1952, when the second Elizabeth came to the throne. No more devoted or courageous person than she could carry on the monarchy which is the enduring strength of Britain and the envy of the world.

As his son has said of him, Richard Dimbleby's 'belief in the monarchy was not dispassionate; it was to partake in an emotional experience in which his whole being was involved'. As an immensely popular television commentator, all his professional expertise would now go into conveying this personal emotion. He had already shown what he could do in the much-praised radio account of the lying-in-state of George VI, and the sort of historical scene-painting he excelled in matched the mood of a nation already in the mental fancy-dress of New Elizabethans. Once the Queen agreed to having television cameras in the Abbey, it was generally agreed that only Dimbleby could do the great occasion justice.

He knew as much himself, and long before the great day dawned reverently prepared himself. A keen sailor, he moored his Dutch sailing barge beside Westminster pier and, although he had a wife and family in a comfortable house on Richmond Green, stayed like some nautical recluse, communing with the monuments of royal London that surrounded him, read all he could of kings and coronations, and majestically prepared his script.

June 2, Coronation Day, proved overcast and wet; but as the morning's papers said, 'it would take more than the English weather to dampen the spirits of the enthusiastic crowds' (estimated by the Metropolitan Police at more than a million) who for several days had been assembling along the royal route. This was London's largest ever gathering for a royal event, just as the actual Coronation was the most ambitious and superbly organised royal ceremony in the history of the English monarchy, His Grace of Norfolk's masterpiece.

For having lost so many of its ancient claims to fame, Britain had finally become the world's repository of public ceremonial. The skills and pride that once produced the greatest trading empire in the world now went into ensuring that the minutest detail of that day's elaborate pageantry was perfect. The original State Coach, built for George III, had been rebuilt, regilded and resprung, and its panels, painted by the Venetian Cipriani, had been meticulously restored under the supervision of the Surveyor of the Queen's Pictures, the distinguished art historian, Professor Sir Anthony Blunt.

Special camps had been erected in the royal parks for the 60,000 troops brought in to line the route and the contingents from every section of the Commonwealth who marched in the procession. Seven extra coaches had to be hired from a film company for the occasion. The Brigade of Guards, each officer, NCO and common soldier with brand new scarlet uniform and bearskin, had been practising its special drill for months. So had the regiments of the Household Cavalry, who would make up the body of the procession, and the Yeomen of the Guard, who marched beside the coach in Tudor uniforms identical to those worn for the crowning of Elizabeth I.

The noble congregation, with many of its members in their robes of state, had been in their places in the Abbey since 8 a.m. The royal regalia had been taken to the Abbey by a hand-picked team from Scotland Yard, the Duke of Norfolk was confident that nothing had been left to chance, and the principal participant was as cool as anyone. Wakened early by the loudspeakers in the Mall, and asked by a lady-in-waiting if she were feeling apprehensive, the Queen replied, 'No, not at all'.

Few of the watchers and participants can have been aware, however, of the other preparations that would make this Coronation so important and significantly different from any of its predecessors. Seeing the opportunity for what it was, BBC TV had put all available resources into preparations for by far the greatest outside broadcast it had ever mounted. So had ITV, who for once would be relaying the full BBC TV report on commercial televison, and using its expertise to market the film version throughout the world. Interest from abroad had proved immense, and once it was known that the cameras would be allowed inside the Abbey it was clear that the Coronation would become an unparallelled international media event.

Here, too, Britain had surpassed herself, and the arrangements for the nationwide and worldwide television link-up had been engineered on such a scale 'that even American network men, who supposed they knew it all, were left open-mouthed.' For once, statistics give the clearest picture of the overwhelming power of the media now being so adroitly brought together round the British monarchy. More than a hundred different commentators from abroad, speaking in forty-two different languages, would be simultaneously on the air; and BBC engineers had set up eighty separate control points in the Abbey and along the route, feeding five main radio networks for home consumption in addition to the 1,300 sound and 100 vision circuits from abroad.

The Post Office had installed a further 3,280 telephone circuits, 'for use by the biggest international assembly of reporters and commentators ever gathered for a single event.' Television would supply seven and a half hours non-stop live reporting on the actual Coronation, record 60,000 feet of film; and thanks to a further network of specially chartered aircraft, it was calculated that by the end of June 2 over three hundred million viewers, by far the largest audience ever assembled on a single day for any event in history, would have witnessed the impressive crowning of Elizabeth II.

Most of the electronic expertise converged on Richard Dimbleby who, like the perfectionist he was, had arrived at the Abbey shortly after 5 a.m. in time to see the television engineers and cameramen making their final preparations – including one jockey-sized contortionist who was managing to squeeze himself and camera into the tomb of Aylmer de Vallance, in order to record the close-ups of the Queen at the moment of her crowning. Then, long before the congregation had assembled, Dimbleby heaved his bulk aloft, into the isolation of the sound-proofed commentator's box high above the Abbey triforium, to await the most important moment of his whole career.

After his six months' preparation, as his son said later, 'he knew every detail of the service, the history of every ritual, the symbolic point of every movement'. He also had his own unrivalled view of what was happening, with an unrestricted line of sight to the coronation chair and the whole 'theatre' of the Abbey underneath him. Through his headphones he could hear as the royal procession left the Palace, and every move that followed as it approached the Abbey through the cheering crowds along the route. Then to the ringing cry of 'Vivat Regina Elizabetha!' from the Westminster schoolboys, the Queen made her entrance, with her maids of honour supporting her twenty-foot train; and as the glittering procession slowly advanced below him to its set positions round the altar, the moment had arrived for Dimbleby to impart his deepest feelings and encyclopaedic knowledge on the monarchy to an expectant world outside.

This he did to extraordinary effect, with a combination of professionalism and profound emotion and belief. Later, he related how deeply conscious he had been of 'seeing history in the making,' and how, for him, 'the slow, irresistible rhythm' of the Coronation service 'seemed to lift it out of time altogether'. His commentary effortlessly expressed this powerful response, and his familiar, authoritative voice gave his words an authenticity that added immeasurably to the television pictures of the service.

Those images alone were remarkable enough to alter in effect the very nature of the ceremony. For in every previous coronation, the right to witness this ritual crowning of the monarch had been a privilege naturally confined to the Abbey congregation – and of these, only the most privileged would have been able to observe the actual detail of the ceremony. Even then, the significance of the complex ritual and symbolism would have been difficult to follow.

Now this was changed completely, and the privilege of close observation was taken over from the aristocracy by the television cameras. The dukes and marquises and earls became extras to the background pageantry, and any ordinary person with access to a television set could witness what was happening more clearly than any nobleman within the Abbey. For those who heard Dimbleby as well, the complex symbolism behind each movement in the ascending ritual of the Coronation was being reverently expounded with detail and feeling.

Never ones for doing things by halves, and in need of every possible device to enhance their royal authority, the medieval English kings had piled all available arguments for kingship into their coronation service: as a result this 'antique ceremony' had finally become a sort of *omnium gatherum* of almost every symbolic claim to temporal and spiritual authority that monarchy has made in history.

There was the basic feudal element of the medieval monarchy in the acclamation of the sovereign by her ancient aristocracy; there was the imperial Roman element represented by the donning of the tunic of the emperors with four gold-embroidered Byzantine beasts to show dominion over the four corners of the earth; there was the ancient claim of the kings of Israel to divine authority in the repetition by Archbishop Fisher of the Old Testament anointing of King Solomon by his High Priest, Zadok; and there were echoes of medieval belief in the miraculous nature of kingship in the use of the sacred oil, the original of which was entrusted to Archbishop Fisher's predecessor, St Thomas À Beckett, by the Virgin Mary.

As the majestic acting out of ancient ritual around the person of the youthful queen, all this made memorable royal theatre. Against the venerable background of the Abbey, and with Dimbleby's authoritative exegesis, the effect was quite hypnotic. For here as nowhere else one understood the extraordinary power of television and an inspired commentator to create conviction on a truly massive scale from a royal ceremony. The scattered television audience was compulsively involved in the ascending climax of the ceremony, sharing the final drama of Elizabeth II at the centre of this magic ritual of her crowning. This seemed to be the essence of the age-old mystery and sanctity of kingship. What one was watching was the creation of belief by television.

So Dimbleby was right when he wrote of a new era beginning for Britain 'when the second Elizabeth came to the throne' – but not in quite the way he meant. Hillary and Tensing climbed Mount Everest, news of which reached Britain on the morning of the Coronation; but barely three weeks after his sovereign's crowning, Winston Churchill had a major stroke. His doctor, Lord Moran, said it would kill him, but he managed to survive and, although distinctly feeble, somehow clung to the adhesive reins of government. Throughout this period his heir apparent, Eden, was also seriously ill and had to have a bile-duct bypass operation. Politically the worst was still to come for this Britain of the new royal era. Otherwise little changed in the situation of a country supposedly exulting in its Elizabethan renaissance under a charismatic monarch.

But for the monarchy itself, something quite unprecedented had occurred. Thanks to the Coronation, this conservative young queen, guided by her mother and dutifully following what she felt to be the pattern of her father, found herself the sudden centre of a cult of regomania not just in Britain, but throughout the world. The filmed version of the Coronation was to run on Broadway and the Champs Elysées for months to come, and M. Christian Dior spoke for many Europeans of the way 'the Coronation of the young Elizabeth II has filled, not only the British, but rather strangely, the French too, with renewed faith and optimism in the future.'

Naturally it was in Britain that the Coronation had its most profound effect. The day had been declared a public holiday, and since television sets were far from universal, many families that possessed them had invited friends and neighbours in for celebratory parties to watch the great event. Ziegler quotes reactions from the contemporary Mass Observation that show how widespread was the popular identification with the Queen herself at the moment of her crowning. There was much emotion: 'I thought I would cry' was a fairly typical reaction; so was the behaviour of a young American girl 'with communist leanings' who was said to have 'grown ecstatic and close to tears' watching the transmission from the Abbey: 'O gosh, this is *wonderful*, this is like a fairy-tale, this is something America hasn't got.'

Much was made of the idea that the monarchy had become a unique national possession, one of the few remaining things for which Britain was the envy of the world. But something more than this was now involved. Ziegler also writes of 'the magical significance attached by many to having seen the coronation in the flesh', and quotes an optimistic lady from Guildford – 'We're all expecting the Queen to work miracles I think.' Belief in the miraculous nature of kingship is extremely ancient, but had all but vanished in Britain after good Queen Anne had dutifully 'touched' her afflicted subjects as a cure for scrofula. But thanks to Richard Dimbleby, and the widespread sense of personal involvement with the Queen at the moment of her crowning, television audiences could now experience that authentic sense of 'the sacredness of the royal person' with which Queen Mary had habitually approached her husband.

Nor was this attitude confined to emotional ladies and members of the Church of England, like Archbishop Fisher, whose verdict on the Coronation was that 'this country and the Commonwealth, last Tuesday (Coronation day) were not far from the Kingdom of Heaven.' As hard-bitten a spectator as the political commentator, Henry Fairlie, could write later of the Coronation:

> I remember feeling that one had seen something of what, perhaps, one should never see – the terrible prescriptions by which a society holds itself together, the awful assumptions, conventions and laws which it imposes on this one human creature.

Even sociologists were not immune to such emotions. The American Edward Shils, and Britain's student of the Meritocracy, Michael Young, would unashamedly invoke a supernatural element in their joint article for that December's issue of the *Sociological Review*. For them both, the Queen at the moment of her anointing was 'a frail creature who has to be brought into contact with the divine and thus transformed into a Queen,' and their considered view of the ceremony as a whole was that it had somehow formed 'a great act of national communion.'

Ten years later, a writer in the *Observer* would remark that 'the public mood at the time of the Coronation was very peculiar: it has been called hysterical', and suggest that the underlying cause was a lack of self-assurance in the British people 'after the experience of an alarming war and the anti-climax of their post-war situation.'

Perhaps it was. Certainly much of the impact of the Coronation came from its power to create around the British monarchy a compensatory dream for what the nation felt that it had lost – or was terrified of losing. It was powerfully consoling at a time when, in Dean Acheson's much repeated phrase, Britain had lost an empire but had yet to find a role – for the sacred monarchy appeared an effective substitute for both.

In all their public aspects as a family, the Windsors had successfully – indeed, immaculately – maintained the perfect image of the 'ordinary' English family, with its simple virtues wonderfully intact.

Love, goodness, thrift, decency and duty – all were there, and all in a form with which the greatest number could identify. At the same time, the ceremonial and sacred aspects of the monarchy had been steadily advanced as people were encouraged to observe the members of this 'ordinary' family magically transformed in the developing great royal ceremonies of state – crowned, robed, worshipped and revered. Now, with the full, sophisticated power of television around them, the process was complete. Almost by chance, British royalty had stumbled on the greatest source of popularity and interest any king has ever had at his disposal.

Shils and Young were right in pointing out that it was the transformation of the 'frail creature' of Elizabeth II into a Queen at the moment of her crowning which provided the essence of the drama of the Coronation. The theme of transformation remains one of the most basic and persistent human myths, forming the universal essence of fairy-stories, tribal ceremonies and the most elaborate religious exercises and beliefs. Cinderella is transformed into a princess, and the beast into a prince. Leopard men take on the attributes of the animal they worship, and sinners are miraculously made Christian saints through the intervention of the mystic love of god. In Westminster Abbey on that morning in June, the House of Windsor finally perfected its own greatest transformation scene before the television cameras which would henceforth form the basis of its unshakeable mystique and universal fascination, as this familiar young woman, who for years had typified the simplest virtues of British girlhood and young womanhood, was recreated Queen in a moment of intense emotion.

According to Dermot Morrah, who as one of the royal heralds stood near Elizabeth at the throne, 'the sense of spiritual exultation that radiated from her was almost tangible'; and she was widely credited with a religious role to an extent to which no modern European monarch has aspired. According to a leader in *The Times*, she had 'stood for the soul as well as the body of the Commonwealth' throughout her Coronation, so that 'every man and woman in the land was a partaker in the mystery of the Queen's anointing' through the signal blessing of his television set.

It took some while for the full effects of the Coronation to appear – and longer still for the monarchy itself to grasp exactly what had happened. Those interests which had seen the opportunities it offered were quick to benefit at once. The popularity of the government continued, and the status of the BBC was considerably enhanced. It had lobbied effectively for what it wanted, shown unrivalled expertise throughout the ceremony, and chosen an inspired commentator for the greatest occasion in the Corporation's history. The result was exactly what Reith himself would have wanted, establishing the service as that 'junior pillar of the state' more firmly than ever: henceforth the monarchy itself was inevitably linked with television for its presentation and its popularity.

The press had also benefited, not just in Britain but throughout the world. Universal celebrities are rare and form the raw material of circulation; thanks to the worldwide interest created by the unforgettable television images of the Coronation, the Royal House of Windsor was henceforth an inexhaustible source of gossip, articles and journalistic speculation. According to *Time* magazine, 'the whole world is royalist now', and outside Britain this particularly applied to the United States, where a common language guaranteed that the impact of the television film of the Coronation was immeasurably greater than any British royal event before. It was now that America really felt that it had 'got to know' the Queen of England and her family. A new mood of sympathy and interest focussed on the once distant and mysterious members of the House of Windsor, and their royal role as international celebrities began in earnest.

The Anglican church had also had its day of glory at the Coronation. One of the Queen's proudest titles is 'Defender of the Faith', which was first bestowed on King Henry VIII by the Pope, and which every subsequent monarch has carried as head of the established Church of England. This religious role was strongly emphasised within the ceremony, so that although the Church's regular congregation had declined to something less than two percent of the population, the Coronation served to underline its continuing position in the state. It also showed that, even in decline, it was still quite capable of staging the most elaborate ecclesiastical ritual in the world: one doubts that even the Church of Rome could have done it better.

All this apart, it would have taken a perceptive courtier to have appreciated just how much the televising of the Coronation of Elizabeth II had done to change the basis of the monarchy's popular appeal. For the millions who had watched the ceremony, it was as if they had been present at the act itself. Unlike all previous coronations from which the populace had been rigorously excluded, there was now a sense of nationwide participation in the monarchy. Most of those who watched had shared a common feeling that this was *their* Queen, *their* royal family and *their* monarchy; but instead of responding to this general mood, little changed at Court. The attitude of those closest to the Queen and her family remained strongly suspicious of TV and the media in general, and the torrent of enthusiasm for all things royal inevitably produced a sense of considerable complacency. With a young queen capable of rousing such royalist euphoria throughout the world, why change anything?

PART TWO

DECLINE

5

PHILIP

'The position of the Prince Consort requires that the husband should entirely sink his own individual existence in that of his wife; that he should aim at no power by himself or for himself; should shun all attention, assume no separate responsibility before the public, but make his position entirely part of hers, and fill every gap which as a woman she would naturally leave in the exercise of her regal functions.'

Prince Albert, writing on the role of the royal consort

For the Queen herself, the triumph of her Coronation was distinctly flattering, and she was happiest with her mother's reassurance that her father would have been proud of her – as indeed he would. For the Queen Mother, the occasion seemed an overwhelming vindication of her life's work, proof positive, if proof were needed, that she had been absolutely right in the role she had created for herself and for her elder daughter. Her policy towards her family had made them beloved by the nation; her husband's sacrifice to duty had not been in vain; and the dreadful damage done to the monarchy by her unmentionable brother-in-law had been magnificently repaired.

Suddenly the world was royalist; but despite this – or possibly because of it – the strain upon the new Queen was considerable. Grim-faced, she often showed the pressure caused by her position at the centre of this multitudinous attention. In private she could be reduced to tears of nervousness and sheer exhaustion. 'Mummy would do it so much better,' she was sometimes heard to say.

The Queen's dependence on her mother, coupled with a surprising lack of personal self-confidence during these early years of her reign, ensured the continuation of the Queen Mother's role as presiding matriarch of the Royal House of Windsor, and in many ways her influence was every bit as powerful over the Queen her daughter as it ever had been with the King her husband.

Her new residence, Clarence House, was a stone's throw from Buckingham Palace, lying just beyond the splendid ceremonial gates erected by King Edward VII at the entrance to Green Park, and with its fine walled garden facing the beginning of the Mall. Once established there, the Queen Mother swiftly made this elegant, stuccoed eighteenth century house what Buckingham Palace could never be – the most stylish and luxuriously run private house in London, with its croquet set on the Edwardian verandah placed casually beside a perfect English lawn, and its owner's lovingly acquired collection of artistic treasures ranged round the hall, including the splendid series of John Piper paintings of Windsor Castle during the war. (A rare example of royal patronage of a modern artist in this period, they were commissioned on the advice of the Queen Mother's close friend and then Surveyor of the King's Pictures, Kenneth Clark. They were painted against a stormy wartime background, and the King remarked to the artist, 'What a pity you always seemed to have such dreadful weather when you came to Windsor, Mr Piper.') The rooms were comfortably yet superbly furnished, a dedicated staff ensured the smoothest running of the royal routine, and the chef served the best food found in any royal establishment to the Queen Mother's frequent dinner parties.

As a result she stayed very much in touch with events and had a wide and influential circle of acquaintances and friends; and with Clarence House so near the Palace, contact between the two establishments was close. She was a devoted grandmother to Prince Charles and Princess Anne, and the morning telephone discussions between the two Elizabeths remained an all-important part of every royal day.

This was in marked contrast with the role we have seen Queen Mary adopting after her son, George VI's accession, when the Queen Dowager, having done her work, tended to retire into the background. Now, on the contrary, the Queen Mother, as old as the century and in her energetic prime, swiftly created for herself a public role which had not previously existed in the royal repertoire. As Queen she always had the knack of presenting what was known as 'the human face' of royalty: now in her widowhood, and freed from much of the previous protocol, she was gaining new popularity as the genial-seeming, mother-figure to the nation.

This more relaxed royal role was one that suited her, and she made the most of it – as she was soon to show with her solo visit to the United States for the 200th anniversary celebrations of Columbia University, the year after the Coronation. This was very much a royal visit, and with her easy charm she stole the show from the international figures, including Chancellor Adenauer of West

Germany, who were also receiving honorary degrees from the university. She got on famously with Richard Nixon, and even the late Senator McCarthy afterwards went on record describing her as 'one of the most wonderful women I've ever met.' Times had changed from the days before the war when another Irish-American politician won votes by publicly declaring his desire to punch her late father-in-law, King George V, 'on the snout'.

She did not confine herself to politicians and celebrities, and enjoyed concluding her itinerary with a well-publicised visit to the famous toyshop of F.A.O. Schwarz on 5th Avenue where, to the delight of a bevy of reporters, she determinedly explained, 'I'm interested in toys for a six-year-old boy and a four-year-old girl — and I'd like them to be very American.' She emerged from the shop looking very happy with a five-dollar model steam shovel and a three-dollar plastic tea-set; and when she flew on to Canada next day, the *New Yorker* had an editorial saying 'how much we miss her' and inviting her back the following year, 'bringing the whole family along.' Nobody seemed to feel the same about Herr Adenauer.

The unabated presence of this matriarchal figure at the centre of the family was good for royal business and did much to humanise the remoter image of her daughter. The British are a matriarchal people, and this energetic widow could ensure that there was little change in the style her family had so successfully created during her period as queen. Under her influence, the appearances were carefully maintained of the simple, country-loving family, devoted more than ever to their corgis and their ponies, attending church conscientiously each Sunday, and still firmly shunning extravagance, intellectuals and the lure of fast society.

The fact that in her private life the Queen Mother could be decidedly extravagant herself, or that she very much enjoyed society gossip and the conversation of such courtly intellectuals as Kenneth Clark, Harold Nicolson or Osbert Sitwell, was neither here nor there. The public image of the family was what counted, and with that popular left-wing organ, the *Daily Mirror*, naming her its 'Woman of the Year' for 1954, it was clear that her purchase of a Scottish castle or her lavish expenditure as a racehorse owner in no way conflicted with her public standing as that democratic-seeming favourite of the people, Britain's own unique 'Queen Mum'.

Public expectation guaranteed her role, which the press was happy to promote. She had long had a way with press men and photographers that made her virtually immune to criticism, and the combination of her highly professional, popular style with that of her sacred yet dependent daughter ensured that, to the world at large, the royal family remained what people wanted it to be – a much-loved group of familiar and reassuring beings who continued to embody simple humanity with their sacred situation.

During the first years of the new Queen's reign, this was the trusted formula on which the Court continued to rely; but apparently it could not satisfy everyone. The November after the Coronation, the *Sunday Pictorial* appeared with a most unusual front-page article. Under the banner headline, 'ROYAL DESIRE FOR FREEDOM', the paper claimed that the Queen herself wanted 'freedom in her private life to mix with us as ordinary people – if we will let them'.

> The Queen and the Duke want their children to mix around as much as possible. They would like more freedom for themselves and for their family. They would like their reign to be outstandingly democratic; themselves to be part of the people they rule.

These sentiments were based, it was claimed, on 'unusually authoritative Palace sources'. Fleet Street rumour had it that they expressed the innermost feelings of the Duke of Edinburgh himself, who, in a strictly non-attributable conversation, had been using the *Pictorial* to fly a private but important kite. If so, His Royal Highness might have saved his breath; but the desire for 'more freedom' for himself and his family would be reiterated over the years by that fascinating conundrum at the very centre of the family – Philip Mountbatten, Duke of Edinburgh, Earl of Merioneth, Baron Greenwich, formerly Prince Philip Schleswig-Holstein-Sonderburg-Gluckburg of the Royal House of Greece.

After their marriage in 1947, the Duke of Edinburgh and his wife had been counting on a considerable period of freedom from royal responsibilities while their children were growing up. George VI's early death at the age of 57 had daunting implications for the new Queen and her consort, and plunged the Duke into several days of a black depression which was not helped by a subsequent attack of jaundice. But what did he find so deeply depressing in the prospect of his sudden role as royal consort? What was the truth about this radical, outspoken, yet most contradictory of men? And how, in the end, did this clever, handsome, very forthright naval officer manage at the centre of such a profoundly matriarchal court?

During the century since Prince Albert, the last male royal consort, had died and the monarchy was being moulded by its dominating royal ladies, its menfolk had been kept revered but carefully in check as paragons of calm domestic virtue. The one king who successfully defied this rule was the former 'Prince of Pleasure', the present Queen's great-grandfather, King Edward VII; but he was already fifty-nine when he stepped from his mother's all-embracing shadow, and for the nine brief years he ruled, age and excess had calmed him down after a life of fairly constant self-indulgence.

His reign apart, there was an overriding female element within the British monarchy, from Queen Victoria to the present day, which has played a crucial part in its survival and success. One reason that undoubtedly contributed to the disaster of Edward VIII was his style of kingship which, in marked contrast with his father, George V's, threatened a reversion to the manner and freedom of a highly independent male monarch. Claiming to believe in firm royal leadership, and impatient with a passive and symbolic role, he had always hoped to play his part in politics and trusted his people would ignore the scandals of his private life.

Regardless of the problems raised by Mrs Simpson, it is hard to believe that an assertive, controversial male monarch would have succeeded in Britain, when similar monarchies had foundered in the rest of Europe. For under the influence of the Windsor matriarchs, the public image of the British royal males had developed round the dedicated, undemanding figures of those family-loving kings, George V and George VI. Free from controversy and scandal, these shy, retiring men were both perfectly adapted to their role, but they had set an uncomfortable pattern for their successor's husband – particularly for one who was neither shy, nor prepared to be totally dependent on his wife, and who was considerably more intelligent than either of them.

One of the crucial facts about the Duke is that he had passed almost all his formative years in the dependent situation of a very poor relation, and only a most unlikely series of events had brought him to the splendid but uncomfortable position of husband to the Queen of England. Although he shared a common great-great-grand-mother, Queen Victoria, with his wife, other elements within his ancestry were very different from the staid and well-known British members of the House of Windsor.

His connection with Queen Victoria came from his great-grand-mother, the Queen's third child, Princess Alice. She married the Grand Duke Louis IV of Hesse-Darmstadt, one of the great historic German princely houses, which claimed descent from Charlemagne and was variously related to many other courts of Europe. Louis IV's aunt had married Tsar Alexander II of Russia, and her younger brother, another Alexander, had contracted a romantic but disap-proved-of marriage with one of her ladies-in-waiting, a beautiful but untitled Polish girl called Julie Hauke. On their return to Germany in 1852 in relative disgrace, the young couple were given a certain standing by the conferring on them of a defunct and minor title of the Royal House of Hesse – the Principality of Battenberg. It was thus that this new, morganatic princely house began.

Julie and Alexander had five children, and it was their eldest son, Prince Louis, who was to make his home in England. Early on he formed the great ambition to become a sailor, and since there was effectively no German navy at the time, and since the House of Hesse was so closely tied by marriage to the British royal family, the obvious solution for him was to join the British royal navy. This he did, and his career was a great success until, as we have seen, he was forced to resign as British First Sea Lord on the outbreak of the 1914 war with Germany.

By then he had in fact strengthened his ties with his adopted country by marrying one of Queen Victoria's granddaughters, named Victoria herself, the daughter of Princess Alice and the Grand Duke Louis. They had four children, Alice, Louise, George and Louis; and after Prince Louis Battenberg's resignation from the Admiralty, the family followed the example of their kinsman, George V, by adopting a more English sounding surname. Battenberg was trans-lated quite literally into English to become Mountbatten, and the King conferred upon Prince Louis the hereditary English marquisate of Milford Haven. He thus became Lord Milford Haven. His son, George, finally succeeded to the title, but it was his younger son the world would get to know by his courtesy title of Lord Louis Mountbatten. Lord Louis would also be Prince Philip's uncle, thanks to the marriage of his sister, still known as Princess Alice, to Prince Andrew of the Royal House of Greece in 1903.

It was from Andrew that the most fateful element within Prince

Philip's ancestry would come: from this tall, good-looking soldier who managed to combine descent from the Danish Royal House of Schleswig-Holstein-Sonderburg-Gluckburg with his position of a royal prince of Greece. Alice had met him in London and fallen in love with him. King Edward VII, a keen connoisseur of female beauty, had judged her fit to marry any king in Europe, and the marriage took place at Darmstadt, the capital of the Grand Duchy of Hesse, amid a flurry of grand-dukes and continental royalty led by Edward's wife, Alexandra, Queen of England, and Tsar Nicholas of all the Russias. But none of this splendour could disguise the fact that Alice was marrying into one of the most vulnerable dynasties of Europe.

The Royal House of Greece had been created barely fifty years before with the backing of the western powers, as a source of stability and unity when Greece won its freedom from the Turks: and since Greece possessed no royal house, and no mere Greek possessed the *savoir faire* to wear a crown, it was considered prudent to import a foreign king from a family that did. The obvious choice was a member of the British royal family, and the freshly minted crown was offered to Victoria's second son, Prince Alfred, who had the sense politely to refuse. It was finally accepted by the eighteen-year-old younger son of the King of Denmark, who became George I, King of the Hellenes. Since his sister Alexandra was already married to the future King Edward VII, he was viewed favourably by Britain, and George I of Greece also gained the good will of the Russian royal family by marrying Tsar Nicholas's daughter, Olga – thus making her the Queen of Greece. Their third son was Prince Andrew, Philip's father.

Although the Greek monarchy was intertwined with almost every royal family in Europe, it could not save them from the chaos that bedevilled its country's politics. In 1913 the unfortunate King George of Greece joined the growing list of assassinated European royalty when one of his subjects shot him in Salonika. He was succeeded by his son (Prince Philip's uncle) Constantine I, and with the outbreak of the First World War a further complication arose which would haunt the Greek royal house for many years to come – the divided loyalties created by its family connections with Germany. Believed to be in league with the Kaiser, Constantine was deposed, largely through French and British influence, and Prince Andrew and Princess Alice spent the remainder of the war in uncomfortable exile in Switzerland.

By now the couple had four daughters, and it was not until Prince Andrew's brother briefly regained the throne in 1920 that the family returned to Greece. Shortly after this, in 1921, in the family villa on Corfu, Prince Andrew became the father of a son. The child was christened Philip in accordance with the rites of the Greek Orthodox Church, and assumed the title Royal Prince of Greece.

But Andrew and the Greek royal family were as ill-fated as their adopted country. Within a few weeks of Philip's birth Prince Andrew took command of a Greek army corps in a war against the Turks, and after a crushing Greek defeat was made the scapegoat for the national disaster. With Greece humiliated and its monarchy once again collapsing, Andrew faced public trial and execution.

He was saved by his family connections, for King George V, shocked by the murder by the Bolsheviks of his cousins in the Russian royal family, was determined to prevent a repetition with the Greeks. Strong British pressure was exerted, a cruiser was despatched to Greece, and it was aboard this British battleship that Prince Andrew, Princess Alice and the eighteen-month-old future husband of the Queen of England made their escape to freedom and the life of stateless exiles.

For Philip this was the beginning of a life of extraordinary contrasts and ambiguities, all of which stemmed from his uneasy royal inheritance. On the one hand was the grandeur of his royal descent: as a small boy he met his saviour, George V, at Buckingham Palace, and sometimes stayed with his grandmother, Princess Victoria, at her apartment in Kensington Palace. ('Kensington Palace', he said later, 'was a sort of base where I kept my things.') But on the other hand there were the frightful insecurity and muddle that afflicted his unhappy parents.

The cosmopolitan and light-hearted Prince Andrew was dogged, not unnaturally, by a mordant sense of failure which would ruin the remainder of his life: and for the more intense Princess Alice, all the horrors that had surrounded the late birth of her final child had permanently scarred her fragile spirit. Nor were things helped by the traditional affliction of most exiles whether royal or not − a permanent shortage of hard cash. For having saved his kinsman from the firing squad, King George and his advisers felt they had done their bit, and there was no great eagerness within the British family of Windsor to have all that much to do with their potentially embarrassing continental poor relations. There was certainly no financial help, and nothing was done to persuade them to stay on in England. They finally made their home outside Paris in a fairly modest villa in the suburb of St Cloud.

Here, as a small boy, Philip witnessed the breakup of his parents' marriage. It must have been profoundly harrowing. His mother, now assailed by deafness, menopause and the general disappointments of her life, had turned increasingly to God: religious mania ensued, and finally produced a total mental breakdown. When she tried to throw away her clothes and marry Christ, her earthly marriage foundered. Prince Andrew, not surprisingly, decamped to Monte Carlo and a wealthy mistress – but very little else – and his wife was consigned to a succession of discreet nursing homes, first in Switzerland and finally near Munich, where she was close to her youngest daughter, Sophie, who had married her German kinsman, Prince Christopher of Hesse.

All Philip's sisters were to marry into the German upper aristocracy – which was to cause divided loyalties later in his life. When he married Elizabeth, the fact that all her sisters-in-law were by marriage German inevitably revived memories of the German royal connection the Windsors had done so much to forget. His eldest sister, Margarita, married Prince Hohenlohe-Langenburg; Theodora, the Margrave of Baden; and Cecile, the hereditary Grand Duke of Hesse. Cecile and her husband were killed in a flying accident in 1937, but during the Second World War Hohenlohe-Langenburg fought with the *Wehrmacht*, and Christopher of Hesse, a dedicated early Nazi, worked for the organisation that became the Gestapo, belonged to the SS, and was killed flying with the Luftwaffe.

Even for Philip, it was touch and go whether he would be brought up in Germany or England after the breakup of his parents' marriage. With neither parent in much of a position to say what should happen to him, he became something of a shuttlecock between the two sides of his family. His sisters, all soon to become dedicated German subjects by marriage, were anxious to see him brought up in the Fatherland, but the strongest influence proved to be the English side of his divided family. His mother's eldest brother, George, Marquis of Milford Haven, took responsibility for the rumbustious eight-year-old by sending him to his own English preparatory school, Cheam; but in 1933 the German influence prevailed and it was agreed that Philip should complete his education not at an English public school, but at the progressive Salem school founded on the family estate by his sister Theodora's famous father-in-law, Prince Max of Baden, the former German Chancellor.

Philip stayed a year at Salem: had he continued longer he might well have had to fight for Germany five years later. But he was unhappy there. The school was disintegrating, and when Kurt Hahn, its celebrated Jewish headmaster, fled to Britain to set up an offshoot of his school at Gordonstoun in Scotland, Philip followed, with his Uncle George's backing, thus becoming one of Gordonstoun's first and most famous pupils. With its emphasis on leadership and self-reliance, Gordonstoun suited his healthy temperament and he became captain of games and head of school. But even now his education continued to keep him firmly apart from the traditional English upper classes. He had nothing of the English public school mentality, with its sense of effortless superiority and membership for life of an extended gentlemanly club. He was royal, but judged by the unspoken standards of such places, he was fairly firmly an outsider.

Indeed it was hard to say exactly what he was. According to his passport he was 'Philip Prince of Greece', but although the Greek monarchy was once again restored in 1935, he had little to do with that turbulent kingdom and firmly resisted the suggestion that he enter the Greek naval academy on leaving Gordonstoun. He had a Danish surname – which he never used – and rarely visited Denmark. Nor had he much to do with Germany now, although he spoke its language fluently, and visited his relations there on holidays. He also visited his father in the South of France and got on well with that elegant, unhappy man. Relations with his mother were less easy, although she had now recovered from the more alarming symptoms of her breakdown and settled in a small house in the centre of Athens. There, with a godly female for companionship, she lived the life of a religious recluse, surrounded by silver-framed photographs of royal relations. The atmosphere did not appeal to him. When she suggested he might make his home with her, he changed the subject.

For by now he had solved what might have been a lifelong problem of personal identity, and with the practicality of youth had found a model for the sort of life he wanted, in contrast with the muddles and disasters all around him.

Louis, Lord Mountbatten, Philip's favourite 'Uncle Dickie', was then in his mid-thirties and almost too glamorous to be true. Handsome, vastly energetic and immensely charming when he took the trouble, he represented everything a penniless, stateless prince like Philip might have dreamed of for himself. From much the same background as his nephew, he had achieved a life of virtually unrivalled splendour and success by using his intelligence, his looks and his royal connections to their fullest possible extent.

During his early twenties he had carefully cultivated his friendship with his dashing cousin, the Prince of Wales, thus firmly establishing his presence with the royal family. Describing the Prince as 'just about my very best friend', Mountbatten went as his ADC aboard HMS *Renown* on his triumphant royal tour of the empire in 1922, and shared in something of the growing magic of the monarchy. His royal connections certainly assisted his career in the Royal Navy, and by 1934 he had become the youngest destroyer commander with the Mediterranean fleet. And although he had not married royalty himself, he had made what was possibly the shrewdest move of all for a minor member of the royal family living on the pay of a naval officer, by marrying the richest non-royal heiress in the land – Edwina Ashley. As the eldest grandchild of Edward VII's favourite Jewish banker, Sir Ernest Cassel, she inherited a yearly income of £50,000 after tax the day she married him.

For Lord Louis the result was a dazzling amalgam of royalty and mammon, the senior service and very smart society. Home was a thirty-room penthouse suite (private cinema included) at the top of the Park Lane block constructed in 1935 on the site of Sir Ernest's megalithic London house. After the death of Edwina's father, Lord Mount Temple, in 1960, he would also have the use of Classiebawn Castle in Ireland and Broadlands, the Hampshire mansion which was once the home of Palmerston.

He had the *entrée* to the Palace and the friendship of Douglas Fairbanks, Nöel Coward and Charlie Chaplin. There was a luxury yacht, a supercharged Hispano-Suiza, a string of polo ponies, and a splendid villa on a hill in Malta where Commander Lord Mountbatten RN spent his shore leave with his wife and their two daughters, Pamela and Patricia, when duty called him to the Mediterranean.

Sixteen-year-old Philip was impressed. According to his cousin, the future Queen Alexandra of Yugoslavia, who grew up with him, 'he talked to me with passionate excitement of Uncle Dickie's penthouse where the lift from the street level was the fastest in London, and how Uncle Dickie's study had a world map in relief on the walls, and his bedroom was like a cabin in a battle cruiser, even to the portholes.'

All this was very different from the life his mother wanted him to share with her in Athens, or that he saw his father eking out in obscurity in Monte Carlo. It was also very different from that uneasy world of continental former royalty which he had seen in Hitler's Germany on visits to his married sisters. Philip was rapidly discovering what he wanted out of life. Alexandra wrote later of how he sometimes talked to her about the home he dreamed of: 'a country house in England he had planned to the last detail of the fitments and furniture. This was so like Philip. Once he has made up his mind on anything, he always knows precisely where he is going, determined to make every plan come true.'

'I don't think anybody thinks I had a father,' Philip once complained. 'Most people think that Dickie's my father anyway.' In fact Philip's uncle, George Milford Haven, had more to do with his nephew during his time at Gordonstoun than Uncle Dickie, and Philip's relations with Prince Andrew were quite firm enough to offer this very self-possessed young man all he needed in the way of father-figures. Lord Mountbatten's influence on Philip, though of great importance, was quite different from that of an adoptive father. After the beginning of 1938, when George Milford Haven died of cancer and the problem loomed of finding a career for the prince who would soon be leaving Gordonstoun, 'Uncle Dickie' changed from being just his nephew's boyhood hero. Suddenly, for complicated reasons of his own, he became prime mover in his seventeen-year-old nephew's most surprising life.

Vain, ambitious, worldly and extremely clever – Louis Mountbatten was all of these; but behind the glittering, not entirely attractive figure of minor royalty on the make lies an obsession of such curious intensity that in retrospect his life appears as one of romantic and almost painful dedication. At the root of this obsession lay the righting of what he saw as the outrageous wrong inflicted on the honour of the Battenbergs when his father had been 'thrown to the wolves' of popular hysteria, and forced from his position as First Sea Lord in 1914.

For Mountbatten's debonair image as the carefree British naval officer, though carefully maintained, was not exactly what it seemed. In character as well as origins he was essentially German, and his rigid and compelling sense of family honour was similar in many ways to Queen Mary's equally Teutonic feelings for the monarchy. According to this code, he felt obliged to recover his father's old position for himself – as he did in 1954 by becoming First Sea Lord himself – and also to enhance still further the dynastic honours of the Battenbergs, those petty German princelings from the Rhine who had already done so well by marrying into the British royal family, and whose origins Queen Victoria's cousin, the Duke of Cambridge, once maliciously described as 'lost in the mists of the nineteenth century'.

Thanks to his own close friendship with the Prince of Wales and the infinite benefits bestowed by all that lovely Cassel money, Louis Mountbatten's careful plans had been working out as he intended; but he had recently had his setbacks too. One was his lack of a male heir, for after the birth of two daughters the state of his relations with his highly independent wife made further children most unlikely. Luckily his brother George had a son to continue the Mountbatten lineage, but for someone of Mountbatten's almost superstitious sense of family the absence of a personal male heir was a lifelong disappointment.

He had further reasons for dissatisfaction with his wife. By the mid-Thirties she had become a source of such scandal and public speculation as to put at risk his own relations with the court. Although she had won a High Court libel action against the *Sunday People* to clear her name of the imputation of an affair with the black singer and actor, Paul Robeson, this had only fuelled the gossip of her supposed attraction for the dark-skinned races. She made no secret of her sympathy for left-wing causes, and the highly conventional George V had virtually barred her from the Court during the last years of his reign.

Mountbatten had been able to offset this for the future by continuing his friendship with the Prince of Wales. As David's kinsman and one of his oldest, closest friends, he knew he could count on a position of unique royal favour when the old King died – as he was bound to fairly soon. What he had not foreseen was the Abdication, which was a personal catastrophe and affected relations with the Court for the remainder of his life. At the time he seemed to have weathered it with typical panache. He had always got on well with George VI, and after his accession the Court seemed anxious to present the appearance of a thoroughly united family to the world at large. Mountbatten was appointed Naval ADC to the new King, and invested with the highest personal honour of the monarchy – the Knight Grand Cross of the Royal Victorian Order. But things were not as rosy as they seemed. The Mountbattens, who had always been such friends and allies of the exiled Duke of Windsor during his affair with Mrs Simpson, had aroused the profound suspicions of the most powerful figure at the Palace. Queen Elizabeth was most adept at hiding her feelings with a diplomatic smile, but she rarely changed them. For many years to come she would be extremely wary of this former crony of the Duke's, who had switched horses with such accomplished ease. The Mountbatten star, which had been rising in the royal firmament, suddenly seemed to have stopped. Something needed to be done.

According to his own account, Prince Philip, left to his own devices, would probably have opted for the Royal Air Force after Gordonstoun, and it was only when Uncle Dickie suggested it might be easier to enter the Royal Navy through Dartmouth Royal Naval College, that he 'just sort of accepted it'. And from then on Uncle firmly masterminded Philip's early nautical career, selecting the special crammer at Cheltenham to prepare him for the Dartmouth entrance and using all his influence to make it possible for a foreigner – Philip was still officially a Greek – to be considered by the college.

There was already something of a tradition linking both the royal family and the Battenbergs with Dartmouth and the navy, and at Dartmouth Philip was thus adroitly placed to attract the notice and approbation of the King. Mountbatten made certain he received it.

According to the generally accepted version of events, the romance between Philip and Elizabeth was born during a royal visit there in July 1939, shortly after Philip joined the college. The royal family was naturally accompanied by His Majesty's Naval ADC, and from the various accounts of what ensued it is clear that Uncle Dickie was determined that the thirteen-year-old heiress to the throne should see as much as possible of his handsome eighteen-year-old nephew. Because of a college outbreak of chicken-pox and mumps, the two Princesses had to spend the day confined to the house of the officer-in-charge; and Philip, who was conveniently free from infection, found himself picked to entertain them.

It is not known if Uncle Dickie was behind this simple but far-reaching arrangement – but it seems likely: for according to Queen Alexandra, it was he who 'steadfastly procured his nephew an invitation to lunch on the royal yacht' next day, and by then the adolescent and extremely sheltered 'Princess Lilibet' was captivated by the boisterous and god-like Prince of Greece.

'How good he is!' she is said to have exclaimed after a lively game of croquet, and according to Miss Crawford, who thought Philip 'a noisy young fellow, eager to make himself seen and heard', the Princess 'sat pink-faced and enjoying it all very much' at lunch on the royal yacht as she watched her cousin demolishing several plates of shrimps and a banana split. Philip appears to have been less emotionally affected. Many years later he recalled the Dartmouth episode as 'a very amusing experience, going on board the yacht and meeting them and that sort of thing, and that was that.'

Amusing or not, he was soon to learn of Uncle Dickie's very serious plans for his dynastic future. Late that summer he left Dartmouth, having gained the prize for best cadet, and through his uncle's personal initiative was posted as midshipman to HMS *Ramillies*, on convoy duty from the Far East to Alexandria. *Ramillies* was commanded by Mountbatten's old commanding officer from the Mediterranean First Destroyer Flotilla, Captain Baillie-Grohman, and Uncle Dickie had cabled him direct with a request to accept his nephew on his ship.

Baillie-Grohman, who had also served with George Milford Haven, was agreeably impressed by his new midshipman. Soon after Philip's arrival on the ship, the Captain had a private 'avuncular' conversation with him that struck him as so extraordinary that he recorded it in his diary.

I had pointed out that as a foreign subject (he was then Greek), he would only be able to reach the rank of Acting Sub-Lieut. in the Royal Navy, and that to go further he would have to become a British subject. I asked, did he want to go on in the Royal Navy? He replied emphatically that he certainly did, and he wished to become a British subject.

Then came a surprise. He went on to say, 'My Uncle Dickie has ideas for me; he thinks I could marry Princess Elizabeth.' I was a bit taken aback, and after a hesitation asked him, 'Are you fond of her?' 'Oh yes, very', was the reply. 'I write to her every week.'

Uncle Dickie was an energetic and a forceful sponsor, and his own career showed what could be accomplished through a clever marriage and close association with the British royal family. According to his biographer, Richard Hough, 'the match between Prince Philip and Princess Elizabeth was the culmination of years of thought and ambition for Mountbatten, binding the Mountbatten dynasty unbreakably to the House of Windsor.' There were others, too, whose interests were powerfully involved, particularly the members of the Greek royal family once they heard from Uncle Dickie, never the most reticent of men, what was in the air.

Once again that invaluable observer of royalty, Sir Henry Channon, makes it clear in his diaries just how busy Philip's uncle must have been, and how early on the Greek royal family was taking it for granted that the marriage would eventually take place. Channon was in Athens in January 1941, on the eve of the German invasion, and among the assembled Greek royalty he was particularly impressed by the twenty-year-old Prince Philip, who would shortly distinguish himself aboard his ship in the decisive battle with the Italian fleet off Cape Matapan.

> He is extraordinarily handsome, and I recalled my afternoon's conversation with Princess Nicholas. He is to be our Prince Consort, and that is why he is serving in our Navy. He is charming, but I deplore such a marriage; he and Princess Elizabeth are too inter-related.

From a keen student of royalty like Channon, the objection to the idea of the marriage on the grounds of blood relationship is strange; for Philip and Elizabeth are no more 'inter-related' than third cousins, and he must have known that such marriages were almost standard practice in the closely linked network of European royalty. Certainly the Greeks had no such qualms, and it is revealing that Channon should have cited Philip's aunt, Princess Nicholas, as the source of such positive inside information – for as the King's sister-in-law the Princess had the closest links of all between the Greek court and the House of Windsor.

It was her daughter, Philip's favourite cousin, the beautiful Princess Marina, who had married and dramatically reformed George VI's youngest brother, the Duke of Kent. As the one indisputable exponent of European style and female glamour in the British royal family in her day, she was extremely popular in England. She was also intensely proud of her lineage and the fact that, unlike the heiress to the British throne, she had royal blood on *both* sides of her family. This obsession with lineage was something she shared with her friend and cousin, Lord Mountbatten, who had early on enlisted her as a keen ally in his marriage plans for Philip. And it was this same exaggerated obsession which made the Greek royals take the marriage as a virtual *fait accompli*, and almost fatally overplay their hand.

This they did in 1943 at the gathering of English and continental royalty for the wedding of Philip's cousin, Alexandra, with the exiled King Peter of Yugoslavia. The not over-sensitive King George II of Greece (also once again in exile and familiarly known as 'the King of Claridge's') took advantage of the nuptial spirit to urge upon his fellow king of England the virtues of his nephew Philip as a future son-in-law. To his great surprise he got a very unenthusiastic answer.

In truth, King George VI was more put out than he actually appeared, having been hitherto oblivious of what the Greeks were taking so much for granted. They had felt they were doing the House of Windsor something of an honour by offering its daughter so handsome a prince with such impeccable royal credentials. George VI saw the situation differently. As a rather insular Englishman he was not at all impressed by European royalty and its ridiculous concern with lineage and dynasties. That was acceptable for someone like his cousin Dickie, but the King of England was above worrying too much about such things, and what really mattered was his daughter's happiness. He was certainly not going to accept an old-style arranged marriage, worked out by the devious Greeks; and his protective – even jealous – feelings for his teenage daughter were instantly aroused.

Not that he had anything against Philip personally. He quite liked the little he had seen of him, and as an indulgent father saw no greater danger in Philip's friendship with Elizabeth than he would later see in that of Group Captain Townsend with her sister. Throughout the war, Philip had been casually invited to the Palace or to Windsor when on leave – but that was very different from suddenly accepting him as son-in-law-in-waiting; and looks and personality apart, Philip had a number of quite glaring disadvantages which became more glaring still the more one thought about them.

First were those vaunted family connections with the Royal House of Greece. Things had changed radically for royalty from those palmy days when Queen Victoria had benignly married off her children and even her grandchildren into the other royal houses on the Continent, and history had shown how awkward such relationships could finally become. George VI's own marriage into the English aristocracy rather than a European royal house was a great success and had underlined the British nature of the House of Windsor, while his father had already had his problems with the Royal House of Greece. There was nothing to be said for even closer ties, particularly with Greece on the edge of civil war as the German occupation ended.

Nor was Mountbatten's eager sponsorship of Philip quite the asset it had been originally. For Mountbatten's popular success as a war-leader had made him a highly controversial character with jealous enemies in high places, including Churchill and the greatest press-lord politician of the day, Lord Beaverbrook. Within the Court he was seen as not merely vain and potentially left-wing, but overweeningly ambitious: Queen Elizabeth mistrusted him as much as ever, and the more she learned of his attempts to promote her daughter's marriage, the more it appeared as one more attempt by the Mountbattens to 'move in on the monarchy'.

And finally the problem no one liked to mention: that of Philip's three surviving sisters, two of whose husbands had fought gallantly for Hitler in the war. However bravely Philip may have fought for his adopted country, facts like these could not be overlooked.

Faced with this situation, George VI behaved like the simple, rather anxious father that he was, and touchingly produced for Princess Elizabeth's inspection a selection of clean-cut, very well-bred Englishmen with none of Philip's inbuilt disadvantages. Suddenly at parties at Windsor and the Palace, old Etonians from the Brigade of Guards like young Lord Euston (Lord Grafton's heir) or the twenty-four-year-old Duke of Rutland started appearing with suspicious regularity.

The Princess was polite, but found it hard to hide her boredom. With the quiet determination of her quietly determined nature she made it very clear that she was not remotely interested in such nice young men, and soon placed a photograph of Philip by her bed to

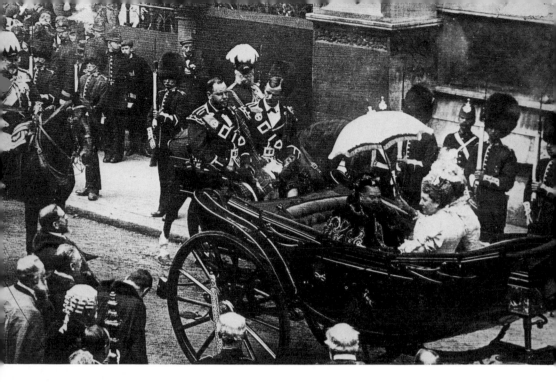

ABOVE: Queen Victoria at her Diamond Jubilee in 1897, with her son resplendently mounted and plumed behind her. Despite the Prince of Wales's attempts to persuade his mother to wear her Jewels of State, she insisted on the simplest black widow's dress *(BBC Hulton Picture Library)*. BELOW: 'Once she was on the throne beside her sailor king, Queen Mary's hour had come.' *(BBC Hulton Picture Library)*

ABOVE: 'To the vast and vulnerable show of royal finery, Queen Mary brought the assurance of sacred destiny.' *(Camera Press Ltd)*

ABOVE RIGHT: The future King George VI leaves his private hut at the annual Duke of York Camp he founded. *(BBC Hulton Picture Library)*

BELOW RIGHT: 'The prospect of a thrice-married lady from Baltimore following Queen Mary as royal consort was hard to contemplate with total seriousness.' The exiled Duke and Duchess of Windsor at the Château de Caude on their wedding day, June 3, 1937. *(Camera Press Ltd)*

ABOVE: 'Mummy, you know, is the most wonderful person in the world in my eyes…' Queen Elizabeth (then Duchess of York) with Princess Elizabeth and Princess Margaret Rose in 1934 (*Camera Press Ltd*). BELOW: 'When his people listen to him they will notice an occasional and momentary hesitation in his speech. But he has brought it under full control, and to those who hear him it need cause no embarrassment, for it causes none to him who speaks.' George VI broadcasts to his people throughout the world on Christmas Day, 1944. (*BBC Copyright*)

ABOVE: 'The majestic acting out of ancient ritual around the person of the youthful Queen made memorable royal theatre.' The moment of crowning of Her Majesty Queen Elizabeth II, as the Archbishop of Canterbury places the St Edward's Crown on her head. *(BBC Hulton Picture Library)*

RIGHT: 'Over the years he had become a convinced evangelist for the British monarchy, believing in his earthly sovereign rather as Billy Graham does in his heavenly one.' 'Gold Microphone-in-Waiting', Richard Dimbleby, outside Westminster Abbey at the time of the Coronation. *(BBC Hulton Picture Library)*

LEFT: 'I don't think anybody thinks I had a father,' Philip once complained. 'Most people think that Dickie's my father anyway.' Uncle and nephew at the National Playing Fields Association dinner in October 1948. *(Popperfoto)*

RIGHT: 'A man of strong emotions which a lifetime at Court had taught him to disguise.' The *éminence grise* behind the ending of the romance of Princess Margaret and Peter Townsend, the Queen's Secretary, Sir Alan 'Tommy' Lascelles. *(The Photo Source)*

'He was a married man, sixteen years her senior. He knew the form.' Group Captain Peter Townsend at the races with Princess Margaret. *(Rex Features Ltd)*

The critics and their quarry. TOP LEFT AND RIGHT: Lord Altrincham *(Rex Features Ltd)*; John Osborne *(Rex Features Ltd)*. BOTTOM LEFT AND RIGHT: Malcolm Muggeridge *(BBC Hulton Picture Library)*; and Sir Richard Colville *(Camera Press Ltd)*.

show the family exactly how she felt. For something unpredictable had happened. The friendship, which for years had been plotted and promoted by Mountbatten and the Greeks with all the unromantic calculation of eighteenth century royal marriage-brokers, had become a genuine romance. From that day at Dartmouth, with the shrimps and the banana split, Elizabeth had never wavered; and she was now determined she would marry Philip and none other.

Daughters in love are difficult to deal with, and George VI, who could deny his daughter nothing, was not the man to thwart her. Old Queen Mary, as befitted a former member of a German princely house, was naturally inclined to appreciate Philip's old-style continental royal connections and came out in his favour: so, more discreetly, did Marina of Kent. A three months' parting, while the Royal Family toured South Africa early in 1947, served only to increase the lovers' ardour; and after a somewhat sticky visit by Prince Philip to Balmoral, His Majesty overcame his evident misgivings and the idea of the marriage was accepted.

During this crucial period, Lord Mountbatten, soon to be appointed Viceroy of India and entrusted by the Labour Government with partitioning India on the eve of independence, was not too much in evidence – which was probably as well. As he later said himself, 'when you plant something you don't keep digging it up to see how the roots are progressing.' But he did have one fascinating contribution to make to the status of his nephew and the reputation of the Battenberg/Mountbatten family. The long-delayed question of Philip's naturalisation as a British subject had to be arranged, and in his breezy, easy-seeming way he offered to take charge of it. The one slight difficulty now was that perennial problem of royalty – a suitable surname. As we have seen, Philip had never really used one, signing himself when necessary, 'Philip Prince of Greece'. His father, who had died in German-dominated Monte Carlo in 1944, had left him (apart from two old suits and a shaving-brush), the resounding Schleswig-Holstein surname, which did not go well in English. No one was over-anxious anyhow to be reminded of that slightly equivocal figure at a time like this, and it was Uncle Dickie, resourceful as ever, who produced the obvious solution. Why didn't Philip use his mother's name instead?

Philip said later that he was 'not madly in favour . . . but in the end I was persuaded, and anyway I couldn't think of a reasonable alternative.' In February 1947, the *London Gazette* announced the granting of British citizenship to Lieutenant Philip Mountbatten RN. And a few days later, Lord Mountbatten flew off to partition India, knowing that with just a little luck he had secured the Mountbatten name its place in European history. With so many other things to think about, no one at the Palace seemed to notice.

Thanks on the whole to Princess Elizabeth's firm insistence, the Abbey wedding duly followed after a short engagement, in November 1947 – this despite a last-ditch effort by the King to make the couple wait until June 1948 'when the weather would be better.' With the King's refusal to allow television cameras inside the Abbey, the actual wedding lacked the public impact of the Coronation five years later, but as the first grand royal ceremonial occasion since the war it was highly popular and a sign of things to come.

Despite a Labour government in power still pledged to post-war austerity, the Secretary of State for War, that shrewd working-class politician, Emanuel Shinwell, had the sense to appreciate the popularity of royal spectacle and ensured that sufficient scarlet uniforms were found for the Household Cavalry to ride in splendour in the royal procession. Churchill described the wedding as 'a splash of colour on the hard road we have to follow', *Picture Post* called it 'the greatest day of national rejoicing since victory was won', and no one missed the bridegroom's sisters who were not invited and remained in Germany.

But his mother was there, a hieratic figure now apparently very much herself in the nun-like habit of a sister of the Church of Greece. So were his Uncle Dickie and his Aunt Edwina, who had just finished their vice-regal work in India, which resulted in partitioning the sub-continent into India and Pakistan. With the widespread inter-racial violence that ensued, Edwina thought it wrong for them to come, but her husband argued that their presence would appear a gesture of their confidence in India and Pakistan's ability to settle their problems for themselves. Besides, it was too much to expect the architect to miss the triumph of his plans sketched out so many years before.

As far as Philip was concerned, the marriage was the climax to one of those sudden transformation scenes which are inseparable from the myth of the modern British monarchy. Before the wedding he had not been over-popular; his Greek and German connections told against him, and a poll conducted by the *Daily Mirror* showed forty percent of its readers supposedly against the marriage. Now this was changed abruptly. With barely a mention in the press of any German element in his background or family, the bridegroom found himself fulsomely described as 'the Viking Prince from beyond the seas'.

Thanks to the love of a very pure princess, the handsome Viking was magically translated from his Nissen hut near Portsmouth, where he had been teaching petty officers navigation, and almost overnight emerged as a Knight of the Most Noble Order of the Garter, together with the triple rank of Duke and Earl and Baron and the gratifying style of Royal Highness. With the couple obviously in love, the fairy-tale Princess had achieved the happiness that everyone felt that she deserved, and Philip's image as the rugged, forthright sailor-prince at the centre of this royal romance now brought him widespread popularity.

At first the reality was not so very different from the fairy-tale – the romantic honeymoon in the rural luxury of Broadlands, the Mountbattens' private, very stately country home; the official income of £10,000 a year in addition to the annual £50,000 his wife received from the Civil List on marriage; a valet and a very smart Lagonda of his own. After the marriage the couple had to spend some months living at the Palace, which Philip apparently did not enjoy, but he was soon supervising extensive renovations to his own home, Clarence House, much as he had dreamed of doing with his ideal English country residence during his days at Gordonstoun.

For in a way those expectations he had confided to Baillie-Grohman as a young midshipman had come true, and he had actually achieved a life in most respects richer and more glamorous than Uncle Dickie's. But it was also much more complicated: for by his marriage he had entered two quite separate worlds, one which centred round the Court, and another which he and the Princess were able to create outside it.

Philip did his best to get on well with George VI, and to a point succeeded, particularly once he proved himself a first-class shot at Sandringham. But in character the two men could hardly have been more different, and the long-established, very private home-life of the Windsors, with its forbidding combination of extreme formality and unsophisticated cosiness, took a while to understand and was really not for him. Nor were the majority of courtiers, whose beliefs had been instilled neither at Gordonstoun nor in the Royal Navy.

Only within his own world could Philip really be himself, and once he and the Princess had set up home in Clarence House, life could finally proceed according to his boyhood dream. The happy production within a year of marriage of a male royal heir, Prince Charles, in November 1948, added greatly to his self-confidence, as did the chance to continue with his nautical career. For the navy was the ideal outlet for his many qualities – his extrovert energy, his lively powers of leadership, his natural toughness and a highly professional attitude to life. These were qualities he shared with his Uncle Dickie, and when he reached Malta, first as second-in-command of a destroyer and later in command of his own ship, HMS *Magpie*, he seemed to be following uncannily in Mountbatten's footsteps.

As his cousin Alexandra noticed, Philip even spoke like Mountbatten in his brisk impromptu after-dinner speeches, so unlike the usual utterances of the tongue-tied Windsors. He learned his uncle's favourite game of polo (and was soon playing it better than his mentor), and afloat showed much the same effective style of command, with forthright and demanding contact with all aboard his ship. A great achiever, he enjoyed competing and succeeding on equal terms with those around him; yet off-duty, and again like Uncle Dickie, he unashamedly relished all the extras of his situation – money, status, and the luxurious Mountbatten villa on the island, where the Princess came to stay like a highly honoured naval wife just as Edwina had before her. The birth of their daughter, Princess Anne, in 1950 brought further satisfaction; and later Philip would talk nostalgically of this period as one of the happiest of his life.

One wonders if he really had an inkling of what he would soon be in for when, by 1951, the King's declining health abruptly made it clear that Philip's successful independent naval life would have to end. For now he faced the likelihood of his wife becoming queen far earlier than either had envisaged. Certainly he must have learned the facts of his future royal life by the time of Elizabeth's accession early the year following – hence the days of black depression that ensued, and his efforts to retain his home at Clarence House away from the dominating influence of the Palace and the courtiers.

For any husband, the transformation of his wife into the Queen of England would have brought its problems; but for one as active and forthright as this former Prince of Greece, the situation now was fraught with genuine humiliation. Life would have been much easier had he been the one thing he patently was not – a royal cypher – for the Palace hierarchy calmly assumed from the start that he should have no influence or power at all over the settled, sacred institution which was invested in the Queen, his wife.

Things were very different from those days, not all that long before, when the future Queen Mary had been given access by her father-in-law, King Edward VII, to those all-important 'boxes' containing documents of state, in preparation for the time when she became royal consort. The Duke was permitted no such access – although it is hard to see that anything but benefit would have ensued – and his status as the monarch's husband was markedly inferior to that which the previous two consorts had enjoyed as the monarchs' wives.

Once he was settled at the Palace, this was made uncomfortably clear. He found he had no secretary of his own, no office and no staff, for he had very little positive to do. According to a courtier's explanation at the time, the theory behind this was quite simple: 'The Duke of Edinburgh is head of family but Her Majesty is head of the nation'. The two roles, according to the accepted wisdom at the Palace, were to be kept in very watertight compartments. The Duke would naturally support the Queen in his personal capacity, take on such public duties as were deemed appropriate, act as a handsome clothes-horse for the uniforms he wore so well on ceremonial occasions – and that would more or less be that.

Some of the reasoning behind this very cagey attitude would have applied to any royal husband. The Queen, by inheriting all the state functions of the King, her father, at her accession, had left no obvious male role for the Duke within the monarchy. The close presence of a very active and experienced royal matriarch, in the person of his immensely influential mother-in-law, blocked any chance of Philip's becoming an effective power behind the throne, as his great-great-grandfather, Albert, was to Queen Victoria; and the awesome public image of the Queen herself, soon to become yet more enhanced at the Coronation, pointed up his own inferiority as he walked the requisite royal pace behind her at their joint royal functions.

But there were other factors too which aggravated the Duke's unenviable position, and these lay in his background and his character. He was not a docile man and the Court was not a ship. In many ways it was highly inefficient and old-fashioned, with a complement of under-worked palace staff and courtiers who were jealous of their power and privileges. Philip was impatient. They became resentful. And when clashes followed, as they did, the Duke became more isolated than he was already.

Paradoxically, he would have found life at Court much easier had he been not royal himself, but one of those rich upper-class Englishmen George VI originally wanted as a son-in-law; for then he would have been instantly at home among the exclusive network of the aristocracy around the throne and in the country. He would have talked their private language, relished their jokes, known and enjoyed their enormous country houses, and possessed an automatic set of friends and allies to rely on. Lacking this, he was very much alone. His closest friend at Court of his own age was the Australian he soon appointed as his equerry, his former shipmate, Commander Michael Parker, and what power and influence he did possess came inevitably from a single source – his wife, the Queen.

This placed her in an unenviable position too. Her instincts and her sense of duty – not to mention the advice of her mother – urged her to protect the royal *status quo*, now sanctified by the memory and example of her father and the mystique of the Coronation. But she also wanted her husband – increasingly frustrated by the loss of his career – to be happy and fulfilled in some suitably demanding role beside her. Since none existed – or could be created without terrible disruptions – it was all extremely difficult.

Nor was the situation eased by the presence now of Uncle Dickie. For having, as he thought, achieved his grand ambition of installing his *protégé* beside the throne, and having finished off his work in India, Philip's exuberant uncle was basking in his status as the nearest thing the Queen had to a royal father-in-law. He was particularly excited by the thought of what he had achieved for the name and standing of his family – and it was this that brought Philip his bitterest embarrassment during the first fraught months after the accession.

As an obsessive genealogist, Uncle Dickie had plainly known exactly what he was up to when he had casually suggested that his nephew took his mother's name in 1947. But in another of those curious lapses which afflict the royal family from time to time, none of its members or advisers understood the simple implications of this very simple event. As we have seen, surnames have always been a blindspot of the British royal family; but as L. G. Pine, the editor of *Debrett's*, pointed out in a fascinating newspaper article just after the accession, Philip's adoption of his mother's name meant that the House of Windsor had been succeeded by a new royal house, the House of Mountbatten.

Anyone at court who read the article clearly did not dare mention this appalling fact, and two whole months went by before the truth sank home. And typically the one who mentioned it was Uncle Dickie. Early in April he was heard boasting that since February 7, 1952 a Mountbatten had been sitting on the English throne. When his words were reported to Queen Mary, the royal penny dropped – and regal hell broke loose.

Frail and aged though she was, the old lady was outraged and, according to the Queen's biographer, Lady Longford, roused herself to state that 'her husband had founded the House of Windsor *in aeterno*, and no "Battenberg marriage", however solemn and effective in English law, could change it.' The matriarch had answered her compatriot. Churchill was informed direct, and apparently egged on by one more of Mountbatten's keenest enemies, Lord Beaverbrook, the old Prime Minister erupted. The Windsors must be saved from this take-over bid by the Mountbattens – and such was the feeling now against Mountbatten that the Cabinet unanimously agreed that Churchill must tell Her Majesty her name: which he duly did, solemnly 'advising' her that her married status notwithstanding, the name of the British royal family stayed what it had been since 1917 – the House of Windsor.

Further eruptions followed, this time from Philip who complained that with even his name expunged, he was left as nothing more than 'an amoeba – a bloody amoeba!' But duty, even for the Queen, was duty, and there was nothing to be done except obey her government, erase her husband's name from the royal family tree and officially proclaim by an Order in Council, dated April 9, 1952, that it was her 'Will and Pleasure that She and Her Children shall be styled and known as the House of Windsor . . .'

If Mountbatten's enemies really thought they had put him in his place, they should have known him better – and acted faster – for by the time they tumbled to what he had done, he had effectively achieved exactly what he wanted: the royal apotheosis of his family. This he made very clear when he published his life work, a curious volume lovingly researched and proudly presented which he entitled *The Mountbatten Lineage*. It laboriously traced his family through forty-four generations, but the book's proudest sentence concerned the accession of 'Elizabeth Mountbatten' to the throne of England. 'The House of Mountbatten only reigned for two months,' he added, 'but historically it takes its place among the reigning houses of the United Kingdom.'

None of this helped marital harmony at the Palace, and although the Queen tried hard to restore her husband's somewhat battered self-respect, he remained furious at what he saw as the high-handed way he had been treated. No one had given a moment's thought to *his* feelings in the matter. It had been suggested that he might adopt the official title of 'Prince Consort' at the time of the Coronation, but after this insult to his name he was in no mood to accept.

With time he was placated by the efforts that were made to redeem his dignity. That November, at the first state opening of parliament of the new reign, the Queen herself overruled the courtiers who insisted that she must sit enthroned alone beneath the canopy of state in the House of Lords, with her husband on a humbler chair below: in the event they were ensconced beneath the canopy together. He was appointed chairman of the Coronation Council, and just before that great event was granted official precedence after the Queen herself. More importantly, he also took the place of Princess Margaret on the Regency Council which, in the unlikely event of Her Majesty's demise, would stand in for the infant Charles as sovereign until his eighteenth birthday. It was clearly common sense for Philip to assume this role with his own son; but although the change was inevitably seen as an advance for Philip at the expense of the Princess, no one commented on a more revealing provision in the Act of Regency: the simultaneous promotion to the Council of the Queen Mother in her daughter's place. Little was being left to chance. Even the Queen's untimely death would still see the royal *status quo* protected by the presence of the royal matriarch, her mother.

His inexperience apart, it is hard to see exactly what the courtiers and politicians feared in Philip. With his glamour, energy and youth, he could so easily have proved the monarchy's greatest asset after the Queen herself – as he demonstrated during the gruelling tour of the Commonwealth with the Queen following the Coronation. The jealousy and pique of those whose ancient toes he trod on cannot entirely account for the way he continued to be 'frozen out' from any position in which he might have changed the sanctified inertia of the Court during these first years of the reign.

Yet once again, like so much in the modern history of the House of Windsor, the answer seems to have its origins in the Abdication. Ever since those anxious days when the matriarchal system of the monarchy was being so effectively consolidated around the gentle family of George VI, Lord Mountbatten, though warily accepted by the Court, had always been regarded as a source of potential danger. The future Queen Mother, a shrewd judge of character, never trusted him, and while her daughters inevitably saw him as a most attractive uncle, she had no intention of forgetting that he had once been the closest friend of the Duke of Windsor – with all that that implied. For he still had many of the qualities of the former king – his popular appeal, his faintly raffish air, his love of luxury and his taste for positive male leadership. But where these qualities had brought disaster on the Duke of Windsor, they had with time and application brought nothing but success to Uncle Dickie.

Whether by chance or by intention, Philip's marriage was the crowning point of this success; and however anguished everyone at court became over his very sharp behaviour with his nephew's name, there was nothing to be done by the time the damage was discovered. Uncle Dickie had achieved exactly what he wanted – as he usually did – and although there was much resentment at the time, regal appearances still had to be maintained. For, thanks to Philip's marriage, Uncle Dickie had become an indispensable member of the royal family. The Queen was extremely fond of him. The infant Charles – who as a baby he had bathed – adored him. And Philip, while always anxious to emphasise his separate identity, was perfectly aware how much he owed him.

The result was something of a stalemate in the family, with the two old enemies, the Queen Mother and Mountbatten, wonderfully polite to one another, yet always carefully protecting their positions. They were well matched – both of them extremely charming, both highly popular, and both accomplished players of the royal game. Mountbatten was possibly the cleverer of the two, but the Queen Mother more than made up for this in sheer experience, in reputation from her past success as Queen, and in the strength of her support.

Mountbatten's major weakness was the opposition he had gathered from the upper reaches of the Conservative establishment. Much had contributed to this, from outright jealousy and rumours of his supposed 'socialistic inclinations', to resentment at the part he played in helping Attlee's Labour government jettison India 'the fairest jewel in the Imperial Crown'. For many years to come, Philip would find himself in checkmate to his uncle's shadow.

It was not a situation he enjoyed. In his school report at Gordonstoun, many years before, Kurt Hahn, after noting how Philip's qualities of leadership could be 'marred by impatience and intolerance' had gone on to predict that he would 'make his mark in any profession where he will have to prove himself in a full trial of strength'. It was this challenge that he lacked. A born achiever, he was in a world that left him little to achieve. A demi-god, he found little left to prove within the engulfing boredom of his female-dominated Parnassus.

One can but admire the way he did his best to find the challenges he needed in a deeply unchallenging environment. He had been piously entrusted with the chairmanship of George VI's favourite charity – the National Playing Fields Association – and revitalized it with his keen involvement. As Chief Ranger of Windsor Great Park, he took on responsibility for managing the royal estates – again with great efficiency. He did his best to follow the example of his great-great-grandfather, the much-maligned Prince Albert, in encouraging industry and science; he also helped design the coinage. One biographer describes him as trying to become 'a sort of national super-manager', and he achieved his greatest notoriety by urging British industry to 'get its finger out!'

Energetic, restless and frequently frustrated, he would do his best to keep extremely busy and to make what he called 'a useful contribution' to the public life of his adopted country. He also acted very loyally, in Michael Parker's words as 'a sort of chief of staff' to the Queen herself, helping, reminding, prompting and supporting her in all her public duties. Within his private family he always played the strict *paterfamilias*.

What he would never do, however, was become a dominating force within the monarchy. The pattern was too set, the matriarchal influence too strong to let his powerful, Mountbatten-style personality achieve the transformation he might have started had he only had the chance. He was emphatically no amoeba – but nor did he become the big fish in the Court he might have been. Those ingrained and emphatic male qualities of leadership were no match for the matriarchal style of the Court, and he would find those real trials of strength he needed, not in fighting battles he could never win, but in personal attempts to prove himself as yachtsman, flier, game-shot and polo-player. He excelled in all he undertook with total dedication, and the only signs of his frustration came from fairly regular brushes with photographers and journalists. He never had been one for bearing fools – or inquisitive outsiders – gladly, and was too direct a man to hide his reactions when feeling vulnerable or bored.

His most determined effort to modernise the image of the traditional Royal House of Windsor would come in 1960, and would show exactly where the true power still resided in the Court. The Duke had never felt at home at Sandringham, which – with some cause – he felt out of date, uncomfortable and vastly inefficient. The time had come, he felt, to change it.

He had been impressed by the work of a modern Cambridge architect called David Roberts, who had recently designed an imaginative and elegant extension to one of Cambridge's most regal buildings – the Fitzwilliam Museum. Who better to create a brand new royal residence at Sandringham, somewhat on the lines of the very modern stately home built for the Duke of Westminster after his immense Victorian Eaton Hall was totally demolished? The new Sandringham Philip envisaged would not only be comfortable for modern royalty to live in – that English country house 'planned to the last detail of the fitments and furniture' which he had talked of as a boy to his cousin Alexandra – but would symbolise the forward-looking nature of the monarchy itself, and offer a unique example of royal patronage to British architects and builders.

At the start, the Queen herself was sympathetic, and encouraged the idea; but the Queen Mother was horrified when she finally heard about it, making it clear that she was irrevocably opposed to the destruction of a building which had always meant so much to her husband and his family. Her Majesty herself began to waver, particularly after seeing the initial plans, and it was then that the Queen Mother thoughtfully suggested that it might be best to use her favourite architect, Sir Hugh Casson, to modernise King Edward's Sandringham without destroying it. To no one's particular surprise, the Queen Mother's influence prevailed. To outward appearances, the house and gardens of Sandringham remained exactly as they had always been. So did a great deal else.

6

MARGARET

'The number one truth... It is the *courtiers* who make royalty frightened and frightening.'

James Pope-Hennesy, official
biographer of Queen Mary

In classical mythology, the most troubling problems on Parnassus arose when its inhabitants were unable to resolve the contradictions between their god-like status and the attractions of ordinary humanity – and what was true of ancient Greece applied equally to the Royal House of Windsor, as Princess Margaret had set out to prove with a sense of timing which horrified the Court, and briefly turned popular attention from the worship of Her Majesty to an earthier interest in the romantic problems of her younger sister.

Margaret must have known at least some of the difficulties she would have to face, having been brought up with the dread example of her Uncle David to show just what happened when the royal rules were flouted. But throughout her life her fatal knack of muddling her royal identity with her private inclinations has brought such dire unhappiness to herself and such scandal to the monarchy that she appears as something of a victim to her royal situation. If Elizabeth II was her parents' great success, Princess Margaret's life appears the price that she, and the House of Windsor, have been forced to pay for it.

For with hindsight one sees just how many of her problems had their origin within that isolated, strangely schizophrenic life 'Us Four' had led since her uncle's abdication. On the one hand lay the sacredness and splendour of the royal situation and the reverence accorded by a deferential court: and on the other, her mother's calm insistence that her daughters must be treated, and behave, like very simple, country-loving, 'ordinary' children. For a clever, self-aware small girl like Princess Margaret, the temptation to play off one side of this royal world against the other must have been almost irresistible.

Nature had made this all too easy by giving her so many of the graces her elder sister seemed to lack. According to Lady Airlie, Queen Mary's down-to-earth lady-in-waiting, 'no two sisters could have been less alike than the two princesses, the elder with her quiet simplicity, the younger with her puckish expression and irrepressible high spirits.' Where Elizabeth was solemn, introverted and distinctly shy, with all the seriousness of an elder child impressed with a sense of the immense responsibilities ahead of her, Margaret was lively, wilful, extrovert and fun. She was also very pretty, 'made to be cuddled and played with', in Miss Crawford's own prophetic phrase; and like so many attractive, rather naughty children, she had swiftly learned to use her charm to get exactly what she wanted.

She knew precisely how to deal with her father, and Lady Airlie has discreetly blamed the King for spoiling and weakly indulging her as something of a favoured *enfant terrible*. For in the end she could always make him laugh: she was a natural mimic with a precocious sense of humour, who could divert him in the middle of an angry telling-off by innocently inquiring, 'Papa, do you sing, "God Save My Gracious Me"?' The king himself described her once as 'able to charm the pearl out of an oyster', and even Germanic old Queen Mary was not entirely immune, admitting that she found her young granddaughter 'so outrageously amusing that one can't help encouraging her'.

Had the House of Windsor really been that ordinary middle-class family it so frequently pretended to be, none of this would have mattered in the least, and its talented, engaging second daughter could have lived happily ever after; but as she grew up with an elder sister who would one day become Queen of England, it was not possible.

This was the crucial fact that ruled her childhood, and there is one apocryphal remark that has been ascribed to so many people in the small court circle – including Princess Margaret herself – that it seems to have expressed the general attitude towards the two princesses: 'Isn't it a blessing Margaret is the younger one?' Courtiers have been quoted muttering this with sanctimonious relief; Margaret herself is said to have repeated it to her mother after some piece of childish misbehaviour; and even the King must certainly have felt it when he compared his adorable *enfant terrible* with her admirable elder sister, who was so conscientiously preparing for the great role she would have to play.

For the young Princess the effect of such an attitude was only too predictable, and it became the basis of her relationship with everyone around her – in particular towards her sister. However outrageously she acted, it would never really matter because Elizabeth was there to do her duty. And because Elizabeth would finally inherit all the power and glory of the Crown, people felt sorry for the younger sister. Since she must positively not be permitted to feel jealous of Elizabeth, allowances were made for her. Elizabeth would one day have her crown, but in the meantime Margaret, a talented actress and musician, was encouraged to express her lively personality – and usually got away with it.

A more sophisticated family might have coped with her, but the House of Windsor, in its regal isolation, was unworldly almost to a fault. Miss Crawford did her best to instill the simpler lessons from the scriptures into the young Princesses; the King was a single-hearted gentleman who believed firmly in the ten commandments and obeyed his wife; and the Queen was so anxious to preserve her children from the worldly habits that had proved the downfall of their Uncle David, that she put her faith in the inculcation of the virtues of the English country gentry she had once been taught herself – courtesy, fresh air, and genteel preparation for the role of loving wife and mother. For Princess Margaret this was simply not enough.

Nor were the courtiers a match for her. By training and tradition carefully obsequious towards the members of the family, this closed community of former guardsmen, old Etonians and professsionally asexual upper-class 'tame cats' would do nothing – and say nothing – that might put at risk the addictive comforts and prestige of life at court. They were very different from the thirty-two-year-old RAF Group Captain who arrived at the Privy Purse entrance to the Palace in May 1944 as newly appointed equerry to the King.

His Majesty had been anxious to pay tribute to the fighting services by having suitable young officers seconded to the Court for a three month period from active service, and Peter Townsend, a slim, good-looking, former fighter-pilot, was a man of action and a hero, who had fought in the Battle of Britain. He was personable and soon found that court life suited him, particularly in contrast with active flying for which, after a form of nervous breakdown, he had by his own admission begun to lose his nerve.

Cold though it was in winter, Townsend enjoyed his grace-and-favour house at Windsor. The King took him stalking at Balmoral, and stood godfather to his second son. He soon picked up the courtier's arts of meticulous flattery and concerned discretion. The Queen enjoyed his company, and as he effortlessly slipped into a position as an accepted member of the family circle, nobody mentioned his return to active service. The King was heard to remark, 'I'd have liked a boy like Townsend'; and before long the full-time life demanded of a courtier had begun to put at risk his wartime marriage with the daughter of a brigadier. He was rapidly becoming that dangerous character apt to crop up in monarchies in days gone by – a royal favourite.

By the unspoken but quite clearcut rules of the Royal House of Windsor, he should have been nothing of the kind; for among the prevailing courtiers, Townsend's background made him a rank outsider. With his father a former member of the Burmese Civil Service and his mother Hugh Gaitskell's aunt, the family was sadly middle-class: he had no private income, no West End club, no family court connections, and his public school – Haileybury – was known, if at all, as the *alma mater* of another dangerous socialist, Clement Attlee. Not that Townsend could be accused of left-wing tendencies (he had once thought of standing as a Conservative candidate for a West Country constituency, but abandoned the idea when the local chairman thought him too 'lukewarm' to make a politician). But although an officer, and possibly a gentleman, everything about him marked him out as subtly different from the other members of that stratospheric social network from which the royal family had always picked its friends and courtiers.

This was primarily a matter of emphasis. The style of the English aristocracy relied essentially on a sort of understatement Townsend never had: he was, if anything, too brave, too clean-cut and too glamorous. He was 'sensitive', enthusiastic and, as events would prove, he failed to understand the private code by which the courtier must always rule his life. Therein, it seems, lay much of his attraction for the royal family – and in particular for Princess Margaret. She was fourteen when he first appeared at court and she admitted later that almost from the start she had 'a terrific crush on him'.

Although she was quick to add that at the time 'there was no question of romance until much later' because he was a married man, it is significant that already she was emotionally attracted by qualities so much the opposite of those around her. She was also being what Queen Mary would have called 'outrageous'. Teenage princesses, in their 'sacred' situation, really had no business with anything as vulgar as a 'crush': and any sensual stirrings they did feel should be sensibly directed where they properly belonged – i.e. towards other royalty or, failing this, to suitable and extremely rich young members of the upper aristocracy like the Duke of Marlborough's chinless heir, Lord Blandford, or the future Duke of Buccleuch, the somewhat solid Lord Dalkeith. To fall romantically in love with a married member of the middle-classes was utterly unthinkable.

It was precisely because of this that Princess Margaret's love for Peter Townsend could continue unsuspected and unnoticed for so long. It also undoubtedly added vastly to the dashing airman's considerable allure, and it was totally in character for the Princess to be so attracted by what others would have found unthinkable. He was a secret challenge for her lively nature, the antithesis of all that bored her in the gilded tedium at court. Unlike so many people round him, he was real.

It was certainly a powerful attraction, for after the Princess's eighteenth birthday there was much competition from the most eligible and richest in the land. The Princess was given considerable freedom by her trusting parents, but throughout this period the Group Captain – who was still married and, as far as one can tell, a very honourable man – stayed in pride of place as the Princess's secret *beau idèal* despite her temptations at the night club, the dinner dance and the very grand country house weekend.

As what is known as 'a man of the world', the Group Captain must have realised what was happening fairly early on, and he was later to be blamed bitterly by older, less attractive courtiers for 'not doing the right thing' and quietly applying for another posting. 'It was his patent duty,' one of them explained. 'Not to have done so was simply unforgivable.' But in fact for several years Peter Townsend seems to have done nothing to 'encourage' the Princess – who apparently required little encouragement, and whose character and position were both stronger than his own. He was flattered by her friendship; she had become, as he has said, 'a girl of unusual, intense beauty, confined as it was in her short, slender figure and centred about large purple-blue eyes, generous sensitive lips and a complexion as smooth as a peach'; and if he was not the sort of eunuch more realistic monarchs than King George VI once entrusted with the care of susceptible royal ladies, he could hardly be blamed for that.

Certainly from the winter of 1947, when he accompanied the royal family on their elaborate and lengthy tour of South Africa, he must have been aware of the feelings of the precocious seventeen-year-old princess. The visit was arranged by the strongly pro-royal General Smuts in a vain attempt to employ the magic of the royal presence to persuade South Africans to stay within the Commonwealth, and throughout the visit Princess Elizabeth was conspicuously pining for the handsome Philip, who was firmly back in England. Princess Margaret, on the other hand, had the man she loved almost constantly beside her as the luxurious white and gold official train steamed its regal way around the Union, and the contrast between the two sisters was obvious for all to see. It was certainly quite obvious to Peter Townsend.

On the return to London, the final annoucement of Elizabeth's engagement to Princc Philip, despite initial opposition from the King, evidently strengthened Princess Margaret's own resolve to continue indulging her love for Peter Townsend; and by the autumn of 1948, continental journalists were already noting signs of unmistakable affection between the young Princess and the unknown British courtier who accompanied her to Amsterdam for the celebrations marking the investiture of Juliana as Queen of the Netherlands. They were described dancing amorously together, 'her head on his chest' at the royal ball; but had any member of the British royal household read the foreign press – which was most unlikely – it would have been considered thoroughly improper, and distinctly hazardous, to have done or said anything about it. The Princess was already something of a law unto herself, and the Group Captain had the trust and the affection of the King and Queen. Besides, he was a married man and sixteen years her senior. He knew the form; there was, of course, no possibility of scandal.

One of the most revealing things about what proved to be a cruelly mismanaged business is the contrast it affords between the naivety of the Court and royal family over Princess Margaret, and their expertise in everything pertaining to her sister.

Throughout the period when the court was so skilfully preparing for the coronation, the romance between the Princess and the courtier reached its crisis; and once again the childhood pattern of the two Princesses was repeated. While the elder sister played her part immaculately, no one seemed capable of coping with the younger one.

What happened was in fact quite simple. During those four years since Townsend had accompanied Princess Margaret to Amsterdam he had been rising as a trusted and successful courtier, appointed assistant Master of the Royal Household in 1950, and Comptroller of the Queen Mother's Household after King George's death. And throughout this period, he and his wife Rosemary kept up the appearances of what he claims was actually a broken marriage. At the same time, Princess Margaret was leading a lively social life outside the Palace in what was known as 'the Princess Margaret Set'; but although he played no part in this, they had become increasingly attached to one another. For as a favoured 'insider' at the Palace, Townsend had an obvious advantage over the richer and more eligible of the Princess's social escorts. He could be a constant companion in her daily life and their friendship could continue unremarked amid the heather of Balmoral, or 'riding in the Great Park at Windsor, along drives flanked with rhododendron and venerable oaks and beeches, or through the pinewoods and across the stubble at Sandringham.'

Indulged as ever, the Princess was permitted this innocent flirtation by her father, who, according to Townsend's own account, once watched them with a 'kind, half-amused' expression when she woke him after a Balmoral picnic by placing 'her lovely face very close, looking into mine.' The King, like everyone who liked and trusted Townsend, must have taken it for granted that there could be no danger in this sort of friendship between his daughter and a much older married courtier, and it was not until shortly after his death in 1952 that the situation changed dramatically.

After five years during which her husband had been fighting back his feelings as he rode among the venerable oaks and beeches, Mrs Townsend sensibly decamped with a gentleman in import-export. What the Group-Captain called their 'calvary' was over, and he promptly sued for divorce. Six months later he was free, and not long afterwards, 'one afternoon at Windsor Castle when everyone had gone to London for some ceremony', he and the Princess found themselves together in the royal red drawing-room. During several hours' conversation in this room where Queen Victoria once received Disraeli, he confessed to her great-great-granddaughter how much she meant to him – and the Princess told him that she felt the same.

Having at last achieved this declaration of their long-maturing love, neither he nor the Princess had apparently considered what would happen next. Marriage, as Townsend candidly admitted later, 'seemed the least likely solution' to their problem of 'how to consummate this mutual pleasure', but both thought it only right and proper to inform the family without delay of what he called 'this poignant situation.'

Given the fact that the whole royal family was in the throes of preparing for the forthcoming Coronation, its members seem to have behaved with commendable restraint. Prince Philip was a little flippant, but he, unlike the female members of the family, had never really cared for Townsend. The Queen and the Queen Mother expressed considerable concern for both the lovers – and a series of what proved to be extraordinary blunders started. For the Court was completely unprepared for dealing with the unexpected where Princess Margaret was concerned, and swiftly turned an awkward but not impossible situation into an open, very painful scandal.

The trouble stemmed from a lack of clear decision, with too many people anxiously involved: and at the heart of all the muddles lay a human conflict which was never properly resolved and which had its origins in the recent history of the House of Windsor. On the one hand lay that family habit established by King George VI of always indulging Princess Margaret, and on the other the boring but persistent nightmare of the Abdication.

It was a dilemma that particularly affected the one person with the strength and standing to have settled the situation one way or the other – the Queen Mother. More than anyone, she had tried to make her family the antithesis of all those weaknesses that destroyed the Duke; yet more than anybody else, she understood her second daughter. She was also very fond of Townsend, who was now in charge of her private household. This left her deeply sympathetic but profoundly torn, and on this one occasion the royal matriarch, irresolute, was seen to falter. It was the only time a courtier actually witnessed her in tears, and since she refused to give a clearcut lead, neither could anybody else.

The Queen, as so often in the past, simply wanted her sister to be happy, and her husband breezily assured the lovers that 'everything would work out in the end': but there were others in the Palace who were far less sanguine and sentimental, and who wanted nothing of the sort.

The most influential power behind the throne was still the Queen's veteran private secretary, Sir Alan Lascelles. An old-style courtier *par excellence*, and related by marriage to the royal family, he had been deeply involved in the Abdication of King Edward – whom he had heartily disliked. A formal man, with nothing of Townsend's glamour and ease of manner, he was as dedicated to the young Queen as he had once been to her father, and had little sympathy with the unpredictable and disruptive Princess Margaret. He was a man of strong emotions, which a lifetime at court had taught him to disguise in the presence of the royal family; but when Townsend came quite sensibly to ask him for advice, nothing could mask his sense of outrage at what this member of the royal staff had done. Almost beside himself with fury, he could only offer what he felt to be the truth: 'You must either be mad or bad,' he muttered grimly.

Whether justified or not, such an attitude was dangerous from Her Majesty's principal Court adviser, particularly one as obsessed – as were most of the older members of the Court – by that death's-head of the Abdication. Not surprisingly, there was already much latent suspicion and jealousy within the Palace of the too successful Peter Townsend: this surfaced and began to spread once his dreadful secret was revealed.

He was very vulnerable of course: divorced, a social outsider and an envied royal favourite, he was now regarded as what he obviously was not, an irresponsible sexual bounder. But it was all too tempting to detect similarities with another divorced outsider and royal favourite who had brought turmoil to the House of Windsor thanks primarily to sex – the former Mrs Ernest Simpson: and for courtiers who had often slyly noted in the past how much the sharp-tongued Princess Margaret seemed to be taking after Uncle David, the next step was to see her unconventional love-affair as the start of a re-run of the Abdication crisis.

In fact it was nothing of the kind. Princess Margaret was not the monarch, any more than Townsend was remotely like that socially ambitious 'adventuress', the Duchess of Windsor. Should anything happen to the Princess's young and very healthy sister, Prince Charles and Princess Anne both stood before her in line for the accession, so there was barely a conceivable chance of Princess Margaret ending up as Queen of England and head of the established church with Townsend as her royal consort. In other words, the situation really had none of those dire repercussions which in King Edward's case had brought such genuine divisions in the country. On the contrary, later opinion polls revealed that a Townsend-Margaret marriage would have been extremely popular, and since they had known each other for so long and weathered such opposition and temptation it should have had every prospect of success.

But with Townsend seen as either 'mad or bad', and Lascelles able to enlist the jealousy and social prejudice of certain courtiers and leading politicians, it had little chance: and the trauma of the Abdication was a perfect weapon for Lascelles to employ – which he did quite ruthlessly behind the scenes. For the courtier's art is a slippery one with a lot of innuendo and a large element of fudge. When the Queen asked for his advice, Lascelles did not speak his mind. Instead he told her what was only legally the truth – that under the terms of the 1772 Royal Marriages Act, Princess Margaret was unable to marry until the age of twenty-five without the permission of Her Majesty.

In giving or withholding this, the Queen should properly be guided by her government; and Lascelles adroitly set to work to ensure that the government advised the Queen firmly against. Again he did not work directly, but relied for an ally on the former private secretary to the then Princess Elizabeth, Sir John Colville. Colville was now private secretary to the Prime Minister, and as a very honourable man was easily convinced of Townsend's unspeakable behaviour and the disaster any thought of marriage would bring upon the royal family. He duly agreed to speak accordingly to Churchill.

Lady Longford tells what happened next. Over lunch at Chequers Colville started to explain to Churchill what was going on, and to the old man's credit he immediately exclaimed: 'What a delightful match! A lovely young royal lady married to a gallant young airman, safe from the perils and horrors of the war!'

While Colville was trying to explain that this was not the reaction Lascelles wanted, Mrs Churchill angrily broke in with a fascinating ultimatum: 'Winston, if you are going to begin the Abdication all over again, I'm going to leave! I shall take a flat and go and live in Brighton.'

With the spectre of the Abdication raised even here to threaten the Churchills' marital felicity, the Prime Minister swiftly changed his mind and Lascelles got exactly what he wanted – a recommendation from the Cabinet to Her Majesty that the question of Princess Margaret's marriage be quietly postponed in accordance with the

Royal Marriage Act until she was twenty-five. It was now the spring of 1953, and Princess Margaret would be twenty-five in September 1955. All could be dealt with most discreetly in the interval in ways a courtier would understand – no unseemly ultimatums to Her Majesty, no upsets and no fuss. Even Princess Margaret could be tactfully informed that her marriage was 'not impossible', if it kept her happy. The chief aim of the courtier is the happiness of royalty, and Sir Alan Lascelles must have felt by now that he had more than done his duty. Two years is a long time in a love affair, and Townsend had made some very influential enemies.

But if Lascelles had displayed considerable guile, there were other members of the Palace staff who were painfully incompetent, and incompetence and guile have always been a dangerous combination, particularly for royalty. In this case the incompetence was rapidly revealed in the one area where the monarchy needed particular skill to cope with the worldwide curiosity engendered by the coming Coronation: the Palace Press Office.

A cynic might easily have thought that behind the great wave of royal popularity and interest that swept the country after the Queen's accession there must have been some all-powerful, immensely clever hidden persuader at the Palace, massaging the media and skilfully presenting the royal family's most favourable aspects. This was not so. Instead, as Press Secretary to Her Majesty, there was Commander Richard Colville, DSC, RN (retd.), a former naval paymaster.

Unlike most former sailors, he was stiff, irascible and something of a snob: but like so many members of the court he owed his appointment to his family connections – he was a first cousin of Sir John Colville – and his chief professional qualification was an almost universal suspicion of journalists in any shape or form or sex. There was something to be said for such an attitude. In a closed monarchy like the House of Windsor, the purlieus of the royal Parnassus needed to be kept as clear as possible from the prying eyes of inquisitive outsiders, particularly if the eyes belonged to journalists intent on finding details of the sacred private lives of those within.

As a cross between a filter and a guard-dog, the Commander acted adequately in straightforward situations, and his resolute denials and official 'no comments' had driven off many an unwelcome story in the past. But a situation as far-reaching and potentially explosive as the one involving the Princess and her lover called for more sophistication and awareness than Colville habitually displayed in his dealings with his enemies, the press. For rumours had inevitably begun, some of which were very near the truth. Some had been published in the American and continental press, and every editor in London was on the watch to see what happened.

Incredibly, one of the few organisations in London intimately concerned with both the press and the royal family which remained unaware of these reports was the Queen's own press office; and that stately ostrich, Richard Colville, kept his head buried deeply in the Palace sand, a position which absolved him from the need of reading foreign press reports (which were bad for his digestion), often written in a foreign language (which he did not understand). As his private contacts with journalists and editors were tenuous or frankly hostile, he had no way of knowing what those low-bred, energetic gentlemen were up to.

In fact, they were monitoring every move of Princess Margaret and Group Captain Peter Townsend, who were completely unaware that their love had suddenly become an open secret for the British press. For as in the lead-up to the Abdication, the British newspapers were remaining loyally discreet until they were absolutely sure about the growing rumours. Had Townsend only known this, there is no reason to doubt his later statement that he would instantly have taken steps to get well clear of what the former airman called 'the target area'. Instead he and the Princess went innocently ahead, and with an unconscious sense of timing gave the attentive journalists the conclusive confirmation they required on the very morning of the Coronation.

This happened just after the ceremony, when Townsend and the Princess met in the Abbey annexe and a journalist, Donald Edgar, saw Townsend holding out his hands to her, and 'Margaret almost falling into his arms, a half-embrace', before flicking a speck of dust from his lapel. Next morning an account of this made headlines in the New York press in competition with the story of the actual Coronation. Even Commander Colville heard about it now.

For the Palace it was an acute embarrassment, for the world press an invaluable scoop, and for Townsend and the Princess a personal disaster which could have been easily avoided. Instantly, their love affair became the one thing the House of Windsor feared with almost pathological intensity – a public scandal –and coming at the very moment of the Coronation it was doubly damaging. Suddenly it seemed as if the fears were justified of those like Lascelles who had seen it as a mini-Abdication crisis from the start; and Townsend could finally and bitterly be blamed for damaging the monarchy and embarrassing the Queen at the very hour of her greatest triumph.

Hell hath no fury like a courtier's towards a fallen favourite, and in the panic that ensued Townsend was fortunate to be rapidly packed off to a pointless but comfortable posting as Air Attaché to the British Embassy in Brussels. The initial plan had been to send him to Singapore – regardless of the effect upon his two young children – and he owed this stay of execution primarily to the Queen and the Queen Mother, who remained loyal to their former friendship.

But even now the muddle created by the courtiers and politicians over Princess Margaret was destined to continue, with further painful consequences for almost everyone concerned. Nobody, least of all Sir Alan Lascelles, was prepared to spell out the obvious but unpalatable fact to any member of the royal family – that influential opposition to the Townsend-Margaret marriage had become so strong that all hope for it should be abandoned. Instead, with consummate cruelty and tact, Princess Margaret was respectfully encouraged to believe that with just a little further patience her romance could still achieve its happy ending. Brussels was close enough to London for the lovers' contact to continue – as it inevitably did, with letters, telephone conversations and secret meetings.

In the end, of course, the truth had to be revealed to the Princess and the royal family. She had been waiting, as originally suggested, for her twenty-fifth birthday, when by the terms of George III's unpleasant Act, she would no longer need the permission of the sovereign for her nuptials. Not unnaturally she had continued in the blithe belief that she would then be free to marry as she wished; but this was not entirely the case. Again, one would have thought that someone at the Palace – even Sir Alan Lascelles, who knew the situation perfectly – might in all fairness have told the Princess, or her sister, the Queen, that there remained one small but treacherous legal hurdle to surmount before wedding bells could ring. But like the well-trained flunkeys that they were, the courtiers smiled and stayed silent.

It was left to a politician to tell Princess Margaret the facts of royal life early in October 1955, and with some irony and even more hypocrisy this cheerful task was entrusted to none other than

the new Prime Minister, the divorced and now happily remarried
Anthony Eden, during a weekend at Balmoral as guest of the royal
family with his new wife, Churchill's niece, Clarissa.

In his statesmanlike opinion, and that of his upright Cabinet
(which contained two further *divorcés*, Thorneycroft and
Monckton), Townsend's status as the innocent party to a divorce
made him permanently and totally unacceptable as a husband for
Princess Margaret. Since the Queen was head of the established
church, such a marriage by her sister would 'irreparably damage the
standing of the Crown.'

Quite so – but surely Princess Margaret, having reached the age
of twenty-five, was free from the restrictions George III had placed
on his descendants, and at liberty to marry as she wished? The
statesman shook his handsome head. Under a further section of the
Royal Marriages Act of 1772, the government of the day possessed
the right, through parliament, to place certain penalties upon royal
persons, even over the age of twenty-five, who contracted marriages
of which it disapproved.

And in this present case?

In the present case, because of the danger to the Crown and the
serious principle at stake, he would reluctantly have no alternative
– should the Princess persist – to asking parliament to pass a bill in
accordance with the Act, to deprive her and her children of all rights
to the succession and any income from the Civil List.

In fact the Prime Minister was bluffing; for as he knew quite well,
he would not have dared present so unpopular a bill to parliament,
risking defeat on an issue where public opinion would be overwhelmingly against him. What really counted was passionate opposition
to the marriage from within his Cabinet, primarily from the
Conservative leader in the House of Lords, Lord Salisbury, who was
threatening resignation if the government permitted it to go ahead.
The trouble was said to be his lordship's conscience, which permitted
him, as a devout Anglican, to serve under a divorced Prime Minister,
but became deeply troubled at the thought of being ruled by a
monarch with a divorced brother-in-law.

Perhaps it really did: the Salisbury conscience has always been an
unpredictable element in British politics. But perhaps Lord Salisbury's contacts with Sir Alan Lascelles also played their part in
convincing him that Townsend really was as 'mad or bad' as his
enemies believed. And perhaps his fellow member of the House of

Lords, Archbishop Fisher, had pointed out to him his duties as a devoted Anglican and keen defender of the monarchy. For Archbishop Fisher certainly agreed with Lascelles that the marriage was deeply undesirable, and would threaten that new 'communion', miraculously engendered at the Coronation, between people, Church and Crown.

Whatever the pressures on Lord Salisbury's beliefs, there was no question of his obstinacy once he had made up his mind. Unlike his fellow members of the Cabinet, he had no House of Commons seat to lose if the government collapsed, and, as the realistic Eden knew quite well, Salisbury's resignation and the bitter public row that would ensue could split his party and easily bring down his fragile government. So one can understand why the Prime Minister listened so attentively to the murmurings of Lord Salisbury's conscience, and used whatever means he had to deflect the Princess from her still intended marriage.

These means were considerable, and now that the whole issue had been permitted to get so out of hand as to threaten the very future of the government itself, they were mobilised quite ruthlessly to squash all chances of the Princess's marriage once and for all. The events of the next few days provide a revealing if unedifying insight into the concerted power of the establishment to get its way when feeling threatened, even to the extent of sacrificing the happiness and future of a leading member of the royal family in the process.

Not unnaturally, Princess Margaret's first reaction to the Eden ultimatum was an angry sense of having been cynically betrayed – as she unquestionably had been. She had now known Townsend for eleven years, and after all the publicity and fuss at the time of the Coronation had scrupulously observed the conditions placed upon her, on the tacit understanding that she and Townsend would finally be free to marry if they wished. Now she was coolly told that she was not. As someone accustomed to getting what she wanted, she was hardly likely to accept without putting up a fight.

So she cut short her Balmoral holiday, and on October 12 returned to London. Closely followed by a regiment of alert reporters, Peter Townsend did the same, and after their two year wait the lovers were publicly reunited. It took a day or two for them both to find out what they were really up against, days during which press speculation mounted. The royal family were still extremely sympathetic, and particularly kind to Townsend, but now there was a crucial difference from the atmosphere two years earlier, when the crisis created by their love affair had started.

In the interval the opposition to the marriage had been able to organise itself to considerable effect. The success of the Coronation had strengthened traditional feelings that nothing should be permitted to endanger the widespread reverence for the Crown, and Lord Salisbury, a close personal friend of the Queen Mother, had been able to express to her his conscientious scruples and deep misgivings for the monarchy, should a *divorcé* become her son-in-law. The Abdication arguments were deployed to considerable effect, and with deep reluctance the royal matriarch was finally convinced that Princess Margaret should follow the example of her father, placing her duty to the monarchy before her private happiness.

This was a theme reiterated in royal circles during the next few days while Archbishop Fisher, who was in close contact with the family, privately explained to the Princess his Church's teachings on such matters as the remarriage of a *divorcé* – which it could not sanction – and the problems involved in her sister's position as head of the established church and Defender of the Faith. Then *The Times* weighed in with a solemn editorial, emphasising the 'symbolic' nature of the royal family for the nation, and claiming that the vast majority of the peoples of the Commonwealth would be sorely troubled by the prospect of the marriage.

The fact that 'the vast majority' of the population of the dwindling Commonwealth had more serious matters on their minds than the marital status of their sovereign's sister's future husband was neither here nor there. However, this sudden and determined unanimity between the Church, the government, *The Times* and certain influential courtiers, was disturbing for the Princess, a convinced member of the Church of England, brought up in the strong belief of her duties to the Commonwealth.

More disturbing still were the threatening comparisons being made between her situation and the Duke of Windsor's. Now for the first time it was quietly suggested that should she and Townsend still persist in marrying, she would inevitably find herself in a situation similar to that royal outcast's (but without his consoling private fortune), deprived of her rank, her status and her duties, and condemned, according to one persistent and unpleasant rumour, to a long period in exile.

With the future of the government seriously at stake, no holds were barred in the campaign to make her change her mind. The Queen Mother's change of heart was all-important now, and the Princess herself began to waver as she wondered if at least some of the arguments being used against her could be right. Suddenly it seemed that not even life with Townsend could justify the crisis and upheaval everyone insisted would ensue. Suddenly the prospect of reality, in the once alluring form of life as Mrs Peter Townsend, must have seemed extremely grim.

The outcome was inevitable. After a few days of such pressure, said Townsend later, 'we were both exhausted, mentally, emotionally and physically. We felt mute and numb at the centre of the maelstrom': and on October 24, 1955, during a hopeless meeting with the Princess at Clarence House, it was Townsend who made what had now become the only possible decision. He had scribbled out a statement for the Princess, ending the affair – and with obvious emotion she agreed to it.

Ironically, mounting speculation in the press was by now bringing increasing popular support for the marriage, but on October 27 the Princess was driven to Lambeth Palace to inform the Archbishop that he and his powerful allies had succeeded after all. She had made up her mind. She met him in his study, and as he reached for a book she is credited with saying: 'You can put your books away Archbishop. I am not going to marry Peter Townsend. I wanted you to be the first to know.'

The Archbishop is said to have replied, 'What a wonderful person the Holy Spirit is!'

As events would prove, this was a little hard on God, but at the time the decision brought predictable relief to those with the greatest interest in maintaining the royal *status quo* and the sacred and 'symbolic' aspect of the monarchy revealed at the Coronation. When the decision was made public, *The Times* somewhat unctuously assumed the right of congratulating the Princess, not just on behalf of Britain, but for those far-off multitudes who owed allegiance to the Crown and whose minds it read with such unanswerable assurance. 'All the peoples of the Commonwealth will feel gratitude to her for taking the selfless, royal way which, in their hearts they had expected of her.'

Greater gratitude should have come from the Prime Minister, who was saved from the prospect of a split in his Cabinet and serious political disaster. And Sir Alan Lascelles, who had done more than anyone to scotch the marriage, must have felt that he had done his duty to preserve the moral image of the monarchy by saving the House of Windsor from the contamination of everything that Peter Townsend represented. If Lascelles had been guilty of duplicity – as Princess Margaret still believes he had – he might claim that the end had justified the means: and if she refused ever to speak to him again, and 'cursed him to the grave' for his behaviour, it would not stop that tough old gentleman from living contentedly on to the age of ninety-one as her near neighbour in his grace-and-favour flat at Kensington Palace, where he died peacefully in 1981.

But for anyone with the long-term interests of the monarchy at heart, there was little for rejoicing in this bruising, melancholy business. The Queen's sister had been cynically misused – and ill-advised – by those who ought to have supported her; malice and incompetence at court had produced a quite unnecessary scandal which had got dramatically out of hand; and in the outcome, those who still hoped for the Princess's happiness had been outmanoeuvred by the politicians, by the Church, and by members of the establishment, largely for reasons of their own.

In the long run, the greatest danger to the standing of the Crown would prove to be such facts as these, and the effect of the affair upon the Princess herself. She had been forced to sacrifice her feelings for a man she had loved for eleven years, in theory to preserve the 'sacred' nature of the monarchy. Like her sister, she had opted to remain a being set apart, a member of this unimpeachable royal family. But she had now revealed that she was vulnerable. She was still headstrong, young and very glamorous. She was embittered and the object of considerable guilt from those around her. The first crack had appeared in the glittering façade created round the Royal House of Windsor.

7

'THINGS FALL APART'

'Most of the monarchies of Europe were really destroyed by
their greatest and most ardent supporters. It was the most
reactionary people who tried to hold on to something without
letting it develop and change.'

Prince Philip

October 15, 1956, proved in retrospect a date of some significance
in the private history of the House of Windsor. Preparations had
been made for it with all the efficiency the Palace secretariat reserves
for major members of the family. Schedules had been rearranged,
innumerable bags and trunks meticulously packed, the Foreign
Office and several High Commissioners consulted, the Cabinet officially informed. A loose-leaf book of over a hundred pages had been
compiled to cover arrangements which included such items as
security, dress (formal and informal), communications, gifts, local
contacts in a number of foreign countries, press facilities and medical
arrangements. The royal yacht, *Britannia* – which four years earlier
had replaced the old royal yacht, *Victoria and Albert* at a cost to
the taxpayer of £2 million – had sailed east in readiness, a rear-
admiral on the bridge, and 275 officers and specially selected ratings
under his command. A four-engined VC 10 from RAF Transport
Command had been specially converted to the needs of royalty.

Just after lunchtime, uniformed police appeared at each road
junction and each set of traffic-lights along the Great West Road,
ready to hold up traffic so that nothing would impede the progress
of the two superbly polished limousines with the insignia of the
crown above the windscreen and no outer handles on the rear doors,
which sailed past soon afterwards towards the airport at a stately
60 mph with members of the royal family aboard.

At London, Heathrow, there were none of the formalities
accompanying the departure of lesser human beings. Although the
Duke of Edinburgh has the honour of possessing United Kingdom
passport Number One (as head of state the Queen quite logically
does not need one) he was not required to present it; and by the

time the royal party descended from the cars to be welcomed at the runway by the airport director, Her Majesty's official Baggage Master had already stowed the Duke's remarkable amount of possessions and impedimenta in the waiting aircraft's luggage hold.

Then in the grey light of a mid-October afternoon, the family waited for the Duke's departure. Farewells had been made before in private, and from a tactful distance television cameras picked up the royal faces for the public. Her Majesty appeared distinctly tense and was not observed to smile. Six-year-old Princess Anne seemed very self-possessed, but her brother, Charles, looked painfully self-conscious in grey socks and a dark grey schoolboy suit. With his eighth birthday in a few weeks' time, he was a chubby rather lonely-looking child as he stood beside his mother, knowing all too well how long it would be before he would be reunited with his father.

The departing Duke had not changed at thirty-four from the handsome male presence at the Coronation three years earlier; and he alone seemed able to play up to the cameras, giving a splendid smile and waving from the aircraft steps as the engines started. Then the door closed behind him, and the VC 10, the most elegant large aircraft ever built, sped down the runway, lifted its dolphin tail and headed west. The family beside the runway offered its final muted wave, and Charles alone was seen to brush away a princely tear.

The official reason for the Duke's departure was to open the Olympic Games at Melbourne six weeks hence; but as what he chose to call 'my personal contribution to the Commonwealth ideal', he had built around this one event a 38,000 mile itinerary which included visits to the West Coast of the United States, New Zealand, Papua New Guinea, the Falklands and Antarctica. People could make what they liked of the fact that for five whole months this restless man had freed himself from the limitations and frustrations of his subsidiary life at court. In doing so he had also parted from his wife and children for what in any marriage would be an uncomfortable length of time. Perhaps both monarchy and Commonwealth required this sort of sacrifice; but by a strange coincidence, almost from the day of his departure, troubles started.

It was in many ways an odd life which the Queen and her husband had been living as, now in their early thirties, each appeared to embody a quite different aspect of the monarchy. During those four years since her accession, Her Majesty had still made few concessions to discreet suggestions for a more open, democratic-seeming royal style. Instead, she doggedly maintained the formal and symbolic role she had been trained for and which the world had witnessed at her Coronation. She was, in Robert Lacey's description 'an icon', which the Oxford Dictionary defines as 'the image of a sacred person, itself regarded as sacred'.

As an icon, Elizabeth II appeared more formal and aloof than any of her predecessors since Victoria. Her personal reaction to the inevitable media obsession with her and her family, which had been so heightened by the Coronation, was a definite decision to reveal as little of their private lives as possible. There would be nothing like those homely glimpses of the happy family of Windsor which the Queen Mother had so cleverly encouraged during the childhood of Princess Elizabeth and Princess Margaret Rose. Even the loyalest of journalists and biographers failed to receive the sort of facilities for describing the family's activities which they had cheerfully enjoyed before the war. It was made very clear that Her Majesty wished her children to be able to live 'normal' lives, as free from publicity as possible – which inevitably created a sense of mystery around this family of carefully protected royal recluses.

Philip, however, seemed determined to remain the family's exception to this royal rule. If the Queen was sacred, it took little to make the Duke profane, and away from the stiffness of a state occasion he had been busy doing what the Queen refused to. Informal, hyperactive, and frequently exasperated by the sheer perversity of the world in general, he did his energetic best to put it right. Whether playing an informal game of cricket to raise money for his favourite charity or making his personal suggestions about traffic congestion and exhaust pollution during his spell as president of the Automobile Association, he presented a human, modern face of royalty, not so dissimilar from the Scandinavian style of democratic monarchy which the House of Windsor emphatically was not.

He was in process of becoming the most popular member of the royal family in this period, if not with journalists – with whom he tended to become impatient and abrasive – at least with the educated young, who responded to his obvious intelligence and unfussy, radical approach to life. But he remained very much his own man, generally acting independently of the Queen's advisers; and he had barely dented the solid matriarchal institution of the Court itself, which calmly continued much as it always had.

In some ways this royal division of labour was a sensible solution to the problems that would always stem from the very different characters of the royal couple, and the fact that the Duke was so different from the previous royal males, George V and George VI. To a point, the Queen and her husband complemented one another, and for a while it seemed as if the monarchy was getting the best of two quite separate worlds. Even within the family, the Queen had her horses, her few close friends from the aristocracy, and her regular daily work with the business and documents of state; while the Duke had his helicopters and sailing boats, his multifarious concern with the world in general, his weekly dinners with his old friends from the navy, and the advice of Uncle Dickie. For four years, this had seemed to work quite well. Then suddenly, in 1956, it didn't.

It was inevitable that problems would begin for the monarchy once the memory of the Coronation faded. Quite suddenly, further cracks began appearing in the most unlikely places, almost all of which were aggravated – if not actually produced – by that amazing mood of wishful thinking round the monarchy which had mesmerised the nation and the Court in 1953. Reality had proved quite different from the glowing images then so loyally accepted by one and all. The Queen obviously was not, and could not hope to be, a national redeemer, any more than Britain could patriotically conjure up a royally inspired renaissance in the 1950s. Those who pretended otherwise had produced an unprecedented mood of national euphoria, but in the longer term had done the monarchy a serious disservice.

Just for a while the Crown was set high above controversy, like the deity itself with which people were assured that it had merged at the climax of the Coronation: but lacking another full-scale royal occasion, interest in royalty began to flag. Disillusion followed when the promised New Elizabethan Age refused to dawn, and by 1956 even the faithful Dimbleby might have had difficulty justifying the perennial royal mystique. As he admitted in an article he wrote:

I have struggled many times to find the right words to describe the true meaning of the Sovereign to the nation. When we look at the Queen we see, in fact, the sovereign who in changing human form, has guided and guarded our affairs for 900 years.

It was safe to make such claims when things were going well; but when troubles started, they appeared distinctly hollow. If the Queen claimed credit for her nation's triumphs, she must also take some responsibility for its troubles – which was a dangerous burden for monarchy to have to bear.

The aftermath of Princess Margaret's affair with Peter Townsend showed up another danger area for the prestige of the monarchy. The establishment and the respectably loyal sections of the media – principally *The Times* and the BBC – had done their best to show how the dignified and dutiful ending of the romance had actually bestowed blessings on the Commonwealth, the Church of England and national morality, through the splendid example of Her Royal Highness's 'sacrifice'.

During this period, *The Times* in particular was still presenting its wealthier, established readership with a version of the monarchy embodying precisely those ideals which the hypothetical *Times* reader, with his pin-stripe suit and bowler hat, would supposedly respect. It was now that the newspaper launched its famous advertising campaign to reassure the nation (and more specifically its richer advertisers) that 'Top People Read *The Times*'; and judging by the paper's comment and reports, the whole royal family was still very much a Top People's monarchy – unquestioned defender of Commonwealth, Church and upper-class attitudes in general – and an invaluable example of behaviour to the lower orders.

But the impact of the Coronation also helped create a more engrossing aspect of the Royal House of Windsor. Those fascinating images on television inspired a vulgar interest in the actual personalities of all those regal figures; an interest which would not be satisfied for ever with the view of the monarchy that gave such satisfaction to the courtiers and to Sir William Haley in his headmasterly editorial office at *The Times*.

The Court Circular and the Commonwealth ideal were all very well, but what was the truth about the private lives of the royal personalities with which the great television audience had been encouraged to identify three years earlier? Perhaps Princess Margaret really had 'sacrificed her love on the twin altars of patriotism and religion', as one correspondent put it, but in the process she had been subjected to a very human barrage of gossip and advice from the popular press. It was the first time a member of the intimate royal family had been exposed to such profane press treatment since the days of the Abdication; and it pointed up the vast potential appetite created now for any crumb of gossip on the tensions and emotions of royalty themselves.

For the press is a pragmatic institution, living off the public interest it creates, and the royal family had increasingly become one of its major assets. The media had invested an immense amount of time and newsprint in maintaining the monarchy at the forefront of popular awareness, and having done so was not unnaturally intent on making the most of its investment. It could no longer be relied on to accept the restricted and restrained official view of royalty after the massive popular involvement in the Coronation, and for the first time since the Queen's accession, a note of criticism started to appear in certain livelier sections of the popular press.

Just a week before the Duke's departure, Hugh Cudlipp's *Daily Mirror* evidently felt the time had come to pose the question in its front page headline: 'Is the New Elizabethan Age going to be a Flop?' According to Cudlipp's editorial, the Coronation had produced a widespread longing for a new, more open sort of monarchy 'when kings could mix with commoners and all the protocol surrounding royalty could be swept aside.' Of course this had not happened, and the reason Cudlipp gave formed an argument which would be taken up by an increasing number of critical commentators in the months ahead.

> The circle round the throne is as aristocratic, as insular and — there is no more suitable word for it — as toffee-nosed, as it has ever been . . . The royal circle is much the same as it always was in Queen Victoria's palmy days.

The Queen and her husband were promptly admonished to 'reshape the royal circle so that it is no longer a dreary roundabout.'

To no one's particular surprise they did nothing of the kind. British court life never had been very lively since the liberated days of bold King Edward VII — which was presumably not what the *Mirror* had in mind — and it remained the way it was because it suited the Queen, the Queen Mother and the friends and courtiers they had chosen. The Duke of Edinburgh would certainly have agreed with much of what the *Mirror* said, but possessed no power to change things on his own. Also, his personal segment of the royal roundabout cannot have been altogether 'dreary' for someone who enjoyed flying jets, sailing regularly at Cowes, playing top-league polo, gliding, photographing bird-life and sounding off on almost anything that took his fancy.

But the strains just waiting to be thrust upon the monarchy would prove more serious than a 'toffee-nosed' courtier or two. Scarcely had Philip's VC 10 left British airspace than the country lurched into its greatest international crisis since the war, which threatened to embroil the Queen herself in the last thing modern monarchy requires – political controversy. 'Perhaps it was as well Philip wasn't here,' the Queen is supposed to have said later. 'He'd have been impossible to live with.'

These troubles had their origin in Cairo where, soon after the Duke's aircraft left Los Angeles, Colonel Gamel Abdel Nasser, head of a recent nationalist coup by young Egyptian army officers, decided to take possession for his country of the Suez Canal, which had hitherto been owned and run by an Anglo-French consortium in accordance with a treaty signed by Egypt, France and Britain back in 1904.

British patriotic feelings were aroused, for although the Canal was undoubtedly part of Egypt, it had been originally constructed as part of Disraeli's plan to link the great Queen Empress's Eastern Empire with the West, and it remained a strongly emotive symbol of Britain's former imperial power. British troops had died defending the Canal against the Germans in the Second World War; and for the British premier, Anthony Eden, Nasser's action was a source of even more profound emotion. In 1938, at the time of Munich, Eden had resigned as British Foreign Secretary in protest at his government's appeasement of Hitler's military coup in Czechoslovakia. Now seriously afflicted with fresh trouble from his bile duct, Eden saw Nasser as a second Adolf Hitler and Suez as another Czechoslovakia. Appeasement was again unthinkable for him. Britain had to act.

She did so like the great imperial power she was not, and the disaster that ensued is part of history – the military intervention badly bungled, the Anglo-American alliance placed at risk, the Canal completely blocked by the Egyptians; and Great Britain humiliated as the pound plummeted, the United Nations condemned her, and former friends and allies hastened to desert her.

Nothing now was heard of those 'New Elizabethans', nor of the Coronation mood of 'spiritual exultation' which had so recently sanctified a godly and united nation round the Crown. Even the Commonwealth – or what was left of it – was split, and the Queen's unifying role at home was put seriously at risk as opinion polarised dramatically between the 'pro-' and 'anti-Suez' groups.

There was little direct criticism of the way the Queen herself had acted, for as far as anyone could tell she had behaved throughout the crisis with constitutional propriety – but that was not entirely the point. The sour mood of national disillusion augured badly for the future of the monarchy: so did certain questions which began to be asked about the role and power of the sovereign in the aftermath of these traumatic weeks. They were important questions, since they involved the few vestiges of power the British monarchy possessed through the royal prerogative.

The first of these issues hinged upon the monarch's restraining influence on her government. Few would have gone all the way with the claims of loyal Dimbleby that an anointed Queen enshrined some miraculous ability to 'guide and guard' her nation's deepest interests, come what may: but the accepted wisdom was that the sovereign genuinely existed as a source of shrewd and impartial counsel to her Prime Minister over matters more important than mere party politics. Bagehot's definition of the matter was generally accepted, that the sovereign's right under the royal prerogative was 'to be consulted, to encourage, and to warn' the government in power; and the Queen had been regularly consulted by Eden throughout the period of Suez, in his bi-weekly Prime Ministerial visits to the Palace.

It is not known what transpired on these occasions, but it is hard to picture Her Majesty 'encouraging' the ailing Eden in his act of lunacy. On the contrary, this was clearly an occasion, if ever there was one, for a conscientious and far-seeing monarch to have exercised the prerogative of 'warning' to an obviously sick Prime Minister. Possibly she did – but if so, her warning went unheeded, and this vaunted function of the monarchy had been demonstrably ineffective at the very moment it was most urgently required.

Suez posed another, even more important point for anyone concerned about the Queen's advisory role under the prerogative. As the truth behind the Anglo-French Suez intervention was gradually – if reluctantly – revealed, it became clear that a vital part of Eden's anti-Nasser diplomacy had involved a secret deal made in advance with the state of Israel, to invade Egypt to ensure the passage of

Israeli shipping through the Canal. This armed Israeli intervention, covertly encouraged by Britain and France, would then provide the pretext needed by the British and French to occupy the whole Canal themselves – in theory to protect it against the foreign threat of the Israelis – as they were legally entitled to do under the terms of the Suez Treaty.

Since the legality of the British case for intervention rested on this Israeli threat, the question not unnaturally arose of just how far the Prime Minister had deceived his monarch over this crucial piece of international dishonesty. Hardly surprisingly, it was a point on which Eden himself remained equivocal until his death, airily assuring Robert Lacey that the Queen 'had known and approved in essence what we were doing'.

But we have already seen how less than straightforward Eden himself had been in manipulating the royal family for political advantage over Princess Margaret's marriage hopes in 1955. Now, barely twelve months later, he would seem to have been guilty of something far more serious as he involved his monarch and his country in this whole disastrous stroke of international duplicity. Either the Queen knew what was happening, or she didn't. Either her Prime Minister had lied to her, or he had made her an accomplice to a stupid and dishonest plot. Whatever happened, Eden had placed her in an impossible position once her signature was on the government mobilisation order for her forces.

The most charitable explanation of the Prime Minister's behaviour is that chronic ill-health and the strain of office had seriously unbalanced him, making him unfit for power – as he effectively acknowledged by resigning just a few weeks later. But other members of his Cabinet were naturally involved in what had happened, and the whole episode would seem to make it clear that the very politicians who had been the most vociferous supporters of the myth of monarchy and the rights of the prerogative at the time of the Coronation, would not hesitate to use the monarch for political advantage when and if they got the chance.

No sooner had the British forces limped ignominiously home from Suez than the Queen was once again involved in a decision that demonstrated just how deftly a small group of the upper aristocracy and the Conservative establishment could use her for their own political devices. This was the arcane process of divining a successor for the miserable Eden.

By an odd but not entirely unfortuitous anachronism in the constitution of the Conservative party at the time, there was then no provision for the party faithful to elect themselves a new leader when in power. The Conservatives, who had always prided themselves on greater dedication to the throne than their political opponents, were still happy to rely upon the wisdom of Her Majesty to nominate their next Prime Minister under the power of the royal prerogative.

In fact it was a thankless task for the Queen to have to decide who, among a number of ambitious candidates for office, would command the most support within the House of Commons. It was also potentially dangerous to the monarchy, laying it open to inevitable suspicion of partiality. But the arrangement had obvious advantages for the minute but influential group privileged to be consulted by Her Majesty over the decision. It was a privilege they made the most of in the murky January days of 1957.

Once more, there are fascinating parallels with the behaviour of Court and politicians in the Princess Margaret crisis: for once more the keeper of the Party's conscience turned out to be none other than that impenetrable aristocrat and lifelong friend of the Queen Mother, Lord Salisbury. And instead of doing anything as democratic or demanding as canvassing Conservative MPs for their opinions, the Court relied upon his lordship's sage advice – backed by yet another right-wing Tory from the House of Lords, Lord Kilmuir – as a pointer to the deepest wishes of the party for its next Prime Minister.

After peering fairly swiftly into the entrails of his party, the noble marquis duly pronounced in favour of its Chancellor of the Exchequer, Harold Macmillan, and the Queen accepted Salisbury's advice. By her powers under the royal prerogative Macmillan was invited to succeed as Prime Minister.

At the time it seemed a surprising and controversial choice for the Queen to take, with the worthy R. A. Butler – 'the best Prime Minister we never had' – thought by many to possess far stronger claims to office than the victor. Whether he actually did remains hypothetical. What is indisputable is that the way the choice was made had cast the Crown in an unfavourable light, rightly or wrongly making it appear as something of a pawn in the grimy game of party politics.

For those with suspicious minds, worse was still to come; for while Butler, from the left-wing of the Party, had been the strongest critic of the Suez intervention inside the government itself, Macmillan had trimmed discreetly during the affair. Thus it might seem as if, by choosing him, the Queen was condoning the disaster. Also Macmillan, unlike Butler, possessed close social ties with the royal family by marriage, through his wife, Lady Dorothy Macmillan, sister of the 10th Duke of Devonshire. Lady Dorothy's sister-in-law, the Dowager Duchess of Devonshire, was the Queen's most influential female courtier, her Mistress of the Robes; and the immensely wealthy Devonshires remained one of the small group of favoured families at the apex of the aristocracy who had been included in the magic royal circle from the days when Edward VII was a regular and cherished guest at Chatsworth, their ancestral home in Derbyshire. George V, too, had often spent his summer holidays at another of their splendid houses, close to Beachy Head.

Now, for the first time since the beginning of her reign, the Queen found herself openly criticised in the press for plainly favouring the aristocracy and the right-wing of the government in power. 'Why should she have to do the dirty work for the Tories?' asked the *Sunday Pictorial's* political editor, Sydney Jacobsen, and he went on to inquire why she had chosen to rely almost exclusively for her advice on her mother's friend, Lord Salisbury, 'who comes straight off the upper glaciers of the Tory nobility'.

Justified or not, such criticism was a dangerous warning of the way the tide could turn against the monarchy once it lost its reputation for political impartiality. Things were not made any better when Macmillan started to appoint a surprising number of his wife's relations to positions in his government, and his brother-in-law, Lord Cobbold to the Governorship of the Bank of England. His nephew, Andrew Cavendish, the young 11th Duke of Devonshire, became a junior minister and was soon responsible for Commonwealth relations, while the political ramifications of the family would even appear in Washington. The Duke's dead elder brother, William Cavendish, Lord Hartington, had been married to Kathleen Kennedy. She herself was killed in an air crash in 1948, but a close relationship between Cavendishes and Kennedys had been established; and when Kathleen's brother, John F. Kennedy, became President in 1960, Macmillan rapidly appointed one more kinsman of the Cavendishes, David Ormsby-Gore (later Lord Harlech), as British Ambassador in Washington. He was in fact a great success, thanks in no small degree to his family friendship with the Kennedys, but the presence of so many Cavendish relations in and round the Government had given rise to talk of something rather sinister called the 'Cavendish Connection'. There was an uneasy feeling that the country was returning to the style of eighteenth century politics, when a handful of extremely rich and influential families ran the country with the court in their capacious pockets.

Such fears were naturally exaggerated, but the fact that they were voiced at all shows how dangerously the Court itself was veering from the attitudes by which the monarchy had grown in popularity under the earlier sovereigns of the House of Windsor. Both Georges had worked hard to give at least the impression of classless, very ordinary Englishmen, who as kings had held themselves aloof from the habits and the interests of the old nobility. But now the monarch appeared increasingly associated with a favoured group within her landed aristocracy. These were the people among whom the Queen was known to pick her private friends, theirs were the houses where she stayed from choice. With the Queen beginning to appear so insulated from her people, it was hard to remember the uncritical popular excitement built around her at the Coronation. Unlike her mother, she was never seen as 'one of us'; and sacrosanct no longer, both the institution and the person of the Queen were suddenly in the firing line.

The trusted Windsor formula of the united matriarchal family had also come under threat with Princess Margaret now a source of scandal; and soon scandal seemed to be threatening the throne itself. Ever since George V succeeded his lively father, one of the great strengths of the royal family had been the freedom from public gossip and innuendo of the royal marriage. But now trouble flared in even this unlikely quarter; and once again the royal advisers showed disastrous ineptitude over the whole embarrassing, unnecessary business.

Five months is a long period apart, even in a royal marriage, and the Duke of Edinburgh was plainly a far more independent husband than uxorious George VI or 'Henpecked' George V. During his absence it was inevitable that rumours would be floated in the foreign press, for whom speculation on the private lives of members of the British royal family was rapidly becoming something of a way of life. But no one at court had the temerity to mention this self-evident fact to the royal couple, and when rumours duly started to appear in *Oggi, Stern* and *Paris Match*, trouble started. For in his office at the Palace, Her Majesty's press secretary, Commander Colville, had evidently learnt one lesson from the disaster over Princess Margaret and Peter Townsend – to pay attention to the gossip in the foreign press. The gossip was considerable.

Had the royal marriage really been 'on the rocks' as the German press was cheerfully reporting? Did the Duke maintain a bachelor apartment 'close to London's famous Berkeley Square'? And had his weekly dinner parties 'in the infamous Soho district' really been confined to old friends from the Royal Navy?

Both the Abdication and the Princess Margaret-Townsend scandal had been sparked off by 'revelations' in the popular foreign press, and the Court was nervous. The royal press advisers were also maladroit. For having failed to prepare the Duke against the inevitable reactions of the foreign press to his five month absence from the Queen, they then did nothing to protect them both against still further personal embarrassment on the very eve of the Duke's return.

This involved his old friend and companion on the trip, his Australian private secretary, Michael Parker. A few days before the Duke was due to be reunited with the Queen – who was flying specially to meet him at Gibraltar – news leaked out that an irate Mrs Parker was suing her absent husband for divorce on the grounds of his adultery. Panic followed at the Palace as the press picked up the story, and foreign newspapers in particular interpreted the news as proof of what they had been hinting at already, with the adulterous Parker cast in the role of the Duke's partner in wild behaviour in Australia.

Hoping to save his employers more embarrassment – but in practice making matters worse – the unfortunate Parker decided on instant resignation. Nothing was done to stop him, so that the Duke's reunion with his wife, instead of being the romantic occasion everyone had hoped for, was overshadowed by the departure in evident disgrace of the close friend with whom he had spent his five month travels. Had Her Majesty insisted Parker should go? In fact, she had known nothing of the poor man's troubles until she heard about his resignation; but it was not hard for the press to speculate again upon the Queen's acute displeasure, particularly with photographers recording the Duke and his friend bidding a grim farewell on their arrival at Gibraltar.

'Philip and Mike clasp hands in silence', stated the *Mirror* in the caption to its picture, while the *Sketch's* reporter, who had better powers of hearing or imagination, quoted the Duke as saying, 'Good luck and God's speed, Mike – whatever happens and whatever you do!'

But once again it was the foreign press which made the most of the poignant royal situation – and none more so than Joan Graham writing for the *Sun* in distant Baltimore. Under the banner headline 'QUEEN, DUKE IN RIFT OVER PARTY GIRL', Miss Graham, in a notable piece of creative journalism, bundled together all the current rumours with the fact of Parker's resignation and concluded that it was mysteriously linked to 'whispers that the Duke of Edinburgh had more than a passing interest in an unnamed woman and was meeting her regularly in the apartment of the royal photographer', the Duke's friend, Nahum Baron.

No one ever did explain what was so special about Baltimore that made the Court so sensitive over what its citizens were told of the 'passing interests' of the Duke of Edinburgh. Perhaps it was some Pavlovian response to the fact that Baltimore was the home town of the Duchess of Windsor. But for whatever extraordinary reason, the Queen's own private secretary, Sir Michael Adeane himself, chose to bring the offending article to the attention of the world by issuing a strong denial of any 'rift' in the royal marriage: and human nature being what it is, it was instantly assumed that something had been very wrong for someone in Adeane's position to try so very hard to put it right.

The whole incident was particularly unfortunate with the monarchy, after so many recent troubles, needing the Duke's intelligence and popularity more than at any time since the accession. But he was now angry and bitter with the press, frustrated by the blunders committed in his absence, and starting to regret his five months' happy freedom from the worries of the royal roundabout.

The Suez Crisis, followed by the Duke's return, marked the beginning of the open season for critics of the royal family and the monarchy in general. Both suddenly seemed vulnerable, and 1957 would be a uniquely miserable year in modern royal history. It was the year when most of the calm assumptions which the Queen took over from her parents at the accession seemed under threat, and there had certainly been nothing like it since the Abdication. The cleverest royal publicist of all, the Queen Mother, was not in evidence, and the Court found itself at the mercy of the very forces which had helped create its worldwide triumph at the Coronation – the popular media.

Indeed, the events of 1957 made clear how vulnerable the House of Windsor had actually become through its dependence on both press and television for the propagation of its central myth. For the media is fickle and voracious. It requires most skilful handling – something the Court had yet to learn. And once things started going wrong, it could be relied on to make the most of the sheer news value of any royal weaknesses.

So something of a battle royal began, with the press thriving on an emotional, highly-charged situation in which it had things both ways: reporting criticisms of the Court and royal family with apparent shock and horror, sensationalising the reaction, and gaining yet more readers in the fuss and indignation that ensued. Within four years of the most popular royal event in history, the Court seemed heading for a situation uncomfortably like the years of Queen Victoria's widely criticised retirement, with the Crown itself less an object for deference and magic than for speculation and controversy on almost any point that took a commentator's passing fancy.

The extent of the criticisms soon became distinctly ominous. The rumblings produced by Suez and the Duke's return had barely faded before Lord Beaverbrook was launching an attack on the philistine nature of the Court. 'Is the Queen fair to highbrows?' asked the front-page headline in his organ, the *Express*. Whether the popular *Express* itself was fair to highbrows was neither here nor there. What had happened was that his smart old lordship had recently had his portrait painted by Graham Sutherland, enjoyed both portrait and painter, and, something of a closet republican himself, swiftly detected what he always secretly enjoyed – a useful stick with which to beat the monarchy. Having previously confined himself to attacking Lord Mountbatten, he sensed the time had come to turn his attention to the Queen on the subject of her preference for horses over modern art.

'Why shouldn't Sutherland paint the Queen?' he impishly suggested in an article in the *Express*. Why, for that matter, did the Queen, Prince Philip and Princess Margaret never patronise the opera or the arts? 'No one in their senses', the *Express* concluded, 'wants a pompous, pedantic family of intellectuals round the throne

. . . but more than anybody they could set the stage . . . for a grand flowering of talent on the highest level.'

As Beaverbrook knew quite well, there was precious little chance of that occurring; but within a few weeks of this attack on the Court for its lack of culture, other journalists were weighing in with a series of much wider-ranging suggestions and complaints. According to the *Women's Sunday Mirror*, the monarchy was too expensive and should cut its costs; the royal family's holidays were far too long, with the Queen spending nearly five months every year at Windsor, Balmoral or Sandringham; and Prince Charles, who was just finishing a spell at a London preparatory school – itself a considerable innovation for a royal heir – 'should be sent to a non-snob school where he can mix with other classes.' Most interesting of all, the article suggested 'a joint monarchy' between the Queen and her husband, 'before he's stifled'.

That something of a national debate on the monarchy had started was clear when even the *Church of England Newspaper* complained of how the 'monarchy has become a sort of substitute religion'. More surprisingly, it even questioned the whole hereditary basis of the monarchy, on the practical grounds that 'no man would be allowed to take over effective direction of a large business firm with no qualifications other than that of being the son of a particular father.'

This was dangerous talk for royalty – and some indication of the depth of dissatisfaction with the Crown in even the most un-likely quarters. Summer should have brought a lull as the royals retreated for their traditional eight week holiday at Balmoral; but even before they reached the safety of the glens, a bombshell burst from an even more improbable source – the August number of the *National and English Review*, which was owned and edited by a young member of the House of Lords, John Grigg, the 2nd Baron Altrincham.

A Tory radical and genuine devotee of monarchy, Grigg was a youthful peer who had written to *The Times* around the Coronation, to complain at what he felt to be favouritism of the aristocracy in the allocation of seating in the Abbey. Since then he had found an increasing number of faults in the way the monarchy was working – most of which he felt owed their origin to the Queen's advisers, those 'tweedy' country gentry who still formed a 'tight little enclave of English ladies and gentlemen' around her. They were, as he put it later, an unimaginative, 'second-rate lot, simply lacking in gumption,' and it was them he blamed for the disastrous impression Her Majesty was making – particularly in the public speeches they composed on her behalf.

> The personality conveyed by the utterances which are put into her mouth is that of a priggish schoolgirl, captain of the hockey team, a prefect and a recent candidate for confirmation.

Shock, horror, and an increasing summer readership ensued as the press picked up this irresistible story, and the controversy was rendered still more topical when Altrincham was slapped by a rabid Empire Loyalist after a TV debate with Robin Day.

Then in the autumn there was more to come from a very different class of critic – John Osborne, author of the play *Look Back in Anger*, and the original 'angry young man' of the early Fifties, who vented his indignation at what he called 'Queen worship' in another intellectual magazine, *Encounter* (which ironically was later revealed to have had financial backing from the American CIA as part of its propaganda battle with world communism).

For Osborne, the whole panoply of royalty was symptomatic of a deeply sick society, 'the gold filling in a mouth full of decay', and overwhelming evidence of bankruptcy within his nation's culture:

> It bores me, it distresses me, that there should be so many empty minds, so many empty lives in Britain to sustain this fatuous industry; that no one should have the wit to laugh it into extinction, or the honesty to resist it.

Osborne, like Altrincham, was widely and indignantly reported, but the whole controversy really reached its peak when Lord Beaverbrook's *Sunday Express* reported sections of an article Malcolm Muggeridge had written for the American *Saturday Evening Post*. Parts of Muggeridge's article were taken out of context, while others were actually rewritten at Beaverbrook's insistence to make what had been a witty, fairly benign analysis of the whole phenomenon of monarchy appear like a stinging personal attack upon the Queen herself. Typical of this treatment was the headlined statement that Muggeridge had dared to call his monarch 'Dowdy, frumpish and banal', when what he had actually written, with possibly some truth, was that 'it is duchesses, not shop assistants, who find the Queen dowdy, frumpish and banal.'

Not that the truth of Muggeridge's feelings on the monarchy mattered very much by now. The BBC abruptly sacked him, the Press Council cravenly refused to criticise the way the press had distorted his original remarks, and he soon began receiving what Claud Cockburn called 'the ultimate non-fan mail' – letters smeared with the excrement of shocked supporters of the monarchy.

But while they were most unpleasant for Muggeridge – and positively painful for Lord Altrincham – the hysterical reactions of so many of the monarchy's supporters were also a danger signal for the Court itself. Parts of the press had certainly exacerbated the controversy, but it was patently absurd to make the monarchy a subject of such emotional taboos – particularly when so many of the criticisms were clearly justified, and a poll conducted by the *Daily Mail* revealed a majority of its younger readership actually supporting Altrincham's remarks. Passionate controversy was the last thing the monarchy required, and suddenly the source of its greatest emotional appeal at the time of the Coronation was in danger of becoming a grave liability. That 'frail creature' Elizabeth II may have been 'brought into contact with the Divine' at the moment of her crowning, but if the monarchy continued to rely on its appeal as a 'substitute religion' it was in for trouble.

So how did the monarchy itself react to the whole inelegant furore engulfing it in 1957?

One courtier, the Duke of Argyll, Master of Her Majesty's Scottish Household, said of Lord Altrincham: 'I would like to see the man hanged, drawn and quartered!' The Queen on the other hand was genuinely puzzled by Altrincham's behaviour. 'Really,' she said, 'he must be mad!' But behind the unchanging Portland stone façade of Buckingham Palace, the sense of shock and irritation was producing a slow but definite effect.

'We ought to take account of this,' the Duke of Edinburgh is said to have remarked when the criticisms started; and many years later Lord Charteris (formerly Sir Martin Charteris, deputy to Adeane as the Queen's principal private secretary, a post he occupied himself from 1972 to 1977) told Altrincham, during a debate at Eton, 'You did a great service to the monarchy, and I'm glad to say so publicly.'

There were in fact two things the more enlightened courtiers could do to update the Court and the monarchy itself, although they needed to proceed with care. One was to change the practice of the Court, and the other to find some way of enlivening its lacklustre public image. Both cautiously began around this time. Informal Palace luncheon parties had recently been arranged so that the Queen and members of her family could meet a more varied section of the public than those courtiers and 'tweedy' members of the peerage with whom Her Majesty undoubtedly felt most at home. One of the sillier royal social relics – the presentation of socially acceptable debutantes at Court – actually ended in the autumn of 1957. And as something of an answer to those accusations of the 'philistine' nature of the Court – not to mention more serious objections that Her Majesty was sitting on one of the greatest national art collections in the world while few of her subjects ever had a chance to see it – her Surveyor of the Royal Pictures, Professor Anthony Blunt, was actively engaged in plans for an art gallery at the Palace, which finally opened to the public five years later.

But it was more difficult to make royalty themselves appear exciting, especially now that relations with the press were obviously strained. Prince Philip tended to become more exasperated than ever with journalists, openly referring to Lord Beaverbrook's *Express* on one occasion as 'that bloody awful newspaper', and the personal criticisms of the Queen had undoubtedly made her even more defensive in public than before. Commander Colville loyally reflected this. As Anne Edwards wrote around this time, 'No dictator ever muzzled the press quite so tightly as the Queen of England muzzles hers today on every aspect of royalty.'

Colville even tried 'muzzling' American journalists during that autumn's royal visit to the United States – with fairly disastrous results, despite strong initial sympathy for the Queen from the American press. The *Louisville Courier* described her at the start of her trip as 'an English rose with a little of the morning dew on its petals', and the *Chicago Daily News* as 'a doll, a living doll'; but this was not, however, how the Commander wished America to see his monarch, and when she reached Washington he did stalwart service in keeping an estimated 2,000 reporters and television men at bay. The result was that they 'ended up interviewing one another over nothing very much', as *Time Magazine* remarked; and the most indulgent verdict on the Queen was the guarded comment of the *Washington Post* – 'She's not as regal as Helen Hayes playing Queen

Victoria, and obviously she's not Einstein, but as far as we can tell, she's human.'

But even that was something the Queen's subjects might by now have doubted, despite her game attempt to beat her critics by making her first live television Christmas broadcast to the nation at the end of 1957. As with everything she did, she took the task extremely seriously, making a number of television tests and recordings in advance, only to reject them later. But as with her father's Christmas broadcasts, she found television a considerable ordeal. 'I am *not* an actress,' she remarked impatiently, and it would be many years before she felt able simply to be herself before the cameras. Her TV producer, Peter Dimmock, found that try as he might to put her at her ease, her whole expression 'froze' throughout the actual broadcast, only to relax when it was over, and her first televised royal Christmas message did little to dispel Altrincham's impression of the captain of the hockey team in action.

The Queen's deep dislike of appearing live on television began on this occasion and placed a further bar between her and her subjects for many years to come. As one of her courtiers put it, 'Television in the Queen's opinion is an uncongenial medium: she doesn't believe she will ever be able to talk to a camera like an old friend.'

There was, however, at least one imaginative attempt within the Palace to act on Altrincham's advice by improving the liveliness of the speeches written for the Queen. This came from Martin Charteris himself, who invited his new brother-in-law, Ian Fleming – now married to Charteris's cousin, Anne, the former Lady Rothermere – to try his hand at speech-writing for Her Majesty. It would have been a most interesting situation to have had the Queen of England scripted by the creator of James Bond – and it might have worked wonders for her public image. But Ian Fleming, like many a lesser man before him, found the prospect of dealing with Commander Colville hard to take, and retired gracefully to Goldeneye, his holiday retreat in Jamaica where Eden had convalesced after his retirement the year before. The talent that might have worked wonders for the royal word went into writing *Doctor No* instead.

8

THE SNOWDON FACTOR

'For better or for worse, Royalty is excluded from the more
settled forms of domesticity.'

The Duke of Windsor

It is some indication of the part sheer chance could play in royal
popularity that, at the beginning of 1958, what seemed to be the
badly needed panacea to the ailments afflicting the public image of
the monarchy would not be found among the efforts of the courtiers,
nor would it issue from the self-serving labours of the politicians,
the prayers of the Church of England or the staunch endeavours of
the loyal establishment. And until the evening of February 20, no
one could possibly have guessed the form that it would take – not
even Lady Elizabeth Cavendish as she welcomed her guests to a
dinner party at her home on Cheyne Walk.

Lady Elizabeth was one of Princess Margaret's oldest friends and
her lady-in-waiting, but she was an unusual courtier and a far from
typical example of the 'Cavendish Connection'. Tall, humorous, and
at thirty-one still resolutely single, she was the youngest sister of the
11th Duke of Devonshire; and while her mother was Mistress
of Her Majesty's Robes, she was the mistress of Her Majesty's
future Poet Laureate, John Betjeman – thus combining intimate
experience of royalty, the landed aristocracy, and fashionable
bohemia. That evening, round her dinner-table, all three elements
were represented.

Princess Margaret was guest of honour, and other guests included
the theatrical designer, John Cranko, and a twenty-eight-year-old
photographer called Armstrong-Jones. Being asked for dinner by the
daughter of a duke was a sign that the new year had started rather
better for the Old Etonian photographer than it had for the royal
family. Five years earlier, he had been sent down from Cambridge
University for failing his architecture examinations; since then, with

growing ambition and considerable social push, he had begun to make his mark as a social and theatrical photographer.

As a photographer, he would not have claimed to be in the class of a famous contemporary like David Bailey, but he was a cut above him socially and, with his looks and considerable charm, had hopes of getting near the sort of lucrative position of one of his earliest photographic heroes, Cecil Beaton. He had already got to know that susceptible and worldly bachelor, whose highly flattering studies of the royal family had brought him the friendship of the Queen Mother and played a vital part in his glamorous career: and with a cool effrontery of which Beaton would have thoroughly approved, he had set his foot on the first rung of the long ladder of royal portraiture himself. After Cambridge he had first learned his trade from Nahum Baron, the Court photographer; then out of the blue had asked the young Duke of Kent if he might take his official photographs in honour of his twenty-first birthday. The photographs were a success, and led to the photographer's first arrival at the Palace – in November 1957 – to take birthday photographs of nine-year-old Prince Charles with Princess Anne.

He got on well with the royal children. The pictures when published in the press were widely praised, and his chances of following in Beaton's gilded footsteps seemed distinctly bright. For Armstrong-Jones, despite his easy manner, was rather a formidable young man, possessed of certain qualities that Beaton lacked. Although many of his friends were homosexual, he was not; but he was somewhat camp in manner, very sexually aware, and not averse to making the most of his attractions. Also, unlike Beaton, he was very tough, emotionally and physically.

His father, a rich and modestly successul Welsh QC, was in the middle of changing wives for the second time, and his mother, sister to the stage designer, Oliver Messel, had long since ascended into the aristocracy by marrying the Irish peer and former coal-mine owner, Lord Rosse.

The marital mix-ups of his parents had left Armstrong-Jones highly self-sufficient, with a cold and practised eye for the vagaries of human nature. They also made him difficult to place in the English social scheme of things, something of a fringe character on the edge of the aristocracy and the artistic world, but actually part of neither, the sort of amphibious, slightly louche Etonian who can be counted on to spot personal advantage in the most unlikely situation. He was worldly, ambitious and extremely smart.

He had other useful qualities for the aspiring society photographer – connections, nerve, a quick eye for the *mise en scène* (like his Messel uncle) and that element of his of sheer effrontery. He was all but impossible to faze, even by royalty, who had begun to fascinate him – which was important at a time when royalty themselves were increasingly dependent on the skills of the photographer.

In the past, monarchs had relied on their Court painters to present a favoured version of their features to the world, so that the mental pictures we possess of historic royalty are largely the creation of the painters they patronised – Holbein's King Henry VIII, Velasquez's sinister Philip IV, the sad profile of Van Dyck's royal martyr, Charles I, and the fecund stateliness of Winterhalter's young Victoria.

With the development of press techniques in the twentieth century, the photographer has tended to displace the painter in creating these important images – but only to a point. The most popular impression we possess of the young Elizabeth II is the work of the most accomplished portrait painter of his time – Pietro Annigoni's romanticised and highly flattering portrait, painted in 1955. And the millions of photographs taken of royalty throughout their lives have done little to detract from the importance of the accomplished Court photographer who, like the old Court painter, is still needed to produce some sort of visual consensus of his royal subjects, showing them as *they* would like the world to see them.

This is not easy, for whereas an Annigoni could rely on painterly technique, imagination and more than a dozen sittings to create the royal image he desired, the photographer can work only with what is actually before his camera. As Norman Parkinson has shown, wonders of discretion can be accomplished with lighting and technique, but in the last resort the photographer's success depends on how his subjects actually respond to him. If he wants a happy royal photograph, he must make them happy. Should he require a picture that conveys human warmth and relaxation, he must be able to create an atmosphere of warmth and relaxation too. The first requirement of the Court photographer is the ability to remain entirely at ease with royalty, to get effortlessly behind the deference and awe with which even the most accomplished courtiers regard them.

This tends to give the royal photographer a special status from the start, which a writer in the *Observer* described rather well:

Photographers, like portrait painters, not only have a side-door access to palaces, away from the stiffness of court etiquette. They also have the social ease that comes with the camera – a kind of professional liberation, with a touch of Bohemia, which breaks down the barrier between royalty and commoners, and provides a link with the world outside.

This was very much the case with Armstrong-Jones. He had already shown himself wonderfully at ease in the Palace with the royal children; and that evening at Lady Elizabeth's dinner party he had no problem being equally at ease with their temperamental aunt – despite the fact that they had never been introduced before, and that she was notorious for her ability to 'freeze' any hapless mortal she felt to be guilty of undue familiarity. Armstrong-Jones was amusing and relaxed, and he charmed her in a way few other young men would have done at their first meeting with the sister of the Queen of England. Just as his camera had already proved his passport into the world of royalty, so there was suddenly the chance of stepping from behind his viewfinder into the royal scene itself. During the weeks to come, and as his meetings with Margaret grew more frequent, he made the most of it.

As might have been predicted, by that evening Princess Margaret had become a problem for those seriously concerned with the loyal presentation of the royal family. Talented, extremely pretty and still by far the liveliest female in the family, she was potentially a natural asset to the monarchy, possessing just those public qualities her sister noticeably lacked – glamour, lack of shyness, skill at repartee and the ability to talk of other things than horses, palace protocol and the affairs and interests of the aristocracy. But the potential had been dwindling.

This was only partly the Princess's fault. Ever since the breakup of the Townsend love affair, she had been regarded as a wronged and romantic royal figure. According to the *Guardian*, 'thousands of ordinary Englishwomen felt personally bereaved' when she and Townsend parted; and around that time *Readers Digest* could still refer to her as 'the personification of British womanhood: the ideal to which every British woman aspires.'

Since then she had made it fairly plain that, far from living up to this ideal of noble sacrifice, she was a rich young woman with a grudge. Because her sister happened to be Queen and Defender of the Faith, she had done what was said to be her duty and parted from the man she loved; but as Nöel Coward wrote in his diary, it was 'arid comfort' to have 'half the world religiously exulting, and the other half pouring out a spate of treacly sentimentality. I hope she will not take to religion in a big way and become a frustrated maiden princess. I also hope,' he added, 'they had the sense to hop into bed a couple of times at least, but this I doubt.'

The unrewarding role of 'frustrated maiden princess' was definitely not for Margaret, and the rest of the family, who treated her with an awkward mixture of solicitude and guilt, had less influence than ever over her private life.

In return for her annual £5,000 from the Civil List she more or less performed the minimum of public royal duties – as Colonel-in-Chief of several regiments, patron of assorted worthy charities and the Royal Ballet, and the Chief Guide of the United Kingdom. Apart from this she made it clear that her private life was very much her own affair as she picked up her social life with what was left of the old 'Princess Margaret set', many of whose members had now vanished from the scene. She lived with her mother, who tended to indulge her. To the rest of the family she was unpredictable, particularly when with friends and having drunk a little – as she showed at the Queen's party for the tenth anniversary of the royal wedding in November 1957, when she arrived at the Palace from the theatre noticeably late, departed early, and attracted unfavourable speculation in the press as a result.

Exigent and vulnerable, 'difficult' yet curiously naive, the Princess seemed intent upon rejecting the ideal of royal womanhood so conscientiously created by her mother and Queen Mary. Making the best of a situation they could do nothing much about, some of the royal advisers seemed to think that this might even prove an asset. At best, the spirited Princess might liven up that 'tweedy', rather solemn royal image there had been so much fuss about: at worst, she could always prove a useful scapegoat to deflect unfavourable comment from the Queen herself.

Others strongly disagreed. As George VI had realised with his emphasis on 'Us Four', much of the strength of the Windsors resided in the tight nucleus of the family. Ever since the Abdication it had resolutely offered a united front to the world outside: once it was split, trouble could ensue. For once any member of the inner royal family was criticised – as over who did what in return for payment from the Civil List – the criticism might spread to other members of the family. It was vital to retain the royal reputation as a caring, self-denying, highly moral family, still utterly immune to the faintest breath of scandal.

After the troubles heaped upon the monarchy in 1957, the last thing the Palace wanted was fresh embarrassment from an aggrieved and unpredictable princess, and as the new year started quite a lot of fingers were being kept firmly crossed over what would happen next with HRH.

Much of the interest of the romance that rapidly developed between photographer and princess after that evening at Cheyne Walk lay in the way it broke so many of the ordinary assumptions about royal behaviour. Both participants were acting totally outside what were generally accepted as their proper roles, and therein lay much of the excitement.

The Princess was in fact acting much as she had with Peter Townsend, by secretly rejecting the rich, titled suitors whose company she kept and cleverly conducting an affair with a lover who possessed a perfect alibi. For just as the Palace courtiers refused to think that any of their number would have dared cast lustful eyes upon a creature of the royal blood, so none of the photographers and journalists who worked with Armstrong-Jones suspected that a mere photographer would dare transcend the rules of his photographic calling.

Each, in a sense, was moving in forbidden territory. Princesses were not generally supposed to help with the washing-up in Thames-side flats at Rotherhithe, where Armstrong-Jones now had a secret hideaway; and photographers who took portraits of princesses were not supposed to go to bed with them. Clearly for both the undercover element was strongly aphrodisiac, and each could introduce the other to an unknown and exciting world. Both were attractive, both have been described as 'rebels,' and both were ready to enjoy a most exciting and enriching love affair.

None of this was particularly surprising: but what was interesting was the reaction of the Palace and the family when, in the early autumn of 1959, the relationship showed signs of turning from romance into something much more serious. For by now it was clear that the couple were intent on marriage. Jocelyn Stevens, one of the few close friends of Armstrong-Jones to hear of this, was seriously shocked, and having known the photographer since their days at Eton angrily advised his friend to think again. So did Armstrong-Jones Senior, despite the fact that he was contemplating his own third marriage at the time. His son, he said, was far too 'free' a spirit to be happy for long in the gilded cage of royalty.

But the reaction of the royal family itself could not have been more different. At best, one might have thought they would have stoically decided to adopt a brave face at the prospect of this unconventional addition to the royal ranks: instead they were genuinely delighted. After the Princess's shabby treatment over Peter Townsend it seemed she had found true happiness at last and the perils of the unattached Princess were over.

However, there was more to the royal attitude than this. From the very start of the romance, the Princess had been careful to take her mother into her confidence. Armstrong-Jones was brought to Clarence House barely three weeks after they had met, and he and the Queen Mother got on famously together. She responded to the young man's charm; she felt his lively personality matched her daughter's, and as something of a virtuoso in the gentle art of the public presentation of royalty's personal relationships, she sensed the benefits this personable photographer might offer to the monarchy.

As far as the lovers were concerned, their affair had happened at a most propitious moment, when a slightly baffled royal family was still attempting to adapt itself to the controversial publicity and criticisms it had silently endured. After those dangerous rumours of the royal 'rift', the Queen and her husband had both done their best to make it clear that they remained a united and devoted couple. The Duke's standing had been publicly enhanced by the Queen's personal decision to create him a full royal Prince of the United Kingdom. (From the first days of their marriage his position had remained somewhat anomalous, for George VI had created him a royal duke, with the style of Royal Highness, and had always referred to him in public as 'Prince Philip', which he wasn't. Now at last he was.) The ancient slight to the Mountbatten name was also rectified when the royal family renamed itself Mountbatten-Windsor; and Prince Philip, as he now indubitably was, had not chosen to repeat that five month winter absence from his wife which caused such speculation on his return in 1957.

By that late summer of 1959, when Armstrong-Jones was invited to Balmoral (theoretically to take yet more official pictures of the family) and he and the Princess discussed the possibility of marriage, the Queen herself was resolutely pregnant after the eight year gap since Princess Anne was born. But despite the widespread reassurance this news had brought, there seemed little chance of recreating anything remotely like the public image of that joyful, classless family of Windsor which had been so universally beloved before the war.

Public attitudes had changed decisively. Sentimental deference to the royal family itself was giving way to rampant curiosity – and the family was ill-equipped to cope with it. Lacking her mother's ease and expertise with journalists, the Queen had made it clear that she and Prince Philip were determined to guarantee their royal offspring as 'normal' a childhood as possible, untroubled by intrusion from the press and television; and when Prince Charles went off to boarding school in 1958 Commander Colville made valiant efforts to order off the press.

As so often with the good Commander, little of this had worked. Before Prince Charles arrived at his father's old preparatory school, Cheam, Colville had taken the unusual step of summoning the Fleet Street editors and giving them a headmasterly no-nonsense lecture on their responsibilities to His Royal Highness. He pointed out the 'extraordinary' nature of Her Majesty's decision to send the heir apparent to an ordinary school together with other ordinary (if somewhat privileged) small boys. But this 'experiment' would now depend for its success upon the responsibility of the media. Should they continue to intrude upon the Prince's school life, his education could be made impossible; Her Majesty might well be forced to consider having him schooled in privacy, and the blame would lie firmly with the press.

For good measure, the Commander had recently complained to the Press Council that the lives of individual members of the royal family were increasingly disrupted by the press, which brought a loyal rejoinder from at least one paper early in 1958.

Can the Royal Family be allowed lives of their own? Have they a right to privacy? . . . The *Star* says that no royal tittle-tattle will be found in its pages . . . And Prince Charles will be allowed the right of every boy to have his schooling uninterrupted by snoopers. Our Royal Family are the admiration of the world. Let them get on with the job!

Brave words! But as with several later efforts to appeal to the finer feelings of individual members of the media, none of the Commander's weighty words had much effect. The *Star* collapsed soon afterwards, and during the Prince's four years at Cheam there were said to have been fifty-four separate 'incidents' involving so-called intrusion by members of the press.

For what Commander Colville and the royal family failed to understand was that appeals to the patriotism or sense of decency or deference of separate 'media-persons' would always miss the point. Like it or like it not, the royal family was news. It was their self-appointed task to be so, and with an international public avid for every detail of their lives, there would inevitably be just one reporter or photographer who would break a self-denying press embargo – and in this most competitive and lucrative of worlds, one would be enough.

Commander Colville's pained exasperation was no answer to the problem. Nor was the active irritation of Prince Philip, who was gathering a reputation as the scourge of press photographers. Never a patient man when feeling hounded by the press, he sometimes broke the royal rules by showing his resentment. This was understandable but ill-advised for a major public figure who depended largely on the press for his popularity, and he might have taken lessons from his mother-in-law whose ready smile and gracious manner made her the darling of the press photographers. Partly as a result, the Queen Mother has always had the most flattering public image of any member of the royal family; which was something Prince Philip was unlikely to achieve from incidents like the famous row that followed his appearance at the Chelsea Flower Show in 1959, when two particularly persistent press photographers were mysteriously drenched by the gardens' sprinkler system.

Whose finger turned the tap? Suspicion pointed at the Prince, and few were terribly convinced when Commander Colville turned a schoolboy prank into almost an affair of state with one of the most solemn and least convincing official denials ever to issue from the Palace:

> The Duke of Edinburgh did not, in fact, press the sprinkler button control at the Chelsea Flower Show. He had no idea on what part of the lawn the sprinkler would operate. Someone else must have pressed the button.

Whoever did – and jokiness apart – things were clearly going very wrong when the royal press secretary found himself issuing such statements. The malaise which had hit the monarchy in 1957 would not go away, and for the Queen herself, now pregnant with Prince Andrew, that summer marked a low-point in deteriorating relations with the media. Feeling her family's private life increasingly disrupted by press intrusion, she was determined to withdraw as much as possible from the limelight to enjoy her next child's earliest years. Her sister's marriage would conveniently slot in with this decision.

The Queen Mother was not only the first to get the news of the impending marriage, but also the first to realise a number of distinct advantages that Tony Armstrong-Jones could offer as her second son-in-law. As well as making Princess Margaret happy, he and the Princess could soon take much of the public pressure off Prince Philip and the Queen at this vulnerable moment in their lives. They would provide invaluable distraction for the troublesome press; and the image of a happily extended and united royal family should help the Crown recover much of its failing popularity. More important still, those very facts about the young photographer which would previously have ruled him out for ever from the sacred inner circle of the family, might now be just as firmly in his favour.

His lack of wealth and title would instantly riposte Lord Altrincham's remarks about that tweed-clad 'shintoistic sect' who danced attendance on the monarch. He did not shoot, had never been seriously astride a horse, and could not have been more different from a chinless duke had he tried. He may have been at Eton, his mother might be married to an Irish peer, but Armstrong-Jones himself possessed a strangely classless flavour: in accent, looks and even in his eager manner, he seemed ideally patterned on that great amorphous British group, the rising meritocracy.

Other facts were in his favour too. He was lively, intelligent and unconventional. He had 'artistic' tastes and genuinely artistic friends. As a childhood polio victim, he had known physical suffering; and even the divorces in his family and the presence of his last exotic girl-friend, the well-known Chinese-Trinidadian model, Jackie Chan, could now appear as evidence of royal broad-mindedness, where they would once have black-balled him for ever from the Court.

His overriding asset was that he was acceptable and yet completely different from anyone previously admitted to the family; and at a moment when the Mountbatten-Windsors seemed dangerously out of date, the arrival of this highly original addition to their ranks could signal to the world that the British royal family were really changing with the times. No longer hidebound, negative and rather stuffy, they might even start to swing at the start of a swinging new decade.

The Queen Mother's warm support for the lovers was to prove of great importance for the future, and the way their news was finally revealed to the public bears all the signs of that distinctive flair which she had long perfected in projecting the happy, human face of royalty. It was quite different from the uncomfortably defensive style of the Palace Press Office which had grown up around her daughter. Supervised by the Queen Mother – and with the dread hand of the Commander just as firmly kept away from things – the public announcement, when it came, would prove the most romantic royal coup until the arrival on the scene of the future Princess Diana. For none knew better than the royal matriarch the importance in such matters of an element of sheer surprise, and that the time had come for a touch of old-style royal showmanship.

Although the engagement was first made known to the Queen Mother as early as October 1959, she firmly counselled absolute discretion for a while. With the Queen's confinement still not due until the beginning of the new year, there must be not the faintest chance of Princess Margaret's news upstaging her sister's joyful moment. And nor did it. For by now the lovers were both highly skilled at conducting their undercover affair beneath the very noses of the eager journalists, most of whom were personally acquainted with the young photographer. Regarding him as firmly one of themselves, they never for a moment entertained the quite outrageous thought of what was actually taking place. It was the perfect camouflage, and although the press had a network of well-paid contacts among the Palace staff and even in the 'Princess Margaret Set', not the faintest hint seeped out.

It was several weeks before the Queen herself was told. She and Prince Philip were later reported to have been 'absolutely delighted' at the news, and although the new prospective member of the family was actually invited to spend part of January *en famille* at Sandringham, he was officially there simply to take photographs in preparation for the royal birth.

The evening of Friday, January 26, had been set by the Queen Mother's own press secretary, Major Griffin, for the unveiling of the Princess Margaret-Armstrong-Jones engagement. With a touch of army-style forward planning, the gallant Major had calculated the timing that would neatly gain the greatest media coverage – from that evening's television, from Saturday morning's daily press, and from the still excited feature writers who could weigh in for the Sunday papers.

The imminent royal birth had firmly occupied the attention of the press, keeping the most determined royal gossip-hounds off the scent, but the Queen Mother was getting worried at the growing possibility of the secret slipping out and ruining her careful preparations. Security was total until six o'clock that Friday evening, when the Major launched the royal bombshell in the form of a Court Circular from Clarence House:

It is with the greatest pleasure that Queen Elizabeth the Queen Mother announces the betrothal of her beloved daughter the Princess Margaret to Mr Anthony Charles Robert Armstrong-Jones, son of Mr R. O. L. Armstrong-Jones QC and the Countess of Rosse, to which union the Queen has gladly given her assent.

Astonishment ensued – as it was obvious it would – and the sheer surprise of the Princess's choice added vastly to its popularity. Not that one would have guessed this from the reaction in next morning's *Times*, whose chief concern appeared to be to reassure the establishment on the feelings of those ever-present multitudes beyond the seas at the news that *their* Princess was marrying a photographer. The engagement, Top People were authoritatively informed, would be 'enthusiastically welcomed throughout the Commonwealth on the simple assurance that HER ROYAL HIGHNESS is following her own heart, and that the QUEEN is delighted with her choice.'

That was that – but other journalists were less restrained. As a working press photographer, the royal *fiancé* was regarded as virtually one of their own; and while this caused a certain element of pique, it also guaranteed both admiration and incestuous attention to the smallest detail of his background and private life. 'In everyone I spoke to two emotions predominated,' wrote the *Sunday Times* portly and authoritative columnist, Godfrey Smith: 'delight and astonishment ... for quite frankly, Tony Armstrong-Jones seemed such an unlikely candidate.'

Unlikely as he was, there was surprisingly no hint of that mood of genuine foreboding which prevailed among a few of those who knew him best, like Jocelyn Stevens, who struck a note of sombre prophecy on hearing the news by cabling his former friend that 'Never has there been a more ill-fated assignment.'

But it was royal romance the people wanted – and it was a lavishly presented royal romance they got. Even in republican France, a journal like the Parisian *l'Aurore* responded to the happy theme:

England is celebrating and so is France, because we love Kings and Princesses – especially perhaps the latter – and we also love love stories.

There was more to celebrate than this, and everything went beautifully to plan. On February 19, Her Majesty was safely delivered of a son, and as if to make the ultimate amend to Prince Philip for those slights at the beginning of the reign which had left him feeling 'like a bloody amoeba', the new Prince, second in line to the throne of England, was graciously named after his paternal grandfather, the penniless and long-forgotten Andrew, Prince of Greece.

A royal birth is a natural time for national rejoicing, one of those all-important moments when royalty appear most human and most hopeful; apart from a royal wedding there is no other time which so combines the traditional dynastic role with an appeal to basic human emotions. This was the first birth to a reigning sovereign since the birth of Princess Beatrice to Queen Victoria in 1857, and the sudden mood of genuine affection for the thirty-three-year-old Elizabeth II was reflected in the shower of presents – many of them tiny garments lovingly knitted by extremely humble fingers – which descended on the Palace. Even the press transformed itself in response to the changing public mood. Intrusive and menacing no longer to the royal privacy, but loyally celebrating the arrival of the Prince with maximum publicity, the media was now as royalist and well-behaved as even Commander Colville could have wished, as goodwill flowed around a happy and united royal family.

This was very much the mood the court was actively encouraging when, on March 1, the couple made their first eagerly awaited public appearance together, appropriately presented by a radiant Queen Mother at a gala evening at the opera. Television viewers watched the scene at Covent Garden, a dreamlike sequence from a perfect Ruritanian romance as the lovers, happy and transfigured in the spotlights, graciously acknowledged a standing ovation from the cheering audience below the royal box.

During the weeks that followed, this enthusiasm spread to include the whole royal family. They seemed magically transfigured in the glow of childbirth and storybook romance. The sentimental feeling for the House of Windsor as a cherished national possession seemed to have revived, and – while it lasted – all the criticisms of the Altrinchams and Osbornes were forgotten. For like the Coronation, it was a prime example of something the royal family always manages extremely well – the romantic transformation scene *par excellence*, most skilfully presented and brought up to date. With the whole world fascinated now, the characters involved could proceed to play their parts to inimitable perfection.

It would have been hard to pick a more topical male Cinderella than this attractive young photographer to be magically translated into the fabled realms of royal splendour through the love of a beautiful princess. He had everything required of the part – youth, looks, a hint of motor-cycle-riding macho glamour, the polio victim's vulnerability, artistic sensitivity, and proven ability to earn his own quite ample living: while in the words of a startled writer in the *Guardian*, the Princess really was 'a devastatingly attractive girl – more attractive than any other princess in this century', who could effortlessly invest 'the most discreet smile at the most blameless royal occasion with a hint of bedroom eyes.' More reverently, the historian, Arthur Bryant, described her as 'the fairy princess for millions hungry for romance.'

The lead-up to the Maytime wedding was certainly a time when those 'hungry millions', by identifying to the full with the principal participants, could share in all the drama of this piece of living royal theatre; but its appeal went far beyond the love-lorn. The best-known family in the world was publicly engaging in a universal rite of passage – the marrying off of a younger daughter – and as at the Coronation it was hard for even the most cynical to curb his curiosity as these mythic creatures seemed to be stepping through the mists of royal splendour into a very normal happy human situation.

Here more than anywhere at this period one saw the working of the personal mystique of the monarchy and the strangely ambiguous fascination it could wield. Unlike most very famous people, the royal family could still apparently combine the maximum awareness from their public with the maximum mystery over their actual private lives. Everyone believed he knew them: with their public role and their constant media exposure, only a Trappist could have dodged some sense of personal involvement with the various Mountbatten-Windsors. At the same time, such was the immense discretion of the courtiers and family themselves that next to nothing was inadvertently disclosed about their true reactions to the simplest event.

This potent mix of mystery and familiarity reached its full effect in the international excitement during the final weeks before the Princess Margaret wedding. Speculation on the feelings and emotions of the nuptial couple became all but universal, with everyone at perfect liberty to place whatever personal interpretation he pleased upon the individual royal reactions.

Mothers of attractive, temperamental daughters 'knew' instinctively how relieved the Queen Mother had to be that her younger daughter was marrying at last – but how did she really feel about that young photographer? Similarly, middle-aged married men also 'knew' how the impenetrable Prince Philip was feeling at the arrival in the family of somebody like Armstrong-Jones. As for the royal children, anyone who was a parent could guess at their excitement, with Princess Anne to be a bridesmaid and Prince Charles himself a page.

This sort of fascinated speculation could occur only because the royal personnel stayed as usual supremely visible and supremely silent; and, just as at the most humdrum wedding, interest mounted when things started going wrong. Even the embarrassments added to the story, like the extraordinary incident when the bridegroom had to find himself a new best man after a newspaper 'revealed' to its shocked readership that the friend he had chosen had a previous conviction for 'a *minor* homosexual offence'.

Then came inevitable complaints about the public cost of the

Princess's marriage. Neither the Queen Mother nor her second daughter are great believers in personal economy, and although Princess Margaret's personal allowance from the Civil List would rise to an annual £15,000 on marriage, news seeped out of a further £56,000 earmarked out of public funds to restore a small apartment for the happy couple in that 'royal condominium', Kensington Palace. This was soon followed by the news that their Caribbean honeymoon aboard the royal yacht, *Britannia*, would cost a loyal nation £10,000 a day.

Serious complaints about the cost of the royal family were something new, and a symptom of the underlying disenchantment which the marriage was intended to dispel. There was considerable ambivalence towards the royal family over this question of expense. On the one hand was a fairly widespread feeling of resentment – which the press cautiously played up to – that a family as rich as the Mountbatten-Windsors should enjoy such further luxury at public cost. But to counter this, the dream of the unstinted riches of the regal life-style played its own important part in the royal fairy-story which was unfolding round the glamorous Princess. You can't cheese-pare on dreams, and as the Queen Mother sometimes said, she had a duty to live up to the style people had grown to expect of her.

She was certainly experienced enough to know how to deal with the critics, by publicly announcing she would pay the cost of *Britannia* from her widow's savings. In fact she did not pay, but nor was there any further carping over the voyage of the *Britannia*. For by that spring of 1960 it was clear that the wedding would be played up to the full as the greatest celebration of the royal family since the Coronation. Its popularity was guaranteed and, just as at the Coronation, the assorted outside interests who had most to gain from it offered ungrudgingly loyal support.

Foremost were the politicians. The new Macmillan government, soon to assure the British voter that he had 'never had it so good', was eager to share in the euphoric mood that naturally accompanies a royal wedding, and freely donated from public funds to make this the grandest royal weddding since the Queen Mother's own in 1923. London was soon *en fête* with garlanded monograms, A and M, along the Mall. Souvenirs were made and minted showing 'Tony and Margaret' as alarming figures of the popular subculture. The waxworks show at Madame Tussauds speedily admitted the royal bridegroom to its regal hall of fame, and magazines throughout the world boosted their circulations with a lavish show of royal photographs – many taken by the bridegroom, who was doing rather well from reproduction fees – and acres of 'informed' and highly speculative stories of exactly what was happening behind the scenes.

But the Coronation had unshakeably established television in pride of place as a necessary component of such royal celebrations. Far from objecting to the presence of the cameras in the Abbey now, the Palace press office gave all possible assistance to the BBC and ITV, and shrewdly confirmed Richard Dimbleby's position as exclusive commentator-royal within the Abbey. For the Palace was firmly counting on a repeat of the euphoria which had so unexpectedly ensued from the massive audience participation in the Coronation – and knew it could rely on that utterly dependable and utterly devout interpreter of royal myth to voice those sentiments he alone could utter with such majestic conviction.

He did not fail them. The Court provided the glittering spectacle, directed with more finesse than ever by its impresario-in-chief, the Earl Marshal and Butler of England, Marmaduke Norfolk. The Church supplied the ritual, and the royal family themselves were revealed in dramatic close-up in their places in the Abbey, waiting for the bride to enter – the Queen with her strangely unrevealing public face, the bridegroom nervous and the Queen Mother with a look of quiet satisfaction. But as the bridal anthem swelled above the cheering from the crowd outside and the bride's procession entered, it was Dimbleby who gave this royal moment its essential meaning for the masses.

> For one moment we see the bride now as she looks about her at the Abbey in this lovely gown of white silk organza, with the glittering diadem on her head, the orchids in her hand, and the comforting, tall, friendly, alert figure of the Duke of Edinburgh on whose right arm she can rely . . .

As ever, Dimbleby had worked hard to perfect his phrasing in advance. Not long before, he had had the cancer diagnosed that would kill him five years later, but it did not affect the meticulous attention he paid to every detail of the ceremony. Nor did it affect the authoritative reverence of the familiar voice which for millions had become *the* voice of a royal occasion, enunciating what seemed irrefutable verities about the scene before them.

Outside the royal circle, who would ever know Prince Philip's feelings for his sister-in-law? By all accounts, relations had been fairly stormy on occasions. But as Dimbleby spoke those few carefully pondered phrases and one actually saw the Princess on that 'comforting' right arm, rumours were forgotten and Dimbleby's assurance became all that mattered. So it was throughout the whole impressive service. As the *Sunday Dispatch* said afterward:

> Whose voice dominated the broadcast of the royal wedding? Not Tony's or Princess Margaret's – they were barely audible. Not even the Archbishop of Canterbury's – movingly though he uttered the words of the service. The voice we're thinking of belongs to Richard Dimbleby.

It was virtually the only voice. Royalty were the stars of the occasion, but for the 300 million television audience they were as usual mute performers, so that once again it was Dimbleby's own awesomely romantic attitude towards the monarchy that the occasion overwhelmingly conveyed. It served to reaffirm emotions which had surfaced at the Coronation, and he was to demonstrate the scale of his own devotion to the monarchy when the ceremony was over and he was waiting at Westminster Pier for the couple to embark aboard *Britannia*. As so often in their lives, they were late arriving, and for fifty minutes Dimbleby ad-libbed before the cameras. He used his own encyclopaedic knowledge of the most abstruse minutiae of monarchy and royal ceremony to provide his audience with the sort of facts he loved, and which suddenly assumed a strange significance because they were about *them* – the names and history of each horse in the royal procession, the origins of the royal postillion's uniform, the characters and ages of the royal wheelwrights.

By the time the smiling couple did arrive, Dimbleby had performed a memorable coup – and so had the royal family. But the loudest cheers went rightly to the Queen Mother, for she had earned that smile of satisfaction in the Abbey. This had been very much her day. Not only had she helped to make her daughter happy after all her troubles, and gained a son-in-law she really liked; but in the process she master-minded an extraordinary revival of the fairy-tale monarchy she typified herself. She had extended the family to include this dynamic, popular young man, she had restored more genuine goodwill towards the House of Windsor than at any time since the Coronation, and she had helped update its image to include a whole new range of fresh activities. As *Britannia* sailed through the Pool of London bound for the Caribbean, one could only wonder what use the monarchy would make of the fresh lease of badly-needed popularity this amazing matriarch had given to her family.

In the autumn of 1960, the newly-wed Armstrong-Joneses took up residence in Kensington Palace in time to follow the exciting race for the election of the youngest ever President of the United States. And just as the Kennedys would bring some intellectual style and the glamour of Camelot-on-the-Potomac to Washington and the Presidency, so it appeared as if this royal couple would soon be doing something similar for London and the image of the monarchy.

Potentially, they certainly possessed much of the appeal of the Kennedys – youth, energy and a welcome hint of sex to liven up the somewhat musty elevated scene on which they entered. Like the Kennedys they seemed open, self-aware and rather witty. And as the Kennedys offered an exciting contrast to the Eisenhower years with the range and eagerness of their response to the spirit of the Sixties, so the Armstrong-Joneses both seemed ready to step into areas where the rigid House of Windsor had rarely ventured.

They undoubtedly had taste and could not have seemed more up-to-date in everything they did. Though not intellectuals, they were certainly 'artistic'. She sang, and like America's First Lady (but unlike her sister) had her own fashionable ideas on interior decoration; he had just published a successful book of photographs on London, and had ambitions to make films for television. Both were social figures, interesting hosts and lively conversationists. They already had an acquaintanceship with many of the most interesting people in the capital – film-makers, painters, actors, even writers – and it was self-evident that no celebrity invited for an evening with the Armstrong-Joneses was likely to refuse the honour. Nor would the glamorous hosts have to worry overmuch about the expense or who would do the washing-up.

They were in fact ideally set to make royalty the social force it had last been in the 1890s; but in place of the titled philistines who had fawned upon the Prince of Wales at Marlborough House,

Kensington Palace could offer something very different – a focus for revived royal interest in the arts, a centre for modern patronage and a place where royalty would have the freedom and incentive to be truly civilised.

For as the Queen Mother had foreseen when she helped engineer the marriage, the young couple found themselves extremely popular. The Queen had made it clear that with the arrival of a baby son she intended to step sideways into more of the private home life she wanted, so that her sister and brother-in-law could automatically assume the role of 'mini-royals' themselves, with all the prestige and activities this implied. But they would also have advantages the Queen and her husband never actually enjoyed. They would be free from the heavy protocol, the Court officials and the constitutional and political responsibilities that helped make Buckingham Palace such a very different place from that less forbidding royal residence at Kensington.

It was a moment when it genuinely seemed as if the House of Windsor was about to renew itself, with all manner of exciting changes stemming from this unstuffy, unencumbered couple who had the freedom to extend the royal influence as and how they wanted. People were forward with suggestions as to how they might do it. Why, asked Jo Grimmond, the Liberal leader, did the royal family not found a bigger, more ambitious opera centre in the country, patterned on Glyndebourne, 'and promote other and popular arts?' Others expressed the hope that royalty – for the first time since the much maligned King George IV – would again become leaders of fashion and design. And the newly-weds seemed to offer an answer to the fears of the profoundly royalist historian, Sir Charles Petrie, that the monarchy had become 'dangerously out of touch with the leaders of thought' within the nation: 'it is an unfortunate fact that, rightly or wrongly, the royal family is credited with being philistine in outlook, and its members with rarely reading a book.' This had contributed, thought Petrie, to the situation that 'in England the man of letters counts for far less than in any other country in the world': in return, writers, although rarely actively republican, were frequently 'indifferent or inclined to be contemptuous of the monarchy.'

Hopefully perhaps, Sir Charles imagined that the damaging impression of a philistine monarchy could be 'corrected' quite easily 'if only a little trouble were taken'. Who better to take that little trouble than the Armstrong-Joneses?

There was of course much wishful thinking in the happy notion of the House of Windsor winning the hearts and minds of an Osborne or a Muggeridge by discussing their library lists over the *crêpes suzettes* at Kensington Palace. But the fact remains that Princess Margaret and her husband were presented with a unique chance to update both the style and the activities of the now extended royal family at a moment when this was badly needed. Their failure to do so remains one of the major missed opportunities of the reign.

All manner of excuses can be made – the ingrained resistance of the Queen herself to change, the suspicions of the old guard courtiers, and the jealous sniping from the press which, as is its way, could hardly wait to prove that the romantic figures they had eagerly built up had feet, and other parts, of purest clay.

But the fact remains that the failure was essentially a failure of the two main characters involved, for those very qualities which provided such excitement to their courtship and marriage made them increasingly unfitted to perform even that joint role the Queen Mother had envisaged for them. Stevens was proved right almost from the start. His friend's 'asssignment' was ill-fated, and as the marriage went its very bumpy way the 'mini-royals' increasingly became a source of interest more for the pratfalls of their none too private lives, than for any modern image they were bringing to the monarchy.

Almost from the beginning there was trouble as the bridegroom – that 'free spirit' – tried to come to terms with a demanding wife on her own exclusive ground. He had plainly not bargained for the subordinate position he had entered, where almost every item in his life was provided by courtesy of his wife and her somewhat overwhelming family. Nor were things made easier by the Princess, who did not possess that calm, accommodating nature which would have eased the situation. All her life she had enjoyed an unquestioned role of dominance and at thirty she was already far too old to change. An escapist love-affair was one thing, the reality of royal marriage quite another, and she inevitably took for granted the continuation of the life that she had always known.

A night-bird, she barely noticed when her guests grew weary in the small hours, knowing it would be frowned on if they left before HRH went off to bed, from which she rarely rose before eleven.

Another problem now encountered by her husband's friends was how to treat her. She could be perfectly relaxed; or she could be very royal indeed, in the style of 'I take it you mean Her Majesty the Queen' when someone was ill-advised enough to speak about 'your sister'. Her husband always referred to her as 'Princess Margaret', and her father-in-law, on the rare occasions when they met, invariably called her 'Ma'am'. She called him 'Father-in-law'.

Prince Philip had found his entry into the British royal family uncomfortable enough, but he had been royal himself, and as a semi-member of the family had known what to expect. Armstrong-Jones genuinely did not. The family were charming to him, and he remained a firm favourite of his much-loved mother-in-law. But for all the money spent on it, the couple's first apartment in Kensington Palace soon proved cramped and inconvenient, particularly for a rich, demanding wife with an energetic husband who was unemployed.

He had a fairly miserable time of it, for those qualities which had brought him to this strange position – thruster, non-conformist, social-climber – were not the sort to help him cope; and while he developed symptoms of a gastric ulcer (reminding one of Philip's attack of jaundice after his wife's accession), the household round him showed other symptoms of domestic trouble in high places. Staff began tendering their resignations. Ruby the maid, Cronin the butler – both left by Christmas, and both inevitably sold their stories to the press; which was unfortunate because their stories, which were widely read, played up the tantrums and the discontents of their employers, who had not observed that golden dictum of the English upper classes – 'For God's sake, *not* before the servants!' The fairy-tale aura so skilfully created round their marriage was already fading, and the gossip columnists, knowing their Princess Margaret from the past and reading the lurid stories that had inevitably started in the foreign press, calmly waited for the scandal to begin. Television, which had made the couple such perfect surrogate figures of romance, could do little for their image now.

Disaster was averted by the fortunate announcement in March 1961 that the Princess was pregnant, and by now the royal family itself, awakened to the problems of the newly-weds, had begun to take the former photographer in hand. This was the period when Armstrong-Jones, under the unlikely tutorship of Prince Philip, started becoming rather royal himself. He lacked the temperament for polo, but took up shooting at Sandringham and was rather good at it; and soon old friends were amused at the way he appeared to be modelling his public manner on his brother-in-law – the same clipped, somewhat haughty way of speaking, the same way of walking with hands behind the back, and even the adoption of the royal 'one', as in 'One often finds oneself asking oneself . . .'

His greatest source of popular acclaim had been his singularity. He was perceived, quite rightly, as a most original addition to the royal circle; but instead of being able to assert this to update the royal image, he was becoming swamped by royalty himself. In fact he was facing much the same problem all outsiders have on entering the royal circle – the intense pressure to conform to rigid modes of royal behaviour. Prince Philip, a much stronger character than Armstrong-Jones, never really managed to resolve the problem, but had gradually mastered his frustrations and evolved an independent role and style for himself within the Court. But Armstrong-Jones had been cast from the beginning as a semi-royal with a difference, and when in October 1961, just before his wife gave birth, he was created Earl of Snowdon, he seemed to lose another element of his uniqueness. It added nothing to his popularity. The *Guardian* noted a widespread 'tinge of disappointment that the plain, honest Mr Armstrong-Jones should have a title thrust upon him', and the *People* saw it negating much of his original mystique.

> As the husband of the Queen's sister, Tony Armstrong-Jones had one very big claim on the sympathy of the British people. He had no handle to his name. He was, in fact, one of us . . . now he has lost even that most precious asset which was his birthright.

In reply it was argued that he had reluctantly accepted his peerage so that his son – christened David Albert Charles, Lord Linley – would have a title appropriate to an infant who was fifth in line to the throne. But it was also pointed out that the same result could have been as easily effected by creating Princess Margaret a royal Duchess in her own right; and suspicions grew that perhaps the former commoner was already over-eager to enjoy the soft life and privilege of his position. These suspicions grew when, a few weeks later, the Earl and his Countess departed for a winter holiday in Antigua, leaving ten-week-old Lord Linley back in London with his nanny.

ABOVE: Sued for adultery and cast in the press as the Duke's partner in wild behaviour abroad, Commander Michael Parker's resignation only fuelled further rumours. Prince Philip bids his friend and private secretary a grim farewell in Gibraltar. *(Syndication International)*

ABOVE: Not only the tiger suffered as the result of the Duke of Edinburgh's marksmanship on this hunt with the Maharaja of Jaipur in 1961. The outcry back in England from animal lovers severely dented the royal family's reputation. (*Popperfoto*)

ABOVE RIGHT: 'No one could have guessed the form in which the remedy to the ailments of the monarchy would appear at the beginning of 1958.' Tony Armstrong-Jones in theatrical pose. (*Rex Features Ltd*)

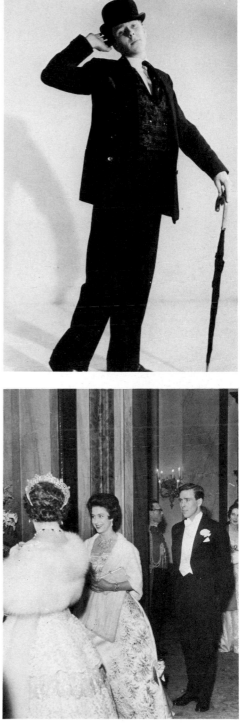

RIGHT: 'Like figures in a Ruritanian romance, the lovers made their first public appearance at a gala evening at the opera.' Princess Margaret and Anthony Armstrong-Jones at Covent Garden shortly before the announcement of their engagement. (*The Photo Source*)

ABOVE: Grandmother with favourite grandchild: the Queen Mother at the time of the Coronation with six-year-old Prince Charles. *(Camera Press Ltd)*

LEFT: 'The generalised perception of Prince Charles was of a lonely child with large ears and unflattering grey trousers.' *(Camera Press Ltd)*

RIGHT: 'You could have put a suit of armour on that lad and sent him off to Agincourt,' said the Mayor of Caernarvon. Prince Charles in full regalia at his Investiture in 1969. *(Camera Press Ltd)*

ABOVE: The snapshot that shook the royal family. Princess Margaret and Roddy Llewellyn beside her by the beach on Mustique, drinking with their friends, the Cokes. With the friends cut out, it was this picture that sparked off the Princess's separation from her husband. *(London Express)*

RIGHT: Princess Margaret at the time of her divorce – 'something of a casualty to life and her royal situation.' *(Rex Features Ltd)*

LEFT: 'Pure operetta,' murmured Norman Parkinson. 'The best of Strauss, but all the characters are real.' Mark Phillips and Princess Anne in Parkinson's wedding photograph in 1973. *(Camera Press Ltd)*

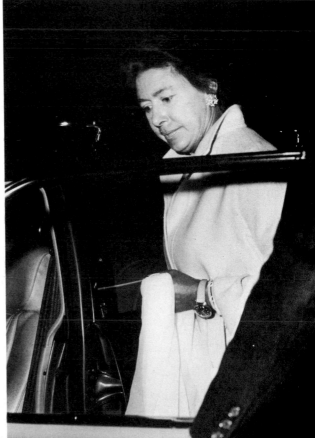

'It was sensibly decided to permit Her Majesty to be herself and meet as many of her subects as she could.' The Queen at Highbury Fields, London, during the celebrations for her Silver Jubilee in 1977. *(Camera Press Ltd)*

The journey seemed remarkably inept, for they travelled in solitary royal splendour in the sealed-off first class area of a BOAC jet, thus depriving BOAC of £5,500 in lost revenue at a time when the state airline was costing the taxpayer £8 million a year. 'Another little touch of apartheid to ensure the democratic idea isn't carried too far', grumbled the *Express*, and another old enemy of the monarchy, Kingsley Martin, smugly pointed out how the Snowdons were also offending the established image of the House of Windsor, by leaving a young baby with a nanny while they departed on a *foreign* holiday.

Working women have been taught to regard the royal family as a model of domesticity, and think they would never have done such a thing themselves.

Eighteen months earlier, Tony Armstrong-Jones had been the most romantic male in the country, and a source of hope for an excitingly modernised royal family. Now, as Lord Snowdon, he and his wife were rapidly becoming media casualties – and a source of gathering embarrassment for the royal family.

Even his attempt to end financial dependence on his wife and pick up his career as a photographer by joining Lord Thomson's *Sunday Times* brought bad publicity. The rival *Observer* not unnaturally objected that Thomson was buying royal prestige in return for Snowdon's £10,000 salary. Moscow's *Izvestia*, rather oddly, called the photographer-earl 'a victim of the beasts that prey in the capitalist jungle', and Jocelyn Stevens in his role as Job's comforter to his former friend gave an unanswerable verdict to the appointment: 'Look at it this way: if Lord Snowdon were not Princess Margaret's husband, would he have been offered the *Sunday Times* job?'

As Princess Margaret's husband, Snowdon certainly brought a touch of royal chic to the glossy pages of his paper's *Colour Magazine*, which was pioneering its appeal to the upwardly-mobile mass readership of the new consumer society of the Sixties. And as a photo-journalist he naturally attracted just the famous faces the paper wanted. (One of the few he failed to get at first was that of the painter Braque, who refused to compromise his principles as an old-style socialist republican by being photographed by a brother-in-law of the Queen of England.)

But the criticisms were perhaps unfair, for some of Snowdon's finest pictures from this period are studies not of famous faces, but of the poor and the unknown. And the fascination of his extraordinary career lies in the way he now began to build a reputation quite apart from his status as a member of the royal family. That easy mingling of the outside world with royalty which some had hoped he would accomplish never really happened. The two worlds stayed quite separate. Even on the *Colour Magazine* his semi-regal status was tactfully preserved, with a larger office than his editor's (specially designed for him by David Hicks) and a separate lavatory which was widely rumoured to have *softer* paper than the standard Thomson House issue.

Whether he realised it consciously or not, he was creating for himself a double life which undoubtedly appealed to his labyrinthine nature. His growing reputation as a star photographer continued to depend upon his royal connection, but did little for the prestige of the monarchy. Nor did the stories that began to circulate concerning his domestic life. But despite the couple's patent incompatibility, and the tensions of the marriage, they had to stay together to maintain appearances. A royal separation was still unthinkable, and there were certain compensations for the husband in his royal situation – the deference he could still command, the use of two Rolls-Royces and an Aston Martin, and free holidays as favoured guests of Niarchos on his private island (with grouse specially brought from Scotland for his royal guests to shoot) or of Karim Khan in a luxurious villa in Sardinia.

Snowdon bravely made the best of things, while at the same time skilfully creating his own separate reputation through the *Sunday Times*, and this independent life not merely helped to cure his ulcer, but would offer his escape route for the future. It also started to shift the balance in his marriage, by ending his dependence on the status of his wife, who increasingly was forced to bear the brunt of public disapproval when the dreams built round her by those 'millions hungry for romance' were not fulfilled. There was fairly constant carping at the cost of her establishment, and in 1962 she appeared on America's list of the world's worst-dressed women, her clothes described as 'a schizophrenic mixture of chic and sheer disaster'. This was a bad sign for a dream princess. So was the front page comment in the London *Daily Mirror* early the same year:

Her petulant decisions and her personal insistences are bound to raise the question sooner or later of whether she should retire from public life.

The Snowdons' failure to live up to the high hopes built around them ushered in a fairly dismal period for the whole royal family. Not merely had they lost their former glamour, but they began to appear fallible and accident-prone to a startling degree. Almost all the criticisms that had mushroomed round the Court in the late fifties, to be briefly stemmed by Princess Margaret's marriage, now returned with a vengeance – despite the birth of a fourth and final child to the Queen, Prince Edward, on March 10, 1964.

Public disappointment was by no means the only reason for this sour mood towards the Court. The sheer insensitivity of royal advisers to changing attitudes within the nation also played its part, and throughout the Sixties the undeniable impression grew of a monarchy that was out of touch with the times and even culpably indifferent to popular opinion.

Typical of this was the egregious stupidity of the royal entourage in managing to ensure that in 1961 the royal visit to achieve by far the most publicity was not Her Majesty's important state appearance in N'Krumah's Ghana, but the elaborate state trip to the Indian sub-continent, which would always be remembered for the fuss about the tiger shoot. In Udaipur, Prince Philip, the ecologically-minded future President of the World Wildlife Fund, shot a crocodile. In Rajasthan as guest of the Maharajah of Jaipur, he despatched a nine-foot male tiger 'with a single shot through the head'. And in Nepal, both Prince Philip and the Queen were actually permitted to take part in a tiger-shoot which also bagged one of the world's most valuable and rarest animals – an Indian white rhinoceros.

When this was first reported in the press and to the outrage of animal lovers round the world, Commander Colville blandly stated that, in Nepal at least, Prince Philip had not actually shot anything himself as he had been suffering from a painfully infected trigger-finger. But instead of leaving it at that, several members of the royal party cheerfully claimed responsibility, with Prince Philip's private secretary, Admiral Bonham-Carter, admitting he had bagged a tiger, and Lord Home, then Her Majesty's Foreign Secretary, blithely sharing the rhino with the Queen's own private secretary.

Sir Michael Adeane and I both hit the rhinoceros, and I am certain it was my shot that killed it. We are sharing it. I am having the horn and the front feet, and Sir Michael is having the back end. I am not certain what I will do with the feet. Probably make them into wastepaper baskets.

His Lordship gave no hint of what he was doing with the rhino-horn, famous for its aphrodisiac properties, and presumably he failed to realise that his future wastepaper baskets had belonged to one of at most forty creatures which were all that then remained of an entire endangered species – or that his 'bag' had been a female with a calf, which must have died without its mother. But the Earl's ignorance appeared as unacceptable as his unconcern, and the incident did untold and unnecessary damage to the royal reputation as caring conservationists. Worse still, it smacked of royal hypocrisy, for not only had Prince Philip come out strongly in the past in passionate defence of wildlife, but the Queen herself was patron of the British Fauna Preservation Society.

The British can be every bit as sentimental over animals as over their royal family, and the Palace postbag had rarely seen so many angry protests. Others were published in the press, of which the following is fairly typical:

There was sadness in our crowded suburban train when we opened our *Evening News* and saw the picture of the animal destroyed as part of the 'entertainment' laid on for the royal visit to Nepal. Staid businessmen were so revolted at the display of barbarism, that they were actually moved to cry out loud!

The fuss, of course, subsided, but more significant and vocal protests were to come when, hard to imagine as it must seem today, and barely a month after the tenth anniversary of the Coronation, the Queen and Prince Philip found themselves being booed in public. The occasion was the visit of Prince Philip's uncle, King Paul of Greece, in 1963. Few objected to bumbling King Paul, but his wife, Queen Frederika, was a vehement and tactless lady whose apparently pro-Nazi sentiments had been widely reported in the past.

Whatever her real feelings – which to be fair were not that clear – the royal Greek connection was an area for the Mountbatten-Windsors to proceed with caution. Instead, the whole royal party attended a gala performance at the Aldwych Theatre of the least politically contentious of Shakespeare's plays, *A Midsummer Night's Dream*, to be greeted by a thousand-strong demonstration and a storm of personal abuse. More scuffles followed outside the Palace. While Elizabeth II at a full state banquet was delivering a speech which praised the 'unremitting struggle' of the Greek royal family 'against foreign domination or occupation', her Metropolitan Police were dragging off demonstrators bearing banners which proclaimed 'London says NO to ex-Nazi Queen!' There was predictable embarrassment, and however angrily the perpetually flustered Home Secretary, Henry Brooke, denounced 'the whole disgraceful episode' as 'the work of a handful of communists and anarchists', the fact was that there had been ninety-four arrests in a protest at an official royal occasion, something that had not occurred in London since the Reform Bill riots in 1832.

It was a damaging episode which, like the royal rhino hunt, could well have been avoided: the failure of the royal advisers to foresee it could only add weight to the attacks now being made by a new breed of left-wing critic led by a very active politician, Willie Hamilton MP. Echoing the erstwhile Lord Altrincham's assault on that 'shintoistic set' of tweed-clad courtiers (Altrincham had by now happily resigned his peerage), Hamilton described the royal advisers from the Queen's private secretary down as being 'as reactionary and blinkered as any in history', and the Queen herself as 'caught in a web of her own creation – a web of flattery and flummery and as far from ordinary people as the outermost planets.'

He seemed to have a point; and it was yet further emphasised later in the year in a much more serious affair that finally confirmed the gathering impression of the monarchy as socially insensitive and politically inept. This was the murky business of the Queen's appointment of that keen shot, upright gentleman, but unelected and obscure statesman, the 14th Earl of Home, as successor to Macmillan as Prime Minister in October 1963.

There was sharp jockeying for power within the government following Macmillan's decision to resign in the aftermath of the Profumo scandal, a decision hastened by the Prime Minister's unexpected and disabling prostate operation. As at the time of Macmillan's own appointment to succeed the ailing Eden, the absence of any electoral process in the Tory party to select a leader when in power gave the Queen the unenviable role of referee, using her royal prerogative to appoint the most acceptable and suitable successor. This power should clearly have been used with circumspection to avoid the faintest hint of royal favour or of constitutionally improper influence from the departing premier. Instead Her Majesty, closely counselled by her private secretary, Sir Michael Adeane, personally visited Macmillan in hospital, and was unquestionably influenced by his strange conviction that the man best fitted to lead the nation and bring harmony and peace to his disjointed party was none other than the Earl of Home.

We will never know how much the Queen herself was also influenced by the fact that the Douglas-Homes, great Scottish land-owners, were old friends of that other ancient Scottish family, the Bowes-Lyons. Probably not at all; but the connection should have made the royal advisers wary. So should the memory of the criticisms that had followed Macmillan's own appointment by the Queen seven years earlier, when it was suggested that the prerogative had been used in the interests of those 'upper glaciers of the Tory nobility'. For Lord Home's precipitate appointment gave the strong impression of a Palace still firmly in cahoots with the upper aristocracy, and from almost every point of view – save that of Her Majesty's loyal opposition – it proved disastrous.

It did little for the government. Two of its ablest members instantly resigned rather than serve under the ill-fated Sir Alec Douglas-Home (as Lord Home, having given up his earldom, now became); Sir Alec notably failed to revive his party or inspire the country; and Labour's victory in the 1964 election faced the Queen with the first administration of the left since her accession.

The continuing tremors of the Home appointment helped produce a crucial change in the prerogative powers of the monarchy itself, for even the most royalist of Tories was no longer totally convinced that he could safely entrust the choice of his party leader to the royal discretion any longer. Sadly but sensibly, the party which had always seen itself the grand defender of the monarchy followed the example of the socialists, and in 1965 decreed that henceforth its leader would be chosen by a simple vote among its serving members – which would produce its first two leaders from the lower middle classes, Edward Heath and Margaret Thatcher.

In the long run, this diminution of the royal power has undoubtedly proved to the monarchy's advantage by conclusively removing it from an area of potentially immense controversy. (The only chance of the Queen having to appoint a Prime Minister is in the unlikely situation of a 'hung' parliament, where none of the parties can command a majority, and none can agree among themselves on a leader. It is a situation the monarchy would almost certainly do anything within its power to avoid.) But this was not the Queen's intention when she acted as she did – still less was it Macmillan's and Adeane's when they tendered her their advice. At the time, like so many actions of those most actively concerned with the preservation of the monarchy throughout the Sixties, the whole affair seemed to epitomise an institution riddled with symptoms of serious decay. Inflexible and unintelligent, secretive and chronically defensive, the monarchy itself appeared unable to exploit the immense advantages it did possess, while its hidebound allies and advisers seemed increasingly afflicted by what might be termed the Marie Antoinette syndrome – arrogant aloofness which amounted to a regal death-wish.

The most startling example of this dangerous insulation of the court in this period was not to be revealed until 1979, when, with accompanying shock and horror, it was publicly admitted that throughout the 1960s one of the Queen's courtiers had also been a Soviet spy. Back in 1964 the man responsible for the whole royal art collection, the distinguished art historian and Surveyor of the Queen's Pictures, Sir Anthony Blunt, had confessed to interrogators from the British secret service – of which he was once himself an important member – that he had spied for Russia, and had allegedly held the honorary rank of colonel in the Russian KGB.

In the outcry that ensued, Blunt was deprived of his knighthood by the Queen, and ended his life in fairly comfortable disgrace in 1983. But there was never a convincing explanation of how and why a former Russian spy was permitted to remain among the courtiers around the Queen for so many years after his confession.

The nearest the government came to an excuse was to say that Blunt had made his 1964 confession only when promised immunity from prosecution, and that had he been dismissed from Court the Russians would have been instantly alerted and the secret services have lost their chance to use whatever information Blunt had given them against his former masters.

This is possible, of course – for a period at least. But it does not explain the most worrying feature of this most extraordinary affair – the way this most important former spy, who almost certainly warned his friend and former secret service colleague, the notorious 'Third Man', Kim Philby, to defect to Moscow in 1961, was then permitted to remain happily at Court in charge of the Queen's art collection until his own honourable retirement in 1972. Even that was not the end of it, for although retired, Sir Anthony was able to continue with his work in the royal art collection, with a lesser but still official royal appointment as Keeper of the Queen's Drawings.

When the scandal broke, there was speculation over whether the Queen herself had known that one of her courtiers was also a prominent traitor to his country. Her private secretary, Adeane, was certainly informed. Had he not told Her Majesty, he would have had to bear a daunting load of personal responsibility. But whether he did or not hardly affects the most disturbing point of this unbelievable affair. For the Prime Minister, the head of the British secret service, and at least one major courtier knew the truth, and a moment's intelligent prevision must have told them that no conceivable advantage to the secret services could possibly outweigh the risks to the monarchy involved in Blunt's continuance at court.

As those who met him will agree, Anthony Blunt was the courtliest of courtiers, urbane, immensely civilised and charming to a degree. He was also very much a member of that 'charmed circle' of trusted palace courtiers. The son of a former chaplain to the British embassy in Paris who had owed his appointment to the friendship of King George V, Blunt was also distantly related to the Queen Mother. His work on the royal collection brought him into friendly and fairly frequent contact not only with the Queen, but with many of the other leading courtiers.

He was very much one of them. He also did invaluable work in the royal collection during his long career at Court, making it hard to avoid the obvious conclusion that, because of who he was and because he was extremely useful as an art historian, his parallel career as a traitor to his country was calmly overlooked and then as quietly forgotten. What made the stories of such traitors from the establishment – like the diplomats Burgess, Maclean, and their friend, Kim Philby – a particular disgrace is that, unlike the more plebeian sorts of spy, they were protected and absolved by members of their class and permitted to escape to Russia. Blunt was also protected by his friends; and counting on everyone's discretion, the Palace played its part in his unique and placid absolution – which continued until the Americans finally and most embarrassingly denounced him in 1979.

Fortunately for the monarchy at least, none of this was known in the 1960s; but with such behaviour from the royal advisers, it is not surprising that an institution so much a law unto itself seemed increasingly insensitive and ineffectual. The resultant dearth of public interest had been demonstrated by the resounding silence that greeted the tenth anniversary of the Coronation in June 1963. BBC television mustered half an hour of loyal nostalgia compèred by the inevitable Dimbleby, but the press barely noticed the anniversary, with the exception of the *Sunday Times* – which rather had to, with the royal brother-in-law the brightest jewel in its journalistic crown. But even here truth compelled that splendid journalist, the late Siriol Hugh-Jones, to note the contrast between the days following the Coronation, 'when it was not unusual to hear reasonable gentlemen declare that they would willingly die for their Queen', with the way the nation had now grown 'bored with the splendidly null, utterly safe and inoffensive middling image of the monarchy.'

Even the national anthem was losing its appeal as the sacred hymn of royalty, and a current survey showed it no longer being played as a matter of patriotic course at major public gatherings and at the conclusion of cinema performances. 'The English are getting bored with their monarchy,' Malcolm Muggeridge was able to assure America on the Jack Parr programme in 1964. Royalty as a cult of emotional belief was on the wane. 'The story goes on and on and the public realise it's been over-exposed. I think it's coming to an end.'

Little seemed to contradict this satisfied prognosis. Too many outside factors were beginning to compound the Court's incompetence – the waning of religious faith, the reaction against the old imperial dreams and the anti-deferential spirit of the liberated Sixties. Some of the monarchy's staunchest allies seemed to have deserted it. Even the BBC, under its new Director-General, Hugh Greene (who shared something of his brother Graham's strong bump of irreverence), had the measure of the times when television's most famous programme of the decade, *That was the Week that Was*, started to use the royal family as target for its sketches. It would have been unthinkable five years earlier.

Just as significant in this period of decline is the fact that between 1960 and 1969 there was no occasion for a full-scale public celebration to revive the myth of monarchy and involve the nation in the drama of a ritual transformation scene around a leading member of the royal family. The most colourful royal event of these years was the marriage of the Queen's most popular cousin, Alexandra of Kent, to the City businessman, Angus Ogilvy, at Westminster Abbey in 1963. The family was there in force, surrounded by the full ceremony of a royal wedding, and Dimbleby, reliable as ever, gave his usual commentary for the television viewers. But this time it proved impossible to generate anything remotely like the crescendo of excitement at Princess Margaret's wedding. Alexandra lacked the top star billing needed to create a royal legend; and, more importantly, the ceremony could not involve television viewers in the magic of a ritual transformation scene. The Princess remained the reassuring, kindly figure she had always seemed, and the bridegroom, younger grandson of Queen Mary's friend and lady-in-waiting, Lady Airlie, knew enough about the court to have already made it clear that, unlike the former Mr Armstrong-Jones, he had no intention of ascending into the ranks of supernumerary royalty himself. Though married to a member of the royal family, he was determined to remain a commoner and very private individual. Even so this did not protect him from the strains that entry into the royal circle imposes upon its male outsiders, and, like Snowdon, Ogilvy was soon afflicted with a gastric ulcer.

The grandest public ceremony of the middle Sixties was not in fact a royal occasion but a tribute to the greatest British commoner of this century, Winston Churchill. His funeral in 1965 came as something of a throwback to the nineteenth century when the most popular and publicly lamented figures had not been royalty at all, but those two great heroes, Wellington and Nelson.

Churchill's funeral pointed up a phenomenon of immense import-ance to the future of the monarchy – the virtual extinction of the cult of human greatness, which had been steadily succeeded by something rather different, the cult of the celebrity. For Churchill was a superhuman figure whose reputation rested on a series of extraordinary achievements which no single personality, however gifted, could conceivably combine today. Statesman, warrior and intellectual, he was the last great individual to have dominated in his day the entire stage of politics, of warfare and of empire, and lived to see this whole stage crumble. Now with that empire lost, with power in all its guises seeming more and more anonymous and warfare synonymous with suicide, people sensed that Churchill's sort of greatness could not come again.

But as some consolation there was the ever-growing cult of the international celebrity and superstar, round whom the media could manufacture images of greatness to satisfy the universal need for heroes, parent-figures, and dreamlike beings of fabulous splendour and romance. Royalty were ideally suited to this role: until television came they had played it to perfection, and their current slump in popularity was largely a measure of their failure to exploit the new mass media technology.

It seemed a moot point if they ever would, and the question now became increasingly important with another death in the same year as Winston Churchill's: that of the prime propagator of royal myth, the intermediary between royal family and television audiences, Richard Dimbleby. So little did the Court appreciate the part he had played in royal popularity that this afflicted, monarchy-besotted servant of Her Majesty never did receive the knighthood he, if anyone, had earned and which would have sent him happy off to meet his Maker. Six half-bottles of champagne – non-vintage – did reach his death-bed from his monarch; but he was then too ill to savour this one gesture from a grateful royal family.

But his death could not be so easily ignored, for there was really nobody to take his place, and in his absence interest in the institution he had served with such devotion continued its decline. By 1967 the royal family itself seemed to accept that it had something of a crisis on its hands, when Prince Philip at a news conference in Canberra mused aloud that 'no one wants to end up like a brontosaurus, who couldn't adapt himself, and ended up stuffed in a museum ... It isn't exactly where I want to end up myself.'

But how exactly could the royal brontosaurus be persuaded to adapt before it was too late? The Prince, who by now had learned the art of publicly presenting questions rather than solutions, failed to elaborate, but few had had more experience than he of the Court's resistance to the whole idea of change. The Queen conceived it as her duty to continue reigning in accordance with the pattern broadly established by her parents, so that any move towards the style of the more open democratic monarchies of Scandinavia was ruled out from the start. Even suggestions from the Commonwealth that the royal family might spend part of their holidays among them were firmly vetoed. For Her Majesty was loyally wedded to the royal routine which included, as it had since the days of Queen Victoria, lengthy family holidays at Balmoral and at Sandringham. They would not change; nor, it was fairly clear, would the essential nature of the monarchy as long as she was Queen.

Writing a century before, Walter Bagehot had speculated on how the British monarchy might meet its end. For him, the real value of the 'ornamental' royal family at the head of what he called a 'veiled republic' lay in the way it gave the country order and stability, thanks to the deference and interest it excited in a population which was, by and large, unthinking and uneducated. Universal education might well change this situation.

> That reverence [for the royal family] could not doubtless continue among a cultivated population, but then, among a cultivated population, a population capable of abstract ideas, it would not be required.

Now it seemed as if this prophecy was coming true and that with increasing education and sophistication among ordinary people, the monarchy was simply not 'required' any longer. The Snowdons had but briefly reversed its decade of decline; the fickle media had transfigured its image only to expose its vulnerability; and its advisers seemed incompetent and out of touch. It was no longer exciting and barely mysterious: it was outmoded, isolated and increasingly irrelevant. How little it was now 'revered' was clear when in 1967, even that stronghold of right-wing attitudes and customary support for the royal family, the *Sunday Telegraph*, unconsciously echoed Bagehot's fears for the fate of the monarchy in a leading article which noted

> a marked change in the public's attitude towards the Crown. Most people care much less than they did – particularly the young, many of whom regard the Queen as the arch-square. They are not *against* in the sense of being *for* a republic. They are quite simply indifferent . . .

The British monarchy will not be swept away in anger, but it could well be swallowed up in a great and growing yawn.

PART THREE

REVIVAL

9

'GOD BLESS THE PRINCE OF WALES!'

'The British royal family is an adman's dream. A unique selling proposition with a pliable market strongly predisposed towards the product.'

Andrew Duncan, *The Reality of Monarchy*

Despite remorseless press attention from the moment of his birth, Prince Charles remained an unknown quantity almost until the eve of his majority in 1969. Court attempts to shield him from epidemic media intrusion into his life at school had failed, but had produced instead an unfortunate impression of his personality based on snatched photographs and random gleanings from the schoolroom and the playing field. There had been unguarded revelations like the overplayed 'Cherry Brandy Episode', when an eager female newshound spotted a naive and under-age Prince Charles together with some wilder spirits from Gordonstoun, requesting an embarrassed glass of cherry brandy in a bar in far-off Stornaway. From the ensuing publicity one would have thought princely depravity could sink no further.

Despite this, the generalised perception of the teenage Prince was of a rather lonely youth with large ears and unflattering grey trousers, who was probably bullied by his sister, spoiled by his grandmother and not terribly successful at keeping up with his high-achieving father. But there had recently been a number of events to suggest that this was not the whole truth about the heir apparent. After a fairly miserable time at Gordonstoun, he had clearly loved his seven months of freedom at school in Australia, where several schoolfriends went on record to describe him as a genuine 'Pommie bastard' – apparently a term of some endearment when used by Australians about the English.

But most of what was known about Prince Charles remained distinctly hypothetical. It was enough to whet the collective appetite for further revelations but gave no hint that he could help bring about a genuine revival of interest and enthusiasm for the royal family. Still less did it suggest the way in which the Palace would soon become the centre for a conscious, highly professional exercise of royal image-building round the person of the Prince. This, when it happened, marked an almost total *volte-face* in royal attitudes towards the public; and although its full significance was not appreciated at the time, it initiated a major revolution in the public awareness and general presentation of the royal family for the future. It was the moment when the first royal superstar was consciously created through the media.

As so often with the royal family, all this happened at least partly by chance, thanks to a number of unrelated incidents which coincided with this period in which the monarchy perceived itself firmly in the doldrums. First came the acceptance by the family that when the Prince left Cambridge in the early summer of 1969, his sheltered life would have to end. Eleven years earlier, the Queen had publicly announced that one day she would 'present' him to her Welsh subjects as their Prince of Wales in some sort of royal ceremony, and this was obviously the time to do it. Part of the accepted wisdom at the Palace was that a major royal occasion invariably produced a rise in popularity, and some regal happening was clearly overdue.

Second was Prince Philip's keen awareness of the brontosaurus factor, for he remained more in touch with outside attitudes than any other member of the family. There was a Labour government in power with a number of potentially dangerous critics of the monarchy on its back benches; and with inflation on the increase and the royal expenses of the Civil List having to secure parliamentary approval, it did not require excessive perspicacity to sense that serious financial trouble might be brewing. Apathy could swiftly turn to something far more dangerous to royalty, and, realising this, the Prince and those around him were more influenced than might have been the case by the third and possibly the most important fact of all in those early weeks of 1968. The long and leaden reign of Commander Colville in the royal press office was reaching its allotted term, and the red-carpeted corridors were already feeling the determined tread of his successor, a thirty-four-year-old Australian called William Heseltine.

A former private secretary to the Australian premier, Robert Menzies, Heseltine had made his mark during a brief secondment to the Palace as a royal equerry in the early Sixties. Since then he had returned to Australia, working as a national organiser for Menzies' Australian Liberal party. At Prince Philip's personal suggestion he had now come back to London, and was being groomed to take full charge of the royal press office.

He could hardly have been more different from Commander Colville had he tried. As an Australian and a complete outsider to the 'charmed circle' of traditional courtiers, he lacked his predecessor's prickly caution where the monarch was concerned. With his easy Queensland manner, he got on well with members of the family; and instead of regarding the Queen herself as a sacred being it was his awe-struck duty to protect against the vulgar world outside, he saw a lively, forthright woman, whose character he thought generally misunderstood by the majority of her loyal subjects. It soon became his self-appointed task to put this right – but how?

Commander Colville had always suffered from a gentleman's dislike of public relations men which exceeded, if possible, his distrust of journalists. This was totally in character, and a standard attitude for any loyal courtier. From the last decades of Queen Victoria, the monarchy had always managed its own public image with consummate success; and the rules that governed everything its members did, from the great ceremonies of state to the simplest personal appearances, all played their part in what until recently had been one of the most successful and elaborate exercises in highly formalised PR the world has ever seen.

For a conservative courtier like Colville, the idea that this majestic system might have anything to learn from the gimmicks and marketing techniques of the ad man and image merchant was almost blasphemy against the magic of the crown. 'If there comes a time when the British monarchy ever needs a *real* public relations officer, the institution of the monarchy in this country will be in a serious decline,' Colville warned in 1964. But to his dismay, his warnings had begun to go unheeded, and in 1966 Prince Philip had insisted on an unabashed and undisguised American PR man, Henry Rogers, to arrange part of his official visit to the United States, thus joining Queen Soraya, Rita Hayworth and Brigitte Bardot on the Rogers Corporation list of celebrated clients.

This marked the start of a crucial change of attitude at court, and smoothed the way for an even more surprising and seminal event in November 1967. Prince Charles had recently been provided with his personal equerry, a man more than twenty years his senior called David Checketts who, like Heseltine, was another markedly atypical courtier. He was a bluff, outspoken former businessman and wartime bomber pilot; and as a resident guide, philosopher and father-figure to the emergent prince, remained his secretary for the next thirteen years, exercising the sort of steady daily influence over the royal heir that the frequently preoccupied Prince Philip never could.

The process started with the trip that played a key part in the Prince's growing up – his period in Australia. Checketts and his family all went with him to provide a familiar supportive base outside the school, and shortly before leaving for Australia, Checketts was approached by a wartime acquaintance called Nigel Neilson with an unorthodox proposal.

Neilson still runs Neilson McCarthy Ltd, a small and carefully selective firm of public relations consultants with an office in the heart of Mayfair. An ebullient New Zealander, he once trained as an actor and his personal publicity handout typically quotes an article describing him as 'The Right Hand Man to the Powerful'. It was a claim he more than earned in many years of advising the late Aristotle Onassis on his public relations and doing much to make the image of that unamiable multi-millionaire acceptable to those who did not know him. These included several highly influential figures in the British oil industry who were persuaded to make profitable use of Onassis's fleet of tankers. Neilson also actively promoted Onassis's lavish hospitality to the aged Winston Churchill, and learned much about the habits of the very rich and powerful that helped him in the gentle art of publicly presenting – and protecting – the bashful tycoons who today form many of his clients. His company is still retained by Christina Onassis, and has prospered with a combination of shrewd media advice, top press connections and a cool assessment of exactly how and when 'better communication' can assist his clients' commercial problems and personal prestige.

Strangely perhaps, his professional success did not alter Neilson's fundamental attitude to life. One of his proudest moments in the war came when he took part in the last cavalry charge of the British army: a deeply patriotic man, he claims that in 1967 he was troubled by the way Prince Charles was being treated by the media. 'Here was a first-class chap, a first-class product, being criminally undersold. Far too much nonsense in the press about the chinless wonder, and his ears which are really no different from anybody else's. So I decided something must be done.'

What he did, as his private contribution to the state of the monarchy, was contact David Checketts and offer him a part-time position as a non-executive director on the board of Neilson McCarthy at a nominal salary of £5,000 a year. Checketts reported back to Heseltine, and amazingly was permitted to accept. For many years to come, the courtier closest to the Prince would also be the salaried director of a firm of West End public relations consultants.

The importance of this extraordinary fact has been curiously over-looked – both by the press, which resents the thought that it can be influenced by shrewd PR, and by the Palace which equally dislikes suggestions that 'the monarchy can be marketed like a packet of detergent.' But it unquestionably played a major part in the public 'launching' of the Prince and his subsequent popularity: in the process it contributed to a number of unprecedented changes which engulfed the monarchy itself.

Neilson's influence was twofold. In the first place, Checketts would conscientiously sit in on working sessions at Neilson McCarthy, thus absorbing much of the company's business philosophy and actual expertise. More important still, Neilson was always at the end of the telephone, waiting and more than willing to advise His Royal Highness's private secretary over anything affecting the Prince's personal relations with the world outside. Very effectively, Neilson McCarthy had appointed themselves public relations consultants to the Prince of Wales.

It was an odd but invaluable relationship, which worked as successfully as it did thanks largely to its informality. Backed by Neilson's advice on how best to deal with Australian reporters, Checketts was already coached to help the Prince achieve an easy relationship with the other boys at his Australian school as well as with the local press. Having held an 'open day' for reporters when the Prince arrived, Checketts then took charge of all contact with the press, efficiently answering queries and telephone calls in person and giving journalists only what he felt they ought to know. He managed this so skilfully that, in marked contrast with Charles's time at Gordonstoun, there were no awkward 'leaks', no incidents, and the Prince's own self-confidence began to grow.

When Charles reached Cambridge the process took a big step

forward. With Checketts at the princely elbow and Neilson in the background with professional support, there was a notable lack of the skirmishes with journalists and press photographers which had come to sour his father's attitude towards the media. As the most famous undergraduate at Cambridge, Prince Charles was treated rather gently by the press. He was to take a good degree in history and archaeology, and may even – if later rumours were correct – have surrendered that most speculative of princely possessions, his virginity, in the Master's Lodge at Trinity. But despite this, there were no dreaded revelations about his love-life, no hints of student indiscretion and nothing remotely like the constant press intrusion which had marred his schooldays.

Instead there was much flattering attention from the London dailies – often tipped off by Neilson in advance – about a number of well-chosen and light-hearted happenings in which the Prince was cheerfully involved. His first attempt at journalism, a contribution to the undergraduate newspaper, 'Varsity', on his life at Trinity, was treated by the press like holy writ; but the greatest interest was reserved for his appearances in amateur college theatricals. Like many in his family, particularly his Aunt Margaret, the Prince is an accomplished mimic, and one of the hazards faced by royal friends at Sandringham and Windsor has always been involvement in the family charades. Something of a devotee of the zany humour of members of the Goon Show, like Spike Milligan and Peter Sellers, Charles was a natural for the Cambridge style of irreverent under-graduate review. It was a further boost to his newly-found self-confidence to be free to act the fool in public, and after a small part as a misused curate in a short play by Joe Orton (who was hardly the sort of playwright one associates with members of the royal family), he had his greatest undergraduate success as Reg Sprott, the singing dustman in his college review called *Revulution*.

Everybody loved it, and the Prince and *Revulution* naturally attracted rave reviews; but more revealing than the Prince's unex-pected stage success was the way the press themselves were treated. For the first time since those early wartime days when the Queen Mother had sanctioned Godfrey Winn to write about the two prin-cesses in 'Old Mother Red Riding Boots', the family pantomime, journalists were actively encouraged to attend these royal theatricals. At Neilson's astute suggestion there was even a special preview for the press, and the Prince himself gave individual interviews about the show.

It was clear by now that Neilson's strategy was working better than anyone had dared to hope, and that the Prince was being 'criminally undersold' no longer. His confidence was steadily increasing; the press were basking in the flattering treatment they were suddenly receiving from the Palace; and public attitudes towards the Prince changed almost overnight. The royal ears and chin forgotten, he had suddenly become what no other member of his family could hope to be. Funny, irreverent and not inclined to take himself too seriously, he seemed firmly on the side of the youthful spirit of the Sixties.

There was of course a danger here which elephantine memories at the Palace were unlikely to forget – the dread example of great-uncle David. For the Duke of Windsor had started his royal rake's progress when he tasted popularity and freedom as an undergraduate at Magdalen College, Oxford. But happily the Prince was made of sterner stuff. He studied; he was actively concerned with important aspects of the world around him; and once again this serious side of Charles's character was skilfully presented through the media.

Checketts was always good at guiding him towards popular but non-controversial projects that would simultaneously catch his enthusiasm and present him to the public as a caring and concerned young man. Rural conservation was a good example; and at the end of 1968, with his time at Cambridge drawing to an end, the Prince graciously accepted the position of official chairman of a Cardiff conference on 'Countryside in 1970'. His first public speech, urging protection of the national heritage, was discussed in advance with Neilson, carefully rehearsed with Checketts, and proved a predictable success.

The Neilson technique was already working even better for Prince Charles than it had for Onassis, but there was more of it to come. For Neilson knew – as Prince Philip notably did not – how susceptible both press and television journalists can be to a little sympathy and royal contact. In the words of Neilson's professional credo, 'The keynote is intelligent communication.'

When it had been his task to convey the message to the world that Mr Onassis was a model of urbanity and civilised good taste, Neilson had invited a handpicked group of journalists to lunch with him aboard the Onassis private yacht, *Christina*. They were distinctly charmed and flattered; 'they could see at once that the yacht was not a floating gin-palace but really very lovely'; and press attitudes towards Onassis started to soften almost overnight.

In some respects the public 'launching' of Prince Charles was easier than the Onassis PR campaign, for the Prince, unlike the rough-hewn shipping millionaire, really was – and is – extremely nice, socially concerned and naturally good-mannered. The biggest problem was simply to avoid the development of those prickly, mutually suspicious attitudes which had reached crisis point between his father and the media.

The problem was solved much as it had been with Onassis. Throughout 1968, surprised journalists from press and televison found themselves summoned to a social gathering oddly reminiscent of those games of football played on Christmas Day in the First World War, between opposing troops in no-man's land: a cocktail party where Prince Charles and the courtiers could meet the media, and vice versa. There never had been anything quite like this before, and journalists were even more surprised when the Palace press office actually suggested that leading editors assign a member of their staff to take a special interest in the Prince. This total switch from the days of the perpetually affronted and defensive Colville produced some strange results. Charles's biographer, Tony Holden once described the way a star-struck lady journalist issued from the Palace, firmly insisting that the Prince was simply 'a sweet virgin boy'.

But for those intent upon the successful public presentation of the Prince, the whole campaign was now proceeding admirably. Charles himself was reassured by the polite attention he was getting from the press, and unhappy memories of the intrusions that had marred his schooldays were forgotten as he read a succession of benign accounts about himself. And while he was starting to feel at ease among reporters, the media was also rapidly adapting to the novel notion that the Prince was likable, approachable and quite possibly human.

None of this had come about by chance, and as the prospect loomed of Charles's Investiture as Prince of Wales, Checketts even started to arrange practice interviews for him with young provincial journalists primed to ask awkward questions. These interviews were tape-recorded, analysed by Neilson and Checketts, and played back later to the Prince to help him learn from his mistakes. Before long the previously tongue-tied heir to the throne had developed considerable skill in playing – or jokingly deflecting – any of a list of questions that could be bowled against him.

Neilson himself also played his part in trying to extend the Prince's experience of the real world outside the Palace. He arranged several gatherings of top industrialists and bankers at his Westminster flat, to meet his Royal Highness over drinks and even singsongs together round the Neilson piano. The Prince apparently enjoyed himself; the industrialists and bankers were impressed; and Neilson's own reputation as 'the right-hand man to the powerful' cannot have suffered.

It would be misleading to see this careful preparation of the Prince in isolation from a number of other changes which were simultaneously affecting other members of his family as well as the general thinking of the Palace. The key date here is February 1968, when Commander Colville – now garnished with a knighthood for those faithful years of defensive service to the Crown – left his office facing Constitution Hill, and William Heseltine finally took charge of the Palace's relations with the press. Heseltine had been working closely with Checketts and the Prince, and their success had naturally confirmed his feelings on how the monarchy as a whole should be presented to the public.

Almost at once he had to take a crucial decision over requests to make a full-scale television biography of Prince Charles in preparation for the Investiture in 1969. Heseltine was much in favour, but saw this as an opportunity for something more ambitious than a film about the Prince alone – who had plainly not lived long enough to fill a satisfactory major programme. Surely it made more sense to have a film about the role of the monarchy itself, which could then be broadcast as a curtain-raiser to the ceremony?

It was an idea whose moment had arrived, with several influential forces moving in the same direction. The most eloquent of these, as so often in the past, was that royal radical and showman, Louis Lord Mountbatten, much of whose time and vanity had recently been devoted to a television series on his 'Life and Times', made by his film-producer son-in-law, Lord Brabourne. He had loved the whole experience, particularly when the programmes were hailed as a personal *tour-de-force*. Keenly watched and enjoyed by the royal family – with the possible exception of the Queen Mother – the Mountbatten programmes showed what could be done; and Prince

Philip, never one for being upstaged by his Uncle Dickie if he could help it, fairly swiftly took the point when Brabourne suggested it was time for something similar on the royal family itself.

There were, however, powerful taboos surrounding the presentation of royalty on television. Despite the worldwide impact of the medium whenever the royals were shown in their god-like ceremonial roles, there remained an almost superstitious dread at the prospect of impromptu revelations of their private lives. This was so rigidly enforced that even when that most trusted of fomer courtiers, Kenneth Clark, had made his television series on the royal palaces, no moving figures were permitted to intrude in any of the scenes in case viewers happened to mistake just one of them for a royal in an unguarded moment.

This attitude was interesting. It stemmed partly from the family's ingrained reaction against constant press intrusion, and partly from the fear of casual remarks or appearances that could lead to subsequent embarrassment; but at a deeper level it reflected the traditional belief that the royal mystique must be religiously protected at whatever cost. In contrast with the life of a monarch like Louis XIV, who was on public view from the moment he took off the royal nightshirt in the morning until his courtiers saw him safely into bed at night, the Mountbatten-Windsors lived like royal hermits. There was not an unguarded moment of their private lives witnessed by the eyes or ears of profane outsiders, and it was totally accepted that only the family and their advisers could decide how much of the mystery of the monarchy might safely be revealed. Once the ordinary lives of royalty were shown in casual detail to the inquisitive world beyond the Palace gates, what would happen to the royal magic? Perhaps, like the emperor's clothes, it might be discovered not to exist.

Checketts' success with Prince Charles had proved such fears were much exaggerated. Heseltine and Brabourne certainly understood as much, but it still required a revolution in Palace attitudes before the sort of film they had in mind could become reality. During the period before Prince Charles's Investiture, some such revolution happened.

The members of the royal family are surprisingly competitive as far as their public is concerned, and once Prince Charles began developing easier relations with the press, those around him soon responded to Heseltine's ambition to present a more human face of the whole family. Somewhat to everyone's surprise they quickly agreed to his idea of a full-scale documentary film about the home life of the royal family and the Queen's activities throughout the year.

It was a tribute to Richard Dimbleby and the BBC's reputation as a pillar of the loyal establishment that – despite aggrieved complaints from commercial television – they were exclusively entrusted with the task, as they had been at the Coronation and Princess Margaret's wedding. The making of the film involved members of the family on and off for almost a year. It was treated, particularly by the Queen and Prince Philip, with utmost seriousness, and its producer, Richard Cawston, came to be a trusted royal adviser and the most important link between the monarchy and BBC TV since Dimbleby himself.

The two men could hardly have been more different, both in character and in their attitudes towards the monarchy. Whereas Dimbleby had been a romantic monarchist, passionately involved in presenting his own vision of the sacred nature of the royal calling, Cawston admits that, like the great majority of people at the time, he was 'really an agnostic over the monarchy' when he arrived at the Palace in the early spring of 1968 to discuss his formidable assignment.

A self-contained and rather quiet man from a BBC department dominated at the time by temperamental Welshmen, Cawston had a reputation as a reliable and down-to-earth professional. He had made his name with a number of major documentaries on important institutions, culminating recently in a mammoth programme on television around the world. He certainly brought no preconceived ideas about the monarchy when he met Prince Philip, Heseltine and Brabourne to discuss the project; but recent advances in documentary film technique made his role unusually significant – and potentially worrying – to the royal family.

The family's film experience had previously been confined to newsreel cameramen and to fixed, elaborately contrived camera locations for ceremonies of state. But Cawston had become an expert in the new techniques of so-called *cinéma vérité*, using hand-held 16 millimetre cameras with synchronised sound-recording to bring greater flexibility and realism to the scenes he shot. This was of great importance, for it meant that, for the first time ever, both the monarch and her family could be filmed quite naturally in any situation exactly as they were. More important still, their casual conversation would be automatically included. Faced with the Cawston cameras, they could effortlessly be themselves.

This was the point at which Cawston's professional concept of the film conflicted with the great taboo about the sacred private image of the royal family. As he himself points out, hardly anyone outside the circle of the Court had ever heard the Queen enunciate a single word, other than from a script and on a thoroughly formal royal occasion. Thus, 'the real break-through was not so much the film as the use we made of sound-track to record the informal dialogue of the family off-duty.'

Interestingly, it was this very point that most concerned Prince Philip in the early stages of production. Cawston had a battle to convince him of its value for the programme, and agreed to a right of veto from the Palace over the finished film. Once convinced, the Prince raised no further problems; and by that summer Cawston and his film crew had also been admitted to the most sacrosanct of royal domains, Balmoral. There they focussed their 16 mm cameras on the Queen, who calmly ignored them as she mixed a salad dressing for the family picnic and her husband barbecued the royal steak.

It was the sort of impromptu family event royalty had always jealously protected in the past: to allow it to be suddenly revealed to a worldwide public in this version of a royal home-movie shows how seriously they themselves had now accepted William Heseltine's idea of presenting that 'human face' of royalty – and how drastically their attitudes had changed towards the media.

Cawston's attitude had changed as well. 'Agnostic' no longer, he had become a dedicated convert to the monarchy as he and his camera crew loyally accompanied the Queen on her state visit to Canada, then back to Britain for the opening of parliament and the ceremonial appearances, official speeches and receptions that comprise the royal year.

This sort of personal 'conversion' frequently occurs with those brought into close and sudden contact with members of the royal family, and no attempt to understand the mystique and influence of the modern monarchy would be complete without appreciating the personal impact of the royal *charisma*. Part of the training royalty endure from childhood is designed to help them cope with the countless, disparate individuals they must meet throughout the year; and, barring occasional lapses, they are very good at it. Granted that their situation permits them few close friendships outside the family circle, there is a Windsor style of affability which combines discreet assumption of the royal dignity with a flattering attention to whoever they meet, considerable reserves of charm and a directness and sense of humour which, backed by the regal aura, usually proves irresistible.

This has always been one of the family's strongest secret weapons, particularly with politicians. Even a theoretical republican like Richard Crossman, who as editor of the socialist *New Statesman* had recently been writing the monarchy off as a more or less absurd anachronism, found himself reluctantly seduced by it during his formal royal duties in the mid-Sixties as Harold Wilson's Lord President of the Council. Cawston had no such preconceptions; and as he found himself not infrequently placed next to Her Majesty at lunch, expertly discussing camera angles and the next stage in the shooting schedule, a genuine *rapport* developed between the Queen and her television film producer.

For one of the qualities about the Queen to remain largely unsuspected at this time was a streak of very simple practicality. Like her husband, she relishes efficiency and enjoys the company of experts able to talk intelligently about their work. Also, like most members of the family, she is fascinated by the world beyond the Palace gates – and television had become a vital way for her to keep in touch with it.

No previous monarch in history had enjoyed this sort of 'window on the world' outside, and the Queen was something of a television addict. Like her subjects, she and her family were keen members of the so-called 'electronic village', and increasingly relied on the small screen for their impressions and opinions of everyday events. They also shared in the popular enjoyment of bread-and-butter television, and one of the favourite programmes of the Queen and Princess Anne was *Crossroads*, the endless television saga of the humdrum lives and dramas of a very ordinary British family.

All this helps explain the ease with which the family cheerfully accepted the role Cawston inevitably wanted them to play. From television they had already learned what to expect and how to behave before the cameras. The mystery and protocol which had previously kept the monarchy so safely shrouded could now yield before the benevolent and universal electronic muse; and instead of looking at the world outside through television, the most famous family in Britain could now reverse the process. They could communicate directly with a nation eager for assurance that the Mountbatten-Windsors were not so very different from anybody else.

Like the natural showman he was, Heseltine was anxious not to waste the element of sheer surprise a film like this could add to the Investiture, and he insisted from the start that Cawston and his colleagues work in strictest secrecy. Cawston had stored his uncut film in a vault at Denham studios, marked with unconscious irony, 'Religious Programmes', and when the completed film was screened in the Palace cinema for royal approval early in the spring of 1969, even the courtiers and members of the family were delighted and surprised by what they saw. For here was the Queen they knew, but as she had never been revealed in public. In some scenes she was acting out her roles of state; in others she was simply the mother of a lively family, on holiday with her husband and children, making them all laugh with an irreverent account of some personage of state she had lately been receiving.

In all earlier appearances on TV, the royal family had kept their casual conversation – and emotions – strictly to themselves. While the world watched their public faces on the television screen, it had been left to some loyal and invariably solemn commentator such as Richard Dimbleby to interpret what they might, or should, be feeling. Now this changed abruptly. Not long before, the theatre critic, Alan Brien, had criticised the way the Queen's appearances, with her spoken words exclusively confined to 'a limited selection of other people's formal clichés', had kept her a stranger from her people. No one could say this now.

In *Royal Family*, as Cawston's film was called, the great taboo against observing the private lives of the Mountbatten-Windsors ended, and for the first time in history people watched and heard royalty behave like normal human beings. Formal and mute no longer, they could now be 'known' as never before; and almost instantly the film appeared to answer the question that is always asked of anyone who meets them: 'What are they *really* like?'

Maybe, as Siriol Hugh-Jones would write, the Queen gave the impression of a determined upper-middle-class lady 'with an account at Harrods', and similar identities could now be given to all the members of the family. To a degree previously unimaginable, anyone who saw the film could identify with one member or another of this very human-seeming family. With the film eventually exhibited in 140 different countries, this would have radical and far-reaching implications for the monarchy, and one wonders just how conscious of this that Palace audience was as it keenly applauded Cawston's film, ignored the royal right of veto, and gave the relieved producer the royal blessing on its screening in a few weeks' time.

As well as his flair for up-to-date publicity, Heseltine's undoubted skills included shrewd coordination. His work as a party political organiser in Australia had made him a clever strategist, and after all those years in which it had been little more than the kennel for the Palace guard-dog, the elegant small office of Her Majesty's Press Secretary was fast transformed into what increasingly resembled a well-run campaign headquarters. This transformation gathered speed as what had started as a fairly simple exercise to 'launch' Prince Charles, and show in the process that the Queen herself was rather human, turned into something more ambitious.

Long before Cawston's film was finished, there was already talk of using it as part of a determined plan to 'relaunch' the jaded monarchy as well, and the Prince's Investiture at Caernarvon Castle in July was accordingly envisaged as some sort of elaborately staged mini-coronation. But whereas the Queen's own Coronation had originally been planned as a solemnly traditional event built round its own historic and religious ritual, this would be something different. Public presentation would be paramount. Television coverage would rule the roost. And everything about it would be deftly dovetailed into the neatest selling operation royalty had ever seen.

The whole campaign offers a fascinating demonstration of something often overlooked by both admirers and critics of the modern monarchy — the sheer efficiency it brings to anything it really puts its mind to. Hidebound attitudes at Court and a lack of royal imagination had contributed to most of the discomforts and disasters since the Coronation; but no one could accuse the royal establishment of idleness, and from now on the timing and arrangements of this royal campaign started clicking into place in a gathering crescendo to make this the most memorable royal spring and summer since the Coronation.

By now the Labour government of Harold Wilson had also scented the political potential of Prince Charles's Investiture, and was all too eager to become involved. It might seem strange to have an administration of self-proclaimed socialists collaborating keenly with a monarchy that embodied much of what it theoretically rejected. This was the party which in 1964 had swept to power in a nationwide reaction against the played-out Tory government of the man the Queen herself had recently appointed Prime Minister, that devotee of grouse-moors, dukes and upper-class attitudes, Sir Alec Douglas-Home: this was the party of the people, pledged four-square against inherited privilege, social inequality and the anti-quated attitudes of an outmoded past, all of which would wither in the new 'white heat' of scientific socialism.

The Queen, on the other hand, owed her entire position to inherit-ance. She was richer than any of her subjects, more privileged, the epitome of seemingly centuries-old tradition, and the keystone and apex of the solidest establishment in Western Europe. But this apparent paradox explains much about the true nature of the monarchy and its role in British politics. For Harold Wilson, like most of his ministers and many of his Labour predecessors, was the most adaptable of socialists, and immensely charmed and flattered by his contacts with the Court. His Tuesday evening audience with Her Majesty was one of the high-points of his week. He found her sympathetic, well-informed and intelligently concerned with current events. The Queen's previous Conservative prime ministers had shared an Olympian tendency to take the support of the monarch for granted, which often irked her. Wilson had no such precon-ceptions, and took extremely seriously his weekly duty of explaining to the monarch what was happening in politics; and the Queen responded to his pithy observations and adroit asides on the Westminster scene.

The Queen's prescribed political neutrality does not mean that she is politically indifferent, and she has always taken seriously her right to 'encourage, warn and be consulted' by her governments. But Churchill had been romantically paternal and verging on senility, Eden impossible and Macmillan distantly avuncular. None had possessed the private style Her Majesty responds to in her statesmen, but Harold Wilson did. That canny Yorkshire power-broker had a cosy knowingness that made his weekly meetings with his monarch a regular success. She was, he said, 'very informal, very well informed, and always very *interested*. On the odd occasion when I'd make maybe, a rather waspish remark about some other politician, she'd have – well – one or two other comments of her own to add.'

With her advancing forties, her experience and interest in politics were growing, and he supplied her with the inside information and political gossip she was learning to enjoy. She, in return, inspired this deeply deferential socialist with an abiding reverence for the monarchy, which would reach its culmination on his retirement as premier in 1974, when the Queen invested him with the plumed hat and dark blue cloak of the most ancient and distinguished honour that is in her gift – the Order of the Garter.

But sentiment and deference apart, Wilson, like all successful politicians, was also conscious of the power of the Crown, and perfectly prepared to use it to maximum political advantage. The atmosphere of national euphoria encouraged by a splendid royal occasion tends to spill over to the government in power – which is one reason why governments of all complexions have long been so lavishly in favour of them. But in 1969 there was an even more compelling reason for the Labour government's enthusiasm for the Prince of Wales's Investiture. The Welsh were increasingly concerned with their national identity. The Welsh Nationalist Party, Plaid Cymru was threatening safe Labour seats. A lunatic fringe of Celtic terrorists were blowing up aqueducts and drawing lessons from the IRA. Now if ever was the time for the Prince of Wales to come to the aid of the Party.

Soon the government was working closely with the Palace over the preparations for the Prince's role. It was suggested that as Prince of Wales he ought to spend at least a term at a Welsh University, to demonstrate solidarity with young Welsh students and learn the basics of their convoluted language. R. A. Butler, now Lord Butler and Master of Trinity, objected to the way the Prince's studies were being sacrificed to political advantage: A. J. P. Taylor went still further, accusing the Prime Minister of imposing on the Prince an ordeal he would not have inflicted on his own son.

But the Prince was a game young man. Anxious to live down his reputation as a softy and to play to the hilt the role his family were now involved in, he stoically endured eight long weeks at the University College of Wales at Aberystwyth. Encouraged by that quintessential Welshman, the Secretary of State for Wales, George Thomas, he mastered some rudimentary Welsh and showed himself perfectly prepared to discuss Welsh aspirations with his fellow students. It was, of course, a calculated risk, relying on his youth, his personality and the vigilance of his personal security men. One must admire his courage and his sense of humour as he rose to the occasion. 'The things I do for England!' he was sometimes heard to mutter.

Prince Charles was scheduled to provide the effective curtain-raiser to that most surprising royal summer; and like everything on the family agenda, his unveiling had been carefully worked out in advance through the combined endeavours of the Palace Press Office, Neilson McCarthy Ltd and the BBC. Together they successfully produced his first full broadcast interview in public.

It was an interesting example of how these things were done, for one of David Checketts' fellow directors at Neilson McCarthy was the veteran broadcaster, Jack di Manio, who also contributed to a highly popular interview programme on BBC morning radio. Who better than this well-known colleague of the Prince's secretary to conduct the interview and ensure that His Royal Highness was presented in the way required? The session was painlessly recorded at the Palace for the BBC, with the questions carefully prepared to let the Prince talk unselfconsciously on the subject he knew most about – himself.

In itself, the interview was not particularly startling, but the Prince was wonderfully relaxed and showed himself something of a natural broadcaster. There were no impromptu revelations and certainly no indiscretions, but when the programme was transmitted in the second week of March, it produced a mild sensation. For just as with the sound-track to the Cawston film, the broadcast broke the terrible taboo against unscripted royal conversation being heard in public. Everyone knew the Prince's face: what was unknown was his personality, and here suddenly one heard (or thought one did, which amounts to much the same) the *real* Prince of Wales, supremely open and unstuffy and an obviously likeable young man.

But the interview was not as artless as clever Jack di Manio made it seem. The questions had been carefully worked out, and the most intriguing point about them was the way they led the Prince to do something royalty had never done before in public – talk freely and intelligibly about the experience of actually *being* royal.

When, di Manio inquired, had the Prince first realised as a small boy that he was heir to the throne?

I think it's something that dawns on you with the most ghastly, inexorable sense. I didn't wake up in my pram one day and say, 'Yippee!' But I think it dawns on you slowly that people are interested in you, and slowly it dawns on you that you have a certain duty and responsibility.

Was the Prince worried at the prospect of the Investiture, with trouble likely from Welsh nationalists?

As long as I don't get covered too much in egg and tomato, I'll be all right. I don't blame people demonstrating like that. They've never seen me before. They don't know what I'm like. I've hardly been to Wales, and you can't expect people to be overzealous about the fact of having a so-called English Prince come amongst them.

It was a smart answer on a tricky subject, for the Prince had been well primed by his advisers; but he also made it plain that he understood the implications and discomforts of his situation, was none too keen on them, but remained determined to do his duty.

As he explained all this, it was as if he were combining two quite separate beings: the amiable Cambridge undergraduate called Charles, and the royal personage he was also forced to be, HRH the Prince of Wales. Charles was real, but Prince of Wales was the role which, 'ghastly and inexorable' though it might be, he was set to play. He was perfectly prepared to talk about it too, in terms which everyone could understand, and in doing so he shared with his audience the problems and the strange experience of being royal.

He was in fact creating much the same reaction as Claud Cockburn had picked on to explain that sudden burst of unexpected popularity for George V at his Silver Jubilee in 1935 – 'fellow-feeling' and the sense of being 'virtually one of US . . . endlessly harried by the bloody politicians.' But whereas his great-grandfather never actually shared his inner feelings with his subjects, Charles did – and at considerable length during the weeks to come, as the television interviewers were encouraged to close in on him in the final run-up to the Investiture. Never before had any member of the royal family chosen to disclose anything remotely like the ordinary humanity Charles revealed during these engrossing weeks.

As well as an interview with David Frost, there was a joint

discussion with Cliff Michelmore from BBC TV and Brian Connell from ITV. Did Prince Philip, Michelmore inquired, ever tell his son to 'sit down and shut up'? 'The whole time' replied the Prince, and very good for him it was, although he was now becoming 'a bit more independent. I think I may be slightly late in developing . . .'

What did he most admire about the Queen?

'She has a marvellous sense of humour and is terribly sensible and wise.'

And Brian Connell, slipping a question in without prior warning, showed Charles attempting to explain the curious dilemma of his *alter ego*, HRH the Prince of Wales.

'Do you have any thoughts about the lady the Prince of Wales should marry?'

Charles paused; then rapidly recovered as he tried to reconcile his private wishes with his public role:

This is awfully difficult, because you've got to remember that when you marry, in my position, you are going to marry somebody who perhaps one day is going to become Queen. You've got to choose somebody very carefully, I think, who could fulfil this particular role, because people like you, perhaps, would expect quite a lot from somebody like that, and it has got to be somebody pretty special; and the one advantage about marrying a princess, or somebody from a royal family, is that they do know what happens. The only trouble is I often feel I would like to marry someone English – or perhaps Welsh.

Charles was also shown on television in Cawston's *Royal Family* film, which was screened twice to audiences estimated at 15 million in the fortnight before the Investiture. Here in the context of the family he appeared an ideal elder son clearly devoted to his parents, and a sensitive and caring brother to his younger siblings. The first important stage of William Heseltine's campaign was virtually complete, and the board of Neilson McCarthy could be satisfied that their 'first class product', Charles Princes of Wales, was 'criminally undersold' no longer.

These had been a hallucinatory few weeks for anyone remotely interested in the monarchy – which by now included a large proportion of the total population. For suddenly it seemed as if real human beings were emerging from behind those familiar public royal masks, and unselfconsciously discussing who they were and what they did and how they felt about the world around them.

But the Investiture itself would provide the culminating ritual which everyone had grown to expect of royalty. The public myth of monarchy now relied upon its cyclical renewal through grand and elaborately staged ceremonies of state in which the family assumed their charismatic roles before their subjects via the television cameras. The last of these royal transformation scenes occurred at Princess Margaret's wedding nine years earlier; another one was clearly overdue.

The Prince's Investiture was a perfect opportunity to mount a magnificent full-scale royal occasion; but it also presented certain problems, and here more than anywhere one sees the royal family's skill at what has been called 'the invention of tradition'. There was, in fact, no genuine tradition of 'investing' the royal son and heir; and, truth to tell, the Queen herself had not been very certain of what she meant when she had publicly declared, in a recorded message to the massed gathering of Welshman at Cardiff Arms Park in July 1958, that she would 'one day present my son, the Prince of Wales, to you.'

The original 'presentation' of the first Prince of Wales, in 1301 was hardly an appropriate memory to revive at a time like this, having been a demonstration of that English domination of the revolting Welsh to which *Plaid Cymru* still bitterly objected. The first King Edward had laid waste their country, killed their tenderly remembered hero, Llewelyn ap Gruffyd, and, after establishing Caernarvon Castle as his military stronghold, proclaimed his son 'Prince of Wales' from its battlements to signify the permanence of English rule.

Subsequent English kings had tactfully refrained from upsetting the susceptible Celts by repeating Edward's public 'presentation', although the title 'Prince of Wales' was generally conferred upon the male heir by simple royal decree; and the first true public 'Investiture' of a Prince of Wales had been the inspired notion of the Prime Minister of the day, Lloyd George, the 'Welsh chameleon', as Maynard Keynes described him. In 1911, anxious to cement his reputation in his homeland by drawing on the current popularity of the royal family, he had suggested to the new king, George V, that the time had come for some sort of ceremony to mark the conferring of this ancient honour on the seventeen-year-old Prince of Wales in the land from which he took his title.

In many ways the situation was not dissimilar to that in which Prince Charles was now involved, with both the monarchy and the government sensing mutual advantage in an act of splendidly enacted royal ceremonial. Lloyd George had wanted the royal presence to enhance his own political mystique in that cradle of Welsh tribal consciousness, Caernarvon Castle; and King George, who loathed and heartily distrusted him, thought that in spite of this such an act might help bind the Liberal party to the Crown, and enhance the aura of both the monarchy and the fledgling Prince of Wales.

The great Court impressario, Lord Esher, had only recently been revamping all the regal ceremonial surrounding coronations and royal funerals, and for courtiers able to concoct the exotic pageantry of King George's Delhi Durbar, the abrupt creation of an appropriately 'traditional' royal ritual round a notional event like this Welsh 'Investiture' was child's play.

Decked out in purple with ermine cloak and satin breeches, like a principal boy in pantomime, the future Duke of Windsor had bitterly resented the whole embarrassing affair. He finally agreed to participate at his father's angry insistence, and said afterwards that he only hoped the uncomfortable business 'would help Papa in his dealings with difficult Mr Lloyd George'.

Prince Charles was three years older and considerably more self-assured than his great-uncle had been. Adroitly coached and then projected at the centre of a brilliant publicity campaign, he was already highly popular. The Caernarvon ceremony would be the climax to this creation of a convincing royal aura round the Prince, but there remained the problem faced by George V and his advisers. In the absence of any historic precedent for a royal investiture, what form should it take?

Lloyd George's pageant was no real answer, and there was now one dominating influence to consider: the eager participation of international television. At the Queen's Coronation it had been reluctantly admitted like an uninvited guest; now the whole ceremony was to be built quite unashamedly around it. But television would not have wielded the influence it did over the actual format of the extraordinary event had it not been for the presence in the family itself of its own communicator-royal, the monarch's brother-in-law, the Earl of Snowdon.

As we have seen, the photographer Earl had failed in his hoped-for role as a supernumerary major royal personality, but here at last was one event in which his interests and undoubted talents could enhance the family mystique. In 1963 he had been appointed Constable of Caernarvon Castle, and as such was now effectively in charge of the Investiture.

For twelve years he had been helping to project the image of the royal family with the informal and official photographs he had been privileged to take as the family's own resident photographer-in-chief. But this was his biggest challenge since his involvement with the monarchy, and in many ways he was ideally suited to make this tricky exercise of royal showmanship the culminating spectacle it had to be. As a royal husband he had failed to reinvigorate the monarchy: now, through the media, he might yet succeed.

He had the Messel flair for theatre, and wide contacts with both stage and television. As an employee of the *Sunday Times* and a television film producer in his own right, he was a 'media person' to his finger-tips. He was also a keen and ingenious amateur designer, famous for the controversial aviary he designed for the London Zoo. On top of this, the home of the Armstrong-Joneses, Plas Dinas, was near Caernarvon Castle, making the Earl an authentic home-grown Welshman – 'Charlie's Uncle Taffy', as one commentator cheerfully described him. What Lord Esher had done for the presentation of the monarchy at the turn of the century, Snowdon looked like doing in the 1960s.

But the Earl possessed one obvious advantage Lord Esher had lacked – his unanswerable authority as a member of the family. He used it to remarkable effect. This was the moment when the whole campaign to modernise the image of the monarchy might have faltered as traditionists at court produced some muted version of the Coronation ceremony. But Snowdon was even more convinced than Heseltine of the need to use the most up-to-date media techniques to propagate the message of the revamped monarchy – so much so that at times it seemed as if the medium really had become the message.

At the time there was some amusement – and more than a touch of outrage from traditionists – at the way the Earl conducted things. Jokes were made about the zippered bottle-green 'royal bell-hop's uniform' he concocted for himself as Castle 'constable', and suggestions made by the Garter King of Arms, head of the ancient College of Arms, for a massed display of various heraldic banners, were briskly overruled. So were suggestions for the sort of mock medieval awnings and miles of royal red carpet which had been rolled out back in 1911.

The Earl was a designer, and he worked like one. He brought in his own team of assistants to create every visual detail of the ceremony, from the plywood knock-down chairs for the audience, to the slate thrones and the space-age laminated perspex canopy, surmounted with gilded Prince of Wales Feathers, built by the ICI Plastics Division and wind-tunnel-tested against gusts of sixty miles an hour. He also supervised the form of the royal souvenirs on sale to the public, insisted that the distinguished audience within the castle be kept to a televisually acceptable 4,000 (as opposed to the 11,000 crammed in in 1911) and persuaded the Queen herself to wear sensible shoes for walking across the uncarpeted expanse of bright green turf. He wanted a splash of colour on the television screens, for this was the first great royal occasion to enjoy the heightened impact of colour television, and he was determined to make the most of it.

'*I* don't regard myself as part of show-business,' Sir Anthony Wagner, Garter King of Arms, peevishly remarked; but having overruled him, Snowdon made no secret of the fact that he was approaching the ceremony like a television film director. 'I have designed the whole thing for television,' he explained. 'We have this great piece of medieval architecture as a set.' As he prepared to use King Edward's ancient castle to maximum effect, the Duke of Norfolk – in what would prove his swan-song as Master-in-chief of royal ceremonial – collaborated closely to produce the format of the actual pageantry; and the result proved to be five hours of top-billing royal television.

That summer of 1969 was important in the annals of international TV. In just a few weeks' time, experimental satellite link-ups would enable viewers round the world to participate 'live' in the landings on the moon. And on July 1 the new transmitter at Goonhilly Down used the same satellite technology to beam the 'Investiture' of the heir to the world's most famous monarchy to an estimated audience of half a billion. This sort of mammoth royal programme was certainly the only show Britain could now produce with an international appeal remotely rivalling the Americans' leap in space: and its success was a tribute both to Snowdon's skill as a director and to the power of television to convey worldwide the illusion and emotion of his carefully created spectacle.

Even more, it showed the extraordinary power of the Mountbatten-Windsors to endow even an invented modern royal occasion such as this with the instant authenticity of apparently time-honoured ritual. From the days of Victoria's far-off Jubilees, the family and their advisers had steadily perfected their public ceremonial: watching them now against the background of King Edward's castle, surrounded by the trappings of the Household Cavalry, the coaches and the trumpeters, it was hard to believe that this was actually not part of some cherished royal ceremony lovingly preserved across the centuries.

The Prince's own procession was particularly grand. It echoed the ancient pomp of the Queen's procession at her Coronation, complete with Heralds, Lords-in-Waiting and assorted Celtic peers bearing his freshly made insignia: and the climax of the ceremony consisted in the Queen's crowning of the Prince with his very modern gold and platinum coronet, after he knelt before her to declare:

I, Charles, Prince of Wales, do become your liege man of life and limb and earthly worship, and faith and truth I will bear unto you to live and die against all manner of folks.

It was the feudal oath his father had sworn at the Coronation, and like much of the Investiture its strict relevance to the Prince's situation – quite apart from its actual meaning – was none too obvious. But as one final piece of royal theatre the sonorous medieval phrases matched the moment, and the emotion they created in the predominantly Welsh audience was palpable. By the time the coroneted Prince had read a final speech in Welsh and been 'presented' by the Queen at the three gates of the Castle, many shared the feelings which the Mayor of Caernarvon had loyally expressed. Prince Charles, he hymned, was no longer 'just a boy. He was a *Prince*! You could have put a suit of armour on that lad and sent him off to Agincourt!'

It would be hard to find an apter tribute, not simply to the Prince, but also to the uncanny power of modern royalty to clothe itself in the illusion of ancient royal glories. But nostalgia and hyperbole apart, the Investiture had been a remarkable success in bringing some very practical and up-to-date results for those involved in it. The Labour government was delighted with the royal family – and so they should have been, for as Harold Wilson had foreseen, the Prince's Investiture achieved its purpose to perfection. The fledgling Prince had done something no politician, Welsh or English, could have managed in a lifetime. Following the ceremony he toured the Principality in person, meeting warmth and great enthusiasm everywhere he went. By the time his tour ended, Welsh separatism – and the faintest sympathy for the Welsh Liberation Army – had been killed stone dead.

For the Prince himself had now emerged as a major force within the monarchy, as both Neilson and Checketts had originally realised he could, given the proper presentation. Within a space of weeks, he had been projected as his family's most popular and charismatic superstar, far surpassing the 'Prince Charming' image enjoyed by his great-uncle David during his period of greatest popularity as Prince of Wales. Indeed, one wonders what that sad-faced phantom felt as he too viewed the ceremony, with his Duchess there beside him, on their television set in Paris.

The contrast between this 'launching' of Prince Charles and the status his great-uncle had gradually achieved as Prince of Wales, points up the crucial role the Palace and the publicists had now assumed in creating the instant myth of royalty. For the Duke of Windsor's popularity as royal heir had gathered its momentum over several years of service in the First World War and his subsequent tours of the empire. But during these extraordinary few weeks, Prince Charles had not been merely 'presented' as Prince of Wales: he had been endowed with a brand new public personality to match – and so efficiently, that public awareness of the Prince was dramatically transformed. He was suddenly shown as the personal embodiment of every princely quality to appeal to the greatest number.

This in itself was an achievement for, as one perceptive observer pointed out at the time, 'in a number of subtle ways, Charles, unlike Anne, is not really in tune with the majority of his generation' with his 'gentlemanly tranquillity', his old-fashioned taste in clothes and music, and his introverted, rather contemplative nature. Despite this, almost overnight the nation was given to understand that Prince Charles was concerned and yet courageous, civilised but something of a stand-up comic, a real swinger, but also a responsible young man with a profound respect for tradition, service, and family.

Nor did this image-building cease with the Prince of Wales. By the time the television films and the Investiture were over, Princess Anne was also 'launched' as a model modern royal daughter, and the whole royal family seemed fully attuned both to the time and to the emotions and ambitions of their subjects. According to the findings of Mass Observation, the film *Royal Family*, even before the Investiture, had already been 'remarkably successful in changing the popular view of royalty; and what is more, in changing it in those fields in which the Queen, in particular, had previously been thought to be weak.' Mass Observation found that she had always been thought to be 'extremely conscientious' and this belief continued: at the same time those who thought Her Majesty 'outspoken' rose from 27 to 42 percent, 'powerful' from 49 to 64 percent, and 'in touch with what is going on' from 69 to 81 percent.

All this had happened in a space of weeks, but it was unquestionably the televised production of the Caernarvon Investiture – 'the most highly publicised royal ceremony held in Britain since the Coronation', as researchers at the University of Leeds described it – that put the seal of true success upon one of the most ambitious and important selling operations ever mounted in this country.

Apart from its coordination – which was directed with outstanding virtuosity – the real triumph of the whole campaign lay in the way it realised its aim without apparently cheapening the monarchy. For it was mounted with immense discretion, so that even to this day few realise quite how much work and careful preparation really lay behind the whole concerted effort to 'relaunch' the British monarchy in 1969.

Only in retrospect does one see the key to its success in the way the sharpest and most up-to-date techniques of PR and the modern media were skilfully combined with the tried and tested methods which the monarchy itself had been perfecting to propagate the royal mystique since the final years of Queen Victoria. Deference, nostalgia, splendid ceremony and religious ritual – all were present in that culminating act of wonderfully invented royal tradition, when the Prince exchanged his familiar *persona* as 'young Charles' for his royal role as the crowned and majestically proclaimed Prince of Wales.

Here was the sanctifying act on which the modern monarchy relies for the ultimate creation of its central myth: the ritual transformation scene as the climax to this piece of never-failing royal drama.

Just as with his mother at her Coronation, the vast television audience shared in the hypnotic process which, for all its deep irrationality, would potently establish Charles Prince of Wales in his superhuman status as presumptive future King of England. Henceforth his official supremacy to everyone except the Queen herself would be unquestioned: automatic deference would be his due from the humblest to the greatest in the land: and as long as the monarchy itself endures, he would be established on his lonely pinnacle at the peak of our curious society.

Because the Investiture appeared so much a part of ancient royal tradition, it disguised the fact that something revolutionary had happened to the monarchy during these extraordinary weeks. Widespread popular identification with individual members of the royal family had long formed part of its appeal, but in the past this process had been rigidly controlled by keeping royalty as largely symbolic figures set carefully above the populace. This had enabled them to stand as the embodiment of clear-cut regal attitudes and virtues such as family morality, service to the Commonwealth and Empire, adherence to the Church of England, and patriotic faith in a united nation.

As these beliefs had faltered, so had interest in the royal family itself, and the PR men and mass communicators headed by Her Majesty's own Press Secretary, had tried to reinforce the monarchy with their original plan to show the 'human face of royalty'. At the time it seemed logical and few had actually foreseen the force it had produced – still less worked out its implications for the future.

For the combination of PR men and courtiers had stumbled on a formula to guarantee virtually unending popularity and worldwide interest in the Mountbatten-Windsors as royal superstars. They were unique and tailor-made for such a role, as the staggering success of these recent weeks had shown. Interest in royalty had never been generated before on anything approaching the sheer scale which television now made possible – nor had it ever been so easy to identify with all the members of one single royal family. Certainly no prince in history had ever been presented with a public role to equal that which television had suddenly created round Prince Charles.

In some ways this was reassuring for the royal family: at least they would never end up now in that museum which had been worrying Prince Philip barely eighteen months earlier. But could they reconcile their superstar role with the more serious elements of monarchy? Could they bear the ballyhoo? And would their evident reliance upon electronic image-making turn them into mere performers for an ever more demanding worldwide audience?

Fears such as these were voiced by several of the more traditional courtiers that autumn. One of them even told the author Andrew Duncan that the film *Royal Family* should be 'locked in the Palace vaults and not be allowed to be seen by anyone for at least ten years'.

Among others who agreed was Cawston's colleague at the BBC, David Attenborough, who, remembering what he had observed in primitive societies, spoke ominously of the troubles that ensued when tribesmen broke the old taboos and peered at the tribal myseries inside the headman's hut.

Less hypothetically, the theatre critic Milton Shulman posed the crucial question which would increasingly concern the court and the royal family itself during the years ahead:

Is it, in the long run, wise for the Queen's advisers to set as a precedent this right of the television camera to act as an image-making apparatus for the monarchy? Every institution that has so far attempted to use TV to popularise or aggrandise itself, has been trivialised by it.

10

THE PRICE OF POPULARITY

'Would you like the Queen to queue in a crowd of shoppers
in a London store, or Prince Philip to strap-hang in a packed
London tube train? Or would you prefer to keep your Queen
and her family just that little bit remote from everybody else?
I think you would. We know them so well.'

Sunday Dispatch

Revived, revivified, and on a peak of popularity it had not known
since the Coronation, the monarchy could face the Seventies with
confidence, but the very scale of the success of the campaign to
'relaunch' the monarchy round Prince Charles's Investiture brought
an inevitable reaction. Just before the new decade began, the *Sunday
Telegraph*, which eighteen months before had called its sovereign an
'arch-square', now had its principal columnist complaining that the
royal family had in fact been 'over-humanised'.

> Being relaxed and informal, unpompous and human is not really
> the essence of the monarchical function . . . So successful have the
> modernisers been in turning the royal family into human beings
> that they seem increasingly ill-at-ease on the occasions when they
> have to be what they are primarily intended to be: symbols of
> authority and majesty.

Thus spoke the paper's own resident 'arch-square', Peregrine
Worsthorne, and, contrariness apart, he had put his finger on a point
of genuine anxiety for the Court. As Prince Philip himself had said,
something fairly fundamental had had to happen if the English
monarchy was to avoid ending up in that 'museum' he had feared
for it in 1967, but might the cure turn out to be even more dangerous
than the disease?

Could one humanise the royal family and yet preserve their
'sacred' and symbolic functions? Would the gathering dependence
on the media – and in particular on televison – end in that 'trivialising' of the monarchy Milton Shulman feared? And had the royal
family allowed themselves to be stampeded into an injudicious

change of policy by the wiles and professional techniques of enthusiastic media men? Had it all been a horrible mistake?

In a Court not previously renowned for its adventurousness towards publicity, there were those who thought it definitely had. It was firmly intimated to William Heseltine that enough had been enough and that for the foreseeable future there would be no repetition of that sort of conscious media engineering he had performed with possibly too much success. Phrases like 'image-making' and 'PR' became – and still remain – strongly taboo within the royal presence, and despite a loyal outcry from her disappointed subjects Her Majesty even vetoed her now traditional Christmas message to the nation on TV that year. Needless to say, that patriotic publicist Nigel Neilson received no decoration for his important work behind the scenes throughout Prince Charles's debut. Awareness of his close relationship with the Prince of Wales and his private secretary had done no harm to Neilson's prestige among his other famous clients, but an honour would have meant officially acknowledging his role – which would have not been politic. Despite this, Neilson McCarthy Ltd were permitted the strange privilege of continuing to employ the Prince's secretary as a supernumerary director at £5,000 a year, such service to the Crown presumably being looked on as its own reward.

But while the Court appeared intent upon forgetting both the methods and the implications of the whole extraordinary campaign created round Prince Charles's Investiture, it did not fail to make the most of the enormous popularity it created, and from now on there is a notable improvement in the sureness with which the monarchy faced and dealt with some of its more controversial problems. Not for the first time in the reign, the chief initiative behind this new mood of royal realism came from Prince Philip; and not for the first time in the history of the monarchy itself, the chief points at issue generally converged in that historic area where crown and commoners have always clashed – finance. With gathering inflation, the costs of maintaining the whole royal establishment had been worrying the Court for some time: at the accession the Queen had been voted £475,000 a year for the annual expenses of herself and certain members of her family. In 1970, inflation brought civil list expenditure up to £745,000, leaving a deficit of £240,000. As Prince Philip remarked on an American television programme late in 1969, if something was not done about it quickly, 'the royal family would go into the red next year' and might have to leave Buckingham Palace. 'We have had to sell a small yacht, and I shall have to give up polo soon. Things like that.'

The Prince was exaggerating, as he sometimes did – although this did not stop a group of patriotic London dockers starting a fund to buy him a polo pony. But nowhere are royal attitudes more ambivalent – or more revealing – than over that magical yet mundane substance, money: and nowhere else, with the possible exception of sexual scandal, is royalty more vulnerable to criticism.

One of the recurring myths about the monarchy is the widely held idea – untrue – that royalty never carry money, for part of the folk-mythology about them insists on their dream-like immunity to commonplace concern with lucre. Within the modern monarchy several residual examples of this old immunity have fruitfully continued, as in the monarch's freedom from taxation and the veil of absolute discretion loyally drawn across the inner mystery at the heart of the royal finances.

At the Palace the Queen's wealth is treated as one of the most sacred attributes of royalty. It is as if royal wealth were in a different category from ordinary money, best treated by the world outside as if it did not actually exist. No royal will is ever published; royal investments, which are shrewdly placed and regularly updated through the Queen's personal stockbrokers, Rowe and Pitman, are the best-kept secret in the City; and no courtier has ever dared divulge the dread secret of just how rich Her Majesty might be.

One reason for this reticence is that no one knows exactly, since the whole question of the royal wealth is something of a muddle in which everything depends on what you actually include and how you value it. At current market rates, the royal art collection alone would make Her Majesty what she is often said to be – the richest woman in the world. But although certain pictures she has bought herself are naturally considered as her private property, and although George V once seemed dangerously impressed by an offer of £50,000 for a royal Rembrandt from the irrepressible dealer, Lord Duveen (only to be later told by the shocked Surveyor of his Pictures, Kenneth Clark, was that the offer was 'unthinkable and most improper'), the royal collection is regarded as part of the nation's heritage – although the nation has no chance of seeing more than a fraction of its treasures. Similarly, the royal palaces like Windsor Castle, Kensington Palace and Buckingham Palace, though used by the royal family, are owned and maintained by the state. Balmoral and Sandringham, however, are the monarch's property.

While the Queen's actual fortune is a secret, so is the income she receives from the last of the historic royal demesnes, the Duchy of Lancaster. (However the income traditionally received by the Prince of Wales from his various possessions in the Duchy of Cornwall is not a secret. In 1984 its properties in Kennington and throughout the West Country brought him just over £1 million, so that *his* polo-playing, on which he spends £80,000 a year, is not at risk.) But following the practice dating back to George III, the monarch at the accession surrenders the hereditary revenues from the rest of the Crown estates for the duration of the reign in return for the annual income voted by parliament under the Civil List.

The nearest the public ever got to an answer on the subject of the royal wealth came from Lord Tryon, the Queen's Treasurer and Keeper of the Privy Purse, to a parliamentary committee after suggestions had been made that she was undoubtedly 'the richest woman in the world' with an annual income in excess of £50 million. 'Her Majesty would like to make it clear,' he said, 'that such suggestions are much exaggerated.' Despite this, with the Queen's freedom from taxation, her immense capital resources and the advice of the City's shrewdest financial consultants on the royal investments, it is not 'exaggerated' to suggest that Prince Charles will inherit a fortune of immense proportions when he finally succeeds his mother.

Naturally it suits the Crown to keep the extent of its wealth a secret, and the royal family has always carefully maintained the habit, first adopted by George V and Queen Mary, of personal economy and even parsimony in its daily life. They seemed to watch the pence, while the millions were very shrewdly taken care of for them.

This was not so much an example of the well-attested avarice of the super-rich, as an effort to project a public image of the royal family sharing the problems of its humblest subjects. While the Crown steadily and secretly increased its wealth, it always managed to avoid the impression of a profligate and wasteful dynasty. From the dresses handed on from Princess Elizabeth to her sister, to Prince Charles's well-known passion for economy, the family has always kept a weather eye on its finances, and courtiers can still find themselves drinking tea from cups with the monogram of George VI. As the well-informed Court correspondent, Douglas Keay, has said,

'Most things last a long time at Buckingham Palace, and nothing is wasted.'

But carefulness apart, and talk of 'going into the red' notwith-standing, the idea of the monarchy in serious financial straits was nonsense. The monarchy was far too rich for this to be a possibility. However, there was the problem of the future; and there was also a strong feeling in the family that since the Civil List was originally based on an excellent bargain for the government, and since the monarchy performed important public functions, the government and public ought to pay for them. As Walter Bagehot wrote on the subject *à propos* of Queen Victoria, 'there is an argument for no Court, but not for a measly Court.'

Despite this, and despite gathering inflation, the Crown might easily have had serious difficulties in obtaining an increase of the Civil List from parliament. For the court was undisguisedly attempting to get the best of two financial worlds – winning its 'pay rise' while retaining all its fiscal privileges and offering parliament no real information on its capital resources or its income from investments, land and property. It could easily become a highly controversial issue, and it is arguable whether the uninspiring monarchy of the 1960s could have got away with it.

Even as it was, in 1971, with a Conservative government back in power, the Queen's request to parliament for additional provision for members of the royal family through the Civil List resulted in a joint parliamentary committee which produced two very different answers. It was unanimously agreed that an increase was justified, but while the Conservatives were all for granting it without conditions, Liberal and Labour members wanted more information about the Court, and a new government department created to deal specifically with matters relating to the Crown.

Such a department might easily have been the thin end of a most unwelcome wedge for the monarchy, leading irrevocably to such royal nightmares as open accounting of the court finances, an end to the Queen's exemption from taxation, and ultimate control by parliament of much of the royal finances. The proposal was rejected and the Queen and her household got their increase from the Civil List to £980,000 a year, along with increased annuities to other members of the family. But what is interesting is that even when a Labour government returned to power, nothing was done to implement its earlier ideas about a government department for the

Crown. Nor, despite some huffing and puffing from Labour back-benchers over the bad example to a much-taxed nation of a tax-free sovereign, was there any real governmental threat to the happy and unique status of Her Majesty's finances.

In terms of parliamentary logic her position was distinctly hard to justify. Over the years, the royal immunity to taxation and death duties had made the royal family richer than the richest of the aristocracy, and while inflation had increased the cost of the royal establishments it had also increased the value of those secret royal investments, and its property and land. As the *New Statesman* pointed out:

> The Queen has astute advisers. Like any other multimillionairess, she seeks and gets prudent advice; and she must be a much wealthier woman, both absolutely and relatively, than she was at the accession.

Or as Willie Hamilton MP was to put it, with a touch of that hyperbole which had rapidly established him as the country's best known, if somewhat solitary, republican:

> Beneath the [Queen's] smooth and shining veneer the machinations are revealed of a shrewd and calculating businesswoman.

But Willie Hamilton could count on the support of a working-class Glasgow constituency where he was popular as an excellent constituency MP. Not all his other left-wing parliamentary colleagues could, and as realists (and even left-wing politicians tend to be realistic when their parliamentary future is at stake) the Labour Party had become as loyally convinced of the new-found royal popularity as any staunch Conservative. Popularity is power, where voters are concerned, and thanks to the popularity that stemmed from the royal revival at the Investiture, the monarch was now able to do something rarely managed by any of her predecessors, effortlessly beating parliament, hands down, over a potentially explosive question of finance.

In 1975 the Labour Government effectively lifted the whole subject of the payment from the Civil List out of controversy for the future, by agreeing to have royal allowances regularly updated in line with inflation. There was no more talk about a royal department in the government, and total secrecy about Her Majesty's finances was never questioned – nor was her freedom from taxation. The Court, relying on its popularity, had stood its ground, and shown in the process that no politician could afford to challenge the monarchy over its privileged position in the state.

The self-confidence and skill with which the Court handled the whole question of the Civil List affair is the best example of the way it increasingly relied on its popularity to consolidate itself throughout the Seventies. 'Over-exposed' its members might be, but people were not, as Muggeridge had predicted, getting bored with them. Quite the contrary: the royal 'story' was not 'coming to an end' but gathering momentum all the time as its public, both in Britain and throughout the world, became increasingly addicted to the antics and the personalities of British royalty.

This needs some explanation, for always in the past the excitement created round a coronation or a royal wedding had invariably been followed by a reaction and a slump in public interest. This had occurred dramatically in both the Fifties and the Sixties, and it might have been expected even more so in the Seventies: for by then most of those resounding qualities which had once been personally embodied in the godlike beings of the pre-war House of Windsor had begun to lose their pull on the collective heart-strings of the nation.

The old Empire died at Suez. The Church of England, of which Her Majesty was still officially 'Defender', saw its congregations dwindling despite the royal family's example every Sunday morning. Those stern concepts, duty and morality, which had earned Queen Mary such ungrudging admiration no longer exercised a more sophisticated nation. Even patriotism, which traditionally inspired the British in their thousands to lay down their lives for 'King – or Queen – and Country', could no longer be the focus for an emotional cult of monarchy.

So what could? The answer undoubtedly resides in that human factor which had been so energetically projected round the royal family during Prince Charles's Investiture; but why should its potency continue to increase, with the Investiture over and forgotten and the Palace showing little inclination to continue William Heseltine's royal exposure programme in its aftermath?

Here we arrive at the most crucial area of change in the whole phenomenon of the modern monarchy.

As the Queen Mother had discovered while still Duchess of York in the early Thirties, the most potent force within a 'democratic' monarchy lay in its power to project itself as a profoundly normal family apparently enjoying simple pleasures in its royal situation. She had carefully encouraged this image, and such was her charm, and such her skill with journalists, that she, her husband and her daughters had become a sort of ultimate English family, much loved two-dimensional characters whom people felt instinctively they 'knew' as they watched and grew up with them through the years.

With the new reign this had changed. A far more private person than her mother, with no intention of submitting her children to the sort of public scrutiny she and Princess Margaret had endured when young, the Queen had done her best to keep the Palace shutters up throughout their childhood. When the shutters were suddenly drawn back at the time of the Investiture, there was once again a human and united royal family on display for a fascinated nation to identify with. But thanks to a sea-change both in public attitudes and in the media, the whole process of identifying with the members of this ultimate family meant something less contrived and decorous than it had in those sentimental days when the good Miss Ring or the gushing Cynthia Asquith penned their dainty tableaux of the royal bedtimes with the young princesses.

For now the grand illusion of the television screen allowed the family to enter that third dimension which their pre-war presentation had lacked, and this sudden revelation of royalty as natural human beings was of the essence of the tribal mystery which David Attenborough warned lay hidden in the headman's hut. One might have thought with him that the effect would prove bathetic, rather like Hans Christian Andersen's small boy pointing out that the emperor was naked after all. But quite the opposite had happened. As the Investiture ceremony proved, the myth of monarchy created in its ritual transformation scenes was as powerful as ever, and so was the public instinct to relate to these regal figures in their human context.

But unlike those long-gone, deferential days before the war, there were no limits to the public curiosity and effectively few taboos on what could now be asked or speculated about these infinitely famous people. Even if *Royal Family* were consigned to the royal vaults for ever, a new way of regarding royalty had been established. That fatal 'glimpse' inside the headman's hut could not be 'unglimpsed', however much some members of the Court might wish it possible; for once royalty had stepped out of their mute, symbolic role, they could not return to it. From living symbols they had been transmuted into living personalities.

This was to prove of infinite importance to the future of the monarchy, affecting both its role and the mainsprings of its popularity. The Seventies would see these implications working out, and it was at this moment after the Investiture, when the Court was still attempting to come to terms with what had happened, that a new member of the family suddenly emerged to carry the humanising process one step further – Prince Charles's twenty-year-old sister, the unrestrained and extrovert Princess Anne.

It is not generally appreciated just how important Princess Anne became during this period, for the future of the royal family. She was essentially a new phenomenon, and it is hard to understand the changes in her family without seeing what was happening to her.

Having been ritually unveiled and presented to the nation as a very human heir apparent, Prince Charles tended to retire from the limelight, to follow the family tradition of service in the Royal Navy. This was not terribly exciting to the public, and as heir apparent he was carefully protected from their inadvertent gaze. His public image having been established, there were no further revelations in this period; nor, to be honest, was there much to be revealed – apart from his love-life, which was pursued with remarkable discretion, thanks largely to the adroit connivance of his Uncle Dickie – and of which, more anon.

But Anne was very different. Far more her father's daughter than her mother's, she had early on exhibited the Mountbatten qualities – assertiveness, outspokeness and independence. She was not the Queen Mother's favourite grandchild, and while Prince Charles had much of that royal lady's ability to keep his private life intact behind a show of charm and impenetrable good manners, Anne did not.

As a child she had also had to face much the same problem as her Aunt Margaret: that second-royal-child syndrome which was always fraught with difficulties. For like the English aristocracy, with its un-European reliance on the principle of primogeniture, the royal family showered its attention and concern on the heir apparent; but whereas Princess Margaret had reacted with her secret teenage infatuation for a handsome courtier, Anne behaved quite differently.

She was very much her father's favourite – and still is. 'Perhaps I did spoil her at times,' he admitted later; and whereas he would sometimes bully Charles in his impatience to 'make a man of him', Anne reacted like a true Mountbatten. She competed. While the Queen taught her stories from the Bible, Prince Philip taught her swimming in the Palace pool, and she soon swam better than her brother. Riding early on a small grey pony at a riding school near Maidenhead, she was off a leading rein before him too.

'When we were children Charles and I used to fight like cat and dog,' she relates. Where Charles was pliant, she was self-assertive; where Charles was a well-behaved small boy, she was considered something of a handful, even for that formidable royal nurse, 'No-Nonsense' Lightbody; and when Charles went off to boarding-school, leaving his sister in the Palace schoolroom with two well-brought up small girls for company, she was frankly bored. As she said later, 'Up to my teens I don't think I went along with the family bit, not until later than everybody else.'

She was also bored much of the time she spent away at school herself, where the consensus was that HRH was 'boisterous, bossy and moody'. This was not good, for as her maternal grandmother had done her best to show by her example, royalty must never show the boredom which is one of the professional afflictions of their regal situation.

This was something the Princess would never totally accept. As she put it in an interview she gave in 1973:

I'm me. I'm a person, I'm an individual, and I think it's better for everybody that I am me and shouldn't try to pretend to be anything I'm not.

Not that she pretended very hard. As a young princess her favourite treat was skating incognito under the worried eye of her governess, Miss Peebles, at Richmond ice-rink. At a school dance she ordered a respectful partner not to treat her 'like a piece of china'. And it was soon clear that the one place where she could absolutely be herself was astride a horse.

The young Princess's hippomania was one thing she could share with all the family, and the intimate relationship between horse and royalty is a fascinating subject in itself. Not for nothing are the splendid and luxuriously appointed royal mews, redesigned by Nash

in the 1830s, such a favoured and important part of the establishment at Buckingham Palace. For the horse has always held a special
place in the traditional ceremonial image of royalty. From ancient
times 'the man on horseback' has been a person in command; the
most impressive paintings and statuary of royalty invariably depict
them triumphantly controlling some sort of mettlesome quadruped;
and in these modern times the horse remains a potent symbol of
nostalgic royal splendour at a ceremonial occasion. Her Majesty is
infinitely more a Queen reviewing the annual trooping of the colour
from the back of her twenty-four-year-old black mare, 'Burmese',
than she could be on her latest missile launcher.

But the horse had other qualities to appeal to a young princess
refusing to 'pretend to be anything I'm not.' It had no consciousness
of rank; nor, like her mother's human subjects, did it treat her like
a piece of royal china. It did not fawn, nor did it expect a gracious
smile and courteous conversation (nor for that matter did horsey
people in their equine connotation). It was, in brief, a means of
achieving contact with a kind of reality which is in short supply for
royalty, and for Princess Anne – who had inherited her mother's
style on horseback – horsemanship rapidly became the ideal outlet
for her desire to compete on equal terms with those around her.
What flying, sailing and polo had been to her father, the challenge
of the day-long horse 'event' became to her. She had reason to be
proud of her success, for she received no favours. 'I learned
"eventing" myself,' she claimed, 'and everything I did, I did for
myself.' Before she left her teens, she was already one of the top
half-dozen competitive female riders in the country.

For the public image of the monarchy, this was something of
considerably more significance than merely proving that the Queen's
daughter had the democratic touch. Eventing, by its nature, is a very
public spectacle, and by dedicating so much energy and interest to
this most exacting sport the Princess was continuing to show that
thoroughly human face of royalty which had first appeared on the
television screens in 1969. Thanks to her competitive riding, Princess
Anne became the most closely observed and commented on member
of her family during the early Seventies.

She was inevitably hounded by the press photographers, all of
them waiting, as she knew quite well, for the priceless picture, not
of her triumph, but of her falling off her horse – which she duly did
on numerous occasions, even cracking a vertebra when thrown from

her mare, Candlewick, at Durweston Horse Trials in 1976. But undeterred both by photographers and falls, she persevered, and in the process established a reputation quite unlike that of any other royal lady of this century. The key to it lay in that refusal to 'pretend' whenever she appeared in public.

The Queen Mother had established something of a pattern of how female royalty were expected to behave – always gracious, always very feminine, always appearing utterly at ease and interested, even when they emphatically were not. This seemed quite beyond the young princess's powers of even rudimentary simulation. When she accompanied Prince Charles to Washington in 1970 as guests of the Nixons, there was much unfavourable comment on the contrast between her lack of enthusiasm on meeting America's first family, and the ever-smiling countenance of the President's enraptured daughter, Tricia. As Mrs Nixon at the time seemed equally enraptured at the prospect of the Presidential daughter being 'dated' by a future King of England, the Princess's lack of rapture was, in retrospect, excusable; but at the time, American journalists competed in expressing disapproval of 'the royal sour-puss' and 'Her Royal Haughtiness'. The Prince's impeccable demeanour received less attention, such being the nature of the press, and the experiment of using the Princess as a roving envoy for the Royal Family was not repeated for some time to come.

At home, the press was almost equally outspoken as they loyally catalogued Princess Anne's failings. These invariably involved behaviour on the riding field – where competitors tend to be profane and highly-strung. She was both, but the Princess always tried to make the point that her riding was her personal affair and that the press really should respect her right to reasonable privacy. Of course they never did. She was regarded as fair game for a battery of cameramen and journalists who never failed to materialise at the sound of royal hoofbeats, making her riding life a genuine ordeal. An understandable vendetta started between the Princess and the press.

A lesser young woman would undoubtedly have given up. She complained that the press, and particularly the photographers, were 'simply a bloody nuisance', always getting in the way, frightening the horses and – the ultimate indignity – 'insisting on asking foolish questions' at the worst possible moment. As she put it angrily, 'when you've fallen off a horse four times, you don't want to be asked what you had for breakfast.'

The fact that she was demonstrating such qualities as courage, grit and a single-minded passion to excel seemed to pass unnoticed. What fascinated press and public was her perverse failure to conform to the old idea of what a royal princess should be. She was not the stuff that dreams of the monarchy are made of; she was not like the 'frail, slender creature' her mother had seemed at her accession; nor was she fodder for those 'millions hungry for romance', like Aunt Margaret on her wedding day. Instead, she was something which would previously have been kept firmly under royal wraps – an uninhibited, extremely tough young woman who, like the majority of unmarried daughters in the Seventies, was determined she would be herself.

When she finally did show signs of conforming to the accepted picture of a storybook princess it was in the one area where not even she could avoid acting the role expected of her – marriage. This took place in November 1973, and briefly and interestingly it seemed as if a brand new image of Princess Anne would supersede the former role of awkward royal daughter to which everyone had grown accustomed by now.

The 'romance' itself had been totally in character with the earlier Princess Anne. Perhaps she should have chosen someone 'suitable' for the daughter of a Queen – English aristocracy or foreign royalty. Instead, like her mother and her aunt, she simply pleased herself, sensibly settling for someone with whom she had most in common – the middle-class, good-looking amateur rider and Olympic gold medallist, Lieutenant Phillips of Her Majesty's Hussars.

Explaining his attractions, one of the Princess's friends said at the time that Mark Phillips was 'one of the very few riders Anne could never actually beat', a motive she herself tended to confirm later.

I thought Mark was the most sympathetic of the good men I'd ever seen riding. He's very, very strong. Horses rarely stop with him, and if they do they wish they hadn't – but he's also sympathetic to different types of horses, which I think is rare in men.

From this equine basis true romance began to blossom; and once it was established, the elaborate machinery of a full-scale royal wedding soon swung into action, with all the key components we have seen in previous major royal spectaculars. The Tory government of Edward Heath was as eager for a touch of diversionary royal magic as the Labour government of Harold Wilson had been at the time of the Investiture. Its rich and sexually adventurous Secretary of State for War, Lord Lambton, had caused fears of a re-run of the disastrous Profumo scandal that autumn, when he was ludicrously driven to resign along with another peer and member of the government in a call-girl scandal. (Tory scandals tend to be concerned with sex, socialist ones with money.) But interest in the royal wedding swiftly edged Lord Lambton from the headlines. 'Les fiançailles de la Princesse Anne viennent à point pour faire oublier l'affaire Lambton', noted *Le Monde* with evident regret, as preparations for this grandest of state weddings went smoothly and steadily ahead.

A significant feature of the reign has been a gathering crescendo in the splendour of these public royal ceremonies, and the Princess's marriage, though lacking the build-up and surprise of Princess Margaret's, surpassed it in its impact at the time. Thanks to satellite link-ups, the worldwide television audience was estimated at a staggering 500 million, making it, as *Time* magazine remarked, 'the most public wedding the world has ever watched'. Apart from the viewers, there were 1600 guests, including 25 foreign royals, most of whom had not seen fit to come to Princess Margaret's wedding. And at the centre of the ceremonial there was once again that all-important glimpse of the Mountbatten-Windsors in their simple human guise. The bride signed the register, 'Anne Mountbatten-Windsor' – one of the few occasions where the new royal surname has been used in public – and no viewer will forget the moment when 'after struggling valiantly for control, Queen Elizabeth dabbed publicly at her eyes for the first time in her official life.'

With scenes like this, the wedding brought its inevitable boost to the popularity and worldwide interest in the royal family, but how did it affect the public standing of the bridal couple? This is a fascinating point, for the wedding demonstrated all the ritual elements of the now classic public royal transformation scene. Not merely was the bridegroom being taken up into the mythical Parnassus of royalty himself, but his bride herself appeared suddenly transformed by something just as magical as royalty – tenderness and love.

At last it seemed she really was the dream princess everybody wanted, and the Palace made absolutely sure that she looked like one as well. As with Prince Charles at his Investiture, nothing was left to chance. Not even Lord Snowdon's considerable powers of photographic flattery were considered adequate to the forbidding task of the official wedding pictures, and the Princess, who had just returned from falling off her horse 'Goodwill' at the three day international horse trials at Kiev, found herself suddenly subjected to the *Vogue*-style treatment normally reserved for the world's top fashion models.

The Queen Mother's favourite photographer, Norman Parkinson, took the pre-wedding colour photographs that suddenly revealed a Princess Anne few imagined could exist. As one incredulous New York journalist wrote, 'the hoydenish sportswoman had become a spectacularly lovely bride.' Her appearance was very much Parkinson's creation. A past-master at the gentle art of transmuting the female countenance into photographic visions of surprising loveliness, he has spoken of the way the camera can 'bring lotion to the heart'. With his photographs of unphotogenic Princess Anne, he used his Hasselblad to to spread lotion on the heart-strings of the nation.

He also used his favourite make-up man, the world-famous Paris cosmetician, Oliver Echaudmaison, to prepare Her Royal Highness for her sitting, and Echaudmaison stayed on to offer all his expertise to Princess Anne on the morning of her wedding. Thanks to this master's highly expert touch, she now appeared before the cameras in the Abbey as she had never been seen on television in her life – a radiant beauty in the bloom of youth, enveloped in the magic of a royal wedding.

The bridegroom made a perfect match, a tall, good-looking figure in his full dress uniform. 'Pure operetta,' murmured Parkinson. 'The best of Strauss – but all the characters are for real.' And therein lay the rub. For the Princess and her bold Hussar had far too much reality for this operatic transformation scene to last.

On the eve of the wedding, in an evident attempt to repeat the success of Prince Charles's interviews before his Investiture, both Anne and Mark had been interviewed by Alastair Burnet and Andrew Gardener on television – but this time television failed to produce the impression the Palace wanted. This was emphatically no dream princess; rather, it was still the Anne the public knew so well – sharp-tongued, intelligent, and not particularly inclined to treat a foolish question lightly.

Could she sew on a button if she had to?

'I'm not totally useless,' came the crushing royal retort. 'I was quite well educated, one way and another.'

Undeterred the questioners pressed on. 'Do you think your marriage can withstand the enormous pressures of public duty and publicity you have to endure?'

To which the Princess realistically but unromantically observed: 'It's got to, hasn't it!'

Like most of Princess Anne's remarks it was a very sensible reply, but it was not what people wanted her to say. A writer in the next day's *Times* reflected the deep disappointment of that loyal organ at this contribution to the image of the monarchy.

Who, watching Princess Anne and her fiancé muttering awkwardly, unoriginal, unglamorous, unexciting, could have felt for one moment that there was anything magical or mysterious left in the institution of royalty?

The Princess was once again refusing to pretend, and in the years ahead this would increasingly become the trademark of her relations with her everlasting public. After her one brief transformation at her wedding, she accepted that the 'glamour, magic and mystery' of the monarchy were not her *forté*, thus leaving the all-important role of royal dream princess waiting to be filled. Nor would she ever manage to resolve the running battle with the press over her angry insistence on her right to lead a private life – particularly where her riding was concerned.

This ensured that she would always be a figure of controversy, whether being regularly attacked as surly, arrogant, and rude – 'why can't she show a little of the charm and grace of her brother and mother?' was a typical press complaint – or criticised by the future Labour leader, Neil Kinnock, when the Queen paid half a million pounds for the Phillipses' country house, Gatcombe Park:

I don't know which is worse – the Queen for being wealthy enough to give it to them, or them for having the neck to take it.

Here was a rare example of a leading politician – as opposed to the addicted and unique royal-baiter, Willie Hamilton MP – openly attacking the royal family's wealth, and with this on record it will be interesting to see what happens should Mr Kinnock ever head a

Labour government in power. If Her Majesty's relations with her previous left-wing Prime Ministers are anything to go by, she will have little difficulty coping to preserve the fruitful mystery round the royal patrimony.

But the Phillipses could count on little of the dignified respect which both the Queen and Prince Charles could still command, and while the Princess fairly rapidly became 'the royal we all love to hate', her husband, an endearingly harmless character and would-be farmer, found himself having to endure the sort of boorish rudeness from the press that Lord Snowdon – who was far more vulnerable but infinitely smarter – always managed to avoid. Indelibly christened 'Captain Fogg' – 'because he's wet and grey and rather thick', Prince Charles is said to have remarked – he still managed to arouse much public sympathy by his firm refusal to accept a title and by his off-the-cuff remark after the birth in November 1977 of his first child, Peter, (the Princess having typically waited to compete in the 1976 Montreal Olympics before conceiving):

'Well, it's good to know I can do something right sometimes!'

But although *The Times* was justified in criticising the couple's lack of glamour, it was profoundly wrong to say that they were 'unoriginal'. For Princess Anne and her gallant husband were quite the most unusual characters to have emerged from the Mountbatten-Windsors to date, and revealed the family's continuing capacity for change. The Princess herself, like her father, is an immensely professional performer of her royal duties, particularly with her fund-raising work for her favourite charity, 'Riding for the Disabled' – which she practically carried single-handed – and for the 'Save the Children Fund', where she has probably done more actual good than any other member of her family.

Even more important was her role in steadily developing the public image of the royal family through the Seventies, as they began to change from their old symbolic figures into public superstars. For she and the much-maligned Captain Fogg remained the most visible and vital members of the royal theatre now emerging through the media. Endlessly quoted, harried, photographed and baited by the press, they could – and did – provide the 'human face of royalty' with a vengeance. Bored they may have been, but they were not permitted to be boring, with the world increasingly regaled with stories of their faintest *mot* or movement: the 'rifts' they were causing in the family, the troubles in their stables (*did* Captain

Phillips *really* kick a horse?), and of course the endless speculation on the state and setbacks of their marriage, which was lived very much in the open. One of Anne's better-looking personal policemen was 'transferred' after much inelegant gossip in the press, and still more gossip followed her husband's close collaboration with the former TV newsreader and fellow horse-fiend, Angela Rippon, who was writing his biography. Miraculously, perhaps, the Phillipses managed to remain together.

This torrent of publicity shows how profoundly William Heseltine and those around him had changed the monarchy in 1969 – and that, however hard the Palace tried, that change could never be reversed. For the Princess and her husband had none of the symbolic role, still less the 'sacredness' so carefully created round the royal family from the beginning of the century. They were quite simply international celebrities, 'famous', like Henry James's character, 'for being famous.' And it was this all-consuming interest in royalty as super-personalities which was rapidly becoming a predominating factor in their popularity. Love them or loathe them, one could never do without them – as was made curiously clear in the hitherto unthinkable crisis which suddenly hit the.very centre of the family of Mountbatten-Windsor early in 1976.

11
DIVORCE

'I am grateful to destiny that I have not been chosen as PRO
to Buckingham Palace, which is in truth a nightmare task.'
Harold Nicolson

With Windsor, Balmoral and Sandringham expensively maintained
as havens from the constant observation of their private lives, the
Mountbatten-Windsors have traditionally avoided holidays abroad.
This dates back to George V's conscious efforts to live down his
German origins and even the Queen Mother, who is something of
a Francophile, makes her occasional trips to France virtually incognito. On one memorable visit to the chateaux of the Loire,
accompanied by her friend Sir Pierson Dixon, the then ambassador
to France, she insisted on spending an informal evening in a typical
French bistro, imagining that nobody would notice her. The
ambassador tactfully suggested she just might be recognised, but
she was adamant; so, like the practised courtier he was, he made
arrangements with the local *préfet*. On the evening of the royal visit
the small working-class French bistro was filled exclusively with
gendarmes and their wives carefully dressed up like ordinary French
couples, and under very strict instructions to take no apparent notice
of Her Majesty, the former Queen of England. Afterwards she told
the ambassador how much she had enjoyed herself, and that the
evening only went to prove how easily she could go abroad in perfect
anonymity.

Her daughter, Princess Margaret, shared something of the same
illusion, but in her case it proved more hazardous when, early in
the new year of 1976, she cut short her holiday at Sandringham
with the rest of the family, caught the night plane from Heathrow
to Barbados, and arrived as dawn was breaking at the Caribbean
island of Mustique.

She still enjoys this regular January holiday at Mustique, which
she calls 'my island paradise'. Her old friend, Lord Glenconner –

then still plain Colin Tennant – bought the entire island for £45,000 in 1952, and long before he made a fortune by smartly developing it as a playground for the very rich, had given the Snowdons six prime acres on a headland as a wedding present. Later he also met the bills, with understandable reluctance, for the construction of a house for the Princess, which she named *Les Jolies Eaux* and which her husband's uncle, Oliver Messel, was persuaded to design for her, also free of charge. It was complete by 1970.

For some reason Tony Snowdon never liked Mustique and visited it once only, early in 1962. Some said that Tennant and his business associates were using the Princess to put the island on the map. Not that Snowdon was averse to being exploited for publicity if it suited him – as it had when he joined the *Sunday Times* – but with the growing tensions of their marriage, he enjoyed the freedom of his comfortably converted cottage at Nymans in Sussex. Similarly, the Princess had grown to love the privacy and independence of *Les Jolies Eaux*, surrounded by its tropical gardens and the cobalt sea. Her regular winter visit there without her husband had become a habit and a relaxation to which she looked forward throughout the year.

For three whole weeks in the middle of a London winter, she could escape – from the advice of courtiers, the attention of the public and the surveillance of the all too vulgar press. For three weeks in the freedom of this easy-going private island, she could relax and be entirely herself – which as Princess Anne had shown is always a tricky thing for modern royalty to do.

As if to emphasise her freedom, and the private nature of her holiday, the Princess took as her companion a startled-looking twenty-eight-year-old socialite turned gardener called Roderick Llewellyn, who was showing understandable anxiety at the publicity engendered by the three years of his indiscreet and often bumpy friendship with the sister of the Queen of England. But, typically, the Princess affected regal unconcern at the growing possibility of scandal.

Only that autumn there had been some fairly risible accounts of her visits to Llewellyn's happy-go-lucky 'hippy commune' at Surrendal in Wiltshire, and the popular dailies – in particular that ancient irritant of royalty, Prince Philip's 'bloody awful newspaper', the *Express* – had interviewed the commune's members at unseemly length, making the most of the entertainment value of embarrassed royalty. Shapely Sarah Ponsonby, 'convent educated niece of the Earl of Bessborough' (and member of a family of famous royal courtiers), was photographed by the *Sun* in jeans and nothing else, hoeing the very cabbage-patch recently weeded by the royal fingers. There was no suggestion, the paper assured its loyal readers, that Princess Margaret had been similarly *deshabillée* during her visits to the commune, but it added that she had spent at least one night at the sparsely furnished farm. Llewellyn had been there as well, and later press reports suggested that he planned to join her on Mustique.

Presumably the time had come for caution, but the Princess scorned the rumours, regally determined to enjoy her holiday exactly as she planned. Her husband could enjoy his freedom, and so could she. She felt her marriage was her own affair; she thought she could ignore the vulgar gossip of the press, and she counted on the privacy Tennant had always guaranteed on her earlier visits to the island. On all three counts she was mistaken.

For Mustique was growing, and with visitors arriving at the island's new hotel the semi-feudal paradise was no longer Tennant's own exclusive fief. He was still bravely keeping cameramen and journalists at bay, but the Princess was too valuable a quarry for the press to leave her in peace for ever. As the wife of a professional photographer herself, she might have known how easily a compromising picture can be taken with a modern camera; and an unknown, unsuspected journalist who just happened to be in Mustique on holiday, and also happened to have worked for Rupert Murdoch, did exactly that when nobody was looking.

It was actually profoundly innocent, a hurried snapshot of the Princess and the gardener, eating with their friends, the Cokes. The photograph was blurred, but since it was recognisably of Princess Margaret it was also very valuable. Within hours it had been wired to London, and expertly touched up; with the Cokes cut out, the exclusive picture of the Princess and her horticultural friend dining apparently *à deux* on a suspicious-sounding tropical island formed the basis of that Sunday's front-page story in that stalwart guardian of family morality, the *News of the World*, now owned by Rupert Murdoch.

Compared with the staple revelations of the paper it was sober stuff, but for Princess Margaret the photograph had disastrous repercussions. In retrospect one wonders why, after so many warnings in the press already, no one at the Palace lifted a finger to avert a situation which now rapidly got out of hand. But as we have seen already, no one at the Palace had ever been particularly good at coping with Her Royal Highness and the risks she often took with her position.

By now there was even more at stake than bad publicity: there was also the attitude of her husband to these public revelations of his wife's unconventional behaviour. It was assumed that he was acquiescent, and his righteous anger on seeing the *News of the World* that February Sunday seems to have caught everyone, including Princess Margaret, by surprise. That same evening she was shocked to hear by telephone that her husband had been in angry contact with her sister over the offending article, and was threatening the unthinkable – a royal divorce.

According to one weary Court official, the following three weeks proved a period of feverish, sometimes furious discussion, mainly at the Palace, as attempts were made to sort the muddle out without an open public scandal. The Princess returned prematurely to discover that her husband had decamped and was staying with his mother, Lady Rosse, in her house off nearby Kensington Church Street. More alarmingly, he was refusing all suggestions of a reconciliation – or failing that, of a continued life of decorous discretion. He was said to be angry. He was certainly standing on his rights. As a friend said later, 'Tony felt he'd been made a fool of publicly just once too often. He wanted out, and knew the strength of his position.'

Under the circumstances – and given that he was now regularly visiting the lady he would ultimately marry in her apartment just around the corner from the Palace – Snowdon's was a spectacularly cool performance. The sheer nerve he demonstrated at the conclusion of the marriage was even greater than in those months before it started. Single-hearted, unafraid, the noble Earl was challenging the royal family in an area still darkly overshadowed by the greatest of the great traditional royal taboos – and posing the royal family its gravest internal crisis since the Abdication in the process.

Divorce had always been anathema to the House of Windsor, and its opposition to divorce and *divorcés* had been a sort of touchstone for its public stance on morality and sex even in King Edward VII's time. Queen Mary refused to countenance a *divorcé* at Court or in the sacred confines of the Ascot royal enclosure, and it was Wallis Simpson's status as a *divorcée* that ultimately cost the King his crown. In 1967, the Queen's first cousin, George Lord Harewood, was divorced by his wife, the former pianist Marion Stein, and married the mother of his youngest son. The result had been Harewood's total ostracism from the Court – and the ending, for a while at least, of much of his public life. He was not invited to Princess Anne's wedding or the funeral of his uncle, the Duke of Windsor, which hurt him deeply. He had also to retire early from his position as Chancellor of York University and even as artistic director of the Edinburgh Festival.

So it was not surprising that the royal family was genuinely shocked by what Lord Snowdon was proposing – apart from Prince Philip who stayed admirably sensible and calm throughout the crisis. But since they could hardly fail to agree that the Princess seemed very firmly in the wrong, the outraged husband stood his ground, refusing to be over-awed or budged from his position. Faced by the Queen's personal solicitor, Matthew Farrer, the one concession he finally agreed to was to save the royal family the trauma of divorce, at least for the time being, by accepting a simple statement of a public separation in its place.

This conceded, he then shrewdly pointed out that, through no fault of his, he had been deprived of his home and even of a place where he could have his children to stay with him: shortly afterwards he received £100,000 from the Princess's private fortune, most of which would go on purchasing a very fashionable house, barely five minutes walk from her own front door.

By the second week of March the negotiations were finished – and so, in effect, was the sixteen-year-long marriage of the Snowdons. The Earl flew to Australia on private business, reaching Sydney on March 18, just in time for the historic announcement from the Palace.

Her Royal Highness the Princess Margaret, Countess of Snowdon and the Earl of Snowdon have mutually agreed to live apart. The Princess will carry out her public duties unaccompanied by Lord Snowdon. There are no plans for divorce proceedings.

After the long journey and the tensions of the previous few weeks, the Earl was edgy with reporters at the airport, even affecting some surprise at their presence; but he finally produced a statement which he read with considerable emotion. Despite his jet-lag, and a show of tearful anguish, his words bore all the signs of shrewd premeditation:

> I am naturally desperately sad in every way that this has had to come. I would just like to say three things; first to pray for the understanding of our two children; secondly to wish Princess Margaret every happiness for her future: and thirdly to express with the utmost humility, the love, admiration and respect I will always have for her sister, her mother and her entire family.

It was a clever statement, which he had carefully worked out before he left; for his years on the *Sunday Times* had taught him something of how to deal with the press, and he was anxious to preserve his reputation as a wronged but still respectful member of the royal family. Princess Margaret and her advisers seemed painfully bereft of such useful expertise, although there was really little they could say. The Queen was reported to be 'understandably extremely sad', and court officials did their best to play down the incident as something that happened in these liberated days in even the best of families, trusting that everyone would simply treat Her Royal Highness with 'sympathy and understanding'. Apart from a few close friends who knew the truth, hardly anybody did.

As the gossip writers had made fairly clear already, the Snowdons had regularly displayed most of the stock ingredients of a marriage on the rocks – infidelities, blazing rows, and short-lived reconciliations covering basic incompatibility. But while the causes of the break were commonplace, the form it took was not, and the interest of this modern fable lies in the royal context which renders it unique.

Like every male who has married into the modern royal family, Snowdon had had his share of stress and worry as he struggled to adjust to his wife's formidable position. It was the classic situation of a relatively penniless young man marrying an heiress – only infinitely more so. Prince Philip, Angus Ogilvy, Mark Phillips – all had finally accepted it and come to terms with it, but Snowdon really was 'too free a spirit' to make any compromise for long, and had learned to solve the problem in his own extremely clever way.

Throughout the Sixties and the early Seventies his was the great example of how to have one's royal cake and eat it, for he made the most of his position and prestige while also living the liberated life he wanted. He had already shown outstanding talent for a double life during his long and undercover courtship of the Princess. Now he employed it with still greater virtuosity to get almost everything he wanted out of life.

He had the deference that went with his position, the eager wooing by the great and the fawning friendship of stars like Peter Sellers. He had his bright red Aston Martin, his own establishment complete with his devoted secretary at Kensington Palace, glamorous holidays abroad, and total acceptance by the royal family during their tribal gatherings at Sandringham or Windsor. (The one exception was Prince Philip, who was never entirely taken in by him, and was actually quite rude about him once in public.)

At the same time he was able to conduct his other life with similar success, building an international reputation as a photographer, winning prizes with his television films, and always having the perfect alibi to contract out of his royal life when it suited him. Free and unencumbered – 'I've been brought up the whole of my life to be alone,' he said in 1974 – he could suddenly turn up in Tokyo, Melbourne or New York on assignments for the *Sunday Times*. He could earn £400 a time from photographs for record sleeves for stars like Shirley Bassey, Adam Faith and Charles Aznavour. He could conduct discreet affairs with young ladies from fashion magazines, who were naturally flattered by his attentions; and there was always the Sussex cottage to escape to when he needed privacy. The nearest he ever got to serious trouble came when a fellow member of the House of Lords, the father of a very pretty daughter, threatened him with a horsewhip in accordance with time-honoured practice in the English upper classes. As the peer was a Sussex neighbour, and the young lady's brother shared a house with the columnist, Nigel Dempster, it is clear that even Snowdon was beginning to take undue risks with his position. (Firm friend and patriot, Dempster kept quiet and did nothing, for the time being, to embarrass his landlord or his sovereign.)

Snowdon's attitude betrays a certain carelessness towards that family for which he would later express so much 'humility, love, admiration and respect'. So, to be fair, did Princess Margaret's, and throughout their marriage both transgressed those firm, unspoken rules on which the respected public image of the royal family had rested since the days of good Queen Mary.

It is strange how the public gradually forms its own impression of members of the royal family. Hidden, confined and separate though royalty may be, they are also the subject of continual gossip and observation. Much is inaccurate and even more of it unfair, but gradually a certain clear impression filters through to form the basis of their public image. With Prince Charles, for instance, little he is known or reported to have done conflicts with the early verdict on his character the Queen Mother gave when asked about him in New Zealand: 'He has a very kind heart, which I think is the essence of everything.' Similarly, with Prince Philip and the Queen the general consensus is that they are serious, dignified, somewhat puritanical and – within certain limits – actively concerned about their subjects.

But with Princess Margaret a very different public profile had emerged. Little that was reported of her habits had dispelled the early impressions of personal extravagance at public expense, created by the publicity around the renovation of her personal apartments at Kensington Palace. She was considered haughty, temperamental and demanding; and unlike her husband she was always particularly vulnerable to criticism, with a public position to maintain in return for her income from the Civil List.

Paradoxically, just because of who and what she was, hers became much the weaker position in the marriage, so that when things started going wrong she could be constantly outmanoeuvred by a husband who held most of the advantages and knew exactly how to use them. Here the difference in their backgrounds was important. Princess Margaret had been spoiled and worshipped, and had grown up in the most sheltered and unworldly family situation any glamorous young woman could enjoy. She was not used to being thwarted, still less to being argued with by those around her. Her husband on the other hand, with parents mixed up in divorces, had learned as a child the tricks of all unhappy marriages. He had enjoyed a liberated sex-life of his own before he married and, as he showed in his relationship with the swiftly discarded Jackie Chan, possessed a very worldly, cool command of his emotions. Vulnerable, emotional, and lacking her husband's skilfully created double life, Princess Margaret found herself increasingly at risk in the rough and tumble of her unrewarding marriage.

With the Snowdons, what was sauce for the royal goose rarely proved sauce for the non-royal gander; and it must be admitted that at times Her Royal Higness acted like a very silly goose indeed. *He* found little difficulty concealing his infidelities: thanks to her nature and her situation, hers were more public and would always be a source of gossip and potential scandal – as with her ill-starred friendship with the night club pianist, Robin Douglas-Home, who committed suicide in 1968. This was followed by the inevitable 'revelations' in the foreign press and hints of blackmail when a batch of letters from the Princess surfaced in New York; and as well as enduring much unhappiness, Margaret seemed to place herself firmly in the wrong with her family.

The contrast with her husband on this occasion could not have been more marked. He was far from blameless on his own account, but by agreeing not to press for a separation or make an unseemly public fuss he earned considerable royal sympathy and gratitude – which was further enhanced by his successful staging of Prince Charles's Investiture. 1969 saw him at the height of royal favour, when the Queen created him a Knight Commander of the Royal Victorian Order, instituted by her great-great-grandmother for those who rendered personal service to the monarch and her family.

The strange imbalance in the Snowdon marriage started showing in the early Seventies. In marked contrast with her sister, Princess Margaret had a strong dependence on both alcohol and nicotine, and the strains of marriage had done little for her looks. She had consulted a psychiatrist during reported 'problems of identity', she was overweight and troubled by a mid-life crisis. Things could hardly have been improved by the glowing image now presented by her husband, who in 1972 came second to Clint Eastwood in an American poll on the world's 'Top Ten Sexiest Middle-aged Men.'

She was something of a casualty to life and to her royal situation, and her friendship with the invertebrate Llewellyn, who was eighteen years her junior, was less an impetuous romance than a desperate solution to that unsuspected royal affliction, loneliness.

Reactions to the news of the breakup of the Snowdon marriage form another pointer to the changes now affecting the whole basis of the monarchy. That there was little sympathy for Princess Margaret can be explained partly by the public lack of understanding for her situation, and also by the virtuosity with which her husband conducted his own exit from the royal family. What public sympathy there was went generally to him.

Against the Princess the outcry seemed alarming – particularly from middle-aged mothers of families who had grown up with

'Princess Margaret Rose'. Having vicariously participated in her role as dream princess, they seemed to feel personally cheated, expressing their anger in letters to the press which were virtually unique in bitterness against a leading member of the royal family.

> That spoiled woman! What a wonderful life she had on other people's money. Her allowance should be stopped at once. It would be good for her to have to work on an assembly-line in a factory.

There were many more. Even at the height of the Abdication crisis, the maladroit King Edward had faced nothing like this sort of outcry from his disappointed subjects, and it is interesting how many of them now picked on that most sensitive point of regal vulnerability – the Princess's income from the taxpayer through the Civil List. It was as if this payment carried an obligation to maintain a happy marriage, and follow the dictates of conventional morality.

Not for nothing has hypocrisy been called 'the English vice', and nowhere does one see its operation quite so clearly as in its attitude to royalty: but for the Court it was a fact of life which had been long accepted, and the alarming spectacle of so many traditional supporters of the monarchy seized by a fit of moral indignation had its effect upon the preparations which were under way to celebrate the twenty-fifth anniversary in May 1977 of Elizabeth II's accession – her Silver Jubilee. First reactions were that this indignation might endanger it, but it was soon realised at Court that whatever else it was, the Jubilee could be a heaven-sent opportunity to repair the damage caused by the Snowdon separation. Because of this William Heseltine now encountered little opposition to his plans for an even more ambitious programme to present that 'human face of royalty' than at any time since Prince Charles's Investiture.

It was obviously what people wanted, and it was also what the monarchy itself required; but this time the emphasis would rightly rest upon the Queen, and instead of relying on some grandiose ceremony of state to emphasise whatever symbolism and mystery still resided in the monarchy, it was sensibly decided to permit Her Majesty to be herself and meet as many of her subjects as she could.

The keynote of a jubilee is celebration, and the only previous royal Silver Jubilee – George V's in 1935 – had shown how the monarch, by appearing in his simple human guise, could suddenly become the object of a national uprush of emotional togetherness – Claud Cockburn's moment when the benevolent but distant king was instinctively felt to be 'one of us'. In King George's case, this had been the unexpected and spontaneous reaction to an old man in the last year of his life; but for Elizabeth II, the even greater impact of her Silver Jubilee came as the result of much careful planning, and can be seen to mark another key development in her reign.

The year began with a series of fairly low-key royal visits to different parts of the country, where for the first time Her Majesty conducted royal 'walkabouts' to meet the people – a role which, though tiring, she discovered she enjoyed and could perform with remarkable success. In early summer she was at the centre of two royal ceremonies, both as usual widely viewed on television – Her Majesty's acceptance of loyal addresses from both Houses of Parliament on May 4, and a full Thanksgiving Service for her reign in St Paul's Cathedral six weeks later. But on both occasions interest centred on the Queen in her human context at this happy moment of her reign, and to emphasise this she and Prince Philip calmly walked among the cheering crowds to the Guildhall luncheon at the conclusion of the service at St Pauls.

It was very much a tribute to the Queen in person, and there was speculation when, contrary to general expectations and the confident predictions of the press Prince Philip was not created 'Prince Consort'. The reason for this was not another of those celebrated 'slights' beloved of writers on the royal family, but simply that it was not a title he remotely wanted. Twenty years earlier it might have been different, but as something of an expert on the previous Prince Consort – his forebear, the lamented husband of Victoria – he had come to feel that the title belonged exclusively to Albert, and had no great wish to be associated in the public mind with that overworked, unappreciated and unpopular German prince.

Prince Philip was distinctly overshadowed in the celebrations – both by the Queen and by his eldest son – and the year seemed to mark the point at which he stepped back slightly from his public role, as Prince Charles started taking on his royal duties as an active Prince of Wales. Charles had now finished his requisite spell of duty in the Royal Navy – which he emphatically had not enjoyed, despite valiant efforts, both by himself and by the press, to present him as a natural sailor in the image of his father and all those other clear-

ABOVE: 'Honorary Grandson' with 'Honorary Grandfather'. 'For Mountbatten, it was the culminating moment of his lifetime to become in old age the philosopher and friend of the future King of England' *(Rex Features Ltd).* BELOW: Enter the glamorous outsider. Prince Michael of Kent and his bride, the former S.S. major's daughter, Marie-Christine von Reibnitz, after their wedding in the grounds of the British Embassy in Vienna. Her controversial father, Baron von Reibnitz, stands between Angus Ogilvy and Princess Anne. *(Camera Press Ltd)*

Prince Charles plays the field: portrait of 'the world's most eligible bachelor' with some of his girlfriends.

LEFT: Lady Jane Wellesley.
(*Camera Press Ltd*)

RIGHT: Sabrina Guiness.
(*Rex Features Ltd*)

ABOVE: Lady Sarah Spencer.
(Rex Features Ltd)

RIGHT: Jane Ward.
(Rex Features Ltd)

'The transformation of Princess Diana, slim-line regal megastar, from the homely, round-cheeked child-bride of four years earlier.' ABOVE LEFT: Diana at the time of her engagement *(Rex Features Ltd)*. ABOVE: portrayed by Snowdon after the birth of Prince Henry. *(Camera Press Ltd)*

LEFT: Diana – 'ready to be awakened by her Prince's love and totally transformed'. *(Rex Features Ltd)*

ABOVE: Dynastic superstar Princess Diana meets *Dynasty* soap-opera star Joan Collins at a charity ball hosted by Bruce Oldfield, dress designer to them both. *(The Photo Source)*

ABOVE: TV's *Spitting Image*
caricatures would have been
unthinkable twenty years ago. Today,
secure in their public standing, the
royal family cheerfully endure them –
on-screen, if not in print.
*(Photograph by Central Television
plc)*

LEFT: 'Silver-tongued' Michael Shea,
Press Secretary to Her Majesty, and
'the courtier with a crucial role
behind the scenes of the great
performing British monarchy'.
(Camera Press Ltd)

'The Queen has not aged particularly well, but nor does she seem particularly bothered —
despite gratuitous advice from self-appointed pundits over how she dyes her hair, applies her
make-up, or chooses her no-nonsense spectacles. If a Queen can't please herself about such
things, who can?' *(Rex Features Ltd)*

eyed, firm-jawed menfolk of the nautical families of Windsor and Mountbatten.

Prince Charle's role in the Jubilee was to head the national Appeal to give thanks for the twenty-five years of his mother's reign, and he did it most effectively. He was helped once again by the professional PR expertise of Neilson McCarthy, who along with several over PR firms had made an official bid to act as consultants to the Appeal Fund – and who, to no one's particular surprise with the Prince's secretary still a member of their board, were finally selected. In its way, the Appeal was cleverly designed to emphasise the original impression Prince Charles had made at his Investiture. Launching the campaign on television, he gave a totally convincing performance as a devoted and admiring son of Her Majesty, his mother; and the form of the Appeal itself – at the Queen's request, it would be used 'to help young people to help others of all ages in the community' – seemed to cast the Prince in the nostalgic, reassuring role of his grandfather, George VI, 'doing something' for the nation's youth with his annual camps and his royal appeal for playing fields.

The Appeal raised more than £16.4 million – in itself a tribute to the Prince of Wales, the Queen and Neilson McCarthy; but it was only incidental to the real purpose of the Jubilee. For the Queen's anniversary was above all the centre and excuse for something a nation needs as part of its collective being – a tribal jamboree in which all manner of irrational forces come together to express benevolence, rejoicing and an overwhelming sense of national identity.

This is a need which politics and politicians alone cannot hope to satisfy, and in 1977 the new Labour premier, James Callaghan, was leading a rather weary government in a struggle with inflation, rising wages and the early problems of the Common Market. It was all profoundly unexciting; and in pointed contrast this national event created round the royal anniversary suddenly released a mood of wonderfully illogical optimism. Neighbours who barely knew each other now united to organise parties in the streets. Trees were planted, village halls dedicated, pageants mounted; special ale was brewed, opening hours extended in public houses, commemorative crockery and medals found an eager market, and as a national event the Jubilee is said to have surprised the Queen herself.

It is intriguing to compare her now with her public image of a quarter of a century before. Then she had really seemed a sacred being, a symbolic figure at the centre of a cult which even the *Church Times* complained of as a form of surrogate religion. As befits a goddess figure, she had been set carefully apart, protected from disclosure of her feelings or her private life, and permitted to reveal only the most formal aspects of her royal stereotype outside the Palace.

With the film *Royal Family* this had changed, and at the Jubilee the process seemed complete. During this year of celebration, the Queen was not worshipped as a royal symbol, but regarded rather as her mother had been in her prime – as an emerging matriarch, particularly that autumn, when her daughter, Anne, made her a grandmother. As the son of a commoner, the Queen's first grandchild had no title, and was firmly *Master* Phillips. More and more was known about her character and role within her family, and as the public interest grew, the myth of royalty began increasingly to change from a cult of traditional belief to one of personality.

There was so much for this new cult to feed on – the non-stop revelations of the trials and tribulations of Princess Anne, the casual remarks Prince Charles would make about his family, and, of course, the running saga in the press about Princess Margaret. Royalty had never been like this before – at least not in public – and the skilful efforts of the Palace publicity machine, in most efficient working order for the Jubilee, now offered yet further television glimpses inside the royal tribal hut.

There were two important royal appearances in television films made around the time of the Jubilee. In one of them, *Royal Heritage*, the Queen, Prince Philip and Prince Charles appeared casually at home to viewers as they conducted that booming broadcaster, Huw Weldon, round assorted treasures in the royal palaces. The choice of title was adroit, suggesting a regal willingness to share at least a glimpse of the priceless royal possessions with the outside world, and the royal hosts seemed wonderfully at home among their fabled surroundings, with none of the eager condescension of so many stately home proprietors before the public. There was a particularly clear impression of the Queen herself – business-like, prepared to be amused, but thoroughly aware of who and what she was – and a still more telling picture was conveyed in the second television film on *The Queen's Garden*, screened in July 1976.

This had a fascinating link with one of the best-remembered items from the sentimental snapshots of the Queen's own childhood, as she was seen showing her niece, Sarah Armstrong-Jones, the secrets of the famous miniature cottage in the grounds of Windsor Royal Lodge. The far-off memory of Princess Lilibet, playing in the cottage with her sister, Margaret Rose, had materialised into this figure of a sympathetic but no-nonsense grandmother, with sturdy handbag and sensible green coat and skirt, accepting a miniature cup of tea from her grandchild and showing the workings of the cottage clock she herself had played with as a child.

On one level the scene was commonplace enough, one more example of that 'trivialising' of the monarchy which had been critcised before; but at a deeper level the close-ups of the Queen in these human situations were projecting something of considerable importance for the royal image. Some time before, the Communist *Morning Star* had posed what it saw as the major problem in the presentation of the modern monarchy:

> How can you defend the business of being head of state of an alleged democracy purely on a hereditary basis, unless you are different from other people? But how can you retain the goodwill of the public unless, in this age of the common man, you can pretend to be the same as everybody else?

For the *Morning Star*, the answer was, you couldn't, and, placed in an impossible position, Her Majesty was best advised 'simply to pack the whole game in and become a private citizen'. This was not exactly likely to occur; but this apart, and not for the first time in its life, the *Morning Star* was wrong in the conclusions it drew from its analysis. For as the immense success of the Silver Jubilee made very clear, the apparent contradictions in the monarch's situation were precisely what made the Queen and those around her such a source of unabated interest for the world in general.

Thanks to the face-to-face encounters of the royal walkabouts and unscripted appearances on television, people were coming to regard the Queen, if not as entirely 'the same as everybody else', as at any rate a normal human being, with a positive character, clearcut tastes and resolute identity. After two decades in which she had seemed to have a personality akin to her unchanging profile on the coinage, she had been quite suddenly introduced to all her subjects.

What they saw was not in itself particularly startling, for she was, as she said, no actress, any more than she was an intellectual, a wit, or a profoundly sensitive lover of the arts. But she appeared entirely of a piece. She was emphatically not 'created' by her press advisers, any more than she was a sort of lowest common multiple of middle-aged British motherhood. She was what the French would call 'une type'; a slightly eccentric, very positive, dog-loving, country-loving lady, clearly devoted to her family, who approached life with the accepted attitudes and mannerisms of the English upper middle-classes.

But the source of this middle-aged mother of four's enduring interest for her public was that while she was utterly familiar, she was also utterly different from anybody else. That apparent contradiction which the *Morning Star* had hit on was the source of all her mystery. 'Princes,' the novelist Dan Jacobson once wrote, 'do what we dream of'; and now that we finally felt we knew so much about her and her family, Elizabeth Mountbatten-Windsor could become the central figure in the most complex and extraordinary public dream of all.

For only now was it possible to appreciate in full the hallucinatory double-life which modern royalty are forced to lead – these ordinary people everybody knows so well, who, along with their ordinariness, are simultaneously endowed with all the mystery and deference preserved within the most impressive of the world's surviving monarchies.

Although bereft of actual power, the myth of kingship remains a potent and universal charge; and the British royal family have shown a kind of genius for making the most of it. Apart from their ritual transformation scenes in the great ceremonies of state, they have embodied legendary attributes from the grandest ancient monarchies – absolute wealth, absolute splendour and respect, tradition, authenticity, and an effortlessly favoured life-style in magnificent surroundings – all of which carry with them the unique, if largely manufactured savour of unspeakable greatness.

Yet at the same time all this centres on a totally familiar country-loving lady and her family. Small wonder that the world was now becoming increasingly obsessed by every detail it could glean about their private lives, or that Princess Anne or Princess Margaret were remorselessly pursued by journalists intent on adding yet another item to the steadily unfolding saga of the royal family.

To describe what had happened to them all as 'trivialising' rather missed the point. Now that the Queen and members of her family seemed to be acting out so many parts of their ordinary lives in public, the curtain had lifted on the most compulsive and original true-life family serial in the world. It was the stuff that great collective dreams are made of; and a running story that had everything required to keep its world-wide audience perpetually entranced.

12

CHANGING FACES

'You *are* a pest, by the very nature of that camera in your hand.'

Princess Anne to a press photographer

As so often in the reign of Elizabeth II, the most controversial figure in the changes continuing to affect the royal family in the aftermath of the successful Jubilee was Princess Margaret. After the Coronation, she had had the uninvited but romantic role of bringing unexpected human interest to the image of the royal family through the revelation of her love for Peter Townsend. Now she was once again to offer an inimitable public epilogue of her own to her sister's triumph, with far-reaching implications for the members of her family as well as for herself.

After the separation of April 1976, she and her husband had continued to enjoy their separate love-affairs – the Earl with his future wife, Mrs Lucy Lindsay-Hogg, and she with Roderick Llewellyn. But as so often in the past, both displayed a markedly different style in their romances, and both acted totally in character. Lord Snowdon was even more discreet than when he had courted Princess Margaret in the Fifties, but Princes Margaret seemed utterly determined to proclaim her hard-won freedom – and to hell with whatever her hypocritical public thought about her now! Llewellyn apparently agreed with her, having taken on his own publicity agent in preparation for an ill-advised change of life from gardener to singing pop star. 'Or course I took advantage of the publicity that surrounds my friendship with Princess Margaret', he was quoted as saying.

That spring the singing gardener found much publicity to take advantage of, in the uncomfortable dramas that ensued from another winter holiday with Princess Margaret in Mustique. It might be thought that they could possibly have chosen somewhere else, or even have employed a little simple common sense. For as Prince

Charles was happily discovering, it is not impossible for royalty, with the wealth and resources at its disposal, to conduct a quiet love affair in private. To go off together to Mustique at a time like this was to issue a virtual invitation to the press as well – and the strain on both of them rapidly began to show.

Instead of the quiet holiday she hoped for, Princess Margaret found herself hiding from press photographers and was soon on fifty cigarettes a day. Llewellyn proved more vulnerable still to nervous tension, and fell victim to that occupational affliction of so many men who enter the world of the Mountbatten-Windsors – a gastric ulcer. At the beginning of April it precipitately burst, and the assembled Princess Margaret watchers were presented with the real-life drama of her lover, now seriously ill, being flown to a Barbados hospital to save his life. The Princess followed and the press were already at the hospital to greet her, so that readers of next morning's London papers learned of how 'a worried Princess Margaret fussed around the hospital bedside of her friend, Roderick Llewellyn, last night. And she made it plain that his sickness would not keep them apart.'

However touching, there was too much absurdity in the spectacle of the Queen of England's sister dancing attendance on a lacklustre lover eighteen years her junior for the incident to gain her any sympathy; and a spokesman from Kensington Palace was quoted by the *Sunday Telegraph*, despondently admitting:

> We are concerned at Princess Margaret's image. There is little we can do about it, and we can't ask the media to love the royal family.

There was certainly little sign of love around for Princess Margaret. The inevitable Bishop – in this case Dr Graham Leonard from the lowly diocese of Truro, later to become Bishop of London – rapidly weighed in with the inevitable episcopal reproof. The Princess's holiday was somewhat redundantly described as 'foolish', with a firm pronouncement that 'she would have to choose between accepting the limitations of public life or withdrawing from it completely.' Much the same theme was followed by sections of the press and House of Commons.

According to the *Sunday People*, 'Readers Vote NO for Margaret'. Three out of every four letters in a so-called 'mammoth postbag' made it clear that 'she fails to justify the £1,000 a week she gets from the taxpayer.' Dennis Canavan MP, aware that a raise in the Civil List was due, likewise complained of 'the £1,000 a week pocket money we are giving to a royal parasite like Princess Margaret', and his colleague, Willie Hamilton MP, smartly suggested that £30,000 of her £55,000 allowance be diverted to provide a badly needed passenger lift for patients at the Elizabeth Garrett Anderson Hospital in Euston.

The Princess's appalling publicity continued through the spring despite news that she was sick herself and unable to attend her daughter's confirmation with the rest of the family, including, naturally, Lord Snowdon. According to a writer in the *Evening Standard*, Her Majesty took advantage of the occasion

to personally compliment Lord Snowdon, who through all the trials which have beset his wife and his marriage, has conducted himself so impeccably. The official photograph the Queen has chosen to issue on her 52nd birthday was taken by her brother-in-law.

A few days later, Princess Margaret was in hospital being treated for alcoholic hepatitis, which led to a predictable article by the seasoned royal journalist, Audrey Whiting: 'Margaret – Will the Agony Never End? Her grim fight to get well'.

She is a sick woman. The possible gravity of her condition has been known for some time to only a handful of very close friends . . . I am told that while there is no cause for immediate alarm, Princess Margaret's future progress will demand the full cooperation of the patient.

Then at the end of May came what seemed the final blow to Princess Margaret's dwindling public reputation. At the Law Courts in the Strand, Judge Roger Blenkiron Willis of the Family Division (Divorce) – 'one does one's job and I don't think one should talk about these things' – heard case number 5684/78, a £16 so-called 'quicky' divorce by mutual agreement, which painlessly and anonymously ended the eighteen-year-old marriage of the Snowdons and made history by creating the first divorce at the centre of the English royal family since Henry VIII discarded Anne of Cleves.

The unthinkable had finally occurred; and while Queen Mary was presumably spinning in her marble grave at Windsor, the Queen's loyal subjects proceeded to digest the implications of a princess who, having renounced the man she loved twenty-three years before because he was a *divorcé*, was now a party to divorce herself.

The general reaction was that even royalty had been finally compelled 'to keep up with the times' and bow to the inevitable. But there was actually more at stake than this for the public role and image of the monarchy, and these few unhappy weeks of Princess Margaret's life repay some study if one is to understand the rapid changes which were now affecting the whole nature of the institution.

The first intriguing point to note is that, despite the tidal wave of unprecedented scandal and bad publicity which swept over Princess Margaret, the royal family itself had never been more popular since the heady days immediately following the Coronation. A poll conducted on behalf of *Woman* magazine in October of that year revealed over 80 percent 'thoroughly in favour' of the royal family, with the Queen at the top of the popularity league with 73 percent, followed closely by Prince Charles with 68 percent, Prince Philip with 56 percent and the Queen Mother with 52 percent. Princess Anne and Princess Margaret shared the bottom of the league with 30 and 29 percent respectively.

A second point of interest is that, despite her illness and the public calls upon her to give up her official role and her income from the Civil List, Princess Margaret did nothing of the sort. She actually did privately offer to retire from public life, 'feeling it her duty to let the Queen decide herself whether her services were any longer required', after what the royal family itself regarded as the most serious crisis it had had to face since the Abdication. But during a hurried conference at Windsor with Prince Philip, the Prime Minister and the Archbishop of Canterbury, Her Majesty decided that the long-term implications of her sister's retirement would cause such 'frightful damage' to the monarchy that it was best to let the Princess soldier on.

That summer, her income from the Civil List was increased, in accordance with the rising cost of living, to £59,000. By June she was out of hospital and off alcohol, and early in August she was staying in Italy with 'handsome bachelor merchant-banker, Prince d'Urso' at his villa at Conca del Marina, near Amalfi. Variously described as 'a playboy' and 'a tough business-getter with a wide circle of friends', the Prince was reported to have said, 'Marriage is not out of the question.'

'Is this the end for Roddy?' several papers hopefully inquired. It was not − for a while at least − and the optimistic banker-prince was not to follow Tony Snowdon as a member by marriage of the British royal family.

This was probably as well for all concerned, but the central fact about the behaviour of Princess Margaret during these miserable but all-engrossing months was that one of 'Us Four', the very nucleus of the originaly holy family of Windsor, had publicly flouted the essential moral code the family had stood for in its loving private life − and neither the heavens nor the monarchy had fallen. And there was more to the affair than this. In 1955, when Princess Margaret was making up her mind over Peter Townsend, it had been made clear to her, both by her family and the politicians, that the symbolic and moral status of the monarchy could not stand the shock of her marriage to a *divorcé*, so she would have to choose between her public and her private life.

In 1978 she was faced with a similar ultimatum. This time, however, it came neither from the Palace nor the Prime Minister, but from the 'lunatic' Willie Hamilton MP and part of the sensationalist Sunday press. The Palace and the political establishment now stood resolutely by her, and the Elizabeth Garrett Anderson hospital did not get its lift at her expense. Fascinatingly, it was no longer *The Times* which trotted out the ancient arguments about the symbolic and moral nature of the monarchy, but that left-wing bugle, the *New Statesman*, which tootled piously: 'It is a sad day when the symbol loses its dignity.'

'In human terms,' it generously conceded, 'it is possible to feel sympathy for Princess Margaret − but humanity is not what monarchy is about.'

As the late Dr Leavis used to say when pointing out the error of some fellow-critic's ways, 'But this was not so!' For as the *New Statesman* should have understood by now, humanity was rapidly becoming almost everything the English monarchy *was* 'about'. It had already had a good deal to do with it when Walter Bagehot wrote in 1867 of the marriage of the future Edward VII to Princess Alexandra, that 'a princely marriage is the brilliant edition of a universal fact and as such it rivets mankind.' Mankind was now equally riveted by the details of a princessly divorce; for far more than with Princess Margaret's marriage, its breakup offered the unprecedented spectacle of the royal family in its most human public role to date.

From shopgirl to sophisticated socialite, everyone was interested in how the royal family would behave; and as far as anyone could tell the answer was – quite admirably. Prince Philip was understood to have been 'wonderfully supportive' to his sister-in-law, while the Queen was 'simply marvellous' to Lord Snowdon, showing particular concern for her sister's children. The royal workhorse, Princess Anne, took on many of her aunt's personal appearances during her illness, and, according to a favourite royal reporter, the Queen Mother too was hard at work 'supporting her emotionally disturbed daughter' through the crisis. During that June's annual Trooping the Colour, she insisted on having Princess Margaret with her in her open landau, 'as if she was trying to draw from the public and towards her daughter some of the sympathy and affection she had always received herself.'

If this really was the Queen Mother's motive it evidently failed to work, if the poll in *Woman* magazine is anything to go by; but Princess Margaret's personal popularity had little bearing on the *rapport* her misfortunes had now established between the public and the other members of her family. Suddenly, like the old motto of a famous Sunday paper, 'All human life was there' in the stately circle of the Mountbatten-Windsors, as the family coped in semi-public with those everlasting elements of human interest – sickness, scandal, family tension and divorce.

Thanks to Princess Margaret, the royal family had been forced at last to jettison that awkward role Queen Mary had bequeathed to her descendants as unflickering beacons of middle-class morality – at a time when its other roles as symbols for the Church of England, the Commonwealth and the nation were themselves fast losing their importance, too. But also thanks to Princess Margaret, the royal family, discomfited or not, had become in strictly human terms more 'interesting' than at any moment since the Abdication – and from now on it would be this all-absorbing interest, rather than the passing popularity of its individual members, that would count.

The distinction is important, as one sees with Princess Margaret and with Princess Anne. Popularity depends essentially upon a public feeling that a certain personality is 'nice' or 'good'. Princess Margaret was clearly not particularly good and Princess Anne was not felt to be particularly nice, but both had become key characters in the situation dramas now rapidly unfolding round the royal family.

Robert Lacey has described the English royal family as 'a performing monarchy'. Therein had always lain their interest and their true importance, as they acted out their dignified and 'ornamental' roles of state. But now the repertoire was changing in the royal family theatre. The traditional performances remained, but along with them came these new and all-absorbing backstage dramas to keep audiences 'riveted' and guarantee that, come what may, the show would continue by popular demand.

Just as in the legitimate theatre, there were certain royal superstars whose none too private lives would play a vital part in their legendary status with the public. In the late Seventies, Princess Margaret had become the star attraction in this new royal super-show, and as she switched her role from ageing dream princess to middle-aged scarlet woman, the other members of the royal cast in turn became more interesting through their relationships with her. The Queen attracted sympathy and public interest by her dignity and womanly concern for her wounded sister in what everybody understood must be a deeply embarrassing situation for a Queen of England. The very fact that people could participate in this embarrassment added immeasurably to the empathy her subjects felt towards their sovereign, and to awareness of her as an essentially decent and dignified matriarchal figure, coping at the centre of her now fascinating family.

Her private and her public roles seemed absolutely of a piece: so did Prince Philip's, as he appeared to offer Princess Margaret that same 'firm right arm' to lean on that Dimbleby had mentioned at her marriage. And so it was with all the cautiously performing members of this performing monarchy as they acted out their private lives round Princess Margaret.

Not that hers was by any means the only episode of human interest for press and public to enjoy in the new, liberated royal show. Public interest changes fast. The somewhat battered Princess Margaret soon failed to satisfy that demanding public interest she consistently aroused at the time of her divorce, and there were other members of the family to take her place with a public that was getting used to royalty as human superstars.

One hesitates to use the phrase about a 'Royal Soap Opera', which Malcolm Muggeridge coined as early as 1955, to describe this burgeoning phenomenon, for the simple reason that the elements of this rapidly expanding royal show went far beyond the strictly limited conventions carefully adhered to in such television serials. To start with, these were living people with a human ability to surprise and break whatever rules the public expected them to follow – as Princess Anne did, when this supposedly 'selfish and arrogant' young woman insisted on visiting starving children in Somaliland and, later, in Calcutta and Beirut as President of the Save the Children Fund.

Also, the 'script' was infinitely richer and more rewarding for its worldwide audience than the predictable events of *Dynasty* and *Dallas*. The scenery was more authentic, the choreography of the ceremonies of state was matchless in the spectacle it offered, and the complex myth of monarchy offered a dreamlike quotient to the process of identifying with its characters.

But at the same time, this new way of regarding members of the royal family – and the family itself – shared certain features with a prime-time television serial it would be foolish to ignore. The world had grown accustomed to relying on television for the authenticating glimpses it enjoyed of royalty as infinitely glamorous and famous human beings: as a result it tended to regard them much as it regards its best-known television personalities – as familiar 'characters' required to act according to the public's view of them. Just as with fictional television, the public's interest in them was addictive and virtually insatiable. The more it learned of them, the more it wanted – and this fascination centred on those points of maximum involvement such as 'rifts' within the family, marriage, sickness, waning affection and untimely death.

As interest in Princess Margaret flagged, the Phillipses remained the most accessible – and vulnerable – members of the royal show, and it is hard to exaggerate their importance as a point of reference for the public interest in the royal family. For more than any other members of the family, they seemed to have a knack for what Prince Philip once called *dontopedology* – which he translated as 'opening one's mouth and putting one's foot in it'; and when they failed to do this personally, the press was not above doing it for them, usually involving other members of the royal family in the process.

There was, for instance, that role the public had grown to expect of Princess Anne from her earliest eventing days as what the *Mirror* called 'the Frown Princess'; and on countless occasions she was presented as a source of friction or of one of those celebrated 'rifts' within the family. The Queen was reported to have been shocked by her daughter's bad language at the Windsor Horse Trials, and to have publicly reproved her. (In fact she wasn't and she didn't.) In one of many lengthy articles at the end of the Seventies, she was described as 'tactless and graceless – the Royal Family's own little gift to republicanism', with the all-important afterthought, 'Couldn't Grannie have a word?' (the suggestion being that the Queen Mother, in her role of real-life grandmother, would naturally be shocked by Princess Anne's beahviour. Again, it would take much more than Princess Anne to shock that very shrewd old royal lady.) And her husband seemed as firmly saddled as one of his own horses with his role as the royal family's resident buffoon. In January 1979, a reporter traced him to a joke shop in Tetbury buying some surprises for the royal family on their winter holidays. These included 'crapalot teabags, sexy sugar lumps releasing contraceptives when they melt, and Dr Windbreak's Fart Powder'. 'These will certainly liven things up at Windsor', he was quoted as saying. A Palace spokesman's comment on the incident was that 'Captain Phillips has a good sense of humour and enjoys a joke like anybody else.' But that was not the point, the real interest being how on earth the royal family reacted to these ghastly objects at the royal teatime. Outrage? Gales of laughter? Or, perhaps, did no one notice? Here history is mute, but the Phillipses remained by far the richest source of public speculation – and fairly innocent amusement – on the whole royal family for many months to come.

Simply because of the roles they had acquired, they were considered more or less fair game for the most unlikely 'insights' into their would-be private lives. In an article in *Woman* magazine in April 1979 – 'Are Mark and Anne really happy?' – Captain Phillips was described as personally upset by having to live in a house where everything had been provided by his mother-in-law, including some cast-off curtains from the Palace. As a result, 'Mark hates people thinking he's a kept man' and sometimes 'overcompensates' by being tough with Anne. Charles was said to have given him 'brotherly advice' before the marriage, not to let his sister 'get away with too much.'

The Phillipses were also vulnerable, like all the royal family, over the question of their wealth. To be fair, they were infinitely less rich than the Queen, Prince Charles, the Queen Mother and Princess Margaret, all of whom, unlike the Phillipses, possessed considerable and undisclosed private fortunes and untaxed income. But fairness was not, as the *Statesman* might have said, what the royal supershow was now 'about'. The Princess and her husband had their public role as what she herself described as 'the royal whipping post': they also had Gatcombe Park, the Captain's earnings as a farmer since he left the army, and the Princess's income from the Civil List. Since other members of the family were sacrosanct, and their very wealth an accepted part of their mythic situation, the latent public discontent over all the royal finances could always be directed at the Phillipses.

They faced a lot of this in 1979 after building a new stable block at Gatcombe Park. Neither the Queen nor the Queen Mother's far greater expenditure on their equine establishments had ever felt a breath of censure from the press – indeed they are generally regarded as a popular component of the traditional 'sport of kings.' But sections of the press were now aghast at what was presented as the most culpable royal indulgence of the quadruped since Nero made his favourite horse a consul. According to the *Mirror*, Princess Anne had insisted on a swimming pool for her wretched horses – 'arrogant', 'extravagant', what else could one expect? – and when it was later pointed out that the 'swimming pool' was in fact a stable with a concrete floor that could be flooded to a depth of several inches for hosing down the horses' hooves, it made little difference to the public image of the Phillipses as horse-mad, self-indulgent villains in the royal roadshow.

Interestingly, the revelation that this shocking pair were actually short of money, and had paid for the stables on a mortgage, only made matters worse. There is nothing royal or mythical about a mortgage, nor about being forced 'to make ends meet'; and when to do this, Captain Phillips accepted an annual £18,000 sponsorship from British Leyland for his riding, indignation seemed to know no bounds – particularly from Willie Hamilton MP, who would not allow a chance like this to pass unnoticed.

It really shows the complete insensitivity of these people, particularly when British Leyland is literally fighting for its life. Some people say Mark and Anne have not much money. They are rolling in it. They are just grubbing around for anyone to keep them going. They are just parasites.

Not for the first time in his life, Willie Hamilton was going just a little too far in his royal criticisms, and he gave the Court its opportunity to point out that the Princess's income from the Civil List, far from bringing a life of unnatural luxury to horses, was being spent strictly in relation to her royal duties; and that, after her parents, she was actually the hardest working member of the whole royal family. This said, little more was heard about the profligate high-life of the Phillipses.

But there were many other aspects of their open life-style to keep them firmly in the public eye throughout this period. For the Phillipses remained that invaluable asset for a worldwide press eager to indulge the highly profitable public longing for the 'human face' of British royalty – a family at once painfully ordinary yet ineradicably royal – and it was this intriguing combination which made the Phillipses themselves a major source of access to the magic zone of royalty itself.

13

PRINCE IN WAITING

'It would be in keeping with a film star, but not with the
Queen. The monarchy doesn't need that sort of publicity.'
Commander Colville on press conferences

Just as it seemed as if the royal family was awash with trivia about
the Phillipses, a gang of Irish terrorists with eight pounds of gelignite
abruptly gave the world the true-life spectacle of the Mountbatten-
Windsors at the centre of an unforgettable display of regal grief on
an early autumn day in 1979.

The gelignite had been placed inside the engine casing of the
ancient fishing boat used for sailing round Bantry Bay by Lord
Mountbatten and his daughter's family, the Brabournes, during their
holidays at Cassiebawn Castle in southern Ireland. Just before
midday in the morning of August 27, it was exploded by remote
control from the nearby cliffs, killing the seventy-nine-year-old Earl
instantly, together with Lord Brabourne's aged mother, one of his
twin sons, Prince Charles's godson, Nicholas Knatchbull, and a
fifteen-year-old schoolfriend. Admitting responsibility some hours
later, the Provisional IRA claimed the murder as 'a blow for a united
Ireland'.

Few Irishmen agreed, but this apart, the outrage undoubtedly
united the majority of Her Majesty's subjects round the royal family.
Like nothing else, the killing emphasised that the danger of assassination was as great a threat to the modern monarchy as it had once
been to the more vulnerable dynasties of Europe. Three years earlier
Princess Anne had been attacked in her chauffeur-driven car by an
armed maniac in the Mall, and in 1981 the Queen herself would
show typical *sang-froid* when fired on from the crowd with three
blank cartridges as she rode past at the annual Trooping the Colour.
Incidents like these were a reminder that, along with its dreamlike
attributes of wealth and splendour, there was also a permanent
element of risk in the royal situation, and the Queen in particular

was much admired for the regal calm with which she faced it. (Queen Victoria had been much the same, dismissing four attempts on her life as professional hazards, best ignored.)

Admiration, sympathy and public grief were the overwhelming feelings with which people watched the splendid royal ceremony staged at the obsequies in honour of this famous 'semi-royal', as Mountbatten once described himself. A royal funeral arouses even deeper emotions than a royal wedding, and this one was particularly impressive because of who Mountbatten was – immensely handsome wartime hero, outspoken public figure, and intimate counsellor and friend of almost all the members of the family.

The last major public ceremony involving all the members of the royal family had been Princess Anne's wedding three years earlier. Since then there had been the celebration of the Jubilee, and the scandals and the dramas of the Snowdons and the Phillipses – all of which had made the inner circle of the royal family more 'interesting', and more widely appreciated as ordinary human beings, than at any previous point in their existence.

Now as the television cameras showed them all at the centre of this ritual act of nationwide grief and mourning, the effect was palpable. For here the monarchy suddenly embodied all the emotive qualities of the occasion – the nostalgic spectacle of the great memorial service in Westminster Abbey; the solemn funeral procession, complete with the Earl's riderless horse, his favourite charger, Nelly; and the whole royal family there to be electronically observed as they struggled to control the most powerful of everyday emotions. As one reporter noted, 'Only the Queen Mother smiled . . . There was forty years of training in that smile.' None of the others managed it; and the moment everyone remembers came at the subsequent funeral service in Romsey Abbey, when Prince Charles, standing with his father, both in naval uniform, dabbed at his eye with obvious emotion. It was the 'human face of royalty' as rarely seen on any ceremonial occasion; and for the world at large, Prince Charles's note on the wreath he left made clear the largely unsuspected nature of the thirty-year-old Prince's relationship with his Uncle Dickie:

'H.G. with love from H.G.'

It was a reference to the way the Prince had called Lord Mountbatten his 'Honorary Grandfather': Prince Charles had also been 'H.G.' – Mountbatten's Honorary Grandson.

Given the chance, most people easily become voyeurs of royalty, and this glimpse of something so private naturally aroused considerable attention. It tended to confirm the public's impression of Prince Charles as a caring, rather gentle character; it emphasised 'Uncle Dickie's' human role within the family; and it also raised a number of intriguing questions over Mountbatten's actual influence upon the public image of the monarchy during the years before his death.

Certainly, without being cynical, his death and funeral could not have been more impressive had this flamboyant and lifelong showman carefully arranged the final episode himself. Everything about it was in keeping with the drama and the public splendour of his life, and the spectacle of his funeral seemed to set the seal on the great achievement of his life – restitution for the dishonour inflicted on his father, and total acceptance of the Battenberg/Mountbattens into the British royal family. It had been a strange ambition and its fulfilment was remarkable: as Claud Cockburn wrote, 'when one reflects that Lord Mountbatten's father started life as a minor West German princeling with a Polish mother, the thing takes on the dimensions of a minor miracle.'

It is hard to overestimate the extent of this 'minor miracle', or of Mountbatten's influence behind the scenes both as a friend of the family and as a 'walking royal encyclopaedia' as one acquaintance described him; and yet there was one area where he had little direct impact on the monarchy. Surprisingly, this was in the very area in which he had proved himself a master – the gentle arts of self-projection and publicity.

For in many ways, Mountbatten had remained the perfect example of everything a male member of the British royal family should carefully avoid. He was colourful and loved controversy. He was often indiscreet and spoke his mind. He was competitive, assertive and a natural leader; and he exhibited much of the popular appeal of his friend the Duke of Windsor in his prime as Prince of Wales. As Prince Philip soon came to appreciate, this was not the male house-style of the Windsor matriarchy; and although the example of Mountbatten's televised life-story had played its part in convincing Prince Philip and the Queen to agree to the historic television film *Royal Family*, it was not until the aftermath of the Investiture that Mountbatten had a genuine effect on the changing style of the royal family – and this through his growing influence over his 'Honorary Grandson', Charles. Only in relative old age did

Mountbatten come into his own as others began to attempt the techniques of superstardom he had long ago perfected for himself.

Prince Charles's relations with his father were by no means as abrasive as rumour often had it. Prince Philip could be – and often was – short-tempered with his eldest son, still seeing it as part of his paternal duty to exhort him on to greater effort and to live up to those manly virtues both had learned at Gordonstoun. Prince Charles had a different, less exacting range of interests than his father. Since he was also happily more tolerant and less aggressive than Prince Philip, there were none of those celebrated 'rifts' between the two of them which would have offered such a fruitful source of public interest – but equally they were not particularly close. There was too much difference in their characters – and as the hyper-energetic Prince Philip had often been too busy or impatient to provide the royal heir with the sort of understanding he required, Prince Charles had increasingly relied on the example and advice of surrogate father-figures from the world outside.

This was a function his avuncular private secretary, David Check-etts, had performed in Prince Charles's transition from adolescence to early manhood, and Checketts' acknowledged skills as a professional PR man gave him a crucial role throughout this period as protector and adviser in that most alarming quarter for a shy young prince – relations with the media and public. The extraordinary success of the Prince's 'launching' at the time of the Investiture had seemed to reinforce his private secretary's standing – and for a while it did, but only for a while. For with success and constant practice in the public eye, the Prince became an excellent performer on his own account. His shyness went, he rapidly picked up the tricks of his unusual trade, and as he did so his reliance on the expertise of David Checketts and Neilson McCarthy started to decline.

After his work on the Jubilee Appeal, Neilson's closest personal contact with the royal family would come from the fact that he had sent his son to school at Gordonstoun, where he became a contemporary and friend of Prince Andrew. A keen photographer, the young Neilson seemed to be following in celebrated footsteps when he took a portrait of Prince Andrew in full naval uniform, which was widely published on his twenty-first birthday; he also organised the disco at Windsor Castle for the private birthday celebrations.

As for David Checketts, his would be the fate of many favoured courtiers before him, as 'the Boy', as he sometimes called Prince Charles, finally outgrew him. Even at Cambridge, it had been the sophisticated and worldly Master of Trinity, Lord Butler, who had exercised the greatest intellectual influence on the Prince, but after Cambridge it was 'Uncle Dickie' on whom Prince Charles increasingly relied for inspiration and personal advice. Mountbatten always claimed to have bathed the Prince as a baby, and had remained a figure of unique glamour for the younger members of the royal family; but it was not until Prince Charles was commanding his uncomfortable mine-layer, HMS *Codrington* that the 'Honorary Grandfather' role began in earnest.

Those who actually met Mountbatten can attest to the extraordinary power of his personality: and in private, the man who once described himself as 'the most conceited character I know', could seem surprisingly unlike his public image. He could be approachable, very funny, and an endless source of anecdote and gossip about almost anyone who mattered – and many more who didn't – in the last half-century. Mellowing with age, he appeared a far more human figure than the cool careerist who had so ruthlessly cashed in on his rich wife and royal connections in his early scramble up life's glittering ladder. Since then he had commanded armies, governed and partitioned India, married his nephew to the future Queen of England and seen the name Mountbatten at the head of Europe's major royal dynasty.

With age and his wife Edwina's death in 1970, he had become a little bored and lonely. Surrounded by his mementoes and the marble statuary of Broadlands, the chance of imparting what he had learned of life to the future King of England naturally appealed to him. He found Charles less assertive than his father had been in his early twenties; and Charles in turn responded to this infinitely understanding and intelligent great-uncle who had known George V and Nehru, Charlie Chaplin and the Tsar of Russia, and who soon became his personal repository of worldly wisdom and dynastic lore. Each in fact had much to offer to the other.

In Prince Charles the monarchy was fortunate to have an heir-apparent whose character so admirably conformed to the public image he was required to sustain. He had inherited – or learned – the many useful qualities for a future constitutional monarch which the Windsors and Mountbattens had developed in previous generations; equally important, he had managed to avoid the predominant defects of the royal race.

Like both his parents he was something of a puritan – which expressed itself in his unconcealed dislike of too much alcohol or central heating and a positive aversion to tobacco (which had almost certainly played at least a part in the death of all four English kings this century). He had none of Edward VII's gluttony or love of gambling and fast society. He was not a philistine like George VI, nor had he turned against his family and parents like the Duke of Windsor.

Like his sister he actually disliked personal extravagance: she once described economy as having been 'bred into' her, having been 'brought up by my parents and my nanny to believe that things were not to be wasted.' Prince Charles was much the same, a great one for checking bills and turning off electric fires; and while he seemed mercifully free from the Mountbatten vanity, he readily admitted to that love of royal ceremony and the formal trappings of tradition which, with the exception of the Duke of Windsor, had been something of a trademark of the royal menfolk since the days of Edward VII. He rather enjoyed the sight of the fifty-odd different uniforms his valet religiously maintained for him in the Palace wardrobe, and would have profoundly disagreed with his great-uncle David that ceremonies of state were so much 'rot' and a dreadful 'waste of time'. Considering the crucial part they played in the whole mystique of modern royalty, this was just as well.

There was however one important point, which few suspected, where the Prince was vulnerable – a belief in his actual role as Prince of Wales. It was not that he lacked self-confidence: Checketts had helped to give him that, and the adulation that had followed the Investiture had convinced him of his power to do whatever was required of him. So had the success of the various projects his private secretary had suggested with an eye to his public image, as well as to provide an outlet for his energies: schemes such as rural conservation, adventure projects for the young, and even the plans to raise the Tudor flagship, *Mary Rose*, from the seabed of the Solent.

But the Prince still faced the problem which had always been endemic for a Prince of Wales – how to provide a sense of purpose and reality to life while waiting to succeed. Since the Queen, his mother, was extremely healthy, barely in her middle fifties, highly popular and showing not the faintest inclination to abdicate, it was a very real difficulty – especially for a prince like Charles, who was contemplative by nature, and much above the Windsor level of male intelligence.

It was not a problem he could easily discuss with his father – whose answer to the majority of life's worries lay in 'doing something'. But it was very much a subject to excite a fervid monarchist like Uncle Dickie, a sympathetic and unshockable man of the world whose abundant memory was crammed with stories and theories of European royalty. For Prince Charles he was the man who really did know all the answers; and for Mountbatten, with this ready pupil, it was the culminating moment of his lifetime as he became in old age the philosopher and friend of the future King of England.

Mountbatten helped Prince Charles achieve the equanimity that saw him safely through his late twenties with so little public criticism. He was a great calmer-down, and an invaluable guide of the sort Princess Anne and Princess Margaret had notably lacked in coping with the problems of their private lives. He was also very shrewd in the way he helped his nephew to avoid the major pitfalls blundered into with such confident abandon by the Duke of Windsor, during his final years as Prince of Wales. That woeful man was a great example of what his successor should avoid, and with Mountbatten there to point the moral, Prince Charles would rarely fall a victim to the public controversy and scandal which had dogged great-uncle David.

This was particularly so over the subject which had made the Duke of Windsor such a source of gossip, and finally cost him the throne itself – relations with the opposite sex. And with the young Prince Charles, sex could easily have brought untold damage to his public image, for throughout his twenties he was extremely fond of women and keen to make the most of his invincible advantages.

After his sheltered adolescence, it had struck the Prince with all the force of a revelation that he could have virtually any young woman he desired. Not that he did, at first, for he was by nature somewhat cautious and the logistics that surrounded royal seduction were formidable. There were his personal detectives on constant duty, there was the press on almost constant watch, there was David Checketts who was what they called 'old-fashioned' on such matters, and worst of all there was the constant danger of a public scandal. What with Aunt Margaret, the family had had enough of that already. Even as an undergraduate at Cambridge, it was a problem that exercised the Prince considerably. Thanks largely to discreet connivance from Lord Butler, he had enjoyed a little of the sexual freedom practised by most of his contemporaries, but he did so in uncomfortable awareness of the dangers, knowing quite well how much a Sunday newspaper would pay for the story of a night of passion with the Prince of Wales.

So during this period the 'World's Most Eligible Bachelor' – as the press would soon wearily describe him – tended to sublimate his feelings in his work, hoping the problem would solve itself. In fact it did nothing of the sort. Fortunately, since one important function of an heir apparent is finally to father more potential heirs apparent, the Prince was by no means backward in this quarter, and his puritanism emphatically did not extend to sex. But unfortunately it was not the sort of subject he could easily discuss with either his father or with David Checketts. Uncle Dickie, on the other hand, could see the point at once.

It was a problem European royalty had coped with from time immemorial, and the Duke of Windsor's troubles had stemmed largely from his parents' prudery and anxiety to find him an appropriate royal bride, which had driven him by reaction into the arms of a succession of married women. It was yet another awful warning from the Duke of Windsor on how not to deal with the latest Prince of Wales.

The family had long tended to rely on Uncle Dickie for advice about the Prince. In 1965, his had been the moving spirit at the informal conference the royal parents called at Buckingham Palace, together with the Prime Minister and the Archbishop of Canterbury, to formulate a schedule for Prince Charles's education on leaving Gordonstoun, and his advice had won the day. 'Trinity College, Cambridge, like his grandfather; Dartmouth like his father and his grandfather; and then to sea in the Royal Navy, ending up with a command of his own.' He was equally emphatic and realistic in his advice on how to deal with the unusual problems posed by Prince Charles's love-life.

For as he understood at once, the great danger as far as the Palace was concerned was that the Prince would get caught up in the sort of extra-mural 'scrapes' that had dogged great-uncle David. As the scandals round the Snowdons had emphasised, the press could no longer be relied on for the loyal discretion they had cast around the

Duke of Windsor's various amours until the moment when the Abdication crisis burst, and Prince Charles had already shown a worrying inclination to become involved with older married women too.

This was, of course, a great temptation for anyone in the Prince's position – and traditionally it had always offered the royal heir relief before and sometimes after he was married. Edward VII confined himself to courtesans and married women of the upper-classes, all of them available, more than willing, and with far too much to lose to blab of royal favours. (Instructively, the only one who did, Daisy, Countess of Warwick, was ostracised by smart society.)

But morals, society and the inhibitions of the press had all changed from those deferential days of good King Edward. Complacent husbands could no longer be relied on to keep quiet out of patriotic duty; nor could the press; and Wallis Simpson had shown how easily an ambitious married woman could become divorced, then married to a prince in love with her. In his early twenties Prince Charles had a disturbing tendency to fall in love.

As so often in the past, the advice of Uncle Dickie, both to the Prince and to his parents, was extremely practical. He was emphatically against the Prince conducting love-affairs with married women. He was equally emphatic on the need to avoid tarnishing the Prince's admirable image by sordid scandal. As he saw it, there was one logical solution. Unlike the Duke of Windsor, Prince Charles was a responsible young man who enjoyed his home-life with his family, and he must somehow be allowed to carry on his private life, either within the privacy of the Palace or the suitable country houses of rich friends on whose discretion he could utterly rely.

When Prince Charles was still in the Royal Navy, HMS *Bronington* would often be berthed at Portsmouth while its commander, unseen and unsuspected, would be spending a weekend's shore-leave twenty miles away with his Honorary Grandfather at Broadlands – and often with a pretty girl as weekend guest. Everything was wonderfully easy and discreet, and the press caught not the faintest breath of what was happening.

Much the same routine was followed at the Palace where, thanks largely to Mountbatten's down-to-earth advice, Prince Charles had his own separate apartments where no one intruded save at his actual invitation. Even the Queen would always contact him by telephone before seeing him, as she invariably did at some time in the day when they were both in residence. It was firmly understood that the Prince's territory was sacrosanct, so he could please himself entirely over whom he saw and what he did.

It was a system that had obvious advantages, both for security and privacy. The Prince could trust his personal detective implicitly; he could invite anyone he liked for dinner or whatever, and the world was none the wiser. Once the all-important ground rules were established, Charles discovered he had all the freedom he required. He used it cleverly and rather coolly, for as he also rapidly discovered, there were few young women who, invited for an evening at the Palace by the Prince of Wales, would willingly forego that interesting honour.

The Prince deserves credit for the restraint he showed in this enviable situation, and for the skill with which he managed to avoid scandal or lurid revelations from discarded girl-friends to the day he married. Remembering that he was sexually extremely active through this period, and that the press were obsessively concerned about his love-life, this was a considerable achievement which requires some explanation.

The key to it was that Prince Charles, following his Uncle Dickie's sensible advice, rigidly adhered to certain basic rules. First, he invariably chose his girl-friends from that strata of the wealthy upper classes in which he also made the male friends with whom he week-ended, hunted, or played polo. They always tended to be part of a closed circle within which loyalty was absolute, everyone knew each other and discretion towards the world outside was absolutely *de rigeur*. The girls within this circle knew the form: one did not gossip about HRH and, whatever the provocation, the idea of revealing anything to a journalist for money was inconceivable, knowing the total social death that would ensue.

The second rule was that Prince Charles never took the risk of visiting a girl-friend, however much in favour, in her own apartment. They came to him, and within the circle it was always made extremely clear that this happened only when and if he asked them. And the third rule, which Uncle Dickie in his wisdom always emphasised, was the danger of writing compromising letters: the telephone was safer than the pen and, for someone like Prince Charles, equally effective.

But apart from these princely rules, which were fairly rigidly observed, the fact remains that although Prince Charles made abundant use of his pasha-like opportunities, he was not what the Edwardians would have called a cad. He was not the most generous of lovers, but neither did he take unfair advantage to steal girls from others – nor did he make promises he could not fulfil. Several of his former mistresses remained close friends when the affair was over.

The press inevitably followed the changing roll-call of the Prince's girl-friends – and just as inevitably speculated on their actual standing and their prospects. Early in 1976 he *seemed* to be in love with blonde Davina Sheffield; then there was the Queen Mother's goddaughter, Lady Sarah Spencer, who after a skiing holiday with the Prince took the unusual step of telling a journalist that their friendship was 'strictly platonic'; and for some time the most favoured candidate in the royal marriage stakes was the daughter of the Duke of Wellington, Lady Jane Wellesley.

But for the future and for the image of the monarchy itself, the important point was that Prince Charles had managed to achieve something that even hardened PR men would have thought imposs-ible. For more than ten years as the most famous bachelor in Britain, he had enjoyed a thoroughly fulfilling sex life without damaging in any way his reputation as devoted son and princely paragon – decent, responsible, concerned and extremely popular. This was something virtually unique in the history of the English monarchy, for whom unmarried male heirs had almost always been a source of trouble, and with the advent of his thirtieth birthday in November 1978 there was only one important point on which Prince Charles could be seriously faulted: his failure to choose himself a bride. It had become his most pressing public duty: to bestow his love and thus create the dream princess who would one day be the Queen of England.

For by the late Seventies, the lack of female glamour in the royal family had produced a serious gap in the ranks of the performing monarchy. All the other roles were filled quite admirably, and its members seemed increasingly at home in the parts a fascinated public expected them to play. The Queen Mother, with a lifetime's popularity, seemed incapable of a bad performance as national grandmother – warm, smiling, human, understanding, she embodied everything the public could want of a tribal grandmother. Particu-larly admirable was the way she had effortlessly passed on her role as royal matriarch to her daughter at the time of the Silver Jubilee, and the Queen herself appeared increasingly assured at the centre of the royal stage. Prince Philip, now in his late fifties, had kept his looks and seemed an impressive father figure at the head of his energetic family. With his two younger sons now in their teens, and Prince Charles the most envied – or desired – young man in England, there was little danger of the monarchy 'ending up' in that 'national museum' towards which Prince Philip once believed it to be heading. Interest and empathy towards this family of endlessly promoted royal superstars had never been so strong.

But in pointed contrast with the Thirties, when three of the four principal members of the royal family had been young and female, the Mountbatten-Windsors in their mythic role as the nation's ultimate family were clearly failing to provide sufficient feminine excitement for their dedicated worldwide public. Princess Anne was a source of considerable interest, but since her wedding she had never been the sort of legendary princess multitudes of unknown women could dream of being, as they had with the youthful Princess Margaret. And Princess Alexandra of Kent, the Queen's first cousin, though an admirable performer of her royal duties and appearances, lacked the instant glamour of her mother Princess Marina of Greece, who had died of a tumour on the brain ten years earlier.

The Prince's thirtieth birthday passed in November 1978, with Charles still in no apparent hurry to choose himself a wife – which was understandable considering what was involved – and while the nation and the Palace waited, the most unlikely character to have entered the ranks of British royalty since anybody could remember came on the scene to give the royal family a touch of badly needed female glamour on her own highly personal initiative.

The Queen's first cousin, Alexandra's younger brother, Prince Michael of Kent, though six years senior to Prince Charles, had himself remained unmarried until that year. A military man, known chiefly to the public as President of the British Bobsleigh Federation, his principal private interests, tobogganing apart, had long been fast cars and fast young women. Then suddenly, early in the 1970s, Prince Michael's pleasurable if unremarkable life had been totally transformed.

He had a friend from Eton called Tom Troubridge, who was married for the second time to a six foot-tall, Brunhilde-like Australian called Marie-Christine. At least, she appeared to be Australian, having in those days just a trace of antipodean accent, and having spent her girlhood in a Sydney suburb where her mother, Countess Rogala-Kozacorawski, *aka* Mrs Gebhardt, owned a beauty parlour. But accent and background were deceptive, for Marie-Christine was supposedly of Austrian descent, the daughter of her mother's previous marriage to a long-discarded, somewhat shadowy 'Viennese' Baron Von Reibnitz – so shadowy a baron that throughout her Sydney adolescence, his daughter never saw him and generally called herself Marie-Christine Gebhardt.

The Troubridge marriage was unhappy. Prince Michael found himself powerfully attracted to this powerful married lady, and at a certain stage Tom Troubridge quietly departed for New York, leaving Mrs Troubridge free to pursue a two year diploma course in decorative art at the Victoria and Albert Museum in South Kensington. She was also free to pursue HRH Prince Michael of Kent; and before long they were riding incognito every morning in the romantic landscape of Richmond Park, where Prince Michael's sister, Alexandra, had a house. A most extraordinary female royal career had almost started.

As one of Prince Michael's bobsleighing friends remarked, 'What happened then was rather like the Cresta run for Michael – exciting, very fast, and no earthly chance of getting off.' But there were massive problems for a British royal prince who found himself in love with a lady who, as well as being married and a foreigner, also happened to be a Roman Catholic.

Enter Uncle Dickie, who as Marie-Christine admitted later, 'really *made* our marriage'. For Mountbatten, as a cousin of Marina's mother, Princess Nicholas of Greece, had always taken a proprietory interest in the Kents; and the great royal showman, with his eye for spectacular young women, was quick to spot something of a fellow-spirit in this extrovert Teutonic beauty. Like the talent-spotting impresario he was, he saw at once that, for all her handicaps, Mrs Troubridge was a natural actress, and the ideal person to inspire his not terribly inspiring nephew, Michael, thus bringing to the royal family itself a touch of what it badly needed at that moment – feminine allure and genuine bezaz.

Her handicaps, of course, were formidable – just how formidable time alone would tell – and only someone with the natural confidence of Uncle Dickie would have thought them superable. For Mrs Troubridge not only had a husband who was very much alive, but was also a devout believer whose conscience, unlike Princess

Margaret's, would not permit her the let-out of divorce. Prince Michael too, as 16th in line to the throne, was affected by the terms of the original Royal Marriage Act, which was still very much in force and laid down that marriage to a Catholic effectively debarred any member of the royal family from his or her rights to the succession.

For a family which, forty years before, had seen its king consigned to outer darkness for marrying a foreign *divorcée* who was not a Catholic, it was still a lot to swallow. But it was the sort of challenge that rather appealed to Uncle Dickie. Princess Margaret's divorce had established a precedent for greater tolerance over marriage tangles in the royal family itself, and Mountbatten was the most persuasive advocate behind the scenes. Once convinced of the need to regularise the position of Prince Michael and the lady he was now emphatically in love with, Uncle Dickie once again took on the role of *ex officio* royal marriage broker.

Prince Michael's chances of succeeding to the throne were so infinitesimal that he had no qualms about renouncing them – once it was made clear to him that renunciation would not affect the rights of any children he might have. And any qualms the royal family might have had about the relationship were pacified by the persuasive Lord Mountbatten.

This left only the problem of disposing of Mrs Troubridge's unwanted marriage – and here the centuries-old wisdom of the Church of Rome came into play. With that sympathy the Vatican extends to the faithful who are rich enough and patient enough to submit their marriage problems to the moral jurisdiction of its matrimonial court, the *Sacra Rota*, it was finally pronounced from Rome that in the eyes of Mother Church, the Troubridge marriage had not actually existed. *Sub specie aeternitatis*, Tom Troubridge's apparent unwillingness to beget children had rendered it invalid: he and the lady he had called his wife had merely lived in sin, and by 1978 the way was almost clear for Prince Michael to make her his Princess.

The wedding was set for June 30, and meant to culminate with a full nuptial mass in the Great Church of Vienna with Lord Mountbatten, assorted von Reibnitzes, the Vienna Boys' Choir, and even the bride's mysterious father, shadowy Baron Gunther, who had specially arrived from his citrus farm in distant Mozambique: and it was only the last-minute refusal from the Vatican of a dispen-

sation to allow the bride to wed a Protestant that consigned the
wedding to a civil ceremony in Vienna Town Hall. Religiously, this
left the bride in an equivocal position, but under the laws of man
and of Her Majesty's United Kingdom, Marie-Christine from that
moment on was HRH Princess Michael of Kent and a member of
the British royal family.

It was a role she swiftly made the most of, with a flair and instinct
for publicity no previous outsider to the ranks of minor royalty had
ever mustered. In effect she was the first example of an instinctive
show-business personality modern royalty had ever known. She was
beautiful, abundant, and engagingly outspoken. Her size made her
unmistakable, her intelligence made her equally formidable, and she
shared with Lord Mountbatten a Germanic instinct to treat everything about the royal situation with absolute Teutonic seriousness.

Her style could hardly have been more different from the relaxed
regality of the rest of the Mountbatten-Windsors – 'She sounds far
too grand for us,' the Queen is credited with saying on first hearing
of her – and from the start she insisted on being treated with every
courtesy to which her freshly acquired rank entitled her. Two girls
decorating her apartment in Kensington Palace were working up
step-ladders when she made an unexpected entrance; both were
peremptorily ordered down, and told to curtsey properly before Her
Royal Highness. A friend she had known in Australia was invited
to dine, and after an exchange of greetings the Princess said thoughtfully, 'Yes, I think you *may* still be permitted to address me as
Marie-Christine.'

Similar stories about her now were legion, all of which served to
emphasise that Princess Michael was filling an important, previously
unoccupied female role in the royal cast-list which every TV soap
opera addict would recognise at once. She was the beautiful
ambitious outsider with the mysterious past, who traditionally in
Dallas or in *Dynasty* makes her dramatic entry into the rich established family through the attraction she exerts upon one of its weaker
male members. And instinctively, like the born actress she was,
Marie-Christine proceeded to act out this most engrossing role to
maximum effect – thus guaranteeing her constant interest from her
female audience, and considerable, if sometimes grudging,
popularity.

The key to the public fascination with this new Princess was the
total consistency with which she always managed to adhere to all

the rules the American TV sagas have laid down for such a character. She swiftly made her husband seem more positive and manly – by openly encouraging him to find lucrative directorships with City firms, and to grow a most successful beard, which not only covered an unimpressive jaw-line but gave him a brand-new public image as a resurrected version of his grandfather, George V. She was jealously assertive of her status in the family, campaigning (unsuccessfully) for Prince Michael to receive an income from the Civil List and, according to one widely circulated story, personally complaining to the Queen herself over the inadequate room allotted to her and her husband during her first royal Christmas with the whole family at Windsor. She also had to clash with other members of the family she had married into. 'What would you give your worst enemy for Christmas?' someone is supposed to have asked the young Lord Linley, son of her close neighbour in Kensington Palace, Princess Margaret. 'Dinner for two with Princess Michael,' was his widely circulated reply.

Such tales kept her firmly in the news, and she was soon providing an important female sub-plot to the central drama of the main performing monarchy, as she carried her story ever further into realms undreamt-of for members of the royal family, but all too credible to soap opera audiences by now. First came her attempts to find the sort of glamorous, jet-setting life her tastes and personality required. Prince Michael notoriously lacked the income, or the inclination, to provide it; but the Princess soon involved him in her undisguised obsession with the international super-rich, who were delighted to be able to include these two authentic members of the British royal family at their parties or among their house-guests at Houston or New York.

Soon after her marriage, she remarked that she would 'go anywhere for a meal' – and a great deal else. She did – and among the other offerings she received from devoted friends have been a racehorse, exclusive use of a luxury apartment in Antigua, and probably at least part of the £300,000 she and her husband, who possessed no private fortune of his own, somehow discovered for the purchase of their idyllic Gloucestershire mansion at Nether Lypiatt. The source of this money has never been explained. It has been publicly denied that it was a legacy from Uncle Dickie, but there has been no refutation of widespread speculation that it came from Her Royal Highness's wealthy friends, the oil-rich Texan Portanovas, who have frequently flown in Prince Michael and his glamorous Princess as prestigious guests of honour at their most impressive social gatherings.

Such behaviour was very much taboo among the other members of the royal family, but because it was so in character with the role that Princess Michael had adopted it did little to affect her popularity – and certainly added further to her interest value. But in 1985 would come the two events which put her popularity and her status in the royal family itself to the most scathing test of all.

First came the revelations about her father, the shadowy Baron from the citrus farm in Mozambique. Far from being the noble Viennese victim of the Nazis she had always lovingly referred to, he was nothing of the sort. He had been German, an early friend of Herman Goering, and a *Sturmbanfuehrer* in the Nazi SS.

Three months later came an even worse blow to the public image of the glamorous princess – the strongly authenticated report in that watch-dog of royal morality, the *News of the World*, of a love affair with one of her richer friends from Texas, Warren Hunt, nephew of the fabulously wealthy Bunker Hunt from Houston. If the story was true, it must be the most extraordinary example of royal nature imitating TV art, for the Hunts of Texas were the original models for the Ewings of *Dallas*.

These reports, of course, were deeply embarrassing to the Princess and to Buckingham Palace, but both managed to behave with a keen professional awareness of how the public would react and the damage could be best averted. Once again the key to what occurred lay in the deft appreciation by the Palace and the Princess herself of that public role she had to play. In a TV serial both incidents might well have been scripted by a clever writer for a character like her. In her reaction to them it was essential to remain consistent and not to disappoint her audience.

How does the story go when the shocking details of the glamorous outsider's secrets are revealed? She bites her lip and faces the truth courageously; and, suddenly admiring her pluck and new and unsuspected depths within her character, the family, and the fascinated viewers, rally round. Which is exactly what occurred with Princess Michael.

Over the revelations of her father's Nazi past, the Palace issued a brief statement saying it was true, but that she had never known about it. Next day she made a widely-praised appearance on breakfast television, candidly admitting, 'Here I am, forty years old, and

I suddenly discover something that really is quite unpleasant. I shall simply have to live with it.' Live with it she did that very evening when, 'facing up bravely to the most agonising ordeal of her life', as the *Daily Mail* put it, 'the brave princess' donned her glittering tiara to join the Queen herself at a royal state banquet held at Windsor Castle in honour of the President of Malawi. Next day there were further headlines praising 'The Courage of the Princess'; and that, effectively, was that, with Baron Gunther and his Nazi past rapidly forgotten.

The next episode in Princess Michael's interesting life was more difficult to cope with, and at the first hint of a romance between her and Warren Hunt she seemed to falter. Briefly it seemed as if she might be suffering a nervous breakdown, but she swiftly rallied. With the Palace Press Office refusing to comment on what it called 'sewage journalism' – but not actually denying anything – both the Prince and the Princess gamely got their act together to deny the rumours, show that their marriage was intact and face the public. When she and Prince Michael turned up hand in hand to watch the tennis finals at the centre court at Wimbledon, few women watching can have failed to sympathise with her obvious ordeal, and in a moment of pure royal theatre, the Wimbledon crowd was suddenly on its feet to give the Princess – and possibly her husband – a standing ovation.

It was a tribute to the way she had made herself a royal superstar; but while giving constant female interest to the public dramas of this performing royal family, she could never hope to reach the highest ranks of all. Even in 1979, for all her glamour, she could be at best a stand-in for the central role of royal dream princess; and her presence at the beginning of the new decade only served to emphasise the pressure that was now upon Prince Charles to find one – for himself, for the monarchy, and for an increasingly expectant nation. 1980 dawned. The weeks ticked by. 'How long, oh Prince?' the nation asked. 'How long?'

14

A MEGASTAR IS MADE

'I think of my family as very special people. I have never wanted not to have a home life – to get away from home. I love my home life. We happen to be a very close-knit family. I am happier at home with my family than anywhere else.'

Prince Charles

It's awfully difficult, because you've got to remember that when you marry, in my position, you are going to marry someone who perhaps is one day going to become Queen. You've got to choose somebody very carefully . . . People expect quite a lot from somebody like that . . . and it has got to be somebody pretty special.

Those heartfelt words Prince Charles had stammered out in his first television interview, at the age of twenty, were even truer now that he was in his thirties, and they served to underline his curious dilemma. When he was barely out of school he understood that, unlike the rest of his mother's male subjects, he would never be able to make a simple choice of settling for a girl he loved and marrying her. He would be choosing simultaneously a wife and a potential future Queen of England – and the more experience he gained of women during his years as a liberated and unmarried Prince of Wales, the more difficult it seemed to find the ideal person to combine these two roles satisfactorily.

One who might have done so was the Duke of Wellington's intelligent and pretty daughter, Lady Jane Wellesley, with whom he had been in love in his early twenties. Since her father was a Duke and a close friend of the family, she was most acceptable at Court; but in her case intelligence had proved the fatal flaw. The more she understood what marriage to the Prince implied, the more it daunted her – just as the Queen Mother, pondering her own marriage to the future George VI in 1922 had herself been daunted by the prospect 'as royalty, never, never again to be free to think or speak or act as I feel I ought to think or speak or act.' Unlike the young Queen

Mother, this had been something she could finally not contemplate and the romance had foundered.

Inevitably, Lord Mountbatten had been unable to resist the chance of one culminating stroke of royal match-making – by promoting the prospects of his granddaughter, Amanda Knatchbull, with the Prince. But although the two had known each other from childhood, the essential chemistry failed to work and the Prince and his cousin genuinely stayed the best of friends and nothing more.

A very different character was the spectacular and temperamental Anna 'Whiplash' Wallace, with whom the Prince was very much in love early in 1980. To begin with, much of her attraction lay in her extrovert glamour and her independence, for the Prince was challenged by the fact – which she made not the slightest effort to disguise – that she was not even publicly in awe of him. This was both piquant and unusual, but for the tolerant Prince Charles things went too far when she made her displeasure at his lack of constant attention all too clear at a ball in honour of the Queen Mother at Windsor Castle.

Within the family there was still a strong survival of Queen Mary's sense of reverence for the sacred royal person, which extended to the royal heir, and it was painfully obvious that, whatever else she did, Miss Wallace would never place Prince Charles on that all-important 'pedestal' within the family. Although in love, the Prince could understand the trouble this would cause – and did nothing to impede the fiery young lady's abrupt departure.

For the Prince, as a dutiful son and a conscientious heir, was strongly influenced by the private family lore of the Mountbatten-Windsors, and the Queen Mother in particular had always been a trusted source of personal advice. The memory of the havoc caused by Wallis Simpson was still very much alive within the family, and the Prince's grandmother was worldly-wise enough to warn him of the danger to the throne of strong-willed, temperamental ladies. Recognising in him much the same uxorious, devoted nature she treasured in her memories of her husband, George VI, she was convinced that Charles's private happiness and the future popularity of the monarchy both required a wife of unusual gentleness and total dedication.

But how to find one? Although in theory 'the world's most eligible bachelor' had the female world to choose from, his ten years of discreet philandering had made the problem more acute than if he had married in his early twenties, like all male royal heirs – with the exception of the Duke of Windsor – in living memory. He was too experienced to agree to a suitable marriage with a foreign royal princess, which the Queen, as a believer in preserving the blood royal, was said to favour. This had happened with both Edward VII and George V, but since then foreign princesses had become in short supply, and although there was speculation over Caroline of Monaco and Marie-Astrid of Luxembourg (with whom the Queen was said to be 'enchanted'), both were Catholic and neither was a starter in the royal marriage stakes.

Nor, as a courtier privately remarked, were 'the girls Prince Charles goes to bed with'. For with the advent of the contraceptive pill, even the most gently nurtured daughters of the upper-classes invariably had what was once known as 'a past' by their middle-twenties; and another piece of royal lore prescribed it as unthinkable for anyone to supersede the heir-apparent in the favours of his wife, the future Queen of England. For the public myth of monarchy demanded a princess who was beautiful, untarnished and above reproach. This was the essence of the dream princess the royal story called for: as one biographer put it, 'It was the Prince's duty to present his public with perfection.'

As a central figure in the performing monarchy, Prince Charles was all too well aware of his uncomfortable responsibility towards this worldwide and increasingly demanding audience, and by 1980 the pressure on him had become intense. Prince Philip was particularly impatient at what he tended to regard as his son's irresponsibility; and once again there was the Duke of Windsor's ghost as a horrible reminder of what could happen to a Prince of Wales who shirked his marital obligations for the pleasures of his single state, only to end up at the age of forty in total thrall to a dominating *divorcée*. With Prince Charles now rising thirty-three, some such fate was not impossible; and with every year that passed it would patently become more difficult for him to find the virginal and lovely dream princess to fill that all-important role beside him.

And then, quite suddenly, he did.

Earl Spencer's youngest daughter, Diana, was just nineteen in the spring of 1980 and, judging by the Prince's form-book, not the sort of girl to have attracted him. She was gauche, shy and extremely unsophisticated. Having left school at sixteen with two 'O'-levels, she gave little sign of that quick intelligence he had always responded to in women. She liked shopping, dancing and pop-music – none of them high on the Prince's list of interests – and as a sere and worldly bachelor he had not evinced the faintest interest in pursuing unformed, rather simple girls, thirteen years his junior. As a gentleman the whole idea would probably have rather shocked him.

But the two of them had much in common through the close connections that existed between the Spencers and the royal family. The Earl himself had been equerry to the Queen until his marriage to Diana's mother Frances, daughter of Lord Fermoy, in 1954. The Fermoys too were close friends of the royal family. Old Lord Fermoy, an Irish peer and Norfolk landowner, had been something of a crony of his neighbour, George VI, and was actually a member of the final shooting party the King enjoyed so much the day before he died. Lord Fermoy is said to have taught Prince Charles to ice-skate on the frozen pond at Sandringham; and on his death, his wife, Diana's grandmother, Lady Fermoy, continued her friendship with the Queen Mother as one of her permanent ladies-in-waiting.

During her childhood, Diana had lived with her parents in a large house on the Sandringham estate as tenants and close neighbours of the Queen. The family were fairly constant members of that 'charmed circle' of royal friends, and excellent examples of that 'tweedy set of upper-class ladies and gentlemen' the erstwhile Lord Altrincham was once so rude about. Interestingly, her parents' divorce in 1968 did little to affect the friendship, and Diana's childhood continued in close personal proximity to the royal family. An insecure small girl, hit badly by the parental break-up, it would have been surprising had she not had dreams of one day marrying a prince herself.

Throughout her teens the personal connections between the Spencers and the royal family were extended, with her eldest sister, Sarah, spending that 'strictly platonic' fortnight skiing with her friend Prince Charles, and her other sister, Jane, finally marrying the Queen's future assistant private secretary, Robert Fellowes, in 1978. As a contemporary of Prince Andrew, Diana was almost automatically included in the circle of acceptable friends around the younger members of the royal family, and as such was adroitly placed to catch the somewhat jaded eye of a Prince of Wales feeling rather sorry for himself at the end of his romance with the glamorous Miss Wallace.

This must explain the Prince's sudden interest in the simple and emergent English rose he had actually known since her childhood. She was a total contrast to the rather glossy creatures he was used to, and her naive exuberance coupled with her shyness both amused him and aroused the protective interests of the amiable Prince. During that spring they met at Sandringham, and again later when she was invited as Prince Andrew's guest aboard *Britannia* – and it struck Prince Charles how very suitable Diana was. In fact no casting director could have arranged things better for a Prince now seriously in search of his Princess.

Indeed, in many ways she slotted quite uncannily into that old-fashioned pattern of regal femininity originally developed by the House of Windsor. Her birth and breeding were impeccable. She was obviously pure and good. She loved children, animals and living in the country, and while brought up to show unquestioning devotion to the royal family, she was perfectly at ease with them. She was the absolute antithesis of the modern, self-assertive 'liberated' girl; and since she still blushed easily, it was very clear that she was quietly infatuated with the Prince of Wales.

Even her lack of almost all sophistication was in her favour, rather appealing to the Professor Higgins lurking in the Prince, as it often does in experienced bachelors on the borderlines of middle-age. Since her mind and interests were as yet unformed, she could easily become the perfect pupil for a royal Pygmalion. Queen Mary would have heartily approved of her reverent attitude to royalty – although she would certainly have wanted something done about her education. But for the Queen Mother, whose advice as so often in the past was crucial in such matters, education – or the lack of it – was of no particular concern. That could all come later. She had known Diana almost from the day she was born, and had naturally heard much about her from her devoted grandmother, Lady Fermoy. Both ladies had become convinced of her suitability for Charles – and once this had happened, the Prince's quest was all but over.

It was an interesting pointer to the future that, from almost the first faint hint of what was happening, the press appeared convinced as well. This was partly due, of course, to the Prince's situation: ever since his thirtieth birthday he had been living on borrowed time as a bachelor, and public speculation was at a peak. But more important still, Diana seemed to have certain qualities from the start that made her perfect princess material for the media, in ways no other girlfriend of Prince Charles's had ever been before.

She was first 'spotted' by that arch-voyeur of royalty, James Whitaker of the *Daily Star*, who for seven years had been following Prince Charles and all his doings with the dedication entomologists expend on the love-life of the Colorado beetle. Late that summer, he was hiding in the bracken on a hill above the river Dee, observing the Prince of Wales fishing in the stream below with (as his binoculars made very clear) a *new* young lady. Who was she? There was a small fortune in the answer, and within days the sturdy Whitaker had traced Balmoral's mystery female guest to Coleherne Court, the apartment block in Brompton Road where Diana shared a flat with three unremarkable but very well brought-up young ladies. From that moment, Lady Diana Spencer became the possession of the world's media, and she was never going to escape.

For what was fascinating about 'Lady Di' – a name she loathed but which rapidly gave her global recognition – was that she was even more exciting to the worldwide press and public than to the royal family itself.

The reasons for this fascination are not as simple as they might appear, for in many ways Diana was a baffling phenomenon, and much about her was profoundly contradictory. She was very much an aristocrat (always 'Lady Di' and never simple 'Di') and much was made of her semi-regal antecedents through the casual royal encounters of long-dead Spencer ladies, most of which the eager press got rather wrong – but that was neither here nor there. (Her best biographer, Penny Junor, has described her as possessing more English royal blood than Prince Charles himself: but since all the Prince's royal blood is strictly-speaking German or Danish, this is a quality she shares with several thousand other subjects of Her Majesty.)

But blood royal and aristocracy apart, Diana also managed to epitomise the simple qualities of the nicest sort of girl next door. She worked in a kindergarten, had none of the strangulated accents of her class, wore little make-up, and contrived to dress in that safe but rather boring way the older generation hope their daughters will adopt – but hardly ever do.

There were other intriguing contradictions too. Though obviously rich (she had bought the flat in Coleherne Court outright with money inherited from her grandmother), Diana had more or less immersed herself in the most menial of tasks, shopping, often cooking for her flat-mates, and even working for three months as a mother's-help with a family near Hindhead.

Her childhood was another potent source of paradox. For this girl who had grown up in the shadow of the royal family had also spent a rather miserable childhood as the victim of a celebrated upper-class divorce. She was devoted to her father but also missed her mother, and was suddenly presented with a none too popular stepmother, the novelist Barbara Cartland's steely daughter Raine – who, having originally set out as Lady Dartmouth, was now invincibly the Countess Spencer, chatelaine of stately Althorp (the ancestral home of all the Spencers) and an object of some animosity from the Earl's two eldest daughters.

In many ways it was a novelettish situation, and Mrs Cartland herself was soon describing Diana as 'a perfect Barbara Cartland heroine' – which of course she was. For almost every detail of her life added to a picture of an up-to-date and real-life Cinderella, noble yet humble, acquainted with palaces but living a very humdrum private life, virginal but absolutely ready now to be awakened by her Prince's love and totally transformed.

This was the culminating act the world was awaiting from Britain's own unique performing monarchy, and nobody could miss the point that Diana was ideally cast to play the starring part. She was so obviously right that both the press and public had virtually settled matters for themselves some months before Prince Charles did what was now required of him, and formally proposed in his private sitting-room at the Palace early in February 1981. Had he failed to do so, not only Diana and the members of his family would have been bitterly disappointed, but also the millions who by now were emotionally involved in seeing that the courtship and the royal dream came true.

Apart from the Queen's Coronation, the Prince of Wales's wedding was the most impressive ceremonial event the British monarchy has ever staged – and as a worldwide spectacle and the greatest television outside broadcast ever mounted in this country, it infinitely surpassed it.

This was due partly to advancing media technology which, in the course of the past century, had been steadily transforming the whole nature of the monarchy. Just as photography and the penny press had played their crucial part in establishing Queen Victoria's popular image from the 1880s, and radio had helped to make both George V and VI admired household characters, so satellite colour television was now able to project the instant magic of a major royal spectacle like this around the world.

Satellite TV had already brought into prominence certain sorts of happenings and staged events which could wield an astounding supra-national appeal. Major prize-fights and the spectacle of the Olympics, international tennis and World Cup football all possessed the crucial combination of human drama and engrossing mass performance that a shrinking world was ready to embrace. But no mass event was comparable to a royal wedding in the way it offered viewers round the world (and female viewers in particular) emotional involvement in an immensely grand and yet immensely human piece of real life theatre for which they had been so carefully prepared. And for the television companies, there was a singular additional attraction in these royal spectaculars – the TV rights to them were free.

That July wedding of the Prince and his Princess possessed sufficient key ingredients to make it televisually unique. As was to be expected from the British monarchy after so many years of careful practice, it was superbly staged; so that the climax in St Paul's Cathedral was not so much the 'purest Strauss' of Princess Anne's wedding five years earlier, as a royal grand opera, complete with state trumpeters, accompanying orchestra and the operatic *prima donna*, Kiri te Kanawa – and it was acted out with a splendour and panache no other family on earth could equal.

In terms of ritual, music and the architectural splendour of the great cathedral, it was unsurpassable; and there was also an uncanny sense of time-warp which was potently conveyed by the illusion of live television. The Hyde Park fireworks the night before were based on the display put on to celebrate the Peace of Aix-la-Chapelle in 1748, and watching the procession through the crowded streets with coaches, Household Cavalry and postillions, gave one a sense of being present at the start of some splendid regal happening from the pages of the history books. It was what Richard Dimbleby would have called 'living history', and this strange sensation steadily increased as the television cameras unerringly picked out the royal members of the congregation, all of them utterly familiar, and each of them closely watched as they waited for the bride to enter.

During the preceding months since the engagement was announced – not by the Palace but by *The Times*, which had scooped the Palace and the world press with the announcement on its front page on the morning of February 24 – 'Lady Di' had effortlessly ascended into the ranks of international superstardom, simply by being what she was. (How *The Times*, of all papers, got wind of this closely guarded secret is a mystery. Palace opinion is that it was almost certainly leaked, by mistake or by design, by a member of Mrs Thatcher's cabinet – all of whom had been informed but sworn to strictest secrecy some days earlier. The royal family, who were not particularly amused, have always had their suspicions of the identity of the culprit, but the then editor of *The Times*, William Rees-Mogg, is a Catholic with a confessor-like discretion over what is told him, and unlikely ever to reveal his source.) Throughout this period she had been remorselessly pursued, photographed, quoted and misquoted by a world press now intent upon the media equivalent of eating her alive. Her most transitory friends had been interviewed at length, her most jejune habits carefully researched, and two major royal chroniclers, Tony Holden and Robert Lacey, had been hard at work creating full-length books about her from the biographical gossamer her simple life provided.

The Queen had been rude to press photographers pursuing her – 'Why don't you go away?' she shouted – and Willie Hamilton had been rude about the royal family. Diana's uncle, Lord Fermoy, had publicly attested to her virginity – 'Diana, I can assure you, has never had a lover' – and the Queen's gynaecologist, Mr Pinker, to her fertility. Her hair style had been copied, her clothes and stance internationally imitated, and the ladies on *Vogue* fashion magazine had already started giving her advice about her future wardrobe.

Where facts were lacking fiction could be all-providing, and throughout the world the media mills were turning to pour out an acreage of anecdote and 'true-life revelation' about this unassuming teenage girl who was suddenly the most publicised recipient of princely love since Cleopatra. Hers was a face to sell a million million magazines, a story to inspire the love-lorn from Tennessee to Tokyo, and the worldwide media which had in a sense 'created' her regarded her for what she was – their hottest property in years.

For a gently nurtured aristocrat like Diana, it was all quite alarming, and the efforts of Her Majesty's new press secretary, Michael Shea, went chiefly into attempting to protect her from overwhelming press intrusion. From the day her engagement was announced, she was lodged like a nun within the Palace, and there was certainly no need on Shea's part to indulge in any of the skilful media presentation his predecessor, William Heseltine, performed so creatively for Charles at his Investiture. Diana's 'story' sold itself. And when to a fanfaronade of trumpets she appeared at the great cathedral west door in the Spencer family tiara and resplendent ivory-coloured wedding dress (white, though more symbolic of virginity, would have caused 'flare' on colour television) she was already the most famous bride the world had ever seen.

At the wedding the traditional chemistry of a ritual royal transformation scene worked as it had never worked before. 'Here is the stuff of which fairy-tales are made', began Archbishop Runcie in his nuptial address, adding the weight of archiepiscopal opinion to what Barbara Cartland had said already. But never before in history had a fairy-tale been performed on such a scale or with such perfection.

The nearest approach to this had been Princess Margaret's wedding in 1960, with which it had certain elements in common – true-life romance, worldwide pre-marital publicity, and the transformation into royal status of a previously unknown, 'ordinary' member of the wedding. But since then the monarchy itself had changed with the media revolution initiated by William Heseltine at the time of Prince Charles's Investiture. The whole royal family had inadvertently revealed its human face; the world believed that it had come to know them; and here at last they were, performing their majestic role before a fascinated worldwide congregation.

It was a wonderful release from the reality of life. 'We're in the happiness business,' a courtier privately admitted; and for a while at least attention was diverted from three million British unemployed, ten million starving in the Horn of Africa, and whatever danger faced mankind of nuclear annihilation.

And all the attention inevitably centred on the bride who was finally endowed with a mythical *persona* of her own, as she made her vows and thus ascended to the public status of a royal goddess on her own account.

However one regards the wedding, it was a most extraordinary achievement by the Royal House of Mountbatten-Windsor, for here was a full-scale royal occasion which did not merely 'rivet' mankind. It electronically welded it together as it was stratospherically beamed to something like a billion eager viewers in seventy nations round the globe. Having ceased to wield the old symbolic power of Queen Victoria over the largest empire in history, the royal family had rediscovered a unique and indispensable new role as surrogate performing royalty for the world.

What no one had quite foreseen, however, was the effect of this upon the bride, who was suddenly the centre of a worldwide cult, the most envied yet unenviable twenty-year-old married woman alive. There had never been anything remotely like this instant creation of a global megastar, whose girlish looks and simple human qualities were suddenly enhanced before this massive audience with all the dream-like overtones of royalty. It was excessive and more than a touch absurd, but it was also now a fact of royal life; and the problem both for the Palace and Diana was quite simply how to cope with it and make the most of it. Neither would prove particularly easy.

For Diana-fever did not quietly subside, as interest in Prince Charles had after his Investiture. Now that so many were emotionally involved in her dream-like story, it had to be continued – which, of course, it was by the world's photographers and journalists, regardless of the presence of Her Majesty's press secretary, Michael Shea. Shea, a former diplomat, was privately appalled by what was happening. An outspoken and essentially straightforward Scot, he got on rather well with journalists, but was not prepared for the amount of fiction now deployed around the dream princess.

For the simple truth about Diana was that there was not a lot to say – and what there was, she and her husband took great care to keep strictly to themselves as they started married life along with other carefully protected royalty in Kensington Palace and at Highgrove, their country house, fifteen miles from the Phillipses in Gloucestershire. But this reticence did nothing to impede the flood of stories which gushed forth about her. Most of these inevitably concerned relations with the royal family itself, and pursued the well-established patterns the public had grown rather used to with the Phillipses – 'rifts' with her sister-in-law Princess Anne, 'jealousy' against her stepmother, Lady Spencer, and 'problems' with assorted members of the royal family – in particular with the Queen, with whom she was alternatively said to 'get on famously' or be the source of 'considerable anxiety.' What all these stories had in common was that they mirrored basic situations in ordinary families, making it easy for anyone identifying with Diana to feel on terms of continuing familiarity with the rest of the royal family as well.

This was not confined to Britain. She was a princess for the world, and it is particularly interesting to see how the endless stories that appeared about her in the foreign press showed her exemplifying the characteristics of each nation's female readership. The German press quoted her as saying that her chief aim in life was 'learning to be a good housewife' – and proceeded to show her doing it – while the Italians concentrated on relations with her mother and, of course, her sex life. One Italian magazine, quoting the unimpeachable source of a housemaid from the Palace, went so far as to describe her as a 'sexual volcano' studying Japanese erotic manuals, who was wearing out Prince Charles in her efforts to ensure that 'Il Principe Dongiovanni' had no surplus time or energy for other women. French magazines were more concerned about her supposed extravagance, how much she spent on clothes and how she kept her figure.

The French magazine *Point de Vue*, which for months following the wedding had a mandatory article on Diana every week, really gave the key to what was happening, in a long article which posed the question: 'Would you *really* like to be the Princess of Wales?' This distinctly hypothetical question was treated with total seriousness, providing such simple details as her holidays, her habits, how she still met her friends and how she chose her shoes. For more than with any other member of the royal family, women, and particularly those in the Princess's age group, were actually wanting now to *be* Diana.

This widespread international emotion was quite different from the previous female interest in Princess Margaret at her zenith as the royal dream princess; for Princess Margaret, fascinated though the world had been with her, had never managed to combine the powerful components of Diana's irresistible appeal. Born royal, she had lacked the Cinderella quotient. She had never been the centre of the ritual television transformation scene. Rather, like Princess Anne, she was too sharp and too intelligent for widespread empathy; and ironically it was only when she fell from favour at the time of her divorce that she was suddenly revealed as an ordinary woman.

In contrast, one begins to see just how unique Diana had become. Once the simple heroine was so magnificently and so romantically inducted into the fabled world of royalty, that billion-strong audience – or a fair proportion of it – needed to know what happened next, and there was nothing in Diana's nature to impede the simple formulation of an answer. There was nothing threatening about her. She was profoundly unpretentious, and in public seemed to get on best with children. The few words she uttered in the presence of reporters were invariably girlish, kind and simple, so that all interest centred on what seemed to interest her – her clothes and her appearance.

To date, the most extraordinary thing about Diana has been the total dedication and success with which she proceeded to respond to the dream-role the world expected her to play. For judging by everything one knew about her personality before the start of her romance, one would have foreseen her part in the family as somewhat similar to that of the worthy, good, but not enormously exciting Princess Alexandra of Kent.

Instead, with total dedication, the Princess of Wales has managed to achieve an almost total transformation of her style and appearance, from round-cheeked, rather awkward kindergarten teacher, into an elegant, remorselessly-dieted royal fashion plate. It required barely suspected qualities of willpower and exercise to reduce her comfortably covered 5′10″ female frame to a shadow of its reassuring self, and the swift and inevitable creation of the 'Diana look', – echoed in myriad hairdressers and high-street dress shops – says much for the continuing influence and skill of those ladies from *Vogue* magazine who still advise her on these all-important matters. It says even more for the single-mindedness of her reaction to exactly what her worldwide public want of her.

For with unerring instinct she has managed to behave as all those multitudes of would-be Diana look-alikes see themselves behaving in her place, using that unlimited royal wealth and the eager attention of the best photographers, *couturiers*, shoe-makers and stylists in the business for one unliberated, superficial, but universally appreciated female purpose – to make herself as glamorous as possible.

Princess Anne had wanted to prove herself on horseback. Princess Margaret had sought for true romance. But since her marriage, the Princess of Wales has been intent on one abiding public passion – to make herself a picture of perfection for her ever-faithful, worldwide female audience – and the audience has so far never failed to respond. For to everyone's surprise, the most unforceful and unformed of all the ladies in the Prince of Wales's life has somehow made herself the most spectacular female member of the British royal family since an earlier Princess of Wales – Edward VII's beautiful but brainless consort, Alexandra.

The similarities are interesting, and a little worrying. Like Alexandra, Diana lives a jealously maternal private life, totally devoted to her children: and like her, her chief concern in public has centred on her stunning looks and appearance. Similarly, her most important public work has been the patronage of charities for children, and so far Diana has evinced few signs of wishing to advance beyond the range of interests and achievements of her predecessor. Of course she is still extremely young, and although child-bearing and adjusting to her regal situation have so far left her little time for mental self-improvement, time is on her side. She is fortunate to have an intelligent and patient husband, old and shrewd enough to help her, but she will need undiscerned reserves of wit and wisdom to develop during the years ahead in the crucial role she has so rapidly assumed within the family.

For inevitably there have already been tell-tale signs of tension – both on herself and on her marriage – as this strong-willed, child-wife and mother from a troubled background has begun to sense the power and problems of her role as a worldwide megastar of royalty. She was not quite anorexic – but not far off it – as she dieted desperately to regain her figure after the birth of her first child, Prince William, in 1982; and this, coupled with her share of the traditionally stormy Spencer female temperament, has not made her personal situation any easier. (She could still learn a lot from how the Queen Mother handled things in *her* mid-twenties, simultaneously satisfying her public and her appetite.)

Her highly publicised tantrums with her husband in the shooting field and on the ski-slopes in front of the inevitable photographers, coupled with the steady seepage from the Palace of a small platoon of staff who have been in contact with her – from her husband's valet and his distinguished private secretary to her own first Palace tutor, the tight-lipped polo-playing courtier, Oliver Everett ('Keep that man away from me!' she was quoted shouting to the Prince) – give just a hint of the strains involved behind the scenes in keeping up Diana's public image.

Given her youth, her inexperience, and the formidable task she set herself, it would have been surprising had there not been trouble, particularly as Diana reads her press reports avidly – unlike, for instance, Princess Margaret, who has long since foresworn reading hers. This has made her more aware than ever of her public, and done little for her personal serenity. 'When they write something horrible, I get a horrible feeling right here,' she confessed to a sympathetic female Canadian reporter, pointing to her chest, 'and I don't want to go out.' The reporter promptly printed the remark, thus adding further to Diana's problems and her insecurities.

Within eighteen months of her marriage, the presumptive future Queen of England was to be publicly proclaimed 'a spoiled brat' by one patriotic lady journalist, and another dedicated royal watcher was soon assuring American television audiences that Diana had become 'a monster'. This was perfectly predictable, as were the rumours picked up in the press of trouble in her marriage after Prince William's birth; but however upsetting to the principal participants, such incidents have done nothing to diminish the continuing public obsession with Diana. On the contrary, they have helped provide a fascinated world with fresh episodes in the now compulsive real-life global serial on the doings of Diana, for at this point the story positively called for evidence of a 'difficult', or better still, an 'utterly impossible' Princess of Wales. For the important younger female audience, closely identifying with Diana's every mood and move, this is how glamorous young stars are expected to behave (and how they would imagine themselves behaving in a similar situation), so that 'Fiery Di' had infinitely more media appeal than the original 'shy Di' from the local kindergarten.

Once again it is the foreign press, with its freedom of infinite invention and its hot-line to the Highgrove bedroom, which gives the clearest hint of what the world desires of the heroine at the centre of the royal dream machine. The Italian women's magazines in particular have remained exceptionally obsessive and uninhibited in their passion for the princess they still prefer to call 'la Lady Di', alternately presenting her as the most temperamental Italian-style *prima donna assoluta* and a suffering royal holy mother. She has been continually cast at the centre of innumerable family disasters, *al'Italiana*, with impassioned conflicts with her nursery staff over her jealous longing for her children taking second place to dramas with her royal in-laws, particularly Prince Philip. The birth of her second child, Prince Henry, in 1984, was described as having taken place 'on a bed of thorns', thanks to the family intrigues around her, and a particularly persistent theme which also crops up regularly in the French popular press has been Diana's 'desperate desire for the Crown of England', with overwritten stories of her inflamed attempts, generally by pressurising her hapless husband, to force an unwilling Elizabeth to abdicate.

Needless to say, there is not the remotest possibility of this occurring – any more than of Diana's wishing for the cares of queenship for many years to come – but the story has provided such a recurrent source of foreign royal fiction that one must see it in the context of the world mythology which now engulfs the royal family. For Diana herself, myth has all but taken over from reality, and her mother-in-law's abdication would naturally provide the perfect happy ending to Diana's dream-like story, placing the royal megastar once more at the centre of the ultimate in transformation scenes, to be vicariously enjoyed through worldwide satellite TV. Another full-scale coronation would undoubtedly provide the media event of the century.

15

THE ULTIMATE FAMILY

'I have to tell you. Queen Elizabeth is a most charming, down-to-earth person . . . Incidentally, she's a very good rider.'
Ronald Reagan

'Our monarch is not a crowned president. She is anointed. She represents a supernatural element in the nation.'
Enoch Powell

The creation of Princess Diana, slim-line regal megastar, from the homely round-cheeked bride of barely four years earlier, mirrors the transformation of the royal family itself during the reign of Elizabeth II. Although Diana's glamorous emergence from the unlikely chrysalis of English upper-class young womanhood seemed so surprising at the time, it had to happen. She was needed, for the role was empty, and the potent mingling of fantasy and fact around the passive image of this freshly-minted dream princess has marked the culmination of a process that began in earnest at the time of that original decision to 'relaunch' the monarchy at the 1969 Investiture by showing the human face of royalty, and making the royal family appear a sort of ultimate in families, backed with the full resources of the modern media.

Blood royal, and the appeal of centuries-old tradition notwithstanding, the position of a modern queen who reigns but does not rule must ultimately rest on public interest and belief; and the troubles that enmired the monarch in the late Fifties and throughout the Sixties showed all too clearly what occurred when this interest and belief began to go, and the monarchy started to become a bore.

Thanks to the media – and principally to unforeseen technical advances in worldwide colour television – the Mountbatten-Windsors triumphantly avoided Prince Philip's 'museum': but there was a price they were required to pay. During the Seventies, the Palace still seemed able, more or less, to contain the addictive public interest in every detail of the daily lives of royalty; but only for a while. With both Princess Margaret and Princess Anne, the old taboos which had always previously enshrined the royal personel were rudely broken. Anything the press could glean, suggest, or photograph within their private lives became fair game for comment and publication. Almost any fact made news as these infinitely famous and familiar royal characters took their places in an ever more compulsive saga for a fascinated world to follow through the hungry media. The monarchy had made itself the story of a family for the world to follow, and throughout the last few years all its members, in differing degrees, have proved surprisingly accomplished actors in the roles created from their daily lives, and appeared increasingly assured in the modern art of royal self-projection.

It is a strange fate for this most ancient and conservative of monarchies to come to, but with the fading of the old symbolic sources of its popular appeal – religious, patriotic, moral and imperial – it is unquestionably this universal and addictive involvement in the daily lives of British royalty which has now become their principle dynamic. In terms of the public interest they command, the Mountbatten-Windsors have become the world's last truly indispensable celebrities, and the novelty of recent years has been the ease and freedom with which the main members of the family have felt they can safely reveal themselves before their public – with the one exception of the Queen herself.

At the beginning of the present reign, their lives were still rigidly controlled – as far as the public was concerned – by a number of strict conventions and royal taboos, which limited their interest value. Divorce was quite unthinkable for royalty, as was the public possibility of sex outside the bonds of regal matrimony. Indeed, so completely did the puritan ethic still blanket the official presentation of the royal family, that photographers were firmly banned from showing any member of the family with drink in hand, and one of the strongest initial objections from the Palace to the manuscript of Tony Holden's biography of Prince Charles in 1979 was to the shocking revelation that Her Majesty had breast-fed her children. (It was an interesting pointer to relaxing royal attitudes, that the objection was withdrawn when the manuscript was read by members of the family.)

By the mid-Seventies, the great effort to present each member of the royal family as an imperishable paragon had had to be abandoned – particularly after Princess Margaret's divorce and the public problems of outspoken Princess Anne with her marriage, with press photographers, and with other members of her family. 'Naff off!' –

the memorable words shouted by the Princess against offending cameramen – could simply not be squared with any of those earlier images of effortlessly good and gracious royal ladies.

Instead, the different members of the family have found themselves presented with clearcut, fairly human public roles to play; and this extension of the royal bounds of human credibility has unquestionably formed the basis of the worldwide fascination with the members of the family which has steadily increased throughout the 1980s.

Since his appointment as royal press officer in 1980, Michael Shea has played a more important part in this development than he would probably admit, working as he does with considerable discretion and aplomb across the minefield that makes up the buffer-zone between his royal employers and the media beyond the palace gates. As with his predecessor, William Heseltine, much of his success has come from the fact that, as the son of a Scots marine engineer, and married to a Norwegian wife, his whole approach to monarchy is rather different from that of the old 'charmed circle' palace courtier. A smart operator, who has known nothing of Eton, Cambridge or the Guards, he is very much in touch with the world outside the palace, and some of his former diplomatic colleagues were suprised at his appointment, having thought him fairly sceptical about royalty.

Since then he has cleverly maintained his reputation as a down-to-earth and realistic spokesman for the Palace, conveying the impression that, however much he now respects the members of the family, he is not entirely in awe of them. During his early days at the Palace, in what he thought was an off-the-record conversation with a Canadian journalist, he casually remarked that the royal family sometimes refered to the Queen's 'Miss Piggy' expression on television, after the character in the TV show, *The Muppets*. This was not a revelation even he would make today – and when it was published, it appeared the sort of *gaffe* to have brought an old-style courtier to an instant nervous breakdown and prompt retirement. It says much for Shea's position, as well as for the Queen's own private sense of humour, that the incident was genuinely passed off as a joke.

In fact, when the need arises Shea can maintain an iron-clad Palace silence with the force of Commander Colville in his prime, and much of his influence at Court comes from his usually unnoticed membership of the Gordonstoun mafia. Born in 1942, he was at the school a bare six years before Prince Charles, and is naturally attuned to the attitudes and interests of the male members of the royal family. This has enabled him to be particularly relaxed, by knowing instinctively how much should – and should not – be revealed to the media. He can say with perfect confidence things that even Heseltine would once have jibbed at, and he possesses one more interesting asset for a courtier with such a crucial role behind the scenes of the great performing British monarchy. He is an accomplished amateur novelist, who recently wrote a situation comedy (under a pseudonym on a strictly non-royal subject) for BBC TV.

Michael Adeane was a water-colourist, Charteris an amateur sculptor, but Shea is the first courtier whose artistic interests actually extend to creating characters of fiction and presenting them on television. With this ability, he is particularly aware of the royal situation dramas he is regularly involved in at the Palace, and of how the individual royal characters play their parts. At the time of Prince Henry's christening, for instance, he was horrified to learn, at almost the last minute, that despite careful staff-work by the Palace secretariat, the Phillipses had several months earlier fixed a shooting party for the day in question, and were adamantly refusing to forego it.

He insists that this is all there was to their failure to attend – which is as may be – but he knew enough of popular perceptions of Princess Anne's alleged impatience at the fuss made of her sister-in-law and children, to realise exactly what would happen if they did not come. Another 'rift' within the family; 'jealous Anne'; a 'slight' to the Princess of Wales – the headlines were predictable, and Shea spent an anxious afternoon on the telephone to Gatcombe Park telling Her Royal Highness what would happen in the press – to no avail. A shooting fixture was a shooting fixture, and the Phillipses were sticking to it. If the press cared to make more of it than that, let them get on with it.

And so, of course, they did, when the Phillipses failed to arrive at the royal christening at Windsor – almost word for word as Shea predicted. But Princess Anne was also right in her refusal to get terribly worked up about what almost anybody else would have seen as the appalling press that followed. She had been in the business long enough to know exactly how the public would react. She knew her role: and she also knew that, far from such incidents

causing any damage to the monarchy, they actually create the sort
of human interest the institution thrives on now. A few weeks later
the Wales's and the Phillipses met at a pub near Highgrove for a
drink. Shea had made sure the press photographers were there, thus
ensuring yet a further episode in the drama of this simple royal
family. After the 'rift', the 'making up'. Prince Charles and Captain
Phillips seemed to be chatting amiably enough together. So were the
two Princesses. The papers had their pictures and their headlines,
and everyone was happy until the next engrossing episode.

Shea says that when he first arrived at the Palace he was told of
two things he should never talk about before the Queen – horses
and royal PR, both being subjects she knew more about than
anybody else. For one of the interesting things about the Queen, that
has passed virtually unnoticed, is that after the anxious, sheltered
beginning of her reign, during which she seemed so overshadowed
by her mother's personality, she has become remarkably adroit
herself in handling what she would hate to call her public image.

After the royal state visit to the United States in 1983, Alistair
Cooke quoted a staunch Republican lady who conceded, having
watched Her Majesty in action, that although her job must be one
of 'ferocious boredom, it was done with grace and even temper'. It
was a signal difference from her reception in the States during the
bungled visit of 1962 – and the 'job' is also done these days with
the increasing assurance and professionalism which come with age.
Ever since her Silver Jubilee, the Queen has been particularly aware
of the power of her personal popularity and the strength the
monarchy derives from the constant public presentation of the family
around her.

The journalist Neal Acherson wrote recently of how 'all nations
are self-admiration societies'. This particularly applies to Britain and
its monarchy where, thanks to the adulation and the overwhelming
public interest in royalty created by the media, the Queen has become
a most efficient focus through which Britain can admire itself.
Dignified, cool and irreproachable, she has become a sort of national
headmistress, perfectly endowed to place the seal of society's
approval on those institutions and those individuals who are
considered to deserve it.

This extends throughout society, from parliament, which she
opens once a year, wearing her crown and robes of state as she reads
the 'royal speech' (every word of which the government has written

for her), to the fighting services who owe her their allegiance, the judges who are appointed in her name, the currency which bears her effigy and the tax demands which are sent out 'On Her Majesty's Service' – but not, of course, to her. The English language, on its best behaviour, is still referred to as 'the Queen's English' – even sometimes in America, where the phrase remains a strange survival of the old colonial connection. The right to show the royal coat of arms and the magic words, 'By Royal Appointment', is still taken as the acme of achievement by over 800 of the country's leading manufacturers and tradesmen, ranging from Harrods and Rolls-Royce to book-binders and the manufacturers of bottled beer. And as the theoretical 'fount of all honours', it is the Queen who still gives credence both to the titles inherited by the British aristocracy, and to those awarded in her name to the more or less deserving members of our modern meritocracy.

Both Prince Philip and Princess Margaret were reportedly incensed by the way the abrupt unveiling of Diana's latest hair style at the state opening of parliament in November 1984 drew all the attention of the press and the television cameras from the Queen. Here if anywhere was a prime example of that dangerous 'trivialising' of the monarchy Milton Shulman had originally predicted if it relied on television for its popularity. But the Queen stayed very cool and unconcerned. From the beginning, the accepted role of the Princess of Wales has been to bring glamour and fresh interest to the monarchy, while the Queen is there to reign.

For Elizabeth II the roles are complementary, and at sixty she exhibits a most businesslike and enviable absence of female vanity before the public. In this, as in so many other things, she is quite unlike her mother. She has not aged particularly well – but nor does she appear particularly bothered, despite gratuitous advice from self-appointed pundits over how she dyes her hair, applies her makeup, wears her unflattering hats and even chooses her no-nonsense spectacles. If a queen can't please herself about such things, who can? She takes great care of her health – unlike her sister – and one of the reassuring things about her is the consistency with which she simply seems to be herself, impervious to passing fashion.

There is an apocryphal story of how Mrs Thatcher arrived at some royal occasion and was most disturbed to find that she had chosen an identical outfit to Her Majesty's. To avoid this happening again the Prime Minister's office sent a message to the Palace expressing regret, and suggesting that in future Downing Street might be informed of what Her Majesty would wear when the Prime Minister was present. Back came a polite refusal, with the explanation that the Queen never notices what any other ladies wear.

On the other hand, the Queen has shown herself surprisingly perceptive to the changes of acceptable public behaviour within her family – as was particularly obvious in the whole reaction of the Palace to Prince Andrew's behaviour on his return as something of a hero with the Falklands Task Force, where he flew a naval helicopter. In lively contrast with Prince Charles's earlier adherence to those rules of strict romantic royal discretion, Andrew was openly determined to enjoy himself; and after meeting the American movie starlet, Koo Stark, in a London night-club, he took not the faintest trouble to disguise the fact that he was having an affair with her.

In those not so far-off days when the Windsors genuinely thought themselves guardians and paragons of middle-class morality, uproar would undoubtedly have followed – both within the Palace and without – especially when kittenish Miss Stark was revealed to have a past which included various live-in lovers and starring parts in several soft-porn movies. Edward VII would certainly have understood his great-great-grandson's taste in women, but have found the publicity unpardonable. The reactions of Queen Mary surpass all imagination. But the family stayed admirably cool.

With silver-tongued Shea to speak on their behalf to the gossip-writers and reporters who soon jammed the Palace switchboard, they actually made the most of what would previously have been a matter of immense embarrassment and royal scandal. For Shea, like the Queen herself, is very much aware of the entertainment value of the modern monarchy. The most urbane of men, he took the unofficial line of 'Well, you know what sailors are!' when the Prince tried taking the young lady incognito to Aunt Margaret's island of Mustique. The theme was generally accepted by the press, so that the episode finally produced considerably envy, much innocent amusement, but little actual damage to the monarchy, which had suddenly discovered a genuine addition to the ranks of the performing royal supershow – a harmless-seeming, not particularly bright, black sheep of the royal family.

Behind the scenes, the family were somewhat less relaxed about the affair than they appeared, knowing quite well how vulnerable a prince can be if this sort of escapade is all he offers in return for his annual income of £20,000 from the Civil List – as so far it has been. There was still more trouble – and this time less indulgent comment – when he sprayed a number of photographers with paint during a visit to America, and Prince Andrew has not been made Duke of York as previous royal second sons have been. There were in fact strong parental words about his behaviour and responsibilities, and since Miss Stark's departure from the scene as bride of a multi-millionaire, a chastened Andrew has seemed intent on making a fresh public reputation in a less contentious field of royal activity – photography. He has been coached by his former uncle, Tony Snowdon, himself now back where he began as the family's own favourite Court photographer – and once more doing rather well from the worldwide reproduction fees on royal pictures, which he no longer gives to charity as he did when a member of the royal family.

To the Court's considerable relief, the baby of the family, Prince Edward, born in 1964, has shown little sign of Andrew's irresponsibility or his sister Anne's uncomfortable passion to excel in public. A gentle, rather introverted character, he has most in common with his brother Charles. Like him, he went from Gordonstoun to Cambridge University, and though he also acted in his satirical college review, his performance made it seem unlikely that he will have the personality of a future superstar of royalty. Instead he seems to have the qualities most needed now in junior male royalty – moderate intelligence, an ability to learn and a talent for keeping out of trouble, making it probable that he will finally emerge as a useful 'working' member of the family.

Periodically, Michael Shea pretends to be extremely heated over what he and the royal family call the 'fairy stories' which the popular press concoct about them all. He has even lectured Fleet Street editors in his solemnest Gordonstonian manner on their strict responsibilities to truth where the royal family are concerned. In fact the maximum media coverage at whatever level is one of the surest guarantees of the future of the monarchy, simply because it maintains public interest and the addictive process of identifying with its individual members. And now that the international mass media have established the Mountbatten-Windsors as the constant object of their subjects' dreams and aspirations, an element of fiction must inevitably mingle with the somewhat scanty facts which are often all that reality – and Michael Shea – can offer to their dedicated public.

That one word, 'royal', has now become a sort of universal talisman, magically investing the most humdrum incident or story with an instant emotional appeal inconceivable in any other context. A junior member of the staff at Clarence House is arrested with a knife – producing instant banner headlines about 'Royal Servant in Knife Drama'. A woman who once rode with Prince Philip is involved in a colourful divorce – which inevitably becomes 'Woman friend of royalty in sex romps'. This heightened interest now extends across the boundaries of social class, income and political belief. *The Times* rarely lets a week go by without some member of the royal family as the subject of its front-page picture: television news invariably has its mandatory royal item – Diana's latest hat, the Queen Mother eating an ice-cream in Venice, Princess Margaret leaving once more for Mustique: and the popular Sunday papers have to have their weekly royal story.

This unremitting national obsession has produced its problems, and Shea can sometimes sound surprisingly like Commander Colville when he attempts to make the point that his employers are entitled to at least a modicum of private life. He was particularly incensed when his permanent *bête noire*, the journalist James Whitaker – who has never seen exactly eye to eye with him on this – made his long-range presence felt once more with the Princess of Wales, by clambering through bushes with a staff photographer on an island in the Bahamas to take pictures of her on the beach, when she was five months pregnant with Prince William, and wearing a bikini.

With outraged questions asked in parliament, platitudes errupting from the Press Council, and humble apologies even offered by the newspapers *after* they had published Whitaker's pictures, everyone appeared profoundly shocked – but it was all distinctly hypocritical, like most of the criticisms made of the oceans of publicity flowing round the British royal family. The actual pictures of the Princess were deeply inoffensive and rather touching, and however tasteless and tedious this sort of press intrusion must appear to its recipients, it has become an all-important part of the modern royal way of life. As Prince Charles once admitted to a group of genial press photographers, 'It's when you characters *don't* want to photograph me that I have to worry.'

What is always wanted is the informal, unexpected glimpse of royalty reacting in a human situation in whatever circumstances, and the most extraordinary instance in the last few years, when the Palace was exposed in an episode of unbelievable – and potentially dangerous – inefficiency, finally redounded to the credit of the Queen. This was the occasion in July 1982 when the half-crazed and unemployed Michael Fagan, anguished by the break-up of his marriage, found not the slightest difficulty evading the security around the Palace, shinned up a drain-pipe, entered an unlocked window, and at seven in the morning made his barefoot entrance into the royal bedroom where Her Majesty was still asleep. Waking, she was remarkably unflustered and her visitor most respectful; and despite the loyal outrage that inevitably followed when the facts were finally revealed, no one seemed to notice that this bizarre affair was above all something of a tribute to the Queen's own public credibility as a sympathetic human being. All Fagan wanted – apart from a cigarette, which gave the Queen a chance to telephone for the Palace police, who did not come – was the chance to discuss his problems with his sovereign, as he might have done with some understanding member of his private family. Many other people feel the same, but lack the intruder's resourcefulness in gaining such close access to the royal presence.

Public reactions to the incident were interesting too. Fagan, for his pains, was consigned to a lunatic asylum. There was predictable shock and clamour for tighter security at Court and the resignation of almost everyone involved, from the head of Scotland Yard to the Home Secretary himself; but for the worldwide public, the consuming interest lay in what the incident revealed of the domestic arrangements in the Palace.

Where had Prince Philip been throughout it all? In fact he had left the Palace earlier that morning to exercise his horses for his current hobby, carriage-driving, but there was no denying the disturbing fact that the royal couple did not share that happy symbol of domestic bliss, a double bed. This produced some speculation in the public prints, including an exhaustive article in the *Daily Mail*, explaining to its humbler readers that the *real* upper-classes never have believed in double beds and even think them rather common. (As, alas, they do, an intriguing example of the English class obsession in even the most intimate corners of domestic life. Middle-class readers can, however, reassure themselves with the knowledge that Prince Charles and his wife most definitely enjoy a king-sized double bed. One was specially installed aboard *Britannia* for their recent visit to Italy.)

The reaction of the *Daily Mirror* to the Fagan incident was simpler and more to the point.

'Give her a cuddle, Philip!' was its headline on the morning after the affair.

Shea has a theory that public interest in the royal family moves imperceptibly from one key royal figure to the next – as it did when Diana took the starring royal role from Prince Charles even before she married him. Before long one even saw the back of the Prince's head in the occasional picture of the royal couple – an interesting example of how press priorities had shifted. And Shea is currently tipping Princess Anne for an increasingly important public role in future – which, given her quite sparkling appearances on TV chat shows, would appear most probable. The talk of trouble in her marriage has subsided; her dedication, particularly to the work of international child welfare has begun to supersede her former horsey image; and she has now emerged as clearly the most articulate and self-possessed member of the family – especially since her father, now in his middle sixties, spends more time than ever far from the cameramen and journalists he actively dislikes, on such largely unpublicised activities as his Presidency of the World Wildlife Fund.

Certainly the public interest in the leading royal performers now seems set in quite definite and clearcut patterns. Some figures like the Queen and the Queen Mother are fixed stars in the royal firmament, the latter in particular the unshakeable embodiment of everything she has taught the nation to expect from its ultimate royal grandmother. The most human and experienced performer in the 'performing monarchy', she has effortlessly adapted to the new demands the media have thrust upon her. Always a superstar, she has responded both to age and to the razzmataz of royalty by seeming more impregnably herself. Her eighty-fifth birthday showed her as energetic and as much the centre of affection as she has ever been. Smiling and cosy, yet immensely professional, she still seems unable to disappoint her audience.

Prince Philip, on the other hand, remains as ill-at-ease as ever with the media, and has still to make a satisfactory passage from his role as the royal radical who told industry to 'get its finger out', to a comfortable position as the royal grandfather. In the latter role, most of his public interest has arisen from his widely-rumoured lack of interest in Prince Charles's wife and children. Whether true or not, it is hard to imagine the abrasive consort having too much interest in the public doings of Diana – and he has certainly made no public effort to dispel the image of a distinctly distant grand-paternal figure.

Such images, of course, can alter overnight as royal roles adapt to changes in the story. A personal affliction, for instance, forms a sure-fire source of instant sympathy and interest – as was shown by Princess Margaret's recent emergence from relative unpopularity and obscurity at the time of her lung operation. After that much earlier, long-running role as the most romantic female member of the royal cast, she has now made something of a come-back as an entirely different character – the royal who is most as risk. All her disasters and private problems seem to have coalesced to change the public's attitude from critical impatience to genuine concern. People are genuinely worried that she still smokes too much, and, echoing this, the *Daily Mirror* once again conveyed a piece of worldly-wise advice to royalty on its front-page headline as she started her convalescence:

'Give them up, Ma'am!'.

A genuine problem for the future of the royal show could be a shortage of younger members able or willing to perform the lesser royal roles in public, and it is interesting that the two Princesses who have had the maximum exposure to the public, Margaret and Anne, have gone on record to express the hope that their children will be able to step off the royal roundabout. Speaking of her resolutely untitled children, *Master* Peter and *Miss* Zara Phillips, Anne said recently, 'I doubt if the next generation will be involved at all' in royal activities; and a spokesman for Princess Margaret made her feelings on the subject even clearer when referring to her daughter, Lady Sarah Armstrong-Jones: 'She will not undertake public engagements or take on official duties. She is an entirely private person and not a member of the royal family.'

The status of Princess Margaret's other child, Lord Linley, is similar, and at twenty-five he has so far made little public mark except as a furniture designer, and by occasional trouble he has caused at parties. There is, however, a considerable reservoir of royal talent for the future in the offspring of the Queen's own close relations, all of whom have so far been kept firmly from the public gaze. There are the three young children of the Duke of Kent, and the three still younger children of the Duke of Gloucester. Princess Alexandra and her husband, Angus Ogilvy, have two children, James and Marina Ogilvy, and Prince and Princess Michael of Kent have made their own addition to the royal brood, with Lord Frederick Windsor born in 1979 and Lady Gabriella two years later. As the present Duke of Gloucester has shown with his continuing career as an architect, all these minor untried members of the family will have the option of following an active function on the fringes of the royal family of the future, or of settling for a simpler human status.

Those who have no such choice are the central royal characters. For them there can be no escape, and for many years to come the great celebrities are certain to remain the royal megastars, Charles and Diana. Much of their fascination will inevitably increase as the differences between their age and characters become clearer, together with the separate things they represent.

Within the matriarchal British monarchy, Diana's role of triumphant royal goddess appears unshakeable, and her international appeal seems stronger now than ever – witness the near-hysterical reception she received everywhere she went on her first state visit to Italy in the spring of 1985. She is equally popular at home – particularly with the young – and one saw something of the mythical status she has now achieved in popular reactions to her visit with Prince Charles to survivors of the recent Manchester air disaster. There were widespread press reports of how a badly shocked and orphaned child opened her eyes to see the royal couple – which in turn produced a predictable revival of legendary belief in the therapeutic power of royalty. While headlines in one newspaper proclaimed Diana 'The Miracle Worker', a leader-writer in another solemnly invoked the 'healing magic' of the royal touch.

Interestingly, none of this referred to Charles, who was also present. As in the days of good Queen Anne, the magic of the modern monarchy seems to reside exclusively within its female members, and until that day, hopefully far distant, when he becomes King Charles III, he would appear to have a far more difficult and complicated public role to play than 'Lady Di', the sacred superstar.

In 1967, the childless 7th Earl Stanhope bequeathed his spectacular Palladian ancestral home, Chevening in Kent, to the nation, in the hope that when Prince Charles married he might live there, and create a princely social circle round himself and his family. But Charles soon made it clear he was not remotely interested in spectacular country houses, and still less in building up a new 'Prince of Wales Set'. Devoted to his family, he is emphatically no social leader and like all male members of the House of Windsor, he seems in danger of adopting the recumbent role of husband to his infinitely famous wife – and little more. Concerned, intelligent, and always anxious – like his grandfather, King George VI – to 'be of use', his problem is that, during his long period of waiting for the crown, there is no really satisfactory and fulfilling role for him to play.

Were he a stupider or lazier man, his life would be easier. But the faintest evidence of his inquiring mind – as over his interest in comparative religion, telepathy or alternative medicine – tends to be picked up by the press as something of a sign of incipient mental instability in the heir apparent. And should he pronounce in public on any subject that concerns him – as he did in his recent outburst against modern architecture – the outcry and publicity are so intense that both he and his advisers have grown wary of permitting HRH The Prince of Wales to say anything that really matters.

Affairs like unemployment, race relations and inner city decay trouble him deeply, but much of Michael Shea's time is spent in making sure that none of this anxiety appears in public in a manner to involve the royal family in controversy, or even hint at the unthinkable – that at least one member of the royal family is considerably at odds with the current policy of his mother's democratically elected government. As a result, Prince Charles seems doomed to pass the prime of life in a bland and rather boring public role, the recipient of endless adulation, but always overshadowed, like so many of the menfolk of the House of Windsor, by his mother and his wife.

This is certainly not a public role that Charles himself enjoys, although the tradition that royalty never reply to criticisms has made him suffer in silence, even when former *Tatler* editor Tina Brown – from the safety of the pages of America's *Vanity Fair* magazine – characterised him a 'wimp' and Diana a 'restless and demanding woman'.

But their silence did not mean that they were not keenly aware of the damage such impressions could produce. And the Palace's response proves just how much it still relies upon TV as the image-making medium of last resort. For the first time since the historic film *Royal Family* revealed the 'human face' of royalty in 1969, a full-scale television documentary will show Prince Charles and his family, just as his parents and *their* children were revealed to the world a quarter of a century ago. And once again the world will see members of this ultimate family in the most homely yet regal situations – supremely sympathetic, absolutely human, yet ineradicably royal.

With such a cast, and with the Palace guaranteed its power of veto on the film, it will create the definitive reply to any residual impressions of princely 'wimpishness' or a 'restless and demanding' wife. And if it has even a fraction of the impact of *Royal Family*, the film will re-establish all those human virtues of the House of Windsor around the regal couple – whatever the truth when the cameras depart.

Meanwhile, at sixty, Elizabeth II can calmly congratulate herself on having presided over the discreet but most effective resurrection of the House of Mountbatten-Windsor after the crises and disasters of the early years of her reign. Apart from that one brief period of monarchical hysteria at the time of her Coronation, she is more popular and indispensable today than ever. Having learned her lessons from the early blunders of so many of her courtiers and political advisers, and with more than thirty years experience behind her, she is herself firmly in control of what has once again become a most effective matriarchal monarchy.

She has shown herself remarkably adaptable in the way she has taken the immense changes in the public image of her family so confidently in her stride. But while she has overseen an effective revolution in the style and presentation of the monarchy, which would have been unthinkable at her accession thirty-three years ago, she has also shown an increasing sureness of touch in the way she has kept the monarchy itself firmly within the guidelines she has always followed. As she is perfectly aware, two things could still damage it – serious controversy or really sordid scandal – and one detects her recent influence in avoiding both.

During his Italian visit, Charles was extremely anxious to show his sympathy with the ecumenical ideal by attending a Roman Catholic mass celebrated by Pope John in his private chapel in the Vatican, and it was only Her Majesty's direct, last-minute intervention that prevented it. Intense embarrassment ensued, particularly for the Prince himself. But while he was unable to disguise his angry disappointment in front of the reporters and assembled cameramen, one wonders if he recalled the words he spoke on television on the eve of his Investiture about his mother being 'terribly sensible and wise.' For however popular the Prince's gesture would have been in Italy, it was clearly 'sensible and wise' for Her Majesty to insist on playing very safe in one area where, as traditional Defender of the Protestant Faith, the Queen herself could easily become the centre of bitter and impassioned religious controversy – particularly in Northern Ireland, where there is quite enough religious bigotry already.

The Queen has also been extremely shrewd in steering her family through the perils of engulfing scandal on a number of occasions. Here she and her close advisers clearly learned important lessons in the public handling of Princess Margaret's divorce, where a potential royal disaster was defused by the way the Windsors suddenly behaved like a caring, human family, and instead of striking public attitudes, firmly closed ranks round the Princess, and gave her their support. Much the same policy in public was adopted over the peccadillos of Prince Andrew, and even with the far more damaging recent disasters that have afflicted Princess Michael of Kent. Whatever anger they have caused behind the scenes, the troubles of this most erratic Royal Highness, have been carefully contained within the royal family itself. There has been no public comment, no sign of outraged royal disapproval, and once again the family has given nothing but the fairly dignified impression of closing ranks around Prince Michael and his family at a time of hideous embarrassment.

In contrast with the chain of disasters following the Queen's Coronation, the Court now seems profoundly self-aware, professional, and able to avoid the dire effects of controversy and of scandal. And on the things that really matter – royal finance, undue pressure from the politicians, and the excessive influence of any group or class – the Crown has increasingly established a remarkable degree of independence.

With this determined sexagenarian female monarch so firmly on the throne, it is quite inconceivable to think of her today being so shamelessly manipulated by a small cabal of politicians and the upper aristocracy as she was at the ending of the Margaret/Townsend love affair, or over the appointments to the premiership of Macmillan or Sir Alec Douglas-Home. The monarchy has grown smarter, the courtiers shrewder, and the megastar status of the royal family has given it immense international interest and prestige. With so much popularity – and with the royal income automatically adjusted through the Civil List – the monarchy has made itself virtually invulnerable to politics and politicians.

But the true measure of Elizabeth II's extraordinary achievement is that, for all the changes which have happened in her reign, she has surrendered nothing of the essence of the royal myth which she accepted as a sacred trust from that dedicated king, her father, thirty-three disturbed and troubled years ago. Queen Mary's firm belief in the sacred nature of the monarchy has all but vanished – as have most of the great ideals it stood for: but *human* interest, and involvement in the characters and the emotions of the world's most famous family, have become the surest guarantee of its enduring future.

As a human story and a super-human dream remorselessly conveyed throughout the world by all the means of modern mass communications, the monarchy is more than ever indispensable, and probably immortal. Should interest in Diana ever start to wane, there will always be fresh members of the family to carry on the story – the loves and marriages of Prince Andrew and Prince Edward, the Phillipses and the further problems of *their* marriage, the growing up of Prince William and Prince Henry, and the inevitable additions to the Highgrove nursery. Like Queen Victoria, Elizabeth II will grow more dignified and popular with age, Prince Philip conceivably mellower, Prince Charles more worried by the way the world is going, and his wife an everlasting source of royal glamour, journalistic scoops and all-absorbing future 'rifts' within the family.

At regular intervals will come the ritual transformation scenes of the great royal public ceremonies, even more splendidly performed for the television cameras than in the past; more royal weddings and the occasional royal funeral which will continue to involve viewers round the world in the potent myth and unique human situation of the world's last great performing monarchy. For the supreme achievement of the Royal House of Mountbatten-Windsor has been the way it has learned to use the modern media to perpetuate itself. In the process, the monarchy has inevitably become something very different from the one Elizabeth II inherited in 1952. 'Trivialised' it may be, but it has managed to increase its wealth, its independence and its popularity, together with its grip on the imagination of a worldwide audience. What, one wonders, would the world now do without it?

INDEX

Abdication crisis, 23, 25–7, 33–5, 42, 48, 79–80, 93, 103–5, 221–2, 227
Acherson, Neal, 283
Acheson, Dean, 61
Adeane, Sir Michael, 127, 131, 160, 162–4, 282
Adelaide, Princess of Teck, 10
Adenauer, Konrad, 68–9
Airlie, Lady, 24, 97, 166
Albert, Prince, see George VI, King
Albert, Prince Consort, 11, 18, 34, 43, 71, 89, 94, 228
Alexandra, Princess, 166, 256, 257, 275, 291
Alexandra, Queen, consort of Edward VII, 15, 73, 239, 276
Alexandra, Queen of Yugoslavia, 77–8, 81, 83, 88, 95
Alice, Princess of Greece, 72–5, 76, 78, 86
Althorp, 269
Altrincham, Lord (John Grigg), 129–30, 131, 133, 143, 147, 161, 266
Ancaster, Earl of, 50
Andrew, Prince, 143, 146–7, 248, 266, 267, 285–6, 294, 295
Andrew, Prince of Greece, 72–5, 76, 78, 85, 146
Anne, Princess (Mrs Mark Phillips), 68, 104, 148, 183, 251, 273; birth and childhood, 88, 115, 116, 135, 208–9; public image, 197, 211–12, 237, 240, 256; character, 208–9, 250; horsemanship, 209–11, 275; poor relations with media, 211–12, 215–17, 280–81; wedding, 212–15, 222, 246, 270; marriage, 217, 295; television interview, 214–15; children, 216, 230, 290; fund-raising, 216, 241; and Princess Margaret's divorce, 239; press criticism of, 241–4; attacked in the Mall, 245; and Prince Henry's christening, 282–3; future public role, 289
Anne, Queen of England, 10, 60, 291
Annigoni, Pietro, 136
Argyll, Duke of, 131
Armstrong-Jones, Anthony, see Snowdon, Earl of
Armstrong-Jones, Lady Sarah, 231, 290
Asquith, Lady Cynthia, 31–2, 46, 207
Asquith, H. H., 39
Attenborough, David, 199, 207
Attlee, Clement, 93–4, 99
l'Aurore, 146

Bagehot, Walter, 7, 11, 20, 121, 168, 204, 238–9
Bailey, David, 135
Baillie-Grohman, Captain, 81, 87
Baldwin, Stanley, 26, 35
Balmoral, 17, 34–5, 40, 129, 141, 168, 182, 203, 218
Baltimore Sun, 127
Baron, Nahum, 127, 135
Battenberg, Louis, Prince of, 18, 72, 78
Battenberg family, 72, 79, 80, 85, 91, 247
Beaton, Cecil, 135
Beaufort, Duchess of, 9–10
Beaverbrook, Lord, 84, 91, 128–9, 130, 132
Betjeman, Sir John, 134

Blunt, Sir Anthony, 56, 132, 163–5
BOAC, 157
Brabourne, Lady, 245
Brabourne, Lord, 179–81, 245
Braque, Georges, 157
Brien, Alan, 184
Brigade of Guards, 56
Britannia, 114, 149, 151–2, 289
British Broadcasting Corporation
    (BBC), 21, 52–4, 57, 63, 118,
    131, 150, 165, 181, 188–90,
    282
British Empire, 7, 12, 16, 38–9, 40,
    198
British Fauna Preservation Society,
    160
British Leyland, 243–4
Broadlands, 87, 249, 253
Brooke, Henry, 161
Brown, Tina, 292
Bryant, Arthur, 147
Buccleuch, Duke of, 50
Buckingham Palace, 14, 17, 40, 44,
    67–8, 153, 202–3, 204, 210,
    288
Burnet, Alastair, 214
Butler, R. A. (Lord Butler), 50,
    123–4, 187, 249, 252

Callaghan, James, 229
Cambridge University, 172, 176–7,
    249, 252, 286
Canavan, Dennis, 236
Caroline, Princess of Monaco, 265
Cartland, Barbara, 269, 272
Cassel, Sir Ernest, 77, 79
Casson, Sir Hugh, 95
Catholic Church, 4, 10, 49, 257–9,
    265, 293–4
Cavendish, Lady Elizabeth, 134,
    137
Cavendish family, 124–5
Cawston, Richard, 181–5, 188,
    190
Chamberlain, Joseph, 12
Channon, Sir Henry 'Chips', 43,
    50, 82

Charles, Prince of Wales, 68, 92,
    104, 148; birth, 88; Lord
    Mountbatten's influence, 93,
    246–9, 251–4; childhood, 115,
    116, 135, 209; education, 129,
    141–2, 171, 252; cherry brandy
    episode, 171; stay in Australia,
    171, 174, 175; at Cambridge
    University, 172, 176–7, 249,
    252; formation of public image,
    172, 174–9, 196–8, 201, 225,
    248, 292; Investiture, 172, 178,
    179, 185–6, 189–98, 200, 206,
    207–8, 226, 272, 279; television
    films, 179, 230, 292–3;
    broadcast interviews, 188–90,
    214; wealth, 203, 243; in Royal
    Navy, 208, 228–9, 252, 253;
    visit to Washington, 211; and the
    Queen's Silver Jubilee, 228–9;
    popularity, 237; at Lord
    Mountbatten's funeral, 246–7;
    relations with his parents, 248,
    253–4; character, 249–50, 292;
    role as Prince of Wales, 250–51;
    relations with women, 251–6;
    choice of wife, 263–9; wedding,
    3–4, 269–73; marriage, 276–7,
    288–9; future public role,
    291–92, 295; press criticism of,
    292; visit to Vatican, 293–4
Charles I, King of England, 10
Charles Stuart, Prince (the Old
    Pretender), 10
Charteris, Sir Martin, 131, 133,
    282
Cheam, 141–2
Checketts, David, 174–80, 188,
    196, 248–9, 250, 251–2
Chelsea Flower Show, 142–3
Chevening, 291
Chicago Daily News, 132
Christmas broadcasts, 21, 54, 133,
    201
Church of England, 63, 111, 113,
    118, 134, 150, 198, 206, 239

Church of England Newspaper, 129

Church Times, 230

Churchill, Sir Winston, 39–40, 41, 44, 50, 51–3, 59–60, 84, 86, 91, 105, 166–7, 174, 186

Churston, Lord, 50

CIA, 130

Civil List, 44, 87, 109, 138, 139, 149, 172, 201, 203–6, 225, 227, 236, 237, 243–4, 260, 286, 295

Clarence, Duke of, 15

Clarence House, 9, 42, 44, 67–8, 87, 88, 287

Clark, Sir Kenneth, 68, 69, 180, 202

Cockburn, Claud, 22, 131, 189, 228, 247

College of Arms, 193–4

Columbia University, 68–9

Colville, Sir John, 52, 105, 106

Colville, Commander Richard, 106–7, 126, 132, 133, 141–3, 144, 147, 159, 172–3, 178, 179, 281, 287

Commonwealth, 26, 38–9, 56, 62, 92, 111, 115, 121, 167, 198, 239

Connell, Brian, 190

Conservative Party, 44, 50–51, 93–4, 122–4, 161–2, 186, 204, 212–13

Cooke, Alistair, 283

Cornwall, Duchy of, 203

Coronations, 48–64; Edward VII, 48–9; George VI, 35–6, 49; Elizabeth II, 48, 49–64, 67, 89, 92, 103, 107–8, 110, 111, 112, 116–19, 149–50, 185

Coward, Nöel, 77, 138

Crawford, Marion, 45–7, 81, 97, 98

Crossman, Richard, 183

Cudlipp, Hugh, 119

Daily Express, 38, 128–9, 132, 157, 219–20

Daily Mail, 131, 262, 288

Daily Mirror, 69, 86–7, 119, 126–7, 158–9, 242, 243, 289, 290

Daily Star, 268

Dartmouth Royal Naval College, 80–81, 252

Day, Robin, 130

Debrett's, 91

Delhi Durbar (1911), 16, 39, 192

Dempster, Nigel, 224

Devonshire, Dowager Duchess of, 124

di Manio, Jack, 188–9

Diana, Princess of Wales, 144, 284, 287; background, 265–6, 268–9; suitability as Prince Charles's wife, 266–9; wedding, 3–4, 269–73; as 'global megastar', 273–8, 279, 291–92; marriage, 276–7, 288–9; children, 6, 276, 277; press criticism of, 277; Prince Philip's reputed lack of interest in, 290; future public role, 291–92, 295

Dimbleby, Jonathan, 54, 55, 58

Dimbleby, Richard, 53–6, 57–9, 60, 117, 121, 150–51, 165, 166, 167, 181, 184, 240, 270

Dimmock, Peter, 133

Dior, Christian, 60

Disraeli, Benjamin, 12, 102, 120

Divine Right of Kings, 10, 14

Dixon, Sir Pierson, 218

Dorchester Hotel, 3

Douglas-Home, Sir Alec, *see* Home, Earl of

Douglas-Home, Robin, 226

Duncan, Andrew, 199

d'Urso, Prince, 238

Duveen, Lord, 202

Echaudmaison, Oliver, 214

Eden, Sir Anthony, 60, 109–10, 112–13, 120–22, 133, 161, 186

Edgar, Donald, 107

Edinburgh, Duke of, *see* Philip,
　　Prince
Edward, Prince, 159, 286, 295
Edward VII, King of England, 17,
　　26, 34, 67, 71, 73, 89, 119, 124,
　　152; scandals involving, 11;
　　character, 13, 250; and Princess
　　Mary, 15–16; Coronation,
　　48–9; marriage, 239, 265;
　　relations with women, 253;
　　funeral, 47
Edward VIII, King of England, *see*
　　Windsor, Duke of
Edwards, Anne, 132
Elizabeth I, Queen of England, 51,
　　56
Elizabeth II, Queen of England, 6,
　　7; birth and childhood, 29,
　　30–32, 37–8, 45, 97, 116; and
　　the Abdication crisis, 42; in
　　Second World War, 39;
　　marriage, 42–3, 52, 75, 80–88,
　　93, 101; becomes Queen, 9,
　　41–5; Coronation, 48, 49–64,
　　67, 89, 92, 103, 107–8, 110,
　　111, 112, 116–19, 149–50,
　　185; her mother's influence, 67;
　　and Philip's role as consort,
　　89–95; children, 88, 146–7,
　　159, 280; surname, 91–2; and
　　Princess Margaret's character,
　　97–8; and Group Captain
　　Townsend, 103, 105, 108–9;
　　style as monarch, 115–16;
　　maintains family privacy, 116,
　　141, 143, 153, 207; press
　　criticism, 119, 124, 127–33,
　　159–60; and the Suez crisis,
　　120–22; Prime Ministerial
　　appointments, 122–5, 161–3;
　　rumours about marriage, 125–7,
　　140; Christmas broadcasts, 133,
　　201; portraits, 136; and Princess
　　Margaret's marriage, 145, 150;
　　criticism of Greek connection,
　　160–61; and the Blunt affair,
　　163–5; and the monarchy's

decine in popularity, 165–8;
　　Prince Charles's Investiture, 172,
　　184, 191, 194–5; television
　　films, 181–5, 230–31, 247;
　　enjoyment of television
　　programmes, 183; and Harold
　　Wilson as Prime Minister,
　　186–7; Prince Charles on, 190;
　　public image, 197, 225, 229–33,
　　255–6, 283–5; wealth, 201–6,
　　215–16, 243; royal art
　　collection, 202; horsemanship,
　　210; at Princess Anne's
　　wedding, 213; buys Gatcombe
　　Park for Princess Anne, 215;
　　and Princess Margaret's divorce,
　　223, 237, 239, 240; Silver
　　Jubilee, 227–9, 231, 246, 255,
　　283; popularity, 237; relations
　　with Princess Anne, 242;
　　assassination threats, 245–6; and
　　the Prince of Wales's role,
　　250–51; relations with Prince
　　Charles, 253–4; and Princess
　　Michael, 259, 260; and Prince
　　Charles's marriage, 265, 271;
　　relations with Princess Diana,
　　273; Michael Fagan incident,
　　288–9; American visit (1983),
　　5–6; achievements as monarch,
　　23, 293–5
Elizabeth, the Queen Mother,
　　consort of George VI, 92, 164,
　　208, 266; marriage, 29, 149,
　　263; and the royal family's public
　　image, 30–33, 36–8, 116, 207;
　　Queen Mary's influence on,
　　33–4; and the Abdication crisis,
　　33, 103; Coronation, 36; and
　　George VI's public image, 36–7;
　　in Second World War, 39; and
　　George VI's death, 43–4; and
　　Queen Elizabeth's Coronation,
　　67; role as Queen Mother,
　　67–70; distrust of Lord
　　Mountbatten, 80, 84, 93, 179;
　　opposition to Philip's plans for

Sandringham, 95; relations with Princess Margaret, 98, 138; and Group Captain Townsend, 103, 108, 111–12; and Princess Margaret's marriage, 140, 143–5, 147, 148, 150–54; relations with the press, 142; public image, 211, 237, 255, 289; visits to France, 218; on Prince Charles, 225; and Princess Margaret's divorce, 239; relations with Princess Anne, 242; wealth, 243; at Lord Mountbatten's funeral, 246; and Prince Charles's choice of wife, 264, 267

Encounter, 130
Esher, Lord, 47, 192, 193
Evening News, 160
Evening Standard, 236
Everett, Oliver, 276

Fagan, Michael, 288–9
Fairlie, Henry, 61
Falklands campaign, 285
Farrer, Matthew, 222
Fellowes, Robert, 266
Ferdinand, Archduke of Austria, 14
Fermoy, Lady, 266, 267
Fermoy, Lord, 266, 271
First World War, 18–20, 25, 72, 73, 196
Fisher, Archbishop, 49, 52, 53, 59, 61, 110–12
Fleming, Ian, 133
Franz, Prince, 10
Frederika, Queen of the Hellenes, 160–61
Frost, David, 189

Gardener, Andrew, 214
Gatcombe Park, 215, 243, 282
George I, King of England, 11
George I, King of the Hellenes, 73
George II, King of England, 11
George II, King of the Hellenes, 83

George III, King of England, 9, 10, 11, 48, 56, 108, 109, 203
George IV, King of England, 11, 153
George V, King of England, 14, 38, 39, 69, 71, 79, 117, 124, 164, 203, 218, 249, 260; marriage 15, 265; character, 16, 17, 31; Delhi Durbar, 16, 39, 192; family name, 18–19; in First World War, 18–20; radio broadcasts, 21, 54, 270; Silver Jubilee, 22, 49, 189, 227–8; relations with his children, 23–4, 29; and Prince Andrew of Greece, 74; public image, 125; Investiture of Prince of Wales, 191–2; royal art collection, 202; death, 25, 47
George VI, King of England, 8, 9, 52, 68, 71, 80, 117, 250, 266, 292; in First World War, 20; relations with his mother, 24; and the Abdication crisis, 33, 48, 93; becomes King, 26, 27–8, 43; character, 28–9; marriage, 29, 84, 263; Coronation, 35–6, 49; radio broadcasts, 36–7, 270; public image, 36–7, 125; stammer, 36–7; and the Empire, 38–9; in Second World War, 39–40; and Princess Elizabeth's marriage, 83–6, 87, 101, 140; relations with Princess Margaret, 97–8, 103; and Group Captain Townsend, 98–9, 102; death, 43–4, 47, 48, 55, 70
Glenconner, Lord (Colin Tennant), 218–19, 220
Gloucester, Prince Henry, Duke of, 24
Gloucester, Richard, Duke of, 291
Gordon, John, 52–3
Gordonstoun, 76, 78, 80, 87, 94, 171, 176, 248, 252, 281–2, 286
Grace, Princess of Monaco, 3
Graham, Billy, 54
Graham, Joan, 127

Greene, Hugh, 165
Griffin, Major, 145
Grimond, Jo, 153
Guardian, 137, 147, 156

Hahn, Kurt, 76, 94
Haley, Sir William, 118
Hamilton, Willie, 161, 205, 215, 236, 238, 243–4
Hanover, House of, 10–11
Harewood, George, Earl of, 222
Harlech, Lord, 124–5
Harrison, Avril, 3
Harrison, Rosemary, 3
Hastings, Lord, 50
Heath, Edward, 162, 212–13
Henry, Prince of Wales, 277, 282, 295
Henry VIII, King, 63, 237
Heseltine, William, 172–3, 175, 179–82, 184, 185, 190, 193, 201, 206, 217, 227, 272, 281, 282
Hicks, David, 158
Highgrove, 273, 277, 295
Hillary, Sir Edmund, 59
Holden, Tony, 178, 271, 280
Home, Earl of (Sir Alec Douglas-Home), 50, 159–60, 161–2, 186, 294
Hough, Richard, 82
House of Commons, 50, 123, 235
House of Lords, 50, 92, 109, 123
Household Cavalry, 3, 56, 86, 195, 270
Hugh-Jones, Siriol, 165, 184
Hume, Cardinal Basil, 4
Hunt, Warren, 261, 262

Investiture of the Prince of Wales, 172, 178, 179, 185–6, 189–98, 200, 206, 207–8, 226, 272, 279
IRA, 4, 187, 245
ITV, 57, 150, 190
Izvestia, 157

Jacobsen, Sydney, 124

Jacobson, Dan, 232
James II, King of England, 10, 35
John, Prince, 24
John Paul II, Pope, 4, 6, 293
Juan Carlos, King of Spain, 3
Juliana, Queen of the Netherlands, 101
Junor, Penny, 268

Keay, Douglas, 204
Kennedy, John F., 124, 152
Kensington Palace, 10, 74, 113, 149, 152–3, 155, 202–3, 224, 225, 259, 273
Kent, Edward, Duke of, 135, 290
Kent, Prince George, Duke of, 24, 27, 40, 83
KGB, 163
Kilmuir, Lord, 123
Kinnock, Neil, 215–16
Kipling, Rudyard, 12, 21
Knatchbull, Amanda, 264

Labour Party, 50, 86, 93–4, 162, 172, 185–7, 196, 204–5, 213, 216
Lacey, Robert, 116, 122, 240, 271
Lambton, Lord, 213
Lancaster, Duchy of, 203
Lang, Cosmo, Archbishop of Canterbury, 33, 37
Lascelles, Sir Alan, 44, 104–10, 113
Leeds University, 197
Lenin, 47
Leonard, Dr Graham, Bishop of Truro, 235
Liberal Party, 192, 204
Lightbody, Miss, 209
Linley, Lord, 156, 260, 290
Llewellyn, Roderick (Roddy), 219–20, 226, 234, 238
Lloyd George, David, 39, 54, 191–2
Lloyds, 3
Logue, Lionel, 36, 45–6
London Gazette, 85–6

Longford, Lady, 49, 91, 105
Louisville Courier, 132

McCarthy, Senator, 69
Macmillan, Harold, 123–4, 149, 161–3, 186, 294
Margaret, Princess, 5, 92, 168, 176, 208, 243, 251; birth and childhood, 29, 38, 96–8, 116; in Second World War, 39; and Peter Townsend, 83, 98–113, 118, 125–6, 137, 234, 238, 294; character, 97; public criticism of, 128, 138–9, 157, 158–9, 235–6; marriage, 134, 137, 139–41, 143–52, 166, 191, 213, 223, 272; public image, 137–8, 225, 237, 240–41, 256, 274; criticism of public expenditure on, 149; failure to update style of monarchy, 152–4; children, 155, 156, 290; marriage problems, 158; holidays in Mustique, 218–21, 234–5; and Roderick Llewellyn, 219–20, 226, 234; separation and divorce, 221–3, 225–7, 236–41, 258, 280, 294; Civil List allowance, 227, 236, 237; and the Queen's public image, 284; lung operation, 290
Marie-Astrid, Princess of Luxembourg, 265
Marie-Christine, Princess, *see* Michael, Princess of Kent
Marina, Princess, Duchess of Kent, 83, 85, 256, 257
Marlborough House, 9
Marten, Sir Henry, 45
Martin, Kingsley, 157
Mary, Princess Royal, 24
Mary, Queen, consort of George V, 61, 79, 89, 203, 206, 221, 295; transformation of monarchy, 8, 9–10, 15–22; and George VI's death, 9; early life, 14–15; in First World War, 19–20, 39;

relations with her children, 23–4; and the Abdication crisis, 25; influence on the Queen Mother, 33–4; at George VI's Coronation, 36; and George V's death, 43; and Princess Elizabeth's childhood, 45, 49; as Queen Dowager, 68; and Princess Elizabeth's marriage, 85; and the royal family's name, 91; relations with Princess Margaret, 97; death, 47–8
Mass Observation, 60, 197
Melbourne, Lord, 11, 12, 52
Messel, Oliver, 135, 136, 193, 219
Michael, Prince of Kent, 256–62, 291, 294
Michael, Princess of Kent, 256–62, 291, 294
Michelmore, Cliff, 189
Milford Haven, George, Marquis of, 72, 75, 78, 79, 81
Le Monde, 213
Moran, Lord, 59
Morning Star, 231, 232
Morrah, Dermot, 37, 62
Mountbatten, Lady Edwina, 77, 79, 86, 88, 249
Mountbatten, Lord Louis (Uncle Dickie), 53, 72, 87, 88, 128, 208; influence on Prince Philip, 42, 77–8, 93–4, 117; background, 76–8; friendship with Duke of Windsor, 77, 79–80, 93; character, 78–9, 249; the Queen Mother's distrust of, 80, 84, 93, 179; and Prince Philip's marriage, 80–86, 93; and Prince Philip's surname, 90–92; influence on Prince Charles, 93, 246–9, 251–4; television film, 179; influence on public image of monarchy, 247–8; and Prince Michael's marriage, 257–8, 260; Prince Charles's choice of wife, 264; assassination, 245–7

Muggeridge, Malcolm, 53,
130–31, 154, 165, 206, 241
Murdoch, Rupert, 220
Murray, John, 30

Nasser, Gamel Abdel, 120–21
National and English Review, 129
National Government, 21–2
National Playing Fields
Association, 94
NATO, 6
Nazis, 25
Neilson, Nigel, 174–9, 196, 201,
248
Neilson McCarthy Ltd, 174–5,
188, 190, 201, 229, 248
New Statesman, 183, 205, 238,
243
New Yorker, 69
News Chronicle, 32
News of the World, 220–21, 261
Nicholas, Princess of Greece, 82–3,
257
Nicolson, Harold, 13, 69
Nixon, Richard, 69, 211
Norfolk, Duke of, 49, 53, 56, 150,
194
Northumberland, Duke of, 50

Observer, 61, 137, 157
Oggi, 126
Ogilvy, Angus, 166, 223, 291
Ogilvy, Marina, 291
Ogilvy, James, 291
Onassis, Aristotle, 174, 177–8
Order of the Garter, 187
Osborne, John, 130, 147, 154
Osborne House, 12

Paisley, Ian, 4
Palace Press Office, 106–7, 144,
150, 172–3, 178, 185, 188, 262
Paris Match, 126
Parker, Commander Michael, 90,
94, 126–7
Parkinson, Norman, 136, 214
Paul, King of the Hellenes, 160

Peebles, Miss, 209
Peter, King of Yugoslavia, 83
Petrie, Sir Charles, 153–4
Philby, Kim, 164
Philip, Prince, Duke of Edinburgh,
9, 241; marriage, 42–3, 75,
80–88, 93, 101; character, 43;
and Queen Elizabeth's
Coronation, 53; role as consort,
70–71, 88–95, 114–17, 146,
156; background, 71–8; naval
career, 80–82, 88; surname,
85–6, 90–92, 93, 141; titles, 87,
140–41, 228; and Group
Captain Townsend, 103; 1956
Commonwealth tour, 114–15,
119–20, 125; relations with the
press, 119, 127–9, 131, 142–3;
rumours about marriage, 125–7,
140; and Princess Margaret's
marriage, 145, 148, 150–51;
influence on Armstrong-Jones,
155–6; rhino hunt, 159; press
criticism of, 159–60; and the
monarchy's decline in popularity,
167, 172–3; television films,
180–82, 230, 247; Prince
Charles on, 190; Civil List issue,
201–2; relations with his
daughter, 209; and Princess
Margaret's divorce, 222, 239,
240; relations with Lord
Snowdon, 224; public image,
225, 256, 289–90; and the
Queen's Silver Jubilee, 228;
popularity, 237; relations with
Prince Charles, 248; and the
Prince of Wales's role, 251; and
Prince Charles's choice of wife,
265; and the Queen's public
image, 284; Michael Fagan
incident, 288–9; American visit
(1983), 5–6; reputed lack of
interest in Princess Diana, 290;
future public role, 295
Phillips, Mark, 212–13, 214–17,
223, 241–4, 282–3, 295

Phillips, Peter, 216, 230, 290
Phillips, Zara, 290
Picture Post, 86
Pine, L. G., 90–91
Pinker, Mr, 271
Piper, John, 68
Plaid Cymru, 187, 191
Point de Vue, 274
Ponsonby, Sarah, 220
Portanova family, 260–61
Post Office, 57
Press Council, 131, 141, 287
Profumo, John, 161, 213
Punch, 51

Queen's Garden, The, 230–31

Readers Digest, 137–8
Reagan, Nancy, 3, 5–6
Reagan, Ronald, 5–6
Rees-Mogg, William, 271
Regency Council, 92
Reibnitz, Baron von, 257, 258,
   261–2
Reith, John, 21, 54, 63
Reynolds News, 47
Rhodes, Cecil, 12
Richard II, King of England, 29
Riding for the Disabled, 216
Ring, Anne, 30–31, 46, 207
Rippon, Angela, 217
Roberts, David, 95
Rogers, Henry, 173–4
Rosse, Lady, 135, 221
Rowe and Pitman, 202
Royal Air Force, 80
Royal Family, 180–85, 190, 197,
   199, 207, 230, 247, 292–3
Royal Heritage, 230
Royal Marriages Act (1772),
   105–6, 108–9, 258
Royal Navy, 17, 72, 77, 80–82,
   126, 208, 228–9, 252, 253
Runcie, Robert, Archbishop of
   Canterbury, 272

Sackville-West, Vita, 40

St Paul's Cathedral, 3, 12, 228,
   270, 272
Salisbury, Lord, 109–10, 111, 123,
   124
Sandringham, 24, 34–5, 95, 129,
   168, 203, 218, 224, 266
Saturday Evening Post, 130
Save the Children Fund, 216, 241
Schwarz, F.A.O., 69
Schweppes, 51
Second World War, 28, 39–40, 75
Shea, Michael, 271–2, 273, 281–3,
   285, 286–7, 289, 292
Sheffield, Davina, 255
Sheridan, Lisa, 39, 46
Shils, Edward, 61, 62
Shinwell, Emanuel, 86
Shulman, Milton, 199, 200, 284
Silver Jubilees: George V's, 22, 49,
   189, 227–8; Elizabeth II's,
   227–9, 231, 246, 255, 283
Simpson, Mrs, *see* Windsor,
   Duchess of
Sitwell, Edith, 26
Sitwell, Osbert, 69
Sketch, 127
Smith, Godfrey, 146
Smuts, General, 101
Snowdon, Earl of (Anthony
   Armstrong-Jones), 166, 168,
   214, 234, 286; background,
   134–6; photographic career,
   135–7, 157–8, 193, 224;
   marriage, 137, 139–41,
   143–54, 223–4; role in royal
   family, 152–7; marriage
   problems, 154–5, 158; press
   criticism of, 156–8; and Prince
   Charles's Investiture, 192–5,
   226; media relations, 216;
   separation and divorce, 219,
   221–3, 225–7, 236–7, 239
Sociological Review, 61
Spencer, Countess, 269, 273
Spencer, Earl, 265, 266, 269
Spencer, Lady Jane, 266
Spencer, Lady Sarah, 255, 266

Stamfordham, Lord, 18–19
Stanhope, 7th Earl, 291
Star, 142
Stark, Koo, 285–6
Stern, 126
Stevens, Jocelyn, 140, 146, 154,
     157
Strathmore, 14th Earl of, 29
Suez Crisis, 120–22, 127, 128, 206
Sunday Dispatch, 151
Sunday Express, 52–3, 130
Sunday People, 79, 156, 235–6
Sunday Pictorial, 70, 124
Sunday Telegraph, 168, 200, 235
Sunday Times, 50, 146, 157–8,
     165, 193, 219, 223, 224
Sutherland, Graham, 128

Tatler, 292
Taylor, A. J. P., 187
Tensing, Sherpa, 59
Thatcher, Margaret, 162, 271,
     284–5
Thomas, George, 187
Time magazine, 63, 132, 213
The Times, 25, 62, 111, 112, 118,
     145, 215, 216, 238, 271, 287
Tonga, King of, 3
Townsend, Group Captain Peter,
     83, 98–113, 118, 125–6, 137,
     139, 140, 234, 238, 294
Trinity College, Cambridge, 176
Trooping the Colour, 47, 239, 245
Troubridge, Tom, 256–7, 258
Tryon, Lord, 203
Twentieth Century-Fox, 5

Umberto, King of Italy, 14
United Nations, 120
University College of Wales, 187–8

Vanity Fair, 292
Victoria, Queen of England, 7, 10,
     17, 21, 34, 42, 52, 71–2, 84, 89,
     102, 146, 273, 295; role of
     monarchy, 11, 12–13;
     retirement after death of Prince

Albert, 11, 43, 128; Disraeli
     and, 12; jubilees, 12, 13, 16; and
     Princess Mary, 14–15;
     Coronation, 48, 49;
     assassination attempts, 246;
     public image, 270; funeral, 47
Vogue, 271, 275

Wagner, Sir Anthony, 194
Wallace, Anna 'Whiplash', 264,
     266
Washington Post, 132–3
Weldon, Huw, 230
Wellesley, Lady Jane, 255, 263–4
Wells, H. G., 18
Welsh Liberation Army, 187, 196
Westminster Abbey, 29, 35, 48,
     49–50, 52–3, 55–9, 62, 86,
     150, 166, 246
Westminster Hall, 47, 48
Whigs, 10, 11, 35
Whitaker, James, 268, 287
Whiting, Audrey, 236
William, Prince of Wales, 276, 277,
     287, 295
William II, Kaiser, 18, 73
William IV, King of England, 11
Willis, Judge Roger Blenkiron,
     236
Wilson, Harold, 183, 185–7, 196,
     213
Wilson, Sir John, 39
Windsor, Duchess of (Mrs
     Simpson), 25–7, 34, 35, 48, 71,
     80, 104, 127, 196, 253, 264
Windsor, Duke of (Edward VIII),
     51, 96, 98, 111, 247, 250; on
     his mother, 10; in First World
     War, 20; character, 24–5, and
     his mother's death, 48; style as
     King, 71; friendship with Lord
     Mountbatten, 77, 79–80, 93; at
     Oxford University, 177;
     investiture as Prince of Wales,
     191–2; public image, 196;
     relations with women, 251,
     252–3; Abdication, 23, 25–7,

33–5, 42, 48, 79–80, 93, 103–5, 221–2, 227; funeral, 222
Windsor, Lord Frederick, 291
Windsor, Lady Gabriella, 291
Windsor Castle, 6, 19, 68, 129, 202–3, 218, 224, 248, 260, 262
Winn, Godfrey, 32, 176
Woman, 237, 239, 242

Women's Own, 46
Women's Sunday Mirror, 129
World Wildlife Fund, 159, 289
Worsthorne, Peregrine, 200

Yeomen of the Guard, 56
Young, Michael, 61, 62

Zetland, Marquis of, 4
Ziegler, Philip, 60

The Royal House of Windsor

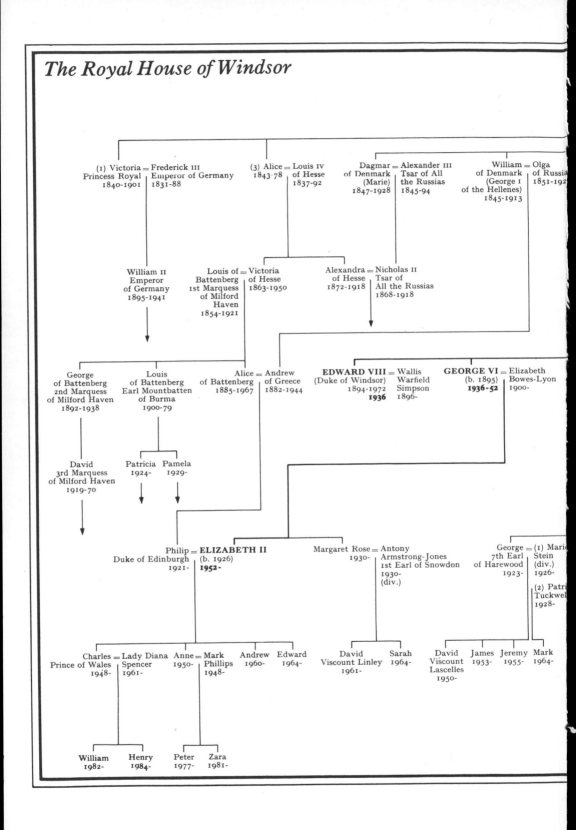